# seductions
## *of rice*

Jeffrey Alford & Naomi Duguid

ARTISAN

NEW YORK

The following photographs are individually copyrighted by the photographers:

COLIN FAULKNER
*page vi*, top right, bottom left | *page x*, top right | *page 19* | *page 290 (1)*, both
*page 290(4)*, bottom | *page 290(6)*, top | *page 290 (7)*, both

BEATRIZ DA COSTA
*page 290(3)*, top

EVAN SKLAR
*page 290(2)* | *page 290(4)*, top | *page 290(5)*, top | *page 290(6)*, bottom

Published by Artisan
A Division of Workman Publishing, Inc.
708 Broadway, New York, New York 10003-9555
www.artisanbooks.com

LIBRARY OF CONGRESS CATALOGING-IN-PUBLICATION DATA
Alford, Jeffrey.
    Seductions of rice / by Jeffrey Alford and Naomi Duguid.
    p.   cm.
    Includes bibliographical references and index.
    ISBN 1-57965-234-4
    1. Cookery (Rice)    2. Cookery, International.    I. Duguid, Naomi.
    II. Title.
    TX809.R5A434   1998                98-3951
    641.6'318—dc21            CIP

Printed in China

10   9   8   7   6   5   4   3   2   1

First Paperback Edition, 2003


BOOK DESIGN BY VERTIGO DESIGN

*Previous page: Rice drying on a road in southern China*

**We're delighted** that *Seductions of Rice* is now in paperback. For us it will always be our *Joy of Cooking,* a collection of recipes that best represents what we cook for ourselves (and for our friends) at home. These recipes from Thailand, China, India, Japan, and from other places all around the world, are for all the foods we most like to eat. And with rice as the backbone of a meal, here is a way of eating that is delicious, inexpensive, healthful, and fun and easy in the kitchen.

Jeffrey Alford and Naomi Duguid
March 2003

To Dominic and Tashi,
*the best traveling companions in the world*

Our favorite way to eat rice is out of a bowl, the way it is commonly eaten in China. We also like eating rice from a small dinner plate using a dessert spoon to pick it up, Thai style. And when we are in South India, we eat it from a banana leaf with our hands, and then we think that is the best way.

But at home we like to use a bowl, a largish one the size of a café-au-lait bowl. We scoop out a generous helping of plain rice from our reliable rice-cooking pot using a wooden rice paddle, and then reach for something flavorful to eat over it: chopped fresh tomatoes from the garden mixed with basil and Vietnamese coriander, or roasted sesame seeds ground with coarse salt, or spicy Sichuan tofu left over from the night before, or a hot Thai curry. We always have on hand a few different condiments to pull out from the refrigerator: *nam pla prik* from Thailand, Japanese pickles, a Chinese *la jiao jang*.

This big bowl of rice is our everyday lunch; occasionally it's dinner, sometimes it's even a midmorning snack. It's our comfort food, and we never get tired of it. It is, in many ways, what this book is most about.

We didn't grow up with rice, we came to know it through travel in Asia, like people who travel to France for the first time and there discover good cheese and good wine. But it took a while for this discovery to happen. We were without all the little sensibilities that people have when they grow up eating rice as a staple food. It took years for us to really appreciate the smells and textures of different varieties, and to have a sense of why one should be cooked one way and another a different way.

Somewhere along the line we found ourselves hooked on rice, on good rice, that is, and on rice as a way of preparing meals. Just like in millions—maybe hundreds of millions—of homes all around the world where rice is a staple food, we fell into the habit of putting rice on to cook first thing in the kitchen. It's effortless. Then we would start thinking about what to serve with the rice, but we'd already be well into preparing our meal.

If you weren't raised with rice, this might sound a bit monotonous. But good rice is just like good bread. It always tastes real and it always sparks an appetite. In fact, this is even truer of rice, as it goes so well with a staggering number of different foods, from Senegalese peanut stew to Yunnanese spicy ground pork. And unlike bread, which requires a grain that has been ground into flour, and that flour transformed into bread, rice is simply cooked!

This, then, is a book about rice, and flavored rice dishes, and eating *with* rice as a staple food. In the chapters that discuss the foods of China, Thailand, Japan, and India, you will find many recipes for dishes where rice is not an ingredient. These recipes are for dishes to serve with rice—plain rice, rice in a bowl, rice on a plate, rice on a banana leaf. From Thai Grilled Beef Salad or Spicy Chinese Greens Salad, from South Indian Lentil Stew to Kerala Coconut Chicken Curry or Kyoto Grilled Peppers, these are some of our favorite foods in the world. Each of these chapters moves from plain rices to dishes to serve with rice, then finally to flavored-rice dishes such as fried rice, sushi, and rice pudding. They are all good home cooking: easy, affordable, and fun.

In subsequent chapters—on Persian and Silk Road rices, the Mediterranean, Senegal, and the Americas—the focus shifts from the Asian tradition of rice being served unflavored to the wonderful world of pilaf, *chelo, pulao*, risotto, paella, *diebou dien*, perloos, and more: flavored rices. Many of the recipes in these chapters are for rice dishes, with only the occasional side dish or accompaniment. Only in the case of Senegal have we departed from this pattern, wanting to give a more complete picture of a fascinating and too unfamiliar culinary tradition.

Entire cookbooks are written on risottos, paellas, and pilafs, so we have tried to concentrate on the tradition of each dish, its essence. When faced with an elaborate version versus a rustic version, we usually gravitate toward the rustic version, as it more often seems to embody the original tradition.

The world of rice is so huge, it would be presumptuous to think that we could include every rice here, or discuss every important rice tradition. Instead we've tried to give an introduction to the world of rice. We hope this book will help you navigate that world with ease, finding your own ways, bringing dishes to your table with confidence and pleasure, day in and day out.

We sometimes laugh when we think about the food we eat at home. It's as unlike the food we ate growing up as any could possibly be. We eat curries from India and tofu dishes from China, seaweed from Japan and little dried fishes. We eat tiny bird chiles—and have a fit if we run out. We have a pantry that looks like a United Nations banquet. But the most exotic food is rice. Without it, none of the other ingredients would be there in our kitchen. It's the great facilitator, unrivaled.

RICE FOR EVERY OCCASION

Rice fields during the rainy season in
western Yunnan, near Dali, China

inset: Grains of rice

# Beginning with Rice

Rice is a grain, the fruit of a grass plant, and the staple food of more than half the world's population. It now grows in more than one hundred countries, on every continent except Antarctica, although over 90 percent of the world's rice is still grown in Asia. Rice grows in all kinds of environments, from northern Japan to Peru, from Australia to Senegal, from Spain to southern India, from sea level to an altitude of ten thousand feet. Rice can be grown in flooded paddies, in rivers, or in dry fields watered only by rainfall. Some varieties of rice will grow in very hot temperatures, others in relatively cool climates.

# Stocking Your Rice Cupboard

Until recently, there had been little demand for a wide selection of top-quality rices, as rice had never been a high-priority food in North America. But times are changing. On a recent trip to our local supermarket, we were pleased to find a fairly good selection of rices, though it required a bit of searching. In the rice section, in addition to Rice-in-a-Bag and Rice-a-Roni, we found plain long-grain American rice. In the Italian specialty section, we found arborio superfino, fine for risotto and as a substitute for Spanish rice in paella. In the "foreign foods" section, along with soy sauces and tempura sauce, we found Thai jasmine, basmati, and Japanese rice. Finally, in the bulk foods area, there were several brown rices and one commercially grown wild rice.

Supermarkets are usually not, however, the best place to shop for good rice. Our favorite place to shop for rice is in ethnic groceries, where the rice is often sold in larger bags and at a lower price. In South Asian groceries, look for Dehra Dun basmati, gobindavog, Patna basmati, rosematta or other parboiled red rices, and more. In Korean and Japanese stores, you'll find plain and sticky Japanese rices usually American-grown. In Southeast Asian and Chinese shops, there is usually a selection of Thai and Vietnamese rices as well as short-grain sticky rice and some American-grown long-grain rices. Try Italian shops for good risotto rices. Natural foods stores are the best source for organically grown rices and brown rices. There too you will sometimes find Japanese rice, basmati, and Thai jasmine, as well as American-grown specialty rices such as Wehani and Black Japonica.

If you are lucky enough to live near a shop specializing in a wide variety of grains and beans, then you won't have to shop around at different stores. You should be able to find or special-order most rices at a specialty grains store. In New York, Kalustyan's has a very wide selection of rices and in Canada, Rube in Toronto's St. Lawrence market and the Madeira brothers in Kensington Market both sell many different rices in bulk. The best place to find exotic varieties unavailable in your local stores is through mail order; a current list of sources is on page 438.

# Buying and Storing Rice

Rice has a relatively long storage life, so we tend to buy our everyday rices in large quantities, in twenty-pound bags. At home we store it in a dry dark pantry or cupboard, in as cool a place as possible. Stored rice will dry out a little more, but should otherwise change little. In some cultures, older rice is prized. Basmati rice, for example, increases in value if it is stored for many years.

At any one time, we usually have six or seven different rices on hand, some in large bags, others in smaller quantities. There are usually twenty-pound bags of Thai jasmine and Thai sticky rice, a big bag of Japanese Kokuho Rose, and smaller bags of basmati, Wehani, Italian rices (carnaroli and arborio superfino), perhaps a Thai black rice, and often rosematta or Bhutanese red. In hot humid summer weather, we buy in smaller quantities, because heat and humidity make grains harder to store.

We do not recommend transferring rice to clear glass jars and storing it in a sunny spot, at least not for months at a time. We do keep smaller quantities of specialty rices in glass jars, but on an inside wall away from the sun. They are very pretty to look at, like the jars with different dals on the shelf beside them.

Brown rice, because of the oil content, will turn rancid if stored in a warm place for too long, just like whole wheat flour, but because it is a whole grain, it does keep better than flour. Like flour, rice will attract grain moths if kept too long. If your rice gets infested, throw it out.

Now, as for just what qualifies as good-quality rice, the rice should be clean, free of stones, and with not too many broken grains. This would meet the standards of a quality-control inspector, but as for great rice. . . ? What is it? Great rice is a little bit like great olive oil. Someone from Tunisia will tell you that the best olive oil is Tunisian, someone from Italy will say the same about Italian oil, and a person from Greece will say the same about Greek oil. Great rice is rice that tastes great to you, and this varies from person to person, and from culture to culture.

Suitability and custom are other related issues. Because different kinds of rices have very different characteristics, each rice lends itself better to certain types of dishes than to others, not to mention the fact that each of us is accustomed to eating a certain kind of rice in a certain situation. Sushi made with basmati rice will taste and look a little strange, as will risotto made with Thai jasmine rice. Eating a Thai salad with Wehani rice might taste fine, but not if we're accustomed to enjoying Thai salads with fragrant sticky rice.

Poor-quality rice is featureless and tasteless. There is a lot of poor-quality rice in the world, especially nowadays. Many of the new genetically manipulated rices, rices that were developed to provide more food for more people, do have increased yields, but at the same time they've suffered from a loss of flavor. If you are eating a rice at home that is only so-so in the taste department, switch to a different rice. *Rice, like bread, should have good flavor, smell, and texture.*

# The Long and Short of It: How Rice Is Classified and Graded

Rice is generally described as being long-grain, medium-grain, or short-grain. *Long-grain* means that the milled grain is more than three times as long as it is wide, as much a description of shape as a measure of size. Well-known long-grain rices include basmati, Thai jasmine, and the old American variety Carolina Gold. *Medium-* and *short-grain* rices, often both sold as "short-grain" to distinguish them from long-grain rices, look fatter and more rounded. Medium-grain rices are from two to just slightly less than three times as long as they are wide. Short-grain rices are less than twice as long as they are wide. Traditional Japanese rice is medium- to short-grain, as are the rices grown in Italy and Spain, such as arborio and Valencia.

Another distinction between rices is between subspecies. Asian rices are divided into three: *indica* (usually tropical and longer-grain, such as basmati and Thai jasmine), *japonica* (usually temperate-climate and shorter-grain, among them Japanese rices as well as Egyptian, Spanish, Italian, etc.), and *javanica*, also known as *bulu* (tropical to subtropical, medium- to long-grain). There are so many varieties of Asian rice—and so much genetic manipulation has been done in the last thirty years to develop disease-resistant climatically adaptable high-yielding strains—that the distinguishing characteristics of the three subspecies have become somewhat blurred.

Finally, rices are also classified as waxy (glutinous/sticky) or nonwaxy. This description has to do with the cooking and eating characteristics of the rice and is a result of the relative amount of amylose, a starch, in the rice grain. *Waxy rices* have a very low proportion of amylose, while *nonwaxy* rices contain higher levels. Waxy rices absorb less water when they cook and then are sticky after cooking; the name "glutinous" describes this sticky texture (which has nothing to do with gluten, for rice has no gluten). Actually there is a continuum of "waxiness," from the nonwaxy relatively high-amylose rices such as basmati, Carolina Gold, Texmati, to low-amylose rices, such as Thai jasmine, and Italian, Spanish, and some Japanese rices, to very low amylose completely waxy rices, such as Japanese, Thai, and Chinese sticky rice (also known as sweet rice). In general, low-amylose rices are japonicas, with the exception of Thai jasmine and related strains; indicas tend to be medium- or high-amylose.

In the United States, milled rice is graded according to grain type, color, chalkiness, degree of milling, bad odors, red bran, impurities, milling yield, proportion of broken grains, moisture content, and aspect or overall appearance. The top grade is given to rice that is uniform creamy white, with a clear glass-like or crystalline look. If there are any white chalky patches, known as white belly or white strip depending on where they are located, a rice my be graded lower. (In Italy and Spain, on the other hand, these white patches are associated with desirable cooking characteristics and so unless the grain has a very large proportion of chalky area, it will not be graded lower.) Any bran left on the grains, especially colored bran, results in a lower grading. Polished rice should have a moisture content of 13 percent or less. Top-quality rice has very few broken grains in it (fewer than 5 percent). "Brokens" are viewed as undesirable because they can make the cooked rice stickier.

Parboiled rices (see page 242) are always rather opaque-looking and are never as white as the top grade of polished rice, but their grading is still based on lightness. The lightest parboiled rices are slightly yellow. Others can be quite brown or grayish-beige in color because some rices (usually those with a darker-colored bran) parboil to a darker color. This does not affect taste, but since consumers generally prefer lighter-colored rices, darker parboiled rice is given a lower grade number and a lower price.

In the United States, the grades of milled rice are from 1 to 6, with the best being 1. The lowest-quality rice is known as sample rice. In Italy, rices are classified into four categories, with the top quality being "*superfino*"; then come "*fino*," "*semi-fino*," and "*originario o commune*." In Spain, rices are graded by color, size, and the proportion of broken grains: "*Extra*" has at least 92 percent whole grains, while the next grade, "*categoría 1*," has a minimum of 87 percent whole grains.

Since U.S. grading is directly related to the completeness of milling and uniformity of appearance, it is not necessarily a reflection of the relative taste or cooking qualities of the rice. For example, if some bran is left on during milling, or if there is any colored bran, the rice is allocated to a lower category. This is why a strain of rice known as red rice is viewed as such a problem among commercial rice growers in the United States. Red rice plants often grow wild, like weeds, in commercial fields and at harvest time, the grains are then mixed in with the cultivated grains. Red rice doesn't polish as easily and so there is often a little reddish bran left on the kernels. This "imperfection" means that a batch of polished rice with some red rice mixed in will be given a lower quality rating and will therefore sell for a lower price.

Some people have clear preferences for particular grades of rice because the grades are associated with particular cooking characteristics such as increased stickiness. For some, the taste and cooking characteristics of a lower-graded rice may be as good as or better than a top-graded rice. In Senegal, for example, the preference is generally for "brokens," usually the lowest grade of rice.

## Rice Family Tree

### LONG-GRAIN TO MEDIUM-GRAIN
*(traditionally tropical to subtropical rices)*

**classic American long-grains:** Carolina rices; long grains, very separate when cooked, nonaromatic

**aromatic rices:** basmati, Persian rices, Texmati, American Della rices; long grains, very separate when cooked, aromatic, tender

**jasmine rices:** Thai and American jasmine; long grains, slightly clinging when cooked, aromatic

**long-grain sticky rices:** Thai sticky rice, black Thai sticky rice; firm grains that clump and stick when cooked

**javanica (bulu) rices:** traditional Balinese rice, many traditional Javanese and Philippine rices, both sticky and nonsticky

### MEDIUM-GRAIN TO SHORT-GRAIN
*(usually temperate-climate rices)*

**Japanese rices:** grown in Japan, the United States, Australia; tender, lightly clumped when cooked

**Mediterranean rices:** arborio, carnaroli, Valencia, Camargue rices, CalRiso, Egyptian rice; absorb lots of liquid while staying firm

**colored japonicas:** Bhutanese red rice, central Asian *devzira*; tender absorbent grains

**short-grain sticky rices:** pudding rice, Japanese sticky rice, Chinese sticky rice; cooked grains shiny and stick together, slightly sweet taste

# Cooking Rice

## Cleaning and Soaking

Traditionally rice, like beans, had to be picked over to check for and discard stones and pebbles. But modern-day commercial rices have usually been well cleaned and sorted before being bagged and shipped, so there's rarely any need for a preliminary check of the rice. To make sure, if you are using a rice that is new to you, place some in a sieve and look at it closely. It should (and usually will) be of even quality, with no stones or other foreign particles.

The second traditional step is to wash the rice thoroughly in several changes of cold running water. Originally, this ensured that any dirt or dust from the threshing floor or impurities from storage would be washed away. Again, with modern cleaning and storage, these reasons may not apply. But preliminary washing also wets the rice and washes off any loose starch prior to cooking. We think it makes a positive difference in the texture of the cooked rice, making it less sticky and helping it cook more evenly. It is also true that after years of washing rice and watching people in Asia wash rice before cooking, we somehow don't feel comfortable cooking unwashed rice.

In the recipes in this book, you'll frequently see the instruction to "wash the rice thoroughly in several changes of cold water until the water runs clear." When the water runs clear, it means that there is no more loose starch or other powder or coating left on the rice that might gum it up or change the texture of the cooked rice.

The case against washing rice is that most rice milled in the United States is coated with extra nutrients (see page 52). The nutrients are applied in the form of a powder that is washed away if the rice is washed. We feel that since in North America we have access to a wide range of vegetables and other foods, the loss is not critical; you should do whatever feels comfortable to you.

Some rices (basmati is the best-known example) cook to a better texture if they are soaked in water first. The soaking makes them less brittle and thus less likely to break during cooking. Others, especially the sticky rices that are steamed, must be soaked in order to cook through properly. Japanese rice is traditionally soaked or left standing wet after washing; like the sticky rices, the grains cook better if they've had a chance to soften slightly first. Most rices, however, and certainly all parboiled rices, can be cooked immediately after washing, with no preliminary soaking.

If you have washed or soaked your rice before cooking, be sure to drain it thoroughly in a fine sieve before starting to cook it so that your water measurement will be accurate.

## Three Methods for Cooking Rice

There are many different methods of cooking rice. Some rices are best cooked in large amounts of water, others are better steamed, and still others are best absorption-cooked in an exact amount of water. Some rices do well with several different methods, others do not. Some of the differences in cooking technique are a matter of culture and taste, but many are dictated or at least strongly determined by the characteristics of the individual rice variety. (For a more detailed description, see page 9.)

We provide instructions for the method most appropriate to the particular rice in the chapter in which it appears. Where more than one method works well, the others are given as options. What follows is a general discussion of rice cooking techniques with some explanation of why a particular method works the way it does.

## Absorption Method

This is the method that most people are familiar with: A measured amount of rice is cooked in a measured amount of water so that by the time the rice is cooked all the water has been absorbed. We always begin by placing the rice in cold water. Once the water heats to boiling, we cover the pot and lower the heat to prevent burning the bottom of the rice. The rice is cooked by the hot water and later, as the water is absorbed and the water level drops, by the remaining steam. (*Note:* Remember, if you have washed or soaked your rice before cooking, to drain it thoroughly in a sieve before placing it in the measured amount of water, or you'll have more water than the rice needs to cook properly.)

To cook rice using the absorption technique, you can use a **heavy pot** or **saucepan** with a tight-fitting lid or a rice cooker. We prefer using a pot, because we think the rice has a subtly better taste and texture. We use a heavy 3½-quart pressed-aluminum pot of 8 to 9 inches in diameter and 5 inches deep. The important thing is a heavy bottom, thick enough to hold and distribute the heat well so that the rice doesn't burn or stick as the water is coming to a boil. The other necessity is a tight-fitting lid that will hold in the steam as the rice cooks. The rice should not be more than 2 inches deep; if it is, you need a larger pot (see larger quantity of rice, below).

We did use a **rice cooker** frequently for about a year, then returned to cooking our rice in a heavy pot. Though we prefer to use a heavy pot, rice cookers do work very well and reliably, especially with Japanese-style (medium-grain) rices. Rice cookers, sold in Asian stores and in many specialty stores, are designed for cooking rice the absorption way, with markings on the inside to show the level of water required to cook a given volume of rice. You simply put in a measured amount of rice, add the amount of water indicated by the marking, put on the lid, and turn on the cooker (or set a timer so it turns on later). The cooker heats the water to a boil, then automatically lowers the temperature and slow-cooks the rice until all the water is absorbed. It then keeps the rice warm until you are ready to eat.

If you are cooking rice in a **microwave**, you are doing a blend of steaming and absorption-cooking. It takes the same amount of time as stovetop absorption-cooking. Wash the rice well, place it in a microwavable bowl with a measured amount of water, and then cook it according to the instructions for your microwave.

**Absorption technique for larger quantities of rice**  If you ever have a problem with a batch of absorption-cooked rice that comes out under- or overcooked, it is probably because you're cooking a bigger volume of rice than usual, or working with an unfamiliar or unsuitable (too lightweight, too small) pot.

One of the adjustments you need to make when absorption-cooking a larger volume of rice is pot size and another is volume of water. We find that a heavy 3½-quart pot manages fine cooking up to 3 cups raw rice. Any larger quantity needs a pot with a larger diameter; we turn to our 4½-quart pot with a 10-inch diameter. The reason is that if the raw rice is more than 1½ to 2 inches deep in the pot (as a rough guide, if you rest the tip of your index finger on the bottom of the pot, the raw rice should not come up past your second joint), it cannot absorption-cook evenly. Consequently, you will have either hard undercooked grains on the top or some mushy grains near the bottom of the pot, especially if cooking a soft fragile rice such as Thai jasmine. (Parboiled rices can generally handle a wider range of circumstances and still emerge intact and well cooked.)

A second adjustment is water quantity. Generally the larger the quantity of rice you are cooking by the absorption method, the less water per cup of rice you will need. Thus if your rough rule of thumb for a particular rice is 1¼ cups of water per 1 cup of raw rice, once you're at 3 cups rice you may need only 3⅔ cups water.

If you don't have a larger pot but you need a big quantity of rice, cook the rice in two batches in your usual pot or rice cooker. When the first batch is cooked, place it in a heavy ceramic bowl and cover it with a lid wrapped in a cotton cloth. The cloth will absorb steam as it rises and prevent the rice from becoming soggy, and the lid will keep most of the heat in as the rice waits.

**High-altitude cookery** Jeffrey grew up in Laramie, Wyoming, at an altitude of over seven thousand feet above sea level. Water boils at just over 200°F there, rather than at 212°F. Consequently, everything takes longer to cook.

How to cook plain rice successfully at high altitudes? One solution is to use a pressure cooker. This compensates for the lower atmospheric pressure and enables the rice to cook quickly without much loss of texture. The alternative, to boil it for longer, risks turning the rice to mush by the time it is cooked through, especially at very high altitudes.

Our friend Deb, who lives in Laramie, increases the "sea-level" amount of water set out in any given recipe a little (changing 2 cups water to 2¼ to 2½ for example) and lengthens the cooking time for plain rice from 15 or 20 minutes to 25 or 30 minutes. She has worked out these proportions just from seeing what works best in her kitchen. If you live at a high altitude (over three thousand feet) we recommend, if you haven't done it already, that you make a note of volumes and times to figure out how much adjustment you need to make.

### Lots-of-Water Technique

Many rices, from arborio to basmati to parboiled American rices, cook very well in plenty of water, like pasta. In the "lots-of-water" technique, a large pot of any kind can be used. Ten or more cups of water (usually salted) are brought to a boil and then the rice sprinkled in. It is important to watch the rice carefully to prevent sticking or overcooking. The rice must be drained immediately and thoroughly in a sieve after cooking, and rinsed with a little tepid water to stop it cooking further. The lots-of-water technique is not recommended for lower-amylose rices, such as Thai jasmine or Japanese rice.

### Steaming

Steaming is the preferred cooking technique for sticky rice and also for some low-amylose rices. The rice is usually soaked in water first, then drained. The grains are then put in a special steaming basket or spread out in a flat steamer. The basket or steamer is placed over a pot or wok of boiling water. The rice does not touch the water; it is cooked only by the steam.

To cook long-grain Thai (and Laotian) sticky rice, you need either a conical bamboo steamer and a narrow-necked pot to steam it over or a flat Chinese-style bamboo steamer lined with a cotton cloth. (See Thai Sticky Rice, page 116, for more details.)

Thai jasmine rice can also be steam-cooked. Many Thais place jasmine rice in small bowls with water to cover. The bowls are then placed in a large steamer and steamed over boiling water. Thai restaurants often cook their jasmine rice in water in large flat trays placed in a steam oven.

## Why Are Different Rices Cooked in Different Ways?

Long before getting deep into research for this book, we knew that different kinds of rice needed different cooking techniques. For example, we soak and steam Thai sticky rice; soak and absorption-cook Japanese rice; soak, then briefly boil and then steam basmati and other long-grain rices; briefly sauté, then stir Italian rice . . . and the list goes on and on. We never really understood, though, why different rices required different treatments. Now we have a better idea, at least.

Some of the differences in cooking technique are a matter of culture and taste. But many are dictated or strongly determined by the characteristics of the individual rice variety. With so many varieties out there, it's hazardous to generalize, but we can roughly distinguish the cooking characteristics of different rices according to two measures: their degree of waxiness—or whether they are high-, medium-, or low-amylose rice—and the gelatinization temperature of the starches in the rice.

High- and intermediate-amylose rices, or nonwaxy rices, are usually indicas, longer-grain rices. They absorb more water than lower-amylose rices and tend to expand more during cooking. When cooked, they are firmer, whiter, duller (less shiny), and generally "drier" or fluffier than lower-amylose rices. Intermediate-amylose rices include basmati rices, Indonesian *bulu* (javanica) varieties, and U.S. long-grain varieties.

Low-amylose rices, or waxy rices, such as Thai jasmine and Japanese rice, absorb less water than intermediate- and high-amylose rices. When cooked, they have a slightly clingy texture.

And very low amylose rices, the sticky rices, absorb so little water during cooking that they are most often steam-cooked. They are often quite shiny when cooked.

Gelatinization temperature (GT) is the temperature at which 90 percent of the starches in the rice have gelatinized (turned liquid and lost their crystalline structure). It ranges from low (about 130° to 155°F, preferred in waxy rices) to intermediate (about 158° to 165°F, preferred over low because the cooked rice is softer) to high (about 165° to 175°F, and uncommon). Rice is cooked when all the starches have gelatinized. The higher the GT, the longer the cooking time. Most long-grain high- to medium-amylose rices have a medium-high GT, which means that the starches in the rice need to be brought to a higher temperature before they soften and cook. These rices tend to need longer cooking times. Others with a medium to low GT cook more quickly. (In India, Bangladesh, Pakistan, and Sri Lanka, these are the preferred rices for parboiling.)

Rices with a medium-high GT, such as basmati, cook better if they are soaked in water first. Rice that has absorbed water during soaking is more easily penetrated by heat. Consequently, the center of the grain heats up more quickly if the rice has been soaked and cooking is then more even. These rices also cook better if the cooking finishes slowly, e.g., by gentle steaming after preliminary boiling. This may explain why the best results with basmati and long-grain rices from the United States come when the rice finishes cooking over very low heat or just by "steaming" under a cloth-draped lid. Jasmine and other related fragrant rices with a lower GT do not need preliminary soaking or a final steaming because they cook through more quickly.

All rices seem to do better if allowed to stand, or rest, for ten to fifteen minutes after cooking is completed. This standing period gives the starches a chance to firm up, in the same way that it is best to allow the softened starches in newly baked bread to set before trying to slice into a loaf.

The starches in parboiled rice have already gelatinized during parboiling (hence the darker and more opaque look of the grains), but the rice has then been dried out. To cook parboiled rice, the whole grain must be reheated and moistened. Since gelatinized starch conducts heat less well than ungelatinized starch, it takes longer for heat to penetrate to the center of a grain of parboiled rice than to the center of an unboiled grain of the same variety of rice. This is why parboiled rice takes longer to cook, up to twice as long as unboiled rice. (Many of the "converted," or parboiled, rices produced in the United States have been precooked, to shorten these relatively long cooking times).

Parboiled rice also absorbs water less easily, so it is less suitable for dishes where flavor absorption is important, such as paella and risotto. During cooking, parboiled rice often "butterflies" or splits open (this is especially noticeable with Louisiana wild pecan rice, in our experience). On the other hand, even split-open parboiled rice grains are completely "unsticky"—bouncy in fact.

## Serving Sizes and Suggestions

There is no magic formula for knowing how much rice to prepare for a meal. Different rices yield very different amounts of cooked rice, so it is important when looking at an individual rice recipe—for the purpose of planning a meal—to look at the yield as opposed to the amount of rice you are starting with. For example, two cups of jasmine rice will yield about four and a half cups of cooked rice, whereas two cups of sticky rice will yield only three and a half cups—and two cups of basmati or Wehani can yield as much as six cups of cooked rice.

Even when you know the yield, it can still be difficult to estimate the amount of rice you will need. People who are accustomed to eating a lot of rice—to eating rice as a staple food as opposed to eating it as a side dish—can happily sit down with an individual helping of two to three cups of cooked rice. For an average lunch in South India, one person will eat over half a pound of cooked rice, which is a lot of rice! But if you were to serve this amount to someone unaccustomed to eating rice this way, they would think you were crazy. When we are cooking rice to serve two adults and two young kids, plain jasmine rice for example, we put on a pot with approximately three cups of uncooked rice, and we usually have a little rice left over.

If you are eating rice as a staple food, the worst thing that can happen is to run out of rice, to have cooked too little. Always err by making too much, as any extra will almost always get eaten later. (See Leftovers and Cleaning Up on page 11 and also in the Index.)

How you serve the rice will affect how much rice you and your guests eat. If it is served as a side dish, it will be eaten as a side dish, and if it is served as the center of the meal (as it is commonly served throughout Asia), it will be eaten in larger quantities. How it is served is also intimately connected to how it will be eaten (i.e., with chopsticks, by hand, with a spoon, or with a knife and fork). In China and Japan, rice is usually served in individual bowls and eaten with chopsticks. In Thailand, it is served on flat plates and eaten with a spoon and fork, using the fork as a pusher to help put the food onto the spoon. In India, rice is served flat on a banana leaf, a plate, or a metal tray, and then eaten by hand. We like all these methods.

Pilafs are gorgeously served on large flat platters, while risotto comes to the table in individual soup plates or flat plates. Paella is meant to be served from the paella pan, an impressive sight. We bring Thai sticky rice to the table in a large wooden bowl. Traditionally it is served in individual baskets with lids, but we find that with young children it's easier to have a generous bowl of rice out and available for grabbing.

## Leftovers and Cleaning Up

Leftover rice should be allowed to cool completely, then stored in a glass or plastic container or a plastic bag, well sealed, in the refrigerator. Most rices harden slightly when refrigerated, but sticky rices tend to get very hard and are then difficult to revive the next day. Consequently, we do not refrigerate leftover sticky rice (anyway, there are rarely leftovers). Rice will keep in the refrigerator for three days, but is best used within twenty-four to thirty-six hours.

To reheat rice, place it in a heavy pot with several tablespoons of water. Break up any lumps with wet hands or with a wooden spoon. Heat over medium heat until you hear the water boiling and see steam rising from the pot. Stir gently, lower the heat, cover, and let steam for 3 to 5 minutes, stirring once or twice. Alternatively, place the rice in a microwaveable container with a tight-fitting lid. Add a little water to the rice, break up the lumps as above, then cover tightly and place in the microwave oven at full power. Depending on the quantity of rice and the size of your oven, it will take one to two minutes to reheat. Be careful of hot steam when you open the lid of the container.

Every rice-eating culture has developed a number of ways of using leftover rice in delicious combinations. Some of our favorite dishes use leftover rice, so we usually cook more rice than we need in the evening in order to have cold cooked rice to work with the next day.

Fried rice, flavored in a variety of ways, is a brilliant and flexible way to transform plain cooked rice into a whole new repertoire. Fried rice is quick to make, and ingredients can vary with the seasons and with what you have available. See, for example, Classic Thai Fried Rice (page 158), Quick Onion Pilaf (page 278), and Leftover Long-Grain Rice, Carolina Style (page 396), as well as leftover rice in the Index.

In the colder months, we often add leftover cooked rice to cooked beans or legumes to make a stew or thick soup. Or, if we have a good chicken or beef stock or broth in the refrigerator or freezer, we heat it up in a saucepan, add leftover rice for body, and then flavor it as we please. In summer, we turn to rice salads: From Italy to Thailand, cold rice salads are a fresh way of using leftover plain cooked rice, combined with herbs and vegetables and a variety of dressings. See, for example, the Italian Rice Salad (page 347) and Multicolored Black Rice Salad (page 404).

When it comes to cleaning up, rice is one of those foodstuffs, like other starches, that needs to be rinsed off dirty dishes before they go into a dishwasher. Otherwise, the heat from the hot water will make the starches harden and stick. If you have a pot with a little rice still in it, fill it with warm water and let it soak. The rice will then come right off.

# The Rice Dictionary

**absorption cooking**   In many parts of the world, rice is cooked by the absorption method: The rice is cooked (in a heavy pot or a rice cooker) in a measured amount of water that boils and then simmers until all the water has been absorbed by the rice. A variant of absorption cooking, used by some households in Thailand, steam cooks the rice by absorption: The rice is placed in several uncovered bowls with a measured amount of water. The bowls are placed in a covered steamer over boiling water, which produces an even heat. Cooking time is a little longer than with the simple absorption method.

**American jasmine rice**   There are a number of good-quality American-grown Thai-style jasmine rices. They have a soft, slightly clingy texture when cooked. They can be served to accompany Thai meals or in place of any plain white rice. Our favorite is organically grown by Lowell Farms in Texas. It is less polished than the Thai rices. Consequently, it needs a little more water and a few more minutes' cooking time; when cooked, it has a more distinctive grain flavor. *See* jasmine rice and Thai jasmine rice.

**American rices**   The United States is an important rice producer and the largest rice exporter in the world. Rice is no longer grown in Georgia and South Carolina, the birthplace of the American rice industry. The major rice-producing states are now Arkansas, California, Louisiana, Mississippi, Missouri, and Texas. The United States produces long-grain, medium-grain, and short-grain rices for use either whole or as an ingredient in processed foods. Many varieties of rice originally grown in other parts of the world are now being successfully grown here, including Japanese rice, basmati and Thai jasmine, Mediterranean rice, and several sticky rices. In addition, rice researchers and growers have developed a number of new specialty varieties. For more information, see page 53.

**amylopectin and amylose**   Rice contains two types of starches, amylose, with long straight strands, and amylopectin, with branching chains. Rices with high levels of amylose and low levels of amylopectin (such as basmati) cook to a firmer, drier texture. Low-amylose rices have relatively more amylopectin and have a stickier, softer texture when cooked (for example, Thai jasmine and Japanese rice). Uncooked grains of high-amylose rice (also known as nonwaxy rice) look translucent. Very low amylose rice (also known as waxy rice) looks more opaque and solid white. In very low amylose rices, there are air spaces between the granules of amylopectin and so the light does not pass through the grain in the same way that it can with the more tightly packed amylose granules. *See also* sticky rice, waxy rice, and nonwaxy rice.

**arborio**   The most widely available Italian rice, arborio can be used for risotto and for other Italian dishes, though many risotto lovers prefer carnaroli or vialone nano. Arborio becomes a little more sticky than these other two and absorbs broth a little less well. Try to find the top grade of Italian rice, *superfino*, for risotto.

**aromatic rices**   Aromatic rices such as jasmine and basmati have a subtle seductive scent as they cook. When the rice is served hot, it is still aromatic. Some aromatic rices are of the

Thai jasmine family, with soft slightly clingy grains when cooked, while others are Della-type rices that cook to a drier, fluffier texture.

**Australian rices**   Australia, like the United States, is a major exporter of rice. The Australian rices available in North America are usually long-grain, though the country also produces Japanese-style rice.

*aval*   Parboiled rice that has been flattened and dried out into flakes is a staple in several regions of India. In Kerala, it is called *aval*. It is available from Indian groceries. See Alternative, page 279; *see also* rice flakes.

**baldo**   This Italian rice is a japonica, like most other Italian rices, medium-grain and not very sticky. It is strong and holds its shape well during cooking. Baldo is also grown in Turkey and is often sold as Turkish rice. See Simple Turkish Pilaf, page 322.

**Balinese black and purple rice**   In Bali, as in most of the rest of Indonesia, rice is the primary crop and food. White rice is cooked fresh every day, but black rice (often purplish-black in color) is used for special offerings at the temple as well as for making fabulous sticky rice desserts sweetened with palm sugar and coconut milk, close cousins of Thai Sweet Black Rice Treat (page 168).

*bash ful*   This is the name under which a good parboiled Bangladeshi rice is being sold in the United States. *Bash ful* is a medium-grain rice, beige-cream in color, and not completely polished. Some of the translucent grains have an opaque white dot; many still have some small flecks of red bran attached. Probably because of the bits of bran, when the rice is cooked in plenty of boiling water, the water foams pink. Because the rice is parboiled, it takes a little longer to cook than regular polished rice, but holds its shape well during cooking. When cooked, *bash ful* has separate grains (like most parboiled rices) that are soft and tender. Available from Kalustyan's in New York City (see Mail-Order Sources, page 438) and sometimes at other specialty stores.

**basmati**   Basmati rice grows in the Himalayan foothills in northern India and Pakistan. It is also grown in some parts of the United States. Basmati is a very long-grain needle-shaped rice, best when it has been "aged" for several years before being milled and sold. When it cooks, it expands greatly in volume, but mostly lengthwise, so it becomes even more elongated.

The California- and Texas-grown basmatis are good but do not expand as much in length as Indian basmatis when cooked and lack the lovely aromatic smell of the original. They are sold in natural foods stores and some supermarkets. The best basmati from South Asia is often labeled "Dehra Dun," since that is reputedly the best growing region. Other basmatis, from West Bengal, are labeled "Patna." Basmatis from India and Pakistan can be found in specialty shops and South Asian groceries. Basmati rice is available white (milled) or brown (unmilled); brown basmati is usually American-grown.

Basmati is the ideal rice for Mogul (North Indian) and Persian cooking, since its grains stay separate and firm even when cooked through and tender. Outside Iran, it is the preferred rice for Persian rice dishes such as *chelo* and *polo*. It can also be cooked plain, then eaten with dal or other savory dishes. See page 236 for a basic basmati recipe and the Index for other dishes.

**Bhutanese red rice**    In Bhutan, which lies north of India in the Himalayas, the staple food is red rice. The rice is medium-grain and slightly sticky and has recently become available in the United States, at specialty stores such as Balducci's and Dean & DeLuca. It's a red japonica rice that has been semi-milled, so the red of the outer (bran) layers is still on the rice in patches. The cooked rice is pale pink when first cooked, soft and tender, and slightly clingy, so it's easy to eat with chopsticks. The rice can be served in place of white or brown rice, accompanied by hearty side dishes such as dal or meat stews. See page 241 for a basic Bhutanese red recipe and also Uighur Autumn Pulao, page 310.

**Black Japonica rice**    This is a specialty rice mixture, developed by the Lundberg brothers of California, of two unmilled rices: about 25 percent black short-grain japonica-type rice and 75 percent medium-grain mahogany-red rice. When you see the raw grain in bulk, it is a mixture of black and rich red. Black Japonica, being unmilled, needs more water and a longer cooking time than white rices. It has the eating characteristics of other unpolished rices, being chewy but tender when cooked, with a mottled reddish-brown color. It is ideal for stuffings and for warm or cold rice salads, and as an accompaniment to strong flavors. For recipes, see page 403.

**black rice**    There are many varieties of black rice. All black rice is rice that has a black-colored bran layer. Underneath the bran, the rice is white. For particular varieties, *see* Balinese black and purple rice, Chinese black rice, and Thai black rice.

**boiled rice**    In India, this is the term used for parboiled rice. Nonparboiled rice is known as *atma* in Bengal. *See* parboiled rice.

**bomba**    Bomba is a premium medium-grain japonica rice from Spain that has relatively large grains and absorbs large quantities of liquid. It is the most prized rice for making paella and related dishes. Bomba generally costs about twice what other rice from Spain costs and is difficult to find in North America.

**brisures**    *See* brokens.

**brokens**    Brokens refers to the lowest grade of rice and also to grains of rice that are broken into smaller pieces. The brokens grade has a high proportion of broken grains in it. It is good rice for congee and for rice pudding, where you want the starches to be released into the cooking liquid.

**brown parboiled rice**    Brown parboiled rice is available from some specialty shops and natural foods stores. Because parboiling drives oils into the bran, unmilled ("brown") parboiled rice is a little oily. If it is stored in a paper bag, you will see smudges of oil on the sides of the bag a few days after you buy it. Because of the oil, parboiled brown rice will go rancid if kept too long or if not stored in a cool place. See page 388 for a basic recipe.

**brown rice**    Brown rice refers to rice that has been taken from its husk but not yet milled and polished. Each grain is still intact, with an outer coating of bran (usually a tawny-brown color, hence the term "brown rice") and the germ too. Some unmilled or "brown" rice is not brown but red or black, because the bran is naturally colored. Brown rice takes longer to cook than milled rice and is somewhat more chewy to eat. It also has more nutrients. (See page 51 for a discussion of the nutritional value of brown rice.)

**bulu**    *See* javanica.

**Calasparra**   This small region of Spain is the only rice-producing region of Europe to have its own *denominación del origin* ("region of origin") designation. Calasparra lies southwest of Valencia, inland from the coast. The most famous Calasparra rice is bomba. *See* bomba.

**caldero**   This is a category of Spanish flavored rice dishes with a moist texture, made in a deeper pan than a paella. See Aromatic Rice and Fish with Two Sauces, page 335.

**Calmati**   Calmati is the brand name for a California-grown basmati-type rice that lacks some of the aroma and the lengthening characteristics of traditional basmati but cooks into a pleasant, fluffy long-grain rice. Sometimes available unmilled, in a brown rice version.

**CalRiso**   CalRiso is a trademarked brand name of Mediterranean-style rice grown in California near Sacramento. The rice is a medium-grain japonica that has similar cooking characteristics to arborio superfino, with a slightly greater expansion of the grains during cooking. It can also be used in Spanish rice dishes.

**CalRose**   Another trademark or brand name, CalRose is a Japanese-style rice. Both plain rice and sweet (sticky) rice are marketed under the name CalRose.

**Camargue rice**   For years, we heard that there was a small rice crop grown in the Camargue. Then a friend brought us some Camargue rice, brown, organic, and delicious. Soon, we hope, supplies of the rice will be available in North America. For now, only if you are in Nîmes or Arles or smaller villages in the Camargue itself do you have any reliable hope of finding the rice. Like the rices of Spain and Italy, it is a japonica type, medium- to short-grain, and slightly rounded at one end. Some Camargue rice has a red-colored bran. *Red Camargue* is difficult to find but has become a gourmet item in some European restaurants. Like *brown Camargue* rice, it is unpolished and is best cooked like pasta, in plenty of salted water, then drained and lightly dressed with olive oil, fresh herbs, and perhaps small pieces of anchovy. *Polished Camargue* rice is translucent white and looks very like arborio. It has a small opaque white spot, like many Spanish and Italian medium-grain rices.

**cargo rice**   *See* paddy rice.

**carnaroli**   A medium-grain japonica grown in Italy, this has the reputation of being the most difficult to grow of the Italian rices. Carnaroli is also the most expensive of the Italian rices. It has a higher amylose content than most risotto rices, so it stays firm during cooking, and perhaps for this reason is preferred for classic risotto except in the Veneto, where vialone nano is generally the rice of choice. Available in some Italian groceries, at specialty stores, and by mail order.

**Carolina rice**   Though South Carolina was once famous not only in the United States but also in Europe for its delicate, white long-grain rice, known as Carolina Gold, commercial rice production gradually died out after the Civil War. However, the name Carolina still evokes a high-quality rice, so some companies now use it to market good-quality generic white long-grain American-grown rices. It is also loosely used to refer to American-style long-grain rices that cook to a dry, separate texture, the classic ideal for Carolina low-country cooks.

**chelo**  This is a classic Persian rice preparation in which rice is soaked, then briefly boiled in plenty of water, then slow-steamed over a flavored crust.

**Chinese black rice**  A recent arrival in North America (see page 438 for Mail-Order Sources), this rice is grown in Zhezhiang in northern China. It is, like Thai black rice, an unmilled rice, what we would call a brown rice here. Local people in the black rice–growing area eat it primarily as *juk* (also known as rice porridge or congee). It has firm non-sticky grains and cooks relatively quickly for an unmilled rice. The cooked grains are tender. See the recipe on page 65.

**converted rice**  *Converted* is a registered trademark of Uncle Ben's and used to identify their parboiled rice. For an explanation of the parboiling process and its results, see Parboiled Rices, page 242, and below.

**Dehra Dun basmati**  This is the most highly prized basmati rice. *See* basmati.

**Della rices**  Della is a category of long-grain aromatic American rices that cook to a dry, fluffy texture with separate grains like conventional (Carolina-type) American long-grain rices. The other aromatic category is jasmine rices (see below). Della rices often have a nutty taste and a roasted nut or popcorn aroma. The two best-known examples are Louisiana pecan and Louisiana popcorn rice. *See* Carolina rice, and Louisiana pecan or wild pecan rice.

**devzira**  This premium pink-red medium- to short-grain rice is the preferred rice for making *pulao* in Turkic parts of Central Asia, such as Uzbekistan and Xinjiang. It is not yet available in North America. See Uighur Autumn Pulao, page 310.

**Egyptian rice**  Egyptian rice is available at specialty stores or by mail order. It is a very pleasant-tasting medium-grain japonica with smaller grains than arborio, excellent as a plain rice, for stuffing, or for Turkish pilafs. See page 322 for a basic recipe.

**enriched rice**  Most polished rice milled in the United States is enriched with a dusting of iron, thiamine, and niacin. Some states require that any milled rice sold in that state be enriched. The process and the requirement date back to the 1930s, when the concern was that the population was not getting adequate nutrition. The American Rice Council advises that enriched rice should not be washed before using and should be cooked by steaming or by the absorption technique, rather than boiling, so the nutrients aren't washed away. This advice runs counter to the practices of many people in the rice-eating world who wash rice to clean it and to improve the texture of their cooked rice. Having learned our rice-eating and rice-cooking habits in Asia, we too wash all our rice because we prefer the resulting texture; suit yourself.

**genmai**  This is the Japanese term for brown rice.

**glutinous rice**  *See* sticky rice.

**gobindavog**  Sometimes labeled "gobindobhog" or "Kalijira," this medium-grain rice from Bengal and Bangladesh has needle-shaped grains, like basmati, but in miniature. It is available from some specialty shops and by mail order (see Mail-Order Sources, page 438). It is cooked plain or can be used for pilafs and also for making rice pudding. See page 240 for a basic recipe and also the Index.

**haigamai**  This is a Japanese semi-milled rice; some but not all of the bran coat is milled off. It should be stored in a cool place because of the oils in the bran. For cooking instructions, see page 178.

**Himalayan red rice**  A long-grain unmilled rice with red bran, Himalayan red looks like Thai red rice. For cooking instructions, see page 241.

**indica**  Most rice that is grown and eaten around the world today is of the common Asian variety, *Oryza sativa*. It is generally divided into two main groups, indica rices and japonica rices, and a third, smaller group called javanica. Indica rices tend to be longer-grain rices that grow better nearer the equator, where day length is more constant. These rices generally have a lower yield per acre than japonicas. Classic indicas include basmati, the long-grain fragrant rices including Della rices, and Carolina-style long-grain rices.

**instant rice**  *See* precooked rice.

**Iranian rice**  *See* Persian rice.

**Italian rices**  Though long-grain rice is grown in Italy, "Italian rices" refers to the varieties used in traditional Italian dishes such as risotto. Italian rices are medium- to short-grain japonicas and include arborio, baldo, carnaroli, lido, roma, rosa marchetti, and vialone nano. Italian rices are graded according to quality, the best quality being *superfino*, then *fino*, *semi-fino*, and *originario o commune*.

**Japanese rice**  Japanese rice is of the japonica type. It is a medium-grain rice and the raw grains are slightly glassy, translucent rather than opaque, with a light powder on them.

Rice grown in Japan is not exported. In this book, "Japanese rice" refers to Japan-style rice.

In the United States, there is a well-established Japanese-style rice production, particularly in California. Our favorite brand is Kokuho Rose, grown in California by Nomura Brothers. Other good California brands are CalRose, Nishiki, and Matsu, available at Asian groceries and specialty stores. Japanese-style rice is also grown in Korea. When properly cooked, plain Japanese rice is very slightly sticky but with distinct firm grains. For cooking instructions, see page 174; for sushi rice instructions, see page 215.

Japanese rice is sold white (polished) or semi-milled or brown. There is also a distinctive and special kind of Japanese rice, a sticky rice, called sweet rice; *see mochi gome* and sticky rice.

**japonica**  Most rice that is grown and eaten today is of the common Asian variety, *Oryza sativa*. It is generally divided into two main groups, indica rices and japonica rices, and a third, smaller group called javanica. Japonica rices are generally medium- to short-grain. They grow best farther from the equator, in temperate climates. Most upland rice is japonica; some japonicas are also relatively tolerant of cold and can be grown in the mountains of northern Japan, for example. Japonicas tend to be higher yielding than indicas and to respond better to applications of fertilizer. Classic japonicas include the rices of the Mediterranean and Japanese rices.

**jasmati**  This is an American "designer rice," developed in Texas as a combination of jasmine rice and basmati. It is aromatic, with the cooking characteristics of Thai jasmine rice (slightly soft and clinging.)

**jasmine rice**   One group of aromatic rices is known as jasmine rices. They are like Thai jasmine rice, low-amylose rices that cook to a soft, slightly clingy texture—unlike the separate fluffy texture of Della rices (see above). They are generally cooked in less water than Della rices. See American jasmine rice and Thai jasmine rice.

**javanica**   Most rice that is grown and eaten today is of the common Asian variety, *Oryza sativa*. It is generally divided into two main groups, indica rices and japonica rices, and a third, smaller group called javanica, sometimes known as *bulu* rice. Javanicas are tropical rices that originated in Java or other parts of Indonesia. They tend to be medium- to long-grain.

**Kalijira**   *See* gobindavog.

**katteh**   This is the simplest plain-cooked rice in Persian (Iranian) cuisine, most typical of the northern coastal region, by the Caspian Sea. See Everyday Persian Rice on page 290.

**Kerala red rice**   *See* South Indian red rice.

**ketipat**   This Malay and Indonesian plain rice preparation is made by packing rice tightly into a small woven basket and then steaming it until done. The rice compresses and compacts as it absorbs water during cooking to make a dense, moist rice "cake," ideal for scooping through sauces. *Ketipat* is traditionally eaten with satay.

**khao neeo**   The Thai word for Thai sticky rice is *khao neeo*. *See* Thai black rice and Thai sticky rice.

**koji**   This is the Japanese word for the fermenting agent, usually made of rice, used in the manufacture of miso, sake, and other products. See the discussion on page 188.

**leftover rice**   There are many recipes that use previously cooked rice to make entirely new dishes (see the Index). To store leftover rice, place it in a plastic or glass container with a tight-fitting lid and refrigerate for up to 3 days. To reheat, place it in a pot with 2 to 3 tablespoons water and as the water comes to a boil, stir gently to heat rice, then cover, lower heat to medium, and let steam for 5 minutes. You can instead add a little water to the rice, then place in a sealed container in the microwave at full power for 1 to 2 minutes to reheat.

**long-grain rice**   The international community has now established standards for the description of rice. Categories are based on the ratio of length to width of grain, not on absolute length. Long-grain rice has grains that are more than three times as long as they are wide. Classic long-grain rices include basmati and Carolina long-grain.

**Louisiana pecan or wild pecan rice**   This is a variety of long-grain aromatic Della rice from Louisiana. We have found it only as a parboiled rice. The aroma during cooking is pleasantly nutty. It is also available as a brown (unmilled) rice. See page 389 for a basic recipe.

**Louisiana popcorn rice**   Like Louisiana pecan, this is a variety of long-grain, aromatic Della rice. It may be parboiled or not, or brown (unmilled). It has a pleasant smell and taste reminiscent of buttered popcorn. For cooking instructions see page 389.

**manohmin**   This is the name for North American wild rice (*Zizania aquatica*) in the Anishnaabe language, meaning "seed." *See* wild rice.

brown basmati

vietnamese red cargo

brown japanese

american short-grain brown

arborio superfino

italian semi-polished

chinese black

brown sticky

american long-grain white

camargue red

louisiana pecan

wild rice (minnesota)

spanish bomba

camargue brown

wehani

american parboiled white

japanese sticky

egyptian

rosematta

turkish baldo

black japonica

bash ful

thai sticky

thai black sticky

thai jasmine

wild rice (saskatchewan)

basmati

japanese white

bhutanese red

himalayan red

obindavog

thai red

american long-grain brown

american parboiled brown

carnaroli

valencia

**above**
Rice stubble just after harvest,
in California's Sacramento Valley

**left**
Irrigated rice terraces in central Bali

Man carrying rice straw home from the fields, in Bengal

**left**
Making offerings at a shrine
in a rice field, in Bali

**below**
Balinese rice terraces

**above**
Pulling and bundling
rice seedlings for
transplanting, near
Luang Prabang, Laos

**left**
Harvesting rice in
central Vietnam

**above**
Smoothing a plowed
and flooded paddy
before planting,
in northeastern Bali

**right**
Ripe rice ready
for harvest, in
Northern California

**clockwise from right**

Karbi woman with her mortar and pestle, used for cleaning rice, in Assam

Newly transplanted rice seedlings in flooded fields near Ubud, Bali

Rice harvest near Quy Nhon, in Vietnam

**medium-grain rice**    The international community has now established standards for the description of rice, long-, medium-, and short-grain. Medium-grain rice has grains that are two and a half to three times as long as they are wide. It may be japonica or indica. A medium-grain indica is the preferred rice for Mexican rice; most Japanese rice as well as the classic Italian risotto rices and Spanish paella rices are medium-grain. About 30 percent of the rice grown in the United States is medium-grain.

**milled rice**    Milled rice is rice that has had the bran layers milled off. It is also known as white rice. Milled rice may be processed one step further, by polishing, to remove every last bit of bran. *See* white rice and polished rice.

**mochi**    Mochi is the Japanese name for cooked sticky rice that has been pounded until it is perfectly smooth. Though it is a traditional New Year's food, it is also eaten year-round. Mochi is sold as a sweet treat to be eaten with tea. It comes in small balls or in fine smooth sheets that may be rolled or folded. It has a slightly sweet taste and a pleasantly smooth texture. Both white rice mochi and brown rice mochi are also sold in dried blocks in natural food stores. These blocks are cut into small pieces and toasted, broiled, or grilled until they puff up, then eaten with a simple dipping sauce. *See* also page 226.

**mochi gome**    This is the Japanese name for Japanese-style short- to medium-grain sweet rice (sticky rice). It is used for making *mochi* (see above) and sweets as well as for red rice (see recipe, page 228). It must be soaked before cooking. When cooked, it is very sticky and clumped together with a slightly sweet taste. *See* sticky rice.

**new-crop rice**    After harvest or parboiling, rice is dried so that it has no more than 14 percent moisture. Even though the grain has been dried (by machine or the sun), it can and does dry still more in the first months after harvest. New-crop rice is rice that has been harvested fairly recently. It tends to have a slightly higher moisture content (so it requires a little less water when cooked by the absorption technique) and it is a little more fragile than older rice. Those who like their rice very soft and perhaps even a little sticky prefer new-crop rice; those of us who don't make sure that the bags of rice we buy in the post-harvest months (November through February) are not marked "new-crop rice."

**nonwaxy rice**    The many varieties of rice (*Oryza sativa*) are generally classed as either waxy or nonwaxy. This classification refers to the proportion of the starches amylose and amylopectin in the rice. Waxy rices are low in amylose and usually sticky when cooked. Nonwaxy rices are high in amylose and usually cook into dry separate grains. They cook at higher temperatures (so usually take slightly longer to cook than waxy rices). *See also* amylose and amylopectin.

**organic rice**    Organically grown rices, like other agricultural products marked "organic," have been grown with no chemical pesticides or chemical fertilizers. Farmers rely instead on natural predators and crop rotation to keep down pests and maintain productivity, and on natural fertilizers such as mulch and green manure to maintain soil fertility. Different countries define "organic" (*biologico* in Italian, *biologique* in French) differently. Organically grown rices are available at natural foods stores and in some supermarkets. When buying unmilled rice in particular, we try to use only organic rice, since we are told that chemical residues may remain in the bran of an unmilled rice.

**Oryza glaberrima**  *Oryza* means "rice" and *Oryza glaberrima* is the Latin name of the dominant African variety of rice. Glaberrima rice is still grown in parts of West Africa, though it has been supplanted in many places by higher-yielding Asian-variety (*Oryza sativa*) rices.

**Oryza sativa**  *Oryza sativa* is the Linnaean name for the Asian rices. Most cultivated rice in the world today is *Oryza sativa* or Asian rice. There are thousands of varieties of *Oryza sativa* that thrive in many very different environments.

**paddy rice**  Also known as cargo rice or rough rice, paddy rice is harvested rice that has not yet been milled to remove the husk. Paddy rice is still a living grain that can be planted. Fifty pounds of paddy rice will yield about twenty-five pounds of white (milled and polished) rice.

**paella**  Paella is both the name of a wide shallow metal pan used to cook certain traditional Spanish rice dishes and the name of the dish. See Index for recipes.

**parboiled rice**  Parboiling is an ancient and ingenious technique for increasing the nutritional value of polished rice. It dates back more than two thousand years and seems to have been developed in southern India. Many people in Bengal, Bangladesh, South India, and Sri Lanka prefer the taste and texture of parboiled rice.

For parboiled rice, paddy rice (rice still in its husk) is boiled, then cooled. This has the effect of driving nutrients from the bran into the center of the rice and at the same time pushing oils into the bran. Parboiled rice is easier to polish by hand than unboiled rice, and perhaps this is why the technique first developed. Mechanical polishers have a little more trouble with parboiled rice because the extra oil in the bran can clog up the machinery. Most parboiled rice is milled (which gives it much better storage qualities—no germ or bran to go rancid), but because of the parboiling process the rice retains much of the nutritional value of unmilled rice.

Because the rice has been heated, the starches in parboiled rice are more glassy and harder in texture than those in nonparboiled grains. The grains have a slightly glassy look to them and tend to be yellowish rather than semi-transparent white. Because the starches are harder, parboiled rice takes longer to cook than polished rice that has not been parboiled. The cooked grains tend to have a slightly bouncy texture and to be completely non-sticky. They are also stronger and stand up better to overcooking or immersion in soup, which makes them a favorite of restaurants and others who must cook rice in bulk.

In North America, parboiling was adopted as a means of improving the nutritional value of rice early in the twentieth century. Most North American parboiled rice is also precooked, at least partially, so that it does not take as long to cook as, for example, parboiled rices from India.

**parboiled brown rice**  *See* brown parboiled rice.

**patna**  This long-grain Indian rice from western Bengal is a kind of basmati rice. It is a very good everyday rice, less expensive than Dehra Dun basmati (*see* basmati). It is available in most Indian and South Asian stores and in some specialty shops.

**pearl rice**  This is a North American term for short-grain rice used in making puddings.

**perloo**   A version of the word *pulao,* perloo is the name of a number of *pulao*-like rice dishes from South Carolina. *See* pilaf and *pulao.*

**Persian rice**   Though Persia—Iran today—has long been famous for its rice and its rice dishes, the best Persian rice has rarely been available outside the country. Outside Iran, Persian dishes are usually made with basmati rice, which is very like the third and fourth grades of Persian rice. Those grades are, starting with the best: *ambar-boo,* amber-scented; *darbari,* imperial court rice; *dom-siah* or black-tailed rice, a variety of basmati; *sadri,* a rice very like basmati that came to Persia from India in the nineteenth century. Iranians use a short-grain rice called *gerdeh* in rice puddings and as a binder in meatballs (*kofteh*).

**pilaf**   *Pilaf* is the Turkish and Turkic-language word for a flavored rice dish that is served on a platter. Partly cooked rice is layered or tossed with meat or vegetables or legumes, or a combination, then slow-cooked until done with a little butter or oil. The dishes in the pilaf family are close cousins of *pulao* and *polo. See polo* and *pulao,* and Index for recipes.

**polished rice**   *Polished rice* is the general term often used for what most of us think of as white rice. It is rice that has had its outer bran layer and germ removed through mechanical or hand milling and has then been further polished to remove all traces of the bran. Polished rice has fewer minerals and vitamins and less fiber than brown rice, but it is quicker to cook, keeps better, and is more easily digestible. (For more on the nutritional values of unmilled versus milled rice, see page 51). *See also* semi-milled rice.

**polo**   The ultimate expression of the pilaf/*pulao* technique, *polo* refers to a category of Persian (Iranian) rice dishes are slow-cooked combinations of rice with meat and/or sour fruits, legumes, or vegetables. See Index for recipes.

**precooked rice**   In the course of marketing rice to North Americans and non–rice eating Europeans, manufacturers and retailers have tried different processing methods to make rice easier to prepare. Many of these techniques result in a loss in flavor and character, but shorten the cooking time.

Many American parboiled rices are also precooked, then dried. All they need is a short immersion in boiling water to become tender and ready to be served. Some rices are marketed as "instant" or "minute" rice; these take only a minute in boiling water to rehydrate and be ready to serve. Boil-in-a-bag rice is usually parboiled rice that has also been precooked and then dried. The cotton bag, with the rice in it, is heated by brief immersion in boiling water. The result is tender fluffy rice, without much character or flavor. To prepare precooked rice, follow the manufacturer's directions.

**pudding rice**   This is an English term that refers to short-grain rices that are often used for making rice pudding. They release their starches as they cook, thickening the cooking liquid. Broken rice can be substituted.

**puffed rice**   More than just a breakfast cereal, puffed rice is a widely used version of rice, especially in India. To make it, polished rice is heated in a metal cylinder under pressure and eventually, like corn, it puffs out to a roundish shape. Puffed rice keeps well in a tightly sealed container or plastic bag. It is available from South Asian groceries. See Spicy Puffed Rice Snack on page 276.

**pulao**   *Pulao* (also *pulau* and *pullao*) is the word usually used for pilaf-style dishes in India and parts of Central Asia. The *pulao* technique seems to have traveled to India with the Moguls. There it is associated with the Moslem community and has developed many different regional versions. *Pulao* is a large category of flavored rice dishes in which long- or medium-grain rice is first fried in oil or butter with some flavorings, then immersed in a large amount of broth and allowed to absorption-cook until done. A *pulao* usually contains meat, though it may be strictly vegetarian; in either case, the meat or vegetables cook together with the rice. *See also polo* and pilaf, and Index for recipes.

**purloo**   *See* perloo.

**quick rice**   *See* precooked rice.

**raspa**   This is the Spanish word for the delicious crust that forms on the bottom of the pot as Cuban rice cooks. *See also tahdig.*

**red rice**   Some varieties of rice have a bran layer that is red rather than the more usual (to us) pale brown. These rices are known as red rices. Because premium polished rice commands a higher price if it is uniformly white, red rice is viewed as an expensive intruder by many rice growers. Even when the rice is polished, some small bits of red bran may remain and thus lower the value of the batch of rice. But some growers have taken advantage of the recent consumer interest in different rices and have successfully marketed red rices. These include Wehani, Thai red rice, and the mahogany rice that is part of the Black Japonica blend. *See* Bhutanese red rice, Himalayan red rice, South Indian red rice, Thai red rice, Vietnamese red (cargo) rice, and Wehani.

**rice bran**   Rice bran is the fibrous outer layer of the grain. When brown rice is milled to become white rice, the bran is rubbed off. Rice bran can be bought at health food stores and is an ingredient in some breakfast cereals. It is composed primarily of fiber (good for the digestion) and also contains some trace minerals and ash. *See also* rice bran oil.

**rice bran oil**   Rice is low in oil, but an oil is extracted from the bran and germ after the bran and germ have been cleaned from the rice during milling. Rice bran oil is rich in Vitamin E, linoleic acid, and plant sterols. India, China (including Taiwan), and Japan are all important producers. Rice bran oil is available in some natural foods stores.

**rice cooker**   Rice cookers are plug-in electrical appliances that cook rice by the absorption technique. They can also be used to make rice porridge (*juk* or congee). An outer pot insulates and protects an electric heating element that sits under an inner pot, usually a light aluminum pot. The lid fits tightly. The inner pot has markings on it to show the level of water required to cook specific quantities of rice. Generally a rice cooker uses a little less water than is required for absorption cooking in a heavy rice pot (probably because there is less evaporation as the rice comes to a boil, since the lid is on the whole time).

The most simple rice cookers have an on/off switch: They bring water and rice to a boil, and then soon afterward lower the heat to maintain a bare simmer until the rice is done. They continue to supply heat after the rice has finished cooking, to keep it warm. More sophisticated rice cookers come with timers, so the rice and water can be placed in the cooker, ready to begin cooking many hours later. Rice cookers have almost completely replaced traditional pots in Japan, Korea, Taiwan, parts of China, Vietnam, and Thailand.

**rice flakes**   Flattened grains of rice are eaten as snacks or breakfast food in many parts of the rice-eating world. The rice grains are heated or parboiled (as they are for southern Indian *aval*) before being rolled and flattened. Rice flakes keep well in a dry place; they absorb water and other flavors very well. *See also aval.*

**rice flour**   After rice has been milled, the remaining (white) grain is the endosperm, made up mostly of starches. Rice flour is ground-up white rice, widely used in Asia to make noodles and for making sweets. It has no gluten-forming protein, so it can be used for flatbreads but must be combined with wheat flour to make risen breads. Rice flour is available in most grocery stores.

**rice oil**   *See* rice bran oil.

**risotto**   Risotto is a northern Italian rice dish, made by cooking an absorbent medium-grain Italian rice briefly in a little flavored oil or butter, then gradually adding hot water or broth, while stirring, until the rice has cooked. Most risottos are finished off with grated cheese—Parmigiano-Reggiano, usually—and often butter too. Most risotto is served as the pasta course in an Italian meal; some may be served as a main course. See Index for recipes.

**rosematta**   Rosematta, a parboiled rice from South India, has slightly fat long grains with some flecks of the reddish outer layers (bran) still on. When raw, even the "white" part of the rice is yellowish because of parboiling. The overall look of the raw rice is pinkish-bronze. When cooked, the grains are separate and almost seem to bounce apart; they fill out and become quite fat, or rounded. The taste of the cooked rice is somewhat smoky-meaty. See the recipe on page 243; *see also* South Indian red rice.

**scented rices**   *See* aromatic rices.

**semi-milled rice**   In Italy, semi-milled rice is called *semi-lavorato;* in Japanese, it's *haigamai.* Semi-milled rice is a wonderful compromise for those who like more taste of the grain and a more nutritious rice than milled white rice, but don't like the very chewy texture of many brown rices. Semi-milled rice is probably very like the rice that was eaten by many rice eaters throughout the world until the advent in this century of mechanical rice milling and polishing. Milled and polished rice is very white and has no trace of the bran left on it. Semi-milled has flecks of bran still clinging to the grain, and may still have the germ attached. Many of the "new rices"—that is, rices now becoming available to North American consumers—are semi-milled or lightly milled: rosematta, Bhutanese red, and Lowell Farms Jasmine are several that come to mind.

Cooking times for semi-milled rices are only slightly longer than those for milled and polished rice of the same kind; since much of the bran has been polished off, the grain absorbs water almost as quickly as milled rice. If you find a semi-milled version of one of the milled rices described in this book, just add 5 to 10 minutes to the cooking time.

**short-grain rice**   Short-grain is one of the categories that the international community has established for the description of rice. Categories are based on the ratio of length to width of grain, not on absolute length. Short-grain rice has grains that are less than twice as long as they are wide. These very rounded grains include many varieties of sweet rice, pudding rices, and some of the Mediterranean rices. Often, however, "short-grain rice" is casually used to refer to medium-grain rices as well, as a way of saying "not long-grain."

**South Indian red rice**   Some of the rices in Kerala, Tamil Nadu, and Sri Lanka have red bran; they are most often rices used for parboiling. Recently one of these has become available in North America, usually sold as "rosematta." It is available parboiled and lightly milled, red-flecked from remaining flecks of bran. Others may soon become available. See the recipe on page 243; *see also* rosematta.

**Spanish rice**   Traditional Spanish rice is medium-grain japonica. It is very absorbent and is almost always cooked in broth or a flavor base known as a *sofrito*. It is used to make paella, *caldoso*, and other Spanish rice dishes. The best-known Spanish rices include Valencia, Calasparra, and bomba. The top grade of Spanish rice is *extra*, the next *categoria 1*. See Index for recipes.

**sticky rice**   Sticky rice, also known as glutinous rice or sweet or waxy rice, may be long-grain or short-grain. It is a different kind of rice from nonwaxy rice (see above), with different starches: more amylopectin and very little amylose. When raw, it has a white opaque look, whereas most white rices have a shining translucent-to-transparent look.

In northern and northeastern Thailand, in Laos, among the Dong people in China's Guizhou Province, and in parts of Vietnam, long-grain sticky rice is the staple grain. It is mostly served with savory side dishes and flavorings, though occasionally it is served sweetened, as in the perennial favorite sticky rice with mango slices. *See* Thai Black Rice Treat, page 168.

In northern Vietnam, in Japan and Korea, and in parts of Burma and China, shorter grain sticky rices are widely used, both as savory dishes and in sweets. Breakfast in northern Vietnam is often *xoi,* sticky rice steamed with peanuts, then eaten with sliced meat, or, instead, with sugar—often as a street food. The sticky rice cakes traditional at New Year's in Japan, much of China, and Taiwan are made from pounded short-grain sticky rice. In Iran, a short-grain sweet rice known as *gerdeh* is used for sweet dishes; in England, sweet rice for use in desserts is known as pudding rice. In North America, the term is more often *pearl rice.*

*See* Balinese black and purple rice, *mochi gome*, Thai black rice, and Thai sticky rice.

**superfino**   This is the top grade of Italian rice. When buying an Italian rice for risotto, try to find this grade.

**sushi rice**   Sushi rice is prepared with plain Japanese rice. The rice is cooked in a little less water than for plain rice, then flavored with a vinegar and sugar mixture. See page 215 for a basic recipe.

**sweet rice**   *See* sticky rice and waxy rice.

**tahchin**   Tahchin is the Iranian term for a category of baked rice dishes in Persian (Iranian) cuisine. See the recipe on page 306.

**tahdig**   This is the Iranian term for the rice crust that forms on the bottom of the pot when rice slow-cooks—for example, in *polo, chelo,* or *katteh.* In Uzbek and Uighur, the crust is known as *kasmag;* in Cuba, as *raspa.*

**Texmati**   A basmati-type rice developed in Texas, this is long-grain and cooks to a dry, fluffy texture, but it lacks some of the aroma as well as the remarkable lengthwise expansion of traditional basmati.

**Thai black rice**   A black variety of Thai long-grain sticky rice, this rice is not milled (i.e., it is a "brown rice"). Though the rice inside the bran is a sticky rice (and white), because the outer (black) bran layers are left on the grain, the grains of rice do not stick together when cooked, but stay entirely separate. The rice turns a most beautiful, slightly purply black when cooked. Thais use this rice for desserts and other sweets. They usually mix it with an equal quantity of white sticky rice and soak them together (see the recipe on page 116). The black rice dyes the white and the white's stickiness helps the blended rice to stick together when cooked. See Sweet Black Rice Treat, page 168.

**Thai jasmine rice**   A low-amylose long-grain aromatic rice originally from Southeast Asia, Thai jasmine is now widely available in North America. Similar rices are grown in Cambodia and Vietnam, but are not readily available in North America. Some American-grown jasmine rices are now very similar in taste, texture, and cooking characteristics to Thai jasmine. Thai jasmine has clear, crystalline long grains. It is usually absorption-cooked, and cooks to soft, slightly clinging grains. For a basic recipe, see page 115.

**Thai red rice**   Red rice grows among jasmine rice plants in Thailand, and a similar "gone wild" red rice also "contaminates" many rice fields in other parts of the world. Red rice is brittle and difficult to polish, so its color lowers the value of any white rice it is mixed in with. Recently, however, this "problem" rice has become sought after as a novelty rice, sold unpolished. It's pretty to look at and good to eat. Red rice is available from many Thai groceries and from specialty stores. Himalayan red rice is very similar and can be substituted. Look for needle-slender grains, mostly a reddish-brown but with the occasional bit of pale white showing through. The rice is unmilled (like brown rice) and so takes longer to cook than polished rices such as Thai jasmine. See page 121 for a basic recipe.

**Thai sticky rice**   Known as *khao neeo* in Thailand and Laos, Thai sticky rice is medium- to long-grain and slightly aromatic. It is cooked by steaming over water, after a preliminary soaking in water. The rice is very low amylose (waxy) rice and may be labeled "sweet rice," or "glutinous rice," or "*gao nep*" (Vietnamese for "sticky rice"). It has opaque white grains when raw rather than the translucent grains of nonsticky Thai rice. Thai sticky rice is also being grown in California.

**Turkish rice**   Turkish pilafs are best prepared with a medium-grain japonica. The Italian variety baldo is preferred in Turkey and often labeled Turkish rice. It is sold in some specialty stores. See Simple Turkish Pilaf, page 322.

**unmilled rice**   This is another term for what we usually think of as brown rice. The outer husk of the grain has been removed, but the bran and germ are still on. *See* brown rice.

**Valencia**   The most widely available variety of Spanish rice, this medium- to short-grain japonica looks very like arborio and other Italian risotto rices. It is ideal for paella and other Spanish rice dishes. Risotto rices and Spanish rices may be substituted for each other.

**vialone nano**   This premium Italian rice is preferred by some for making risotto, especially in the Veneto. Its grains stay firm during cooking. Its name means "dwarf vialone" and its grains are shorter and fatter than carnaroli grains, though with almost as high a proportion of amylose. It is available from well-stocked Italian grocers and some specialty stores.

**Vietnamese red (cargo) rice**   This medium-grain red unmilled japonica rice from Vietnam is now being sold in some specialty stores. Cook it as you would brown Japanese rice.

**waxy rice**   The many varieties of rice (*Oryza sativa*) are generally classed as either waxy or nonwaxy, which refers to the proportion of the starches amylose and amylopectin in the rice. Waxy rices (also known as sweet, sticky, or glutinous rices) have relatively low amylose levels and proportionately more amylopectin. This means they generally cook (the starches gelatinize) at a lower temperature and are most often soaked and then steamed, rather than being boiled. They have a sticky texture when cooked and a slightly sweet taste. *See* sticky rice.

**Wehani**   Wehani is a designer rice, developed by the Lundberg brothers in Northern California. Wehani is a beautiful, red-colored, unmilled rice with long, slightly wide grains, available at natural foods stores, specialty stores, and some well-stocked grocery stores. In the bin at the store it looks like Thai red rice or Himalayan red rice, but a little less fine and needle-like. See page 400 for a basic recipe.

**white rice**   White rice is rice that has been milled to remove its bran. Much white rice is also polished to remove the last traces of bran. The endosperm, or inner layer, of all rice is white; thus, whatever color the bran layer, once a rice is milled and polished, it will be white or cream-colored. Milled parboiled rice tends to have a yellower color, though it is still sold as "white rice."

**whole-grain rice**   *See* brown rice, black rice, and red rice.

**wild rice**   In North America, wild rice is the name given to the rice-like seed of a wild grass (*Zizania aquatica*) that grows wild from northern Saskatchewan into Minnesota, Wisconsin, and Ontario. The Anishnaabe (Ojibway) call it *manohmin*.

Recently, wild rice has been successfully cultivated in California and elsewhere. Consequently, though it has been traditionally harvested from lakes and marshes by people working in canoes, a great deal of the "wild rice" now available in stores is cultivated rather than wild, and harvested mechanically, not by hand. Wild rice grown and harvested in the traditional way is the most expensive and difficult to find.

Grain of wild rice are from half an inch to three inches long, and from tawny-blond in color to almost black. See page 405 for a basic recipe.

**Zizania aquatica**   This is the Linnaean name for North American wild rice, a member of the grass family (*zizania*) that grows in water (*aquatica*). *See* wild rice.

Ifugao rice terraces and small hamlet
near Banaue, Philippines
inset: Ifugao buluh statue holding a staff of ripe rice

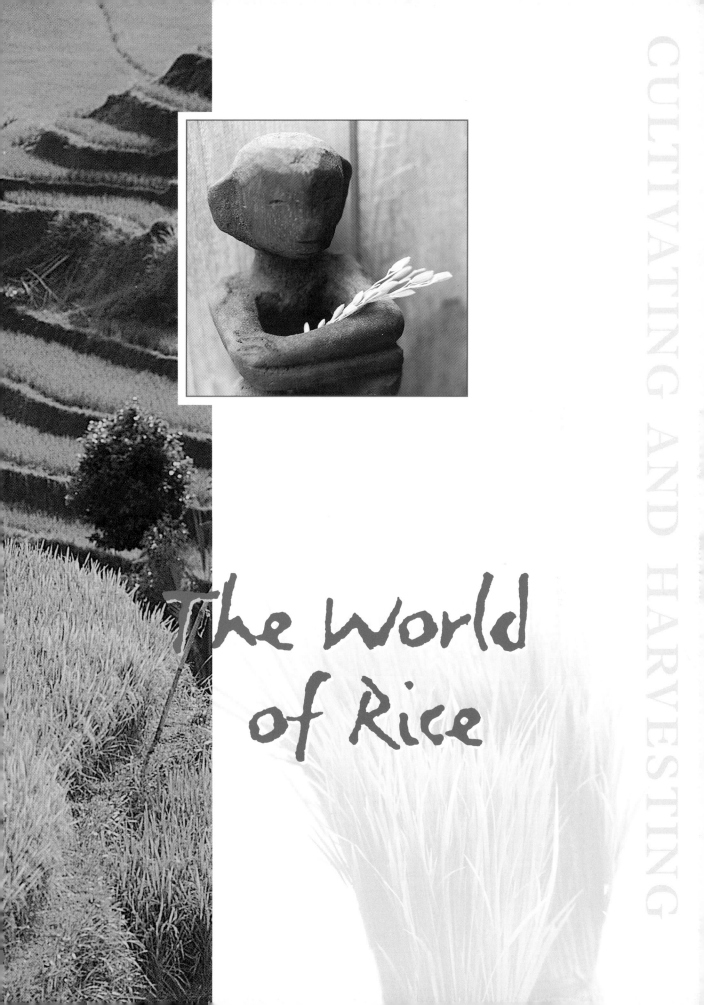

# The World of Rice

# Rice Through the Millennia

The two main cultivated species of rice, *Oryza sativa* (Asian rice) and *Oryza glaberrima* (African rice), first developed from wild species. Rice has been growing wild for millennia, and still does in many parts of Asia and Africa. The first evidence of rice cultivation is hard to pin down, but authorities seem to agree that somewhere in the region stretching from southern China across Thailand and Burma to Assam, the species *Oryza sativa* developed and was cultivated by early groups of people about seven thousand years ago. First written records of rice are Chinese and date from five thousand years ago; archaeological rice remains from India and Thailand date from about the same period. These early cultivators seem to have grown both *indica* (long-grain tropical) and *japonica* (medium-grain temperate) types of rice. The first cultivation was probably dryland cultivation, perhaps on the damp edge of a riverbank, perhaps on lowlying wetlands on valley floors.

The whole of the belt from South China to northern India is subject to the southwest monsoons, the rainy season that lasts from approximately May until September and coincides with hot weather. Since rice thrives in wet and warm conditions, it is not surprising that it should have been first cultivated in an area where natural growing conditions were ideal. Soon after, people learned how to manipulate and enhance growing conditions to extend the areas in which they could grow rice and to increase productivity.

The settled villagers in the rich Asian valleys who first cultivated rice must have selected seed for planting the following year based on observation of which plants were strongest and produced the best grain, as well as on trial and error. The result of that selection

Plowing the paddy with a water buffalo in the Red River Delta, Vietnam

*Woman making an offering to the gods before harvest, at a shrine near Sayan, in Bali*

process over time was a number of rice varieties that flourished in a range of environments. It's not known when people first discovered that flooding rice plants during the growing season helps keep down weeds, stabilize temperatures, and increase yields, but from this discovery came the development of sophisticated systems of irrigation and water management, not just in Asia, but also in West Africa. Later these techniques traveled with the spread of rice cultivation, to Madagascar, to the southern United States, and to South America.

From its origins in China and Thailand, rice cultivation spread to Vietnam and into the Malay Peninsula as well as to the Philippines. The origin of rice cultivation in Java and other islands of Indonesia is not clear, although rice probably reached Indonesia from mainland Southeast Asia over two thousand years ago.

Although archeological remains of rice dating back almost three thousand years have been found under Lake Biwa, near Kyoto, rice cultivation seems to have come to the Japanese island of Kyushu from China only in the first century B.C. Korean rice agriculture also developed from Chinese rice cultivation. In both Korea and Japan, successful rice agriculture in the colder and more northerly regions depended on the development of varieties of japonica rices that were tolerant to cooler temperatures and to varying lengths of day.

Rice also traveled through trade and conquest to present-day Bengal and Bihar and then to southern India and Sri Lanka. It was also cultivated in the Himalayan foothills. Both trade and conquest spread rice cultivation to Persia. The area bordering on the southern end of the Caspian Sea in present-day Iran and Azerbaijan is still an important rice-growing region, and rice dishes are still one of the glories of Persian (Iranian) cuisine. Persian rice dishes eventually found their way back to northern India with the Mogul conquest in the fifteenth century.

Rice cultivation probably reached the oases of Central Asia from Persia along what became the Silk Route; rice also traveled west with traders to the Arab and Turkish lands in the Mediterranean region.

In the seventh and eighth centuries, as the Arabs conquered Northern Africa, Sicily, and the Iberian Peninsula, they brought a love of rice and a knowledge of rice cultivation with them. The legacy of their conquests is the present important rice production in Egypt and Spain, and the Spanish word for rice, *arroz*, from the Arabic *ar-rozz*.

Rice cultivation in Northern Italy began in the late fifteenth century after the draining of the wetlands in the upper Po Valley. There is dispute as to whether rice arrived from Spain or from Sicily or from the East, brought by Venetian traders. Later, as the Turks conquered parts of the Balkans and present-day Hungary, rice cultivation and cookery became established in southeastern Europe as well.

About fifteen hundred years ago, Malay peoples from somewhere in the Indonesian archipelago found their way across the Indian Ocean to Madagascar. There they settled and established an Asian-style rice agriculture, with irrigated rice terraces and a rice-based cuisine. Rice remains the staple in Madagascar, as well as in neighboring Mauritius and the Comoros Islands.

Our knowledge of the history of rice cultivation in West Africa is more sketchy, although red (*glaberrima*) rice from West Africa was known to the Greeks in Hellenic times, long before Asian rice was brought to Africa. It seems to have developed in the Middle Delta of the Niger River (just south of Timbuktu), where rice is still grown, and in the form of floating rice (deep-water rice, page 42) along the riverbanks. It was also cultivated early along the Gambia and Casamance rivers. Asian rice traveled to West Africa sometime in the last seven hundred years, either with Portuguese traders coming back from India or with the Arabs who brought Islam to the region across the desert from Egypt and North Africa.

In the Americas, rice is now grown in Brazil (the largest producer in South America), Argentina, the Dominican Republic, Surinam, Peru, Colombia, Uruguay, Guyana, Venezuela, and Costa Rica, as well as in Mexico, Cuba, and the United States. Production in the Americas began after the Spanish Conquest, with the Spanish and Portuguese establishing rice cultivation in their colonies, while the English brought in slaves from West Africa to work in the rice plantations along the coasts of Georgia and South Carolina. With the end of slavery and the development of machinery for planting and harvesting, American rice cultivation moved to the heavier soils of Louisiana, Arkansas, Texas, Mississippi, Missouri, Florida, and Northern California, ideal for mechanized cultivation and all dependent on irrigation. The United States, which exports from half to two thirds of its rice crop, is the world's largest exporter of rice.

In Australia, most rice production is also highly mechanized and dependent on irrigation. Commercial-scale rice growing began there in 1924 in the Murrumbidgee Irrigation Area, in New South Wales, rice having been successfully introduced by a Japanese settler a decade earlier. Rice is also grown in Queensland and on New Zealand's North Island. Like the United States, Australia exports a large proportion of its rice crop.

Most rice is still eaten in the country, and most often in the small region where it is grown. Only 4 to 5 percent of the world's rice crop is traded between regions and countries. China grows more rice than any other country, 35 percent of world production. Thailand, the United States, and Vietnam are the world's biggest exporters of rice. Pictured are Karen insurgents unloading rice bags by the Moei River on the Thai-Burmese border.

# Growing Rice

Rice can grow in many different environments, from dry hillsides to irrigated paddy fields to deep river water. In each environment, the rice plant develops in a similar way from germination to grain ready for harvest.

Rice plants grow from seed (that is, grains of rice still in the hull), usually seed that has been soaked for a day to soften it and help encourage germination. The seed may be planted directly in the field or started in a seedbed and then transplanted into the field once it has developed a root system. The seed is usually planted in wet soil and then ideally grown in flooded soil. The seed first sends out roots, leaves, and a stalk. The new leaves look like fresh green grass. Then come several more stems or stalks. On each of these develop flowers, which then turn into heads of rice grain, the fruit of the plant. In traditional varieties, the stalks may grow to over six feet in height; in new varieties, the stalks are generally much shorter, often less than three feet. As the grain ripens, the rest of the plant dries out and turns from green to golden.

From planting of the seed to ripened grain ready for harvest takes from three to seven months depending on climate, water, and variety of rice. From the time the rice "heads" (starts forming grain) until it ripens and is ready for harvest takes about thirty days in the tropics and as long as sixty days in temperate regions such as Japan and Italy. In tropical and subtropical regions, provided there is irrigation water or enough rainfall, two and sometimes three crops of rice can be grown in a year. Some rices (mostly japonicas grown in temperate climates) take a fixed amount of time from planting to harvest, while many tropical indicas are mildly or strongly "day-length sensitive," so that they begin to develop and ripen at the same time of year, no matter when they are planted.

## Traditional Dryland Rice

Dryland rice is grown without irrigation, dependent only on rainfall or moisture already in the ground. It is usually planted around the start of the rainy season. Rice plants prefer very moist growing conditions, though there are now many drought-resistant varieties that grow well in areas with relatively little water (for example, in parts of West Africa). Dryland rice cultivation takes place in two ways, depending upon whether it is on an upland hillside area or a low-lying naturally wet area.

**Upland rice cultivation** In the least interventionist method of rice cultivation—swidden ("slash-and-burn") agriculture—people living in the tropical hills roughly clear a small area of jungle and burn off the brush during dry season. They dig up the ground before planting, or instead use pointed sticks to make holes in the ground and plant several rice seeds in each hole. The planted area is kept weeded, but moisture is entirely dependent on whatever monsoon rains fall. Harvest is about a month after the end of the monsoon. The same land will be cultivated for two or three years, then the people move on. The trees and other vegetation grow back until fifteen to thirty years later, when the same patch may be cleared and cultivated again. This method is still used by the Iban and others in Sarawak, Sabah, and Kalimantan on the island of Borneo; by hill tribes in mountainous parts of mainland Southeast Asia; and in parts of Africa and South America.

A less nomadic form of traditional dryland rice cultivation is used in parts of India, Southeast Asia, and Africa, where rice is planted in tilled ground along riverbanks, sometimes just after the river level has dropped. The moisture in the soil, plus rainfall, is the only form of water the plants get.

In established dryland rice fields, often the seeds are started in a well-watered seedbed, then transplanted once the rains have begun and the fields are thoroughly wet. Before planting or transplanting, the ground is plowed and then often the clods of earth are flattened and broken up by a second plowing. Some farmers, instead of plowing, enclose animals such as water buffalo in the fields to churn up the earth before planting.

**Rain-fed lowland rice** Lowland rice is grown without irrigation and is dependent upon rainfall and runoff. Each field is surrounded by a dike, or bund, a small earth wall to keep rainwater in and prevent it from flowing away downhill. Consequently, many dryland fields look like a complex patchwork of small areas, divided by these dikes, to help with water management. During the rainy season, the water can be up to twenty inches deep in lowland rain-fed fields. Maintaining the dikes is an important part of the work needed to cultivate rice. Before planting, the ground is well tilled and then wetted, or "puddled," with water carried to the field by hand, or by early rain if the farmer is lucky. Often animals are used for tilling and also to churn up the mud in the puddled field.

**above**

One study in 1990 estimated the number of person-hours required for each hectare (2.2 acres) of rain-fed paddy using improved seed, some fertilizer, and traditional labor-intensive techniques. The steps in rice production included in the study were seed selection, seedbed and rice field preparation, transplanting, weeding, fertilizing, pest management, harvesting, threshing, drying, and marketing. To produce over 1527 kilos (1.5 tons) of milled rice (almost double the amount of rough rice) from 1 hectare took 84 person-days and 14 animal-days. Twenty-two of those person-days were used for harvesting and threshing by hand. In contrast, in California, mechanical cultivation and harvest of 350 hectares (770 acres) required only 40 person-days to produce over 1,000 tons of milled rice. Pictured is a paddy landscape in Vietnam's Red River Valley.

**right**

Yields of rice can be as high as 7,000 kilos (15,400 pounds) of rough rice per hectare—in well-irrigated and fertilized farms in Australia, United States, and Spain, for example—and as low as 700 kilos (1,540 pounds) per hectare (700 pounds per acre) in tropical dryland rice farms. In warm-temperate areas, yields average about 3,000 kilos (6,600 pounds) per hectare (3,000 pounds per acre); and in the tropics, about 1,500 kilos (3,300 pounds) per hectare (1,500 pounds per acre). Pictured are upland rice terraces on the Chinese-Vietnamese border.

## Deep-Water and "Floating" Rice

In the deltas of the large rivers of Southeast Asia, such as Thailand's Chao Phraya and the Mekong, rices developed (both naturally and through human selection) that can be grown in very deep water. The rice is sown on the riverbank and then as the waters rise rapidly with monsoon rains, the plants keep pace, sometimes growing eight inches in a day. Though many of these rivers have now been controlled with dams and other water management schemes, deep-water rices (also known as floating rices) still grow in many delta areas of Asia. The water depth is from three to six feet during much of the growing season. Yields are lower for deep-water rice than for irrigated or rain-fed lowland rice, but higher than for rain-fed upland rice.

Floating rice also grows along the Niger River in Mali. It is a variety of native African *Oryza glaberrima* that has become well adapted to the river's changing levels. It grows rapidly with the rising river during the rains and then the grain is harvested from canoes as the river falls at the start of the dry season in December and January.

## Wild Rices

We are not here talking about "wild rice," the plant that grows in North America and elsewhere and produces a rice-like seed (see page 384), but about wild varieties of true rices. In a very few places, wild varieties of *Oryza* are still gathered for food. Wild African rices are harvested along the shores of Lake Chad (though decreasingly, with a fall in the lake level caused by years of drought) and wild Asian rices are gathered by hill tribe peoples in South and Southeast Asia. In rice-growing areas of Asia and Africa, wild varieties and cross-breeds of wild strains and *Oryza sativa* grow in among the cultivated grain. Where the crop is commercial (rather than just for domestic use), these are treated as weeds and impurities. However, wild varieties are valuable to plant geneticists looking for hardy characteristics, such as drought- or heat-resistance or resistance to pests and disease, that they can try to build into new strains of rice.

## Irrigated Rice Production

Rice has been grown using irrigation, or water diversion and flow management, for over two thousand years. Recently, traditional techniques have been replaced or supplemented in some regions with machinery and modern technology. Whether the cultivation is traditional or modern, irrigated rice yields are far higher than yields from other methods: an average of 11.3 tons per hectare (5.2 tons per acre). Almost half the land in the world used for growing rice is irrigated land and it produces over 70 percent of the world's rice crop. (These numbers can be a little misleading, however, since a high proportion of these irrigated lands are also in highly mechanized commercial production using new rice varieties grown with fertilizers and pesticides which also increase yields per acre.)

**Traditional irrigated rice** Traditional irrigation requires cooperation between farmers. Many forms of organized cooperation have developed in the densely cultivated and irrigated rice fields of Asia.

In Bali, irrigation water comes from the many streams that flow down from the volcanoes at the center of the island. The water is diverted to flow through the rice paddies on steeply terraced hillsides. In parts of Vietnam, China, and Thailand, irrigation water is diverted from rivers into a complex system of canals and waterways. The water is diverted into fields and then later drained off in a sophisticated sequence developed over the centuries. The use of irrigation water often requires the building of terraces so that the water can flow down through the cultivated rice fields. Maintaining the terraces and the irrigation system is sometimes achieved with communal labor and is always time-consuming.

**Modern irrigated rice** Mechanized rice cultivation is possible only where the soil can support machinery. The soils of the present-day rice lands in the United States and Australia can, whereas the soft coastal soils of the Carolina coast and much of the delta areas in Asia cannot support heavy modern equipment. In the United States and Australia, large tracts of land are smoothed and flattened by machine, then diked around the edges. The flatness and slope, if any, are calibrated and regulated to ensure minimal water loss. Seeding is usually by airplane. Once the land is planted, it is flooded and kept wet until just before harvest.

In other countries with mechanized irrigated rice agriculture, such as Italy, Spain, and Japan, rice may be machine-drilled into dry or puddled soil, then flooded. More traditionally, rice is started in a seedbed and the seedlings transplanted by mechanical transplanter, a machine that saves thousands of hours of backbreaking work. The rice is weeded either by hand or by mechanical weeder.

Irrigated rice is usually started in a seedbed, then the plants are transplanted by hand into the prepared field. The water will be about six inches deep and the soil wet and oozy beneath. Two to six small rice plants are pushed into the mud in a regularly spaced line.

The rice plants can thrive in this wet environment but weeds do not; the water serves as a weed patrol as well as a source of nutrients for the rice plants and a temperature stabilizer. Still, some hand weeding is needed. The rice is usually weeded three or four times as it grows. The rice plants grow very quickly and fill in any empty spaces, and soon the paddy is solid green with little water showing. As the plants mature, the water level in the field is lowered (or the water absorbed by the soil is not replaced). By the time the plants reach maturity and begin to dry out and yellow, the ground is entirely dry and the rice can be harvested easily. Pictured is a Laotian woman pulling up and bundling seedlings for transplanting.

# Harvesting Rice

When the grains of rice have fattened on the stalk and begun drying out, they and the whole plant turn a golden yellow color. It's time for harvest. Harvesting methods depend on culture and technology, climate, terrain, and the variety of rice being grown. In all cases, however, the ripe grain must be cut from the stalk and brought in from the field. The stalks and leaves of the ripe plants are called "straw"; "the grain" refers to the individual rice grains hanging on the stalks. Part of harvest involves threshing, that is, separating the grains from the straw. Threshing may take place right after harvest, or the grain may be stored still on the straw.

In modern industrial farming, large combine harvesters cut the rice stalks near the ground, sweep up the rice and straw, and separate the grain from the straw, all in one operation. The harvested rice goes to a mill to be hot-air–dried and then moves straight on to the husking, milling, and polishing process.

In nonindustrial farming, threshing is often done by animals. The harvested rice, still attached to the stalk, is brought to a flat threshing ground in the field or, more often, in the courtyard in front of the family house. A modern version of the animal-threshing technique has developed among farmers living close to paved roads. The farmers lay the harvested

**below**

Birds, too, are interested in the ripe grain, so farmers all over the world use scarecrows to try to keep losses low. Pictured is a scarecrow in a field of ripe rice ready for harvest in Bali.

**above**

In southern China, the traditional two-crop rice cycle is part of an agricultural "closed circuit." Water ferns are planted in the paddies between crops because they have a symbiotic relationship with the blue-green algae that help fix nitrogen in the soil. Fish, ducks, and pigs are often part of the cycle, providing fertilizer and eating grubs and waste. Food production is maximized at a sustainable level, with little need for expensive inputs from outside, such as commercial fertilizers or pesticides.

In Bali, ducks are a necessary element in the traditional cycle, coming onto the rice fields after the harvest to eat any fallen grains. Then, after the stubble is burned and plowed in and the fields flooded, the ducks eat grubs and insects, at the same time fertilizing the soil. The ducks pictured are feeding on a flooded rice terrace in central Bali.

In Bali, the traditional rice (*padi bali*) grows very tall (five feet or more) and the grains stay tightly attached to the straw. The grain is cut by hand very near the top of the stalk, leaving tall straw standing in the field. The traditional harvesting tool is a small curved knife that is held in the palm of the right hand. At the end of the day, the heads of rice are not threshed but are carried home and stored on their short lengths of straw until needed for cooking. At that time, the grain is threshed off the straw, pounded in a mortar to polish the rice, and winnowed to sift out dust and dirt. Pictured is a man carrying home freshly cut *padi bali* near Tengalalen, in Bali.

**left**

In traditional harvesting by hand, the straw is cut with a sickle or knife, and later the rice is threshed from the straw. Pictured are people harvesting sticky rice outside Chiang Mai, in Thailand. They are carrying rattan strips with which to tie up the rice bundles.

**below left**

Some varieties of rice, including most of the new Green Revolution rices (see page 53), do not grow as tall as traditional rices. The rice is easily separated from the straw, and in fact falls off the straw. Where these rices are harvested by hand, the rice must be cut and then threshed from the straw in the field. The rice stalks are usually cut with a sickle, near the ground. Bundles of the long cut stalks are then threshed immediately or may be left out in the field to sun dry for a day or more before threshing. Hand-threshing involves taking a bundle of rice stalks and slapping the rice-bearing end vigorously and repeatedly on the ground, or on a rock or a wooden platform. The grains are knocked off and fall to the ground; after all the grain has been slapped off, the bundle of straw is set aside for mulch or animal feed. Pictured are women hand-threshing rice in a field near Sideman, in central Bali.

left

In South Carolina, threshing sheds were traditionally used for hand threshing. Now only one threshing shed still stands from the rice and slave era; it is at Mansfield Plantation just north of Georgetown and is pictured here. The shed is on tall wooden stilts and has a slatted floor. The rice was threshed by beating it on the floor in the shed. The rice grains fell through the slats onto the ground below, where they could be collected and further cleaned before being bagged and sold at the market.

### right

In Assam, we saw bundles of freshly harvested rice being piled in a thick layer around a post stuck in the ground, and then a cow (in other places an ox or a donkey is used) was hitched to the post and sent walking round and round on the rice (as is pictured here). The animal is often muzzled to prevent it from taking mouthfuls of grain as it works. Eventually the rice falls off the straw onto the ground and can be swept up, winnowed to clean out bits of dust and chaff, and stored.

### below right

Nowadays, in many parts of Asia, small mechanical treadle threshers have lightened the labor. Harvested rice is fed into the machine (rather like feeding laundry through a wringer), powered by the farmer's foot pushing on the treadle, and the rice is separated from the straw quickly and easily. Often a mechanical thresher will be shared among villagers. Pictured here is a mechanical foot-powered rice thresher being used in central Vietnam.

46

Rice grains laid out to dry are turned over with a rake or with the farmer's bare feet to make sure they all get exposed to the heat and dry evenly. Paved roads are used in some places for drying the grain. Pictured here is rice laid out on a road in the Mekong Delta.

rice, still on its straw, on the highway. Cars and trucks driving over it separate the rice from the straw, in a form of passive mechanical threshing.

After threshing, the grains of rice are swept up into a basket. It may then be spread on a flat surface to dry out in the sun. After threshing and drying, there will be bits of straw and chaff mixed in with the rice. These are winnowed away before the rice is bagged.

On many modern rice farms, mechanical dryers, rather than sunshine, are used for drying the rice. Moisture should be reduced to about 13 percent before the grain is stored, to prevent fermentation.

Once the rice grain is harvested, what remains of the plant is rice straw. It may be gathered for use as animal fodder or for domestic uses such as making bricks or woven mats, or it may be burned or plowed back into the soil as a fertilizer. If the soil is not turned over and the ground stays moist enough, the "stumps" of plants left after harvest may sprout new shoots that can, if the weather permits, produce another, though more meager, crop of rice, known as a *ratoon* crop.

# Parboiled Rice

We were walking early one morning along a narrow path past fields of rice just outside Calcutta in Bengal, in India. It was early November, dry season in Bengal, and the sun was already bright and warm. The rice was golden, it was harvesttime, and in every field out across a large flat plain as far as we could see, there were groups of villagers working hard cutting and threshing rice. Their voices, together with the songs of birds and the occasional bump of a bicycle riding along the dirt path, were the only sounds to be heard. The landscape was entirely human in scale, people perspiring in the sun while harvesting their food, food that they—and their children—would eat for the next six months.

We were there taking pictures, asking the odd question, but mainly just being there. With us were our two sons, Dominic and Tashi, who were soon to turn seven and four years old. They were happy simply to be outside with space to play, but they were also curious, as we were, to see the harvest, to see the water buffalo chomping on the stubble in the fields already harvested, to see farmers slapping long bundles of cut rice against a threshing table so that the grain would dislodge from the straw.

Parboiling rice in a village outside Calcutta

At one point, someone invited us into a compound of small mud houses set just on the edge of the rice fields. In the middle of the compound there was a dung fire burning with a large pot full of water boiling vigorously on top. In the pot was freshly harvested rice that was being parboiled. Each batch of rice was left in the water for just a few minutes, then it was taken out and another batch was thrown in. The parboiled rice was then spread on a sheet and left out in the sun to dry. We were thrilled. We'd never actually seen rice being parboiled, though we'd read about parboiling, and we'd eaten lots of parboiled rice in India and Sri Lanka, as well as the occasional serving of Uncle Ben's.

Parboiling is an ancient and ingenious technique for increasing the nutritional value of polished rice. It dates back more than two thousand years and seems to have been developed in southern India. Many people in Bengal, Bangladesh, South India, and Sri Lanka prefer the taste and texture of parboiled rice; much of the rice sold in the United States is parboiled, using modern industrial techniques rather than traditional village methods.

In parboiling, paddy rice (rice still in its husk) is boiled, then cooled. This has the effect of driving nutrients from the bran into the center of the rice and at the same time pushing oils into the bran. Parboiled rice is easier to polish by hand than unboiled rice, and perhaps

Hand threshing newly harvested rice in a small village in Bengal

this is why the technique first developed. Mechanical millers have a little more trouble with parboiled rice because the extra oil in the bran can clog up the machinery. Most parboiled rice is milled (which gives it much better storage qualities—no germ or bran to turn rancid), but because of the parboiling process, the rice retains much of the nutritional value of unmilled rice.

During the parboiling process, the starches in the rice gelatinize (become liquid). When the rice is cooled, the starches harden again; in fact they become harder and denser than the starches in unparboiled rice. Grains of uncooked parboiled rice are easy to spot: They have a slightly glassy look to them and tend to be yellowish rather than semitransparent white. Because the starches are harder, parboiled rice takes longer to cook than polished rice that has not been parboiled. The cooked grains tend to have a slightly bouncy texture and to be completely nonsticky. They are also stronger and stand up better to overcooking or immersion in soup without getting mushy, which makes them a favorite of restaurants and others who must cook rice in bulk.

In North America, parboiling was adopted as a means of improving the nutritional value of rice early in the twentieth century. Most parboiled rice is also precooked, at least partly, so that it does not take as long to cook as, for example, parboiled rices from India.

# Husking and Milling Rice

Newly harvested rice, once it has been threshed off the straw, is known as rough rice, or paddy rice. The grains are still in the husk. The preliminary cleaning of the grains, or husking, produces unmilled rice, usually known as brown rice in North America, though it can be other colors. Most rice is then milled to remove the bran and germ layers, leaving it white. White milled rice is usually polished to remove the last traces of bran. In India, Bangladesh, Pakistan, and Sri Lanka, some of the rice crop is parboiled (see Parboiled Rices, page 242) before husking and milling.

In many villages in the developing world, the labor of husking rice by hand has been relieved by simple gas- or electric-powered rice mills. Pictured here is a small gas-powered rice mill in an Iban village on the Rejang River in Sarawak, Borneo.

The original way of husking rice was to place it in a mortar and pound it with a pestle. The pounding split the husks, and then the grain was tossed in a winnowing basket so the wind would blow away the lighter husks and leave the grains. The rice would then be pounded again to clean the bran off. This labor-intensive method is still used in West Africa (see Daily Labor, page 363) as well as in rural parts of India, Thailand, Laos, Indonesia, and elsewhere. This kind of low-tech processing just before cooking does have the advantage that the grain is alive, whole and protected in its husk until the last minute. It can be stored in the husk almost indefinitely, for it is much less likely than milled or polished grain to deteriorate or be vulnerable to infestation. In addition, using a mortar and pestle to polish off the bran results in a less complete milling than mechanical milling and polishing. Consequently, some of the fiber and vitamins in the bran layers and some of the germ remain on the rice.

In Banaue, a reasonably prosperous village that is surrounded by the extraordinary Ifugao rice terraces (see page 55), rice husking and milling is still done by hand pounding in deep mortars. When Jeffrey asked why the village didn't have a mechanical rice mill, he was told that the teenagers were given the work of cleaning the rice. The implication was clearly that the physical labor of pounding the rice helps keep them in good physical shape and out of trouble.

In Japan, Italy, Korea, Spain, Australia, and the United States, husking, milling, and polishing have been mechanized for a long time. Modern milling techniques are now employed in many other rice-growing countries as well, such as Thailand and Vietnam, especially when the crop is commercial or for export. The rough rice passes between rubber rollers that crack the husk and then the husk is blown away and separated from the grain. The rice usually passes directly on to the milling and polishing process. The bran is used for animal feed or as a source of rice bran oil, while the polished rice is sorted by grain size. Broken grains are separated out (to be sold separately as a lower grade of rice), then the rice is bagged and labeled, ready for market.

# Anatomy of a Grain

Rice grains are the fruit of the rice plant. They develop from florets on the spikelets that develop at the top of the stem. Flowering takes place over a few days. From flowering to ripening of the grain takes thirty to sixty days. Each stalk bears many grains of rice, each grain encased in a protective coating or outer layer known as the hull or husk. Unhulled rice is also known as rough rice, or paddy rice. Inside the husk is the whole grain, known variously as brown rice, unmilled rice, hulled rice, or cargo rice. Its outer bran layer is often a light brown color (hence the term "brown rice"), but is sometimes red or black or mahogany-colored. The bran is made up of three thin layers, the pericarp (which contains coloring), the seed coat, and the nucellus. Together the bran layers contain fiber, protein, carbohydrates, minerals, and ash.

Under the bran is a thin layer of cells, called the aleurone layer, that covers the endosperm and the embryo, or germ. The endosperm, "the storage area," makes up most of the rice grain by weight and volume. At one end of the endosperm is the germ, or the seed embryo, the part that would, if the rice were planted, develop into a rice plant. The aleurone and the germ are rich in fats and proteins. In milling and polishing, the germ is knocked off and the bran is removed together with remains of the aleurone layers, leaving only the white endosperm, the heart of the rice grain.

The endosperm contains the starches that would nourish the growing embryo if the seed were planted. Most of the food value of the grain—protein and carbohydrate—is in the endosperm. (See below for a more detailed discussion of the nutritional properties of brown and milled rice.) In waxy (sticky) rices the endosperm is a more opaque chalky color, while in nonwaxy rices such as basmati it is almost transparent.

# Nutritious Rice

Rice, like bread and pasta, is high in starches and low in fat. It consists mostly of complex carbohydrates and is a nutritious and sustaining everyday food. It provides us with starches that give energy, and also with protein, minerals such as calcium and iron, and B vitamins. In many parts of the world, rice has for centuries been the main daily food of millions of people, supplemented by vegetables, legumes and beans, and relatively small amounts of oil, fish, and meat.

Rice has the highest protein digestibility and energy digestibility among all the staple foods. The total protein content of rice is about 8 percent in brown rice and 6 to 7 percent in milled rice, lower than in some other grains. Usable protein, however, is calculated by looking at the completeness of the protein. In grains, the limiting or least available amino acid is lysine. Rice (and oats) have the highest levels of lysine of all the grains, and milled rice (as well as wheat) has the highest levels of utilizable protein.

Many people believe that brown rice is "healthier" than white (milled) rice. It is true that brown rice has more calcium and iron as well as higher protein levels and significantly more of the B vitamins (thiamine, riboflavin, and niacin) than milled rice. Black rices have more iron, calcium, and phosphorus than noncolored rices. Rice bran and rice bran oil (found in brown rice, but removed from milled rice) seem to have a cholesterol-lowering effect. Brown rice also contains more fiber than white rice.

But brown rice is less digestible than white (milled) rice. The aleurone layer and embryo, still present in brown rice, contain phytate phosphorus, which seems to interfere with the absorption of calcium, zinc, and iron. Phytate is not destroyed by heating or cooking. Consequently, even though brown rice contains more calcium and iron than milled rice, in recent tests, those fed a brown rice diet had a poor mineral balance compared with those fed white rice.

On the other hand, brown rice has much higher levels of the B vitamins than white rice and they are easily absorbed by the body. As a result, when machine-milled rice replaced the less-polished hand-cleaned rice in many parts of Asia in the last thirty years, the population sometimes suffered from beriberi caused by inadequate levels of the B vitamin thiamine.

It is important to remember that these studies of nutritional balance and deficiency concentrated on rice in a situation of food scarcity, when rice was the only food or one of the few foods in the diet. In fact, a recent study showed that if an adult male ate milled (white) rice for his entire 2400 calories per day, he would get the RDA (U.S. Recommended Daily Average) requirements of protein and phosphorus, though he would get only 50 to 75 percent of the recommended levels of zinc, niacin, iron, magnesium, and pyridoxine and less than 40 percent of the recommended amount of calcium, thiamine, and riboflavin. However, in most households where a wide variety of foods are available, malnutrition is not an issue. When eaten with even small amounts of legumes and vegetables, with or without some meat or fish or dairy, rice is a nutritious staple food, not "empty calories" as an earlier meat-obsessed generation might have thought.

Parboiled rice is rice that has been heated while still in the husk, before husking and milling (see page 242). Parboiling drives water-soluble vitamins from the bran layer into the endosperm. Thus, milled parboiled rice has higher levels of the B vitamins thiamine, riboflavin, and niacin than regular milled rice. In the United States, parboiling techniques were refined in the 1930s to improve the nutritional and keeping qualities of rice.

In 1958, the U.S. government adopted a policy of enriching milled and polished rice, setting minimum and maximum levels of thiamine, niacin, iron, vitamin D, and calcium to be added to rice. (In the seventies, the vitamin D requirement was dropped.) Many states have now passed laws prohibiting the sale of plain nonenriched white rice. Consequently, most white rice produced in the United States is coated with a fine powder containing the B vitamins thiamine and niacin, and for this reason, the packaging is marked "To retain vitamins, do not rinse before or drain after cooking." However, we always wash our rice, partly from habits learned in Asia, partly because it improves the texture—and we are eating our rice with vegetables, legumes, and a little meat, so adequate nutrition is really not a worry.

# Rice in the Present Day

It's hard to give a figure for the number of varieties of rice now growing. The International Rice Research Institute (IRRI), just outside Manila in the Philippines, has collected a bank of rice genetic materials that now has about eighty-three thousand rice cultivars. Most of these are wild strains or established cultivated rices; some are newly developed by plant scientists. However, in any given year most of the world's cultivated rice comes from a small number of varieties. Large-scale modernized rice agriculture brings with it pressures for standardization that many people fear will result in a loss of genetic diversity.

IRRI's rice bank was established in order to try to preserve diversity. Some of the cultivars in the bank have been important contributors to the development of the new "miracle" rices, others may be in future. Characteristics such as resistance to a particular disease or

The traditional rice-growing techniques of pretechnological societies such as those of the Iban in Sarawak (Malaysian Borneo) and the Diola in Casamance (Senegal) were very sophisticated in some ways. In each, there was an appreciation and encouragement of diversity. Traditionally, the Iban saved and sowed seeds from different rice varieties so that if one kind failed there were others that might succeed in producing a good crop. The Diola still grow over fifteen different varities of rice, perhaps for the same reasons but also because different varieties are prized for their different tastes and textures. The Akha people of southern Yunnan and the Golden Triangle area grow twenty-three different varieties of rice. At the other end of the technology spectrum, commercial rice growing, which means growing rice for sale (use outside the family or village), demands standardization and thus discourages diversity. Pictured here is a woman watering rice by a spring near Marsassoum in Casamance.

hardiness in extreme conditions may be found in an "obscure" wild rice variety collected in the mountains of Taiwan or Burma or Peru. By crossbreeding, geneticists can sometimes produce a new rice with the selected characteristics from a number of varieties.

This process produced the first "miracle rices" in the sixties and seventies that launched the "Green Revolution." The new varieties had higher yields than the older rices, so that soon places like Bali and China, which had been importing rice, became exporters. However, a new variety of rice is not a simple solution to food shortages. First, any disease resistance built into a new variety is effective only for a limited time, until the disease or pest finds a way around the biological barriers, or some new disease makes inroads. Consequently, once a new variety is released, work must turn to developing the next generation. Second, the new varieties require fertilizer and pesticides that cost money not always available to the farmers, and they often cause environmental degradation, particularly water pollution. Third, increasing output by changing the traditional crop rotations and by double- and triple-cropping rice can eventually, even with fertilizers, deplete the soil.

Finally, although the new rices are edible and nutritious, they are often different in taste, aroma, and cooking characteristics from traditional rices. Because consumers usually prefer their traditional rice, traditional rice begins to command a premium in the marketplace. With the higher prices, farmers who could initially earn more by planting higher-yielding new rice are tempted to go back to cultivating traditional rice.

Still, with growing populations, many Asian countries have pushed their farmers to switch to the new miracle rices. Increasing production is the goal and new varieties, together with fertilizers and pesticides, are the means. Rice research institutes in Indonesia, Vietnam, and China, as well as IRRI, continue to work developing new rice varieties and producing enough seed to supply millions of farmers. Unfortunately, with the standardization that comes with widespread planting of the newest variety rice, Asian rice farmers may now be more vulnerable to widespread crop failure.

Research institutes in the industrialized rice-growing countries (the United States, Australia, Italy, Spain, and Japan) are also working on developing new varieties with disease resistance or higher productivity or other desirable characteristics. And with the growth of consumer demand in the West for long-grain Asian-style rices, scientists and farmers have also focused on developing varieties that can be successfully grown in, say Spain or the United States, and yet resemble in cooking and eating characteristics rices from Thailand and India. This research has resulted in Texmati, Calmati, and aromatic (nontropical) jasmine rice, and many others. Work has also been done on developing new varieties of medium- and short-grain temperate-climate rices, like the new American- and Australian-grown Japanese rices and American-grown Mediterranean-style rices.

As new varieties are developed and refined by researchers, farmers switch over to them. This trend has not resulted in increased diversity of crops, but just an ever-changing selection of varieties. In any one year, for example, there are only ten or so varieties of rice widely planted in the United States. Of these, four or five are long grain, another four or five are medium grain, and one or two are short grain. Ninety-nine percent of the rice grown in the United States these days is from varieties developed by public rice research centers and experiment stations. Long gone are the days when an American cookbook could call for specific varieties of rice, such as Lady Wright, or Blue Rose, or Early Prolific.

# Banane

The first time I ever really saw a rice terrace, I was staying in a dormitory in a two-dollar-a-night hostel in Hong Kong. Another traveler staying in my room had recently come from Bali, and one day he came back to the hostel with a big batch of color prints that he had taken in Bali and just developed. We sat down on a bottom bunk together and started looking through the shots. He had been living for a year in a relatively isolated village in the interior of the island, so he not only had a lot of photos, but a lot of good stories to tell.

At one particular photograph of a tall, steep hillside covered entirely with lush, green rice terraces, I paused, and at that moment I was suddenly struck: The photograph entered my imagination, sat down, made itself comfortable, and said, "I'm not leaving." Whether it was the magical little trail that wove its way up through the terraces or the tiny speck that turned out to be a house, I'd never before seen anything like it.

Rice terrace near Besakih, in central Bali

Ifugao woman cleaning weeds from a terrace in Batad, near Banaue, in the Philippines

A few days later, as my friend was about to leave Hong Kong, he came to say good-bye and to give me a copy of the photograph. I carefully put it in with my passport and valuables, and for years I carried it everywhere I went.

It's a bug, you know, rice terraces. It's like all those people who follow solar eclipses, tracking them down no matter where they occur. It's like surfers and their waves. It's like certain sailors that you meet, sailors who see the world as a map of tiny islands. Not that we've run into a lot of rice-terrace people, but we know they exist. We know because of the way word spreads, like people describing sand dunes. "You know the one, south-facing coming off the back side of Mt. Tinabalu, yeah, the one that looks a little like the tall narrow one outside Ubud, right." When you're listening for this sort of thing, pretty soon you get to realize that there are rice terraces, and then there are Rice Terraces. There are those in Bali (particularly in the center and the east), and in southern Yunnan Province in China just north of the Vietnamese border, and there are the terraces in central Madagascar, and the ones in Guizhou Province in southeastern China. There are terraces that are simply huge, others that are exquisite in their form, and still others that are particularly wonderful because of how they were constructed, or who farms them and how, or how water moves from terrace to terrace.

And then there is Banaue. Banaue is the name of a small mountain village in Ifugao Province in the northern part of Luzon in the Philippines, but it's also the name most often used to refer to the rice terraces of the region. The rice terraces of Banaue leave all the others in a cloud of dust, they break the bank, they earn their reputation and then continue to amaze, but not in an overpowering sort of way. They aren't the biggest, or the most beautiful; they're simply the best.

In Banaue the village, there is no such thing as horizontal. If you walk, you walk up or you walk down. In all directions all around there are terraces, and if you walk to the next valley over, it's the same, and the next valley. When I first arrived in Banaue, having heard about the terraces for most of my adult life, I was a little bit disappointed, I don't know why. Maybe I was expecting the biggest, the most beautiful.

In the village I found a little hotel with a good view, and each day I set out walking in a different direction. I was there in November, just after a terrible typhoon had ravaged its way across Luzon, so the trails and roads were badly damaged. So too were many of the terraces, and people were working to repair the damage. Some of the fields had tender young shoots sprouting up, but most lay waiting for cultivation.

Ifugao woman planting whole rice stalks on a flooded terrace in Batad

One afternoon the mountains were deep in clouds and it was pouring rain; the trails were awash in mud. So I followed a little sign pointing to a local museum and ended up lost in a book for the rest of the afternoon. The book was the *Ifugao Atlas*, written by anthropologist Harold Conklin (published in 1980). Conklin, who had lived for many years in the region, describes in wonderful detail how the terraces are constructed and maintained, how water is channeled from the top of the mountains to the valleys below, how fields are passed down from one generation to the next. He describes local eating and drinking habits; he analyzes the plant life and animal life of the terraces; he makes a calendar of every day of the year and describes what each day requires in terms of work on the terraces. From Conklin I learned that the terraces weren't simply carved out from the mountainside, as I had always imagined, but they were built onto it, that below the surface of every terrace is eight to ten feet of gravel, gravel that was brought down from the top of the mountain by simple hydraulic technology some thousand years ago or so.

As I read, I was in awe. It struck me as a book someone writes only once in a lifetime, a book that's impossible to describe. It is a book, just like its subject, that is one of a kind.

When I came out of the museum, and walked down a muddy trail in the rain, I was no longer disappointed with the rice terraces of Banaue. And I finally knew why, when I first looked at the photograph in the cheap hostel in Hong Kong, why it had meant so much. It has to do with all that human effort.

Local restaurant in Kunming

inset: Lung Shan Temple in Taipei

# White Rice,
# Black Rice,
# Congee

hinese cookery can involve some of the most elaborate and sophisticated methods and techniques, and some of the most obscure and rare ingredients, of any cuisine in the world, but what we have always found most compelling about Chinese food are its simplest dishes.

A platter of blanched green vegetables lightly salted, a plate of cucumbers dressed with chiles and sesame oil, or a bowl of spicy simmered tofu—these are the dishes that we remember long after having first tasted them. What is it that can give a simple stir-fry that wonderful flavor of the wok, that taste that somehow seems to carry a little of the flavor of all the dishes that went before it, like a sourdough starter keeping a taste alive? And what is it that makes a dish as straightforward as stir-fried bean sprouts turn out so beautifully? These are the techniques we have tried to learn for ourselves, and ones we've tried to pass on here.

**clockwise from top**

Man selling watermelons in Shangai

Market day in Yangshuo, Guangxi

Tofu products for sale at the market in Kunming

**opposite**

Bai woman near Dali, Yunnan

Cooking Chinese food is for us an everyday reminder of the importance of restraint. A Chinese recipe can look almost silly on a page, like a recipe for a tortilla or a chapatti ("flour, salt, and water"). In the kitchen with a Chinese recipe, we are always working against a temptation to add more ingredients, as if making a dish more complicated will somehow make it better. Chinese cooking reminds us always that this is not the case.

We use our wok more than any other skillet or pot in our kitchen except the pot we use to cook rice. It is big, heavy, durable, and totally reliable. We bought it for five dollars on sale in a neighborhood store; it's made from spun steel and it has a long wooden handle to grab onto. It is so big that we have to move other pots off neighboring burners so that it can have room all by itself, the big boss. We turn the gas flame as high as it can go and leave the wok atop the flame to get nice and hot, then we pour in a little oil and we're ready to cook. Right after we finish cooking, we give the wok a quick scrub and a rinse with hot water, quickly dry it off, and hang it back up.

Once you've bought a wok, you'll also want a good Chinese spatula with a shovel-shaped metal end for stir-frying. Though it is not essential, a good sharp cleaver is also wonderful to have, for chopping, slicing, smashing flat a clove of garlic or several scallions. Chinese cleavers come in several different shapes and sizes, but basically there are heavy ones and lighter ones; both are useful, but we end up using the lighter one the most. If you are looking to buy a cleaver, get a Chinese one. (They are great buys, to boot.)

Right beside our stove we have a cupboard with room for tall bottles. (It didn't used to be tall enough inside for bottles, but we cut two shelves into U shapes, so that we can store bottles on the bottom shelf and spices on the little shelves overlooking them.) Here we

store bottles of rice vinegar, rice wine, soy sauce, and sesame oil, as well as olive oil, fish sauce, and other ingredients for other kinds of cooking. It works really well, as everything is right there and handy when we're cooking furiously in the wok and need a quick splash of soy. Beside the stove, we also keep wide-mouthed jars of sugar, sea salt, and cornstarch.

When cooking Chinese food, just remember to have everything ready before heating your wok. And, equally important, only stir-fry quantities that fit easily into the wok. There is no bigger disaster than to be stir-frying four cups of rice for fried rice in a wok that is meant to handle one cup at the most. If you are at all suspicious about the size of the recipe versus the size of your wok, stir-fry it in batches. It is very important that all the food you are cooking come into contact with the surface of the hot wok, which is why the bigger and heavier the wok, the better.

At the table, we generally follow a Chinese way of eating rice, no matter what kind of food we are eating with the rice. We can use chopsticks, or a spoon and fork Thai style, but we almost always eat rice from individual bowls. Depending on how we feel, we'll use small palm-size ceramic bowls, or bigger café-au-lait bowls, or even larger Chinese ceramic soup bowls. The great advantage of eating rice Chinese style out of a bowl is that you can hold it right up next to your mouth. Eating rice from bowls also has that great effect, like a Vietnamese one-dish noodle combination served in a large bowl, of blending together little bits of flavor from all the different dishes on the table, so that when you get to the bottom of your bowl there is a fabulous "stew" of different flavors.

We're also big believers in serving other dishes flat, Chinese style, on plates or platters, if at all possible. Many dishes are so much more visible and attractive this way, as opposed to being served in a bowl. With a simple garnish like a leaf of lettuce, or cucumber or tomato slices, a simple home-style meal can be made that much more special. This also gives us an excuse to keep a eye out for brightly colored plates so that we can match a particular dish with a particular plate!

**left to right**

Woman selling pickles at the market in Kunming

Peanuts, dried noodles, and other products for sale at
Yaumatei market in Hong Kong

# Plain Rice

*fan*

THIS IS A RECIPE FOR PLAIN WHITE CHINESE RICE, RICE BOWL RICE, ORDINARY everyday nonaromatic, reliable rice. The rice we buy in our Chinatown neighborhood and labeled in Chinese for Chinese consumers is usually a plain nonaromatic long-grain or medium-grain rice grown in the United States, often sold without any further identification or special brand or variety marked. This is what you should look for to stock your Chinese pantry. It should have semitransparent grains, not the opaque white grains of sweet rice or sticky rice. You do not want Dehra Dun or Patna basmati for your Chinese meals. They are too dry when cooked, made for eating with the hands or with a spoon, not with chopsticks. Parboiled rice has bouncy separate grains and a too-distinctive taste that intrudes in a Chinese meal. You could use Japanese rice, but that slightly sticky style of medium-grain rice, though preferred by some in Taiwan and easy with chopsticks, is not the majority favorite. If you can't find a Chinese rice, you can use a jasmine. It will be more aromatic than the customary Chinese rice, a little more clingy and soft, and easy to manage with chopsticks.

When you find it, here's how to prepare it. Notice that there's no salt or oil in the cooking. The flavor comes from accompanying dishes.

2 cups long-grain rice
2½ cups water

Place the rice in a heavy medium pot with a tight-fitting lid and wash thoroughly under cold running water, swishing it around in the water with your hand until the water runs clear. Drain in a sieve.

Place the rice in the pot and add the water. Heat to a boil, stirring briefly and gently to ensure the rice isn't sticking; then, when the water is boiling vigorously, cover tightly and lower the heat to very low. Let cook, without lifting the lid, for 20 minutes. Remove from the heat, lift the lid to release steam, and replace it immediately, then let stand for 10 minutes so the starches in the rice firm up.

Turn the rice over gently, using a wet wooden rice paddle or shallow wooden spoon. To serve, transfer to a bowl or serve directly from the pot.

**Rice cooker method:** Rice cookers work by the absorption technique, as in the method above, cooking rice in a measured amount of water. The inner pot of any cooker has marks on it to show the appropriate water level for different amounts of rice. These don't correspond exactly to the volumes of water used when cooking in a pot, for the cooker operates the whole time with the lid on and hence needs a little less water for a given volume of rice.

Because the cooker shuts itself off automatically and then keeps the rice warm, it's very useful if you are rushed or distracted or if your kitchen is small; you just put in the rice and water and plug the cooker in at least 25 minutes before you wish to eat, then forget about it. If you have a sophisticated cooker with a timer, you can put in the rice and water and then can program the cooker to start cooking the rice at a set time.

Wash and drain the rice as above. Place in the rice cooker and add water up to the 2-cup mark on the rice cooker. Cover and plug in or turn on the cooker; it will bring the water to a boil, then simmer the rice until done, after which it will automatically shift to a "warming mode" to keep the rice warm. Serve from the cooker, as directed above.

# Chinese Black Rice

**Makes about 5½ cups rice**

BLACK RICE FROM CHINA HAS RECENTLY BECOME AVAILABLE IN NORTH America. It is a medium-grain unmilled rice, with white kernels inside the black bran. Washing turns the water a deep purple–black. Very tender when cooked, the rice makes good leftovers. It is beautiful served with fresh Chinese green vegetables; its nutty taste pairs well with ripe avocado or with strong meaty flavors. Cooking time is just over half an hour, relatively short for an unmilled rice.

2 cups Chinese black rice
3½ cups water

Place the rice in a heavy medium pot with a tight-fitting lid and wash thoroughly under cold running water until the water runs clear. Drain in a sieve, then return to the pot, with the water. Heat to a boil, stir briefly, and skim off any foam. Cover tightly and lower the heat to very low. Let cook, without lifting the lid, for 35 minutes. Remove from the heat and let stand for 5 to 10 minutes.

Serve from the pot, using a wet wooden rice paddle or wooden spoon, or turn out into a shallow bowl.

**Note:** You can also, if you wish, add ½ teaspoon of salt to the rice as it begins to cook. Because in China plain rice is generally cooked and served with no salt or oil, this would be more appropriate if you were planning to serve the rice with a non–East Asian meal.

# Basic Rice Congee
*juk*

Serves 4 to 6

CONGEE IS BREAKFAST FOOD IN CHINA. IT IS SERVED PIPING HOT IN BIG ceramic or metal bowls, with Chinese-style soup spoons. On the table, or served directly on top of the congee, are various little flavorings such as preserved vegetables and fried peanuts. Congee makes for a good breakfast, especially on frosty mornings.

Early one morning in Lhasa, in Tibet, we came to see it from a new perspective. Two women, one from Hong Kong and the other from Japan, checked in to the hotel where we were staying. Both had the windswept, wide-eyed look that people have when they have been outside at high elevation for a long time. They told us that they had come all the way from Xinjiang Province in western China, through the western part of Tibet and from there all the way to Lhasa: two months on the road, hitching rides on the occasional truck, sleeping out at night, and most of it at fifteen thousand feet or above! It had been a big adventure, but they were happy at last to be in the comforts of "cosmopolitan" Lhasa.

We wanted to ask them more, but they gracefully excused themselves. "Do you know," they asked, with a look both incredibly eager and anxious, "we've been told that we can find congee here in Lhasa? Is it true?"

Pure craving.

Some people like their congee thin, with the rice grains cooked until broken and somewhat shapeless. We prefer it the consistency of a thick soup, with the rice grains intact. You can adjust the consistency by adding extra water.

The list of accompaniments given here is meant as a guideline. Sprinkle them on top of your congee or stir them in; feel free to add other textures and flavors to the array of garnishes and condiments you set out on the table.

*continued*

8 cups water, plus extra boiling water as necessary

1½ cups whole or broken long-grain rice (Thai jasmine or Chinese- or American-grown long-grain; not basmati or any of the parboiled rices)

½ teaspoon salt

### Accompaniments and garnishes

1 tablespoon peanut oil or vegetable oil

7 to 10 cloves garlic, coarsely chopped

¼ pound pork tenderloin or other lean cut, trimmed of all fat and sinew and ground, finely chopped, or processed to a paste in a food processor and then finely chopped, or ¼ pound lean ground pork

¼ teaspoon salt

¼ cup lightly dry-roasted unsalted peanuts (see Glossary), coarsely chopped

1 to 2 red cayenne chiles, finely chopped (or substitute any medium-hot fresh chile, such as jalapeño)

3 to 4 scallions, finely chopped

½ cup loosely packed fresh coriander leaves

½ cup Chinese pickled vegetables (see Glossary), finely chopped (optional)

Soy sauce

Salt and freshly ground black pepper

Bring 8 cups of water to a boil in a large pot, then add the rice and stir gently until the water returns to the boil. Lower the heat to medium, add the salt, and boil gently for 15 minutes. The rice should be cooked but still firm. Remove from the heat and let stand uncovered for 15 minutes, or up to 1 hour. The rice will continue to soften and to absorb water. (If you want your rice grains very soft and broken, use a little more boiling water and boil for 30 minutes, rather than 15.)

While the rice is cooking, heat a skillet or a wok over medium heat. When it is hot, add the oil. When the oil is hot, add the garlic and stir-fry until it is starting to color. Add the ground pork and salt and stir until the pork is cooked through, 3 to 4 minutes. Remove from the heat, place in a bowl, and set aside.

Place the roasted peanuts, chopped chiles, chopped scallions, coriander, and Chinese pickled vegetables in separate piles on a platter, or in small bowls.

Just before serving, stir the cooked rice gently. If you find the congee too thick, add boiling water ½ cup at a time to achieve the desired consistency. Transfer to a serving bowl. Ladle the hot congee into individual soup bowls at the table.

Place the bowl of sautéed pork and garlic on the table, along with a small bowl of soy sauce, salt and pepper, and the platter or bowls of other accompaniments, so that guests can help themselves as they please.

# Rice in China

China is almost identical in area to the United States, a little more than three and a half million square miles. It is also roughly the same shape, so much so that if you could move one country around the globe, it would fit neatly on top of the other. It is by far the world's largest producer and consumer of rice. Archaeologists estimate that the Chinese have cultivated the grain for well over four thousand years, maybe as long as seven thousand years. The country's many different agricultural regions, varying enormously in terms of climate, soil conditions, and availability of water, result in a great many different varieties of rice grown and consumed. In general, wetland rices outnumber dryland rices, and nonglutinous rices outnumber glutinous rices.

Though rice is grown in almost all regions of China, it is most intensively cultivated in the center, the south, and the southwest. In the northern and western parts of the country, where winters can be long and hard, wheat, millet, and sorghum (for noodles and breads) are more commonly cultivated than rice. Most rice grown in China is consumed in the region in which it is grown.

**left to right**

Raked rice drying near Yangshuo

Using a simple rice thresher near Yangshuo

In Mandarin Chinese, cooked rice is called *fan*, while all the other dishes on the table meant to be eaten with the rice are called *cai* (pronounced "tsai"), which is also the generic name for vegetable. There is a wonderful expression in Chinese about how *cai*'s role in a meal is to help "send" the rice. Like a curry in South India, *cai* brings extra flavor to the rice, but it is the rice that is the most important food.

In the rice-producing parts of China, rice is typically eaten at least two times a day, every day. To complement the rice, the other principle foods eaten are soy beans and fresh or preserved vegetables. Soy beans are an essential source of protein; they are eaten as sprouts or converted into different forms of tofu and into soy sauce. Vegetables, green vegetables in particular, are the most common accompaniment to rice in an everyday Chinese meal.

Archaeologists believe that before wok cookery, most Chinese food was slow-simmered. Rice was steamed over the simmering stew (as couscous is prepared in North Africa). With the arrival of the wok about two thousand years ago, stir-frying became a common method of cookery, and the typical preparation of rice changed to the absorption method (the rice cooks, in a heavy pot or a rice cooker, in a small amount of water, absorbing all the water as it cooks and steams). Rice was also at times cooked in the wok, certainly if a wok was the only cooking vessel a family owned. Our neighbor Simon, who grew up in Guangdong Province in the 1950s, remembers how the family wok was also the family rice pot. The rice cooked in the wok had a chewy flavorful crust wherever it had come into contact with the surface of the wok, and this crusty part of the rice was everyone's favorite.

In China, rice is usually eaten for breakfast in the form of *juk,* or congee. At lunch and dinner it is eaten plain, served with one or more side dishes. The rice can be long- or medium-grain. Many Chinese prefer nonaromatic rice, but some prefer a Thai jasmine-style rice. Those who prefer their rice a little sticky don't wash it before cooking, so that the loose starches left on the rice will make it stickier when cooked.

Chinese home-style food is for the most part simple and practical. Cooking utensils are

minimal and cooking times generally short, because fuel for cooking is relatively scarce and expensive. Rice is served in individual ceramic or enameled metal bowls. The accompanying vegetable or meat dishes, the *cai*, are generally served on flat plates or platters. In a normal home-style Chinese meal, you take the food directly from the plate with your chopsticks and put it onto your bowl of rice. Unlike the Japanese style of eating rice, the Chinese custom is to eat *cai* with the rice, not separately. Soup is also a common part of a meal, generally eaten after the rice.

There are, of course, many exceptions to this general practice. With increasing prosperity, people tend to eat less rice and more *cai*. It is not uncommon now in Taiwan to sit down to a meal where rice may never be served, where the entire meal is made up of *cai*. Banquets and festive meals are also exceptions, serving dishes that are as complex as home-style meals are simple and direct. In such meals, the emphasis is on preparing dishes that people seldom enjoy at home, and on creating an atmosphere of fun. One of the biggest compliments that can be paid to a Chinese restaurant is that it is "hot and noisy," meaning people are having fun.

**above**

Walking the water buffalos home to the village at day's end

**opposite left to right**

Freshly cooked rice turned out into a basket in Yangshuo

Plowing under rice stubble in southern China

# Stocking Up on Stock

Freezers tell a lot about what goes on in a kitchen. In ours, you have to get past the Popsicle and ice cream boxes and the snowballs frozen from last winter; they just live there. The important part is all the little plastic bags and yogurt containers filled with coriander roots, cuts of meat portioned out into half-pound helpings, frozen wild lime leaves, etc. . . .

Street vendor serving soup in Taipei

Most important, here are our stocks, usually stored in pint containers. As long as we have rice on the shelf and stock in the freezer, we figure we're okay. Come dinnertime, if our children are tired and we're tired, we can simply cook rice and heat and season a stock, and when the rice is done, we can ladle it into the hot stock for a warm rice soup. If we have a few condiments on hand, like Chinese hot pepper paste or Thai fish sauce with chiles, we can jazz it up just a bit. But often we have it just plain, sprinkled with salt and freshly ground black pepper. It's a delicious, utterly simple meal. It's also a very good way to use leftover rice.

The other great use for stock is in stir-frying. After starting with hot oil, stir-frying garlic or onions and then, say, meat or vegetables or a combination, you will often want to add a little liquid and let the dish simmer before turning it out and serving it. You can use water, but stock gives a much better depth of flavor.

Stock is made when meat or bones, or a combination, are simmered in water, with or without herbs, spices, or other flavorings, until the water has taken on flavor from the meat and bones. Generally, the more meat and bones used, the more flavor. When making pork or beef stock, especially if using bones, you will have to skim off foam as it rises to the surface in the first ten to fifteen minutes of cooking. The stock should be gently simmered once it has come to the boil, because continuous vigorous boiling will make it cloudy. Stocks made from bones generally need long (several hours) simmering, while those made from pieces of meat usually will be flavorful in a shorter time.

# Chicken Stock

SIMPLE BUT DELICIOUS CHINESE HOME COOKING HAS ALL TO DO WITH HAVING a good stock on hand, whether it is a chicken- or meat-based stock or a vegetarian soy-based stock. Stocks give extra flavor and depth to simple seasonal stir-fries and to long-simmered dishes alike. To make a basic chicken stock, you can use a whole chicken, three to four pounds chicken necks and wings, or a chicken carcass.

A whole chicken, 3 to 4 pounds necks and wings, or a chicken carcass, rinsed

8 to 10 cups cold water

1 teaspoon black peppercorns

1 onion, quartered

2 inches ginger, coarsely chopped (optional)

Place the chicken in a stockpot or other large pot and add cold water to just cover. Add the remaining ingredients, bring to a boil, and skim off and discard any foam that has risen to the surface. Lower the heat to maintain a gentle simmer and simmer, partially covered, for about 45 minutes for whole chicken or necks and wings, or 2 to 3 hours for a chicken carcass.

Place a sieve over a large bowl and pour the stock through. Discard the solids and let the stock cool before pouring into one or more well-sealed nonreactive containers for storing in the refrigerator. After several hours in the refrigerator, a layer of fat will have solidified on the surface: Skim it off and discard, then freeze the stock or use in a recipe. If using stock to make a clear broth, warm it slightly, then strain it through a colander lined with a double layer of cheesecloth before proceeding with the recipe.

We freeze our stock without any seasoning, then add salt or fish sauce or a combination (depending on how we are using it) when we reheat it.

# Vegetarian Stock

Makes 5 to 6 cups stock

IN MANY NEIGHBORHOOD RESTAURANTS IN TAIWAN, A LARGE OPEN POT OF SOUP is free for the taking, at all hours of the day. The soups are simple, clear, hot stocks. Large chunks of squash or slivers of tofu sheets might be added, but basically they're just good hot soups to enjoy with your meal.

Vegetarian broths are common in Taiwan and in mainland China, enjoyed not as a substitute for meat broths, but for their own distinctive flavor.

1 tablespoon peanut oil or vegetable oil

1½ pounds soy bean sprouts, thoroughly washed and drained, or 1 cup dried soybeans or fava beans, soaked overnight in cold water

3 scallions, cut into 1-inch lengths

9 dried black mushrooms (approximately ½ ounce), rinsed

3 slices ginger (the size of a quarter)

8 cups cold water

Heat the oil in a stockpot or other large pot and heat over medium-high heat. When it is hot, add the sprouts or beans, scallions, mushrooms, and ginger and stir-fry for 2 to 3 minutes, or until the sprouts have changed color and become somewhat translucent. Add the water, raise the heat, and bring to a vigorous boil, then lower the heat to medium and simmer for 2 hours, partially covered. If using beans, skim off and discard any foam during the first 10 minutes.

Pour the stock through a fine-meshed strainer or a colander lined with cheesecloth and placed over a large bowl. Discard the solids.

Let the stock cool, then store, well sealed in glass or plastic containers in the refrigerator, or freeze in 2-cup plastic containers, until needed. Taste and season the stock when you use it, if you wish.

# Simple Luxury on the Li River

It didn't matter that it rained without stopping for days on end. It didn't matter that my hotel flooded, or even that my room flooded. It only mattered that I was in China for the first time, in a little town called Yangshuo in Guangxi Province, one of the most beautiful places I had ever seen.

Yangshuo is situated on the Li River, downstream from Guilin. The town, and the region, look like an exquisite Chinese landscape painting, with rocky limestone "karst" formations towering in all directions and the Li River and the mist sneaking their way in between the rocks. Sixteen years ago, the time of my first visit, Yangshuo was a decidedly slowed-down sort of place. Every once in a while, a car or a truck would pass on the main road, which went through one end of town, but that was about it for action. The one hotel in town was called Yangshuo Hotel Number One. It was built all on the one floor, which was nice except in case of a flood.

There was also only one place to eat, the People's Restaurant. People's had very rigid hours, so if you missed mealtime by a minute you were out of luck. I never did. For breakfast I would have hot rice congee, hot soybean milk, and delicious buckwheat honey *shaobing* (flatbreads). For lunch I would have a large bowl of rice, in a metal

Fisherman and his net on the Li River near Yangshuo

bowl, along with plates of stir-fried local green vegetables or bean sprouts or tree fungus. There would also be *la jiao jiang* (hot pepper paste) on the table as a condiment. It wasn't that there was any choice in what to order; it was a set menu, but all the food was simple and delicious. Dinner was the same as lunch, only at dinner, local beer was available, served like the rice in a large metal bowl.

Between meals I would put on my raincoat and walk down to a pavillion by the river where I could sit protected from the rain. There was always something to watch: a cormorant fisherman fishing with his birds, a few oxen bathing in the river, a long passenger boat carrying people to and from nearby communes. At that time foreigners were forbidden from taking local transport on the river. It made it all the more mysterious, wondering where the river went.

Well, it never stopped raining, and eventually I left.

Maybe it was the hot rice congee, or the buckwheat honey shaobing (it certainly wasn't the rain); anyway, last year I went back. I arrived well after dark in a taxi from the airport in Guilin. The driver dropped me off on the main road, a place that looked familiar but only just. Yangshuo was busier than before, and bigger, but it had a feel that was the same. Two older women came up and asked me if I needed a hotel, then they led me down a street toward the river. I thought they were taking me to good old Number One, but they weren't. So I got a room on a second floor.

There are moments when you're traveling that make traveling very special, like when you go back to somewhere you've been before and you can't wait to throw your bag on your hotel bed and head back out into the street, just wanting to be there. I knew that People's would be closed, but maybe I'd find something else.

Times are changing in China, at least in Yangshuo. I ended up dining at Susannah's. I could have chosen Serena's, or Minnie Mao's, or Mickey Mao's, or the Hard Seat, even Slim's, but the tables at Susannah's were set out in the street and there was John Coltrane playing over crackly speakers—John Coltrane on a cobblestone street in a small Chinese town that is hundreds of years old.

Woman watering her farm garden outside Yangshuo

"Hi, my name is Lilly," said a waitress who looked like a gymnast and spoke English with an Australian accent. "What would you like to eat?" The menu was printed on a board set over against a wall, next to another board that told about Susannah's:

"*. . . in October '87 the former U.S. President Mr. Jimmy Carter dined here with local VIPS* [sic]. *In December '93, Mr. Arthur Holcobe, resident representative of the United Nations Development Programme, enjoyed losagne* [sic], *one of the specialities of the house. . . .*"

"Do you really accept Visa?" I asked, seeing a sign, yet already aware that dinner could never come to more than a dollar.

"Sure," said Lilly, with an ever-so-tiny hint of a grin.

For dinner I had fish from the Li, a Sichuan-style braised eggplant, a spicy fried cucumber dish, a plate of local green vegetables, a big ceramic bowl of rice, and a bottle of beer, all for about fifteen cents.

Early the next morning I went looking for People's, hoping to find hot congee and buckwheat honey *shaobing* for breakfast. But People's didn't seem to exist anymore, nor did the Number One—at least I couldn't find them. So I ended up renting a mountain bicycle for the day, and I rode straight down to the river. There was the pavillion. I wasn't crazy, my memory wasn't playing

Local traffic by the Li River near Yangshuo

tricks. And there was the river and the fishermen and the boats.

"Are you going up the river?" a boatman called up to me in English.

"With my bike?" I yelled back, amazed.

And before I knew it I was heading up the Li, me and my bicycle. The sun was shining, the glassy Li reflecting the tall rock walls all around. We passed cormorant fishermen with their birds, teetering on tiny rafts made of three long bamboo poles strung together. They would nod or wave at the boat driver, and he would return their greeting. He had made the same trip up the river every day for twenty-eight years, he told me, never missing a day.

Two hours upriver we docked at a village where it was market day. The boatman and his wife disappeared into the market, only to reappear a moment later with an armful of leafy greens. They told me that I could get off the boat farther upriver, and asked if I would join them for lunch. So as we headed on up the Li we dined on rice, green vegetables, *la jiao jiang* (hot chile sauce), and hot green tea.

In the village of Xingping we docked again, and I climbed off the boat with my bicycle, listening intently to directions on how to find my way back to Yangshuo. "But it's easy," they kept saying reassuringly, and it was. I had only to follow the river, downhill, through villages and rice paddies and stands of giant bamboo. It was rice harvest, and everywhere I looked was golden and beautiful. There were birds singing, and in the air there were the smells of land growing food, of harvest straw. I coasted, and pedaled a little, and coasted, all the way back to Yangshuo.

When I at last arrived in town I was tired, but I stayed a little longer on my bike, pedaling slowly up and down the narrow streets trying to get my bearings. Outside one little shop were two big pots set over hot charcoal fires and a tray with a towel over the top. I got off my bike and went up to look. Sure enough, pulling back the towel I discovered buckwheat honey *shaobing*, and there in a pot was hot rice congee!

The day I left, ten days later, it began to rain.

# Hot Chile Paste
*la jiao jiang*

Makes approximately ¾ cup sauce

UNLIKE RAILWAY STATIONS IN INDIA, THOSE IN CHINA USUALLY OFFER relatively little in terms of fun and diversion for a weary traveler, but there are exceptions. Late one night, on a trip from South to North China, we stopped in the town of Changsha in Hunan Province. Changsha is traditionally billed as Mao Zedong's hometown (though technically that honor belongs to a nearby village), so we thought we should at least stretch our legs on the platform.

To our surprise, off in a corner was a vendor in a little booth selling jars of hot pepper paste. Mao was a big fan of hot food, and Hunan has a reputation for delicious *la jiao jiang*, hot pepper paste, so we each bought a jar and climbed back on the train. For the next few weeks, whenever we went to lunch or dinner, we would carry along a jar of hot pepper paste, and before we knew it, both jars were finished. Sadly, we've never found another *la jiao jiang* to compare.

Pounding dried chiles to make chile flakes at a Kunming market

Except, that is, our own. After years of buying jars of pepper paste in Chinese supermarkets, buying different kinds and different brands and never really loving any of them, we decided to make our own. We soaked dried hot chiles, threw them into the food processor, then started tasting and fiddling, trial and error. *La jiao jiang* began to make sense. First and foremost, the taste and quality of the pepper paste depends on what kind of chile *(la jiao)* you use. In Guangxi Province, someone recently gave us a superhot paste made from tiny bird chiles. "That's nothing," she said, seeing our expressions, "these chiles [which are called rice chiles in Guangxi] are much hotter in a neighboring village!"

There is no one recipe for *la jiao jiang*, no more than there is only one salsa in Mexico. Try our version here and then branch out. It keeps well in the refrigerator. You can use it as an accompaniment at the table, or it can be used directly in the cooking process, as in Spicy Cucumber Surprise (page 81) or Spicy Simmered Tofu (page 89).

We highly recommend it, and it is great fun to make. Thanks, Mao.

1 cup loosely packed dried red chiles (see Glossary), rinsed

¾ cup boiling water

1 teaspoon salt

1 teaspoon sugar

1 tablespoon peanut oil or vegetable oil

¼ cup finely minced shallots

1 teaspoon cider vinegar or rice vinegar

Place the chiles in a medium bowl, pour the boiling water over them, and use a wooden spoon or spatula to press the chiles down into the water. Alternatively, place a pot lid just smaller than the diameter of the bowl on the surface of the water to keep the chiles immersed and soaking. Let soak for at least 20 minutes or as long as 2 hours.

Transfer the chiles and soaking water to a food processor or blender and puree. Add the salt and sugar and process briefly to blend. Transfer the mixture back to the bowl and set aside.

Place a wok or heavy skillet over medium-high heat. When it is hot, add the oil. Swirl it around, then add the shallots and stir-fry until well softened and translucent, 2 to 2½ minutes. Add the pureed chile mixture and stir-fry for about 20 seconds, then remove from the heat and stir in the vinegar. Transfer to a clean bowl to cool, then store in a well-sealed glass or other nonreactive container.

# Cucumber-Sesame Salad

THIS SALAD IS SO EASY TO PREPARE, AND NO MATTER HOW OFTEN WE EAT IT, it is never often enough. In Taiwan it frequently comes to the table with a plate of fried peanuts as an hors d'oeuvre, even before you've had a chance to order. (But watch out—you still get charged for it.)

Use the small, thin-skinned varieties of cucumber native to parts of Asia or the Middle East if you can—they have the best flavor.

1 European cucumber or 1 pound pickling cucumbers (6 to 8)

1 tablespoon kosher salt or sea salt

1 heaping teaspoon grated ginger

2 tablespoons rice vinegar or red wine vinegar

2 teaspoons roasted sesame oil

½ teaspoon sugar

½ to 1 teaspoon dried chile pepper flakes

2 to 3 thin strips red bell pepper, for garnish (optional)

Wash the cucumber well. This dish is traditionally made with unpeeled cucumbers, because the contrasting greens are very pretty, but peel the cucumber if you wish. Trim off the ends and cut lengthwise into quarters. Remove the seeds. Cut each quarter lengthwise into 3 or 4 slices, then cut into approximately 2-inch lengths. Place in a colander, sprinkle on the salt, and mix gently with your hands to ensure all the pieces are salted. Let drain over a bowl or in the sink for 20 minutes.

Rinse the cucumber pieces thoroughly with cold water, wrap in a cotton towel, and gently squeeze dry. Place in a shallow serving dish.

In a small bowl, blend together the ginger, vinegar, sesame oil, and sugar. Pour over the cucumbers and toss gently to coat. Sprinkle the chile flakes over. Add the optional bell pepper garnish. Serve immediately, or within 2 hours, or cover with plastic wrap until ready to serve.

# Spicy Greens Salad

ONE OF THE WONDERFUL QUALITIES OF MANY CHINESE LEAFY GREEN vegetables is that they are as delicious served at room temperature as they are hot from the wok. Some are even better cold, for then they've had a chance to absorb flavor from a dressing.

This salad, made with *choi sum* or *bok choi,* can be prepared an hour or more in advance. The amount of chile used in the recipe makes for a pleasingly hot dish, but people who like hotter food will probably want to increase the chile flakes to one teaspoon.

1 pound greens: *choi sum* or *bok choi* (see page 83), cut into 3-inch lengths

1 teaspoon minced ginger

2 to 3 scallions, sliced lengthwise, then cut into 1-inch slivers

1 teaspoon sugar

¼ teaspoon salt

½ to 1 teaspoon chile pepper flakes or crumbled dried red chile (see Glossary)

2 tablespoons soy sauce

1 tablespoon rice wine vinegar

1 teaspoon roasted sesame oil

In a large pot, bring 8 cups of water to a rolling boil over high heat. Toss in the greens and stir to press them down into the water. Cook for 4 minutes, then drain thoroughly.

In a large bowl, mix together the remaining ingredients, stirring to distribute the ginger. Add the drained greens and toss to coat well with the dressing. Transfer to a flat plate and pour the remaining dressing and flavorings onto the pile of greens. Serve hot or at room temperature.

# Everyday Sprouts

THIS IS A QUICK, DELICIOUS, STAFF-OF-LIFE SORT OF DISH. BEAN SPROUTS ARE inexpensive, nutritious, and easily available year-round. At its best, the dish should come to the table with the bean sprouts piping hot and still crisp, but this is not as easy as it might seem, because they can overcook quickly. The trick is to have a very hot wok to start with, and then to work with a quantity of sprouts that is not too large for it. Be sure to have your salt, soy, and vinegar close at hand to add quickly, so as to avoid unnecessary cooking time. In China, the ends of the sprouts are often cut off before cooking, but we think this is unnecessary.

| | |
|---|---|
| 1 to 2 scallions | ½ teaspoon soy sauce |
| 1 tablespoon peanut oil | ½ teaspoon rice vinegar |
| ½ pound bean sprouts (3 cups) | ½ teaspoon roasted sesame oil |
| Scant ½ teaspoon salt | |

Prepare the scallions by slicing them lengthwise into long slivers and then cutting them into 2-inch lengths. Place beside your stovetop together with all the other ingredients.

About 3 minutes before you wish to serve, place a wok over the highest heat. When it is very hot, add the oil. After 20 seconds, toss in the scallions and bean sprouts and stir-fry vigorously, tossing and pressing them against the hot wok to quickly wilt and cook them. After 1 minute, add the salt and continue stir-frying. After another minute, add the soy sauce and rice vinegar. Continue to stir-fry for another 30 seconds to 1 minute.

Turn out onto a plate, drizzle with the sesame oil, toss gently, and serve.

# Spicy Cucumber Surprise

**Serves 4 to 6 as part of a rice-based meal**

WE OFTEN PREPARE THIS DISH, AS EUROPEAN CUCUMBERS ARE ONE OF OUR favorite vegetables to have in the garden, and they tend to flourish. It is also a fun dish to cook for friends; most of them don't realize they're eating cucumbers.

Try it. It's spicy, fun, easy, and delicious—everything a good stir-fry should be.

1 large European cucumber (1½ pounds)

1 tablespoon soy sauce

¼ teaspoon salt

¼ teaspoon sugar

1 tablespoon peanut oil

1 tablespoon minced garlic

1 heaping teaspoon minced ginger

1 teaspoon Hot Chile Paste (page 76), or less for a milder version

Peel the cucumber. Slice lengthwise into quarters, then scrape off the seeds. Slice each quarter lengthwise into thirds, then cut into 1- to 1½-inch lengths. Place by your stovetop.

In a small bowl, mix together the soy sauce, salt, and sugar and set aside near your stovetop together with all the other ingredients.

About 5 minutes before you wish to serve the dish, heat a wok or heavy skillet over high heat. Add the oil and swirl it around, then toss in the garlic, ginger, and chile paste and stir-fry for 15 to 20 seconds. Add the cucumber pieces and stir-fry for 2 minutes. Add the soy sauce mixture and cook for 2 to 3 minutes, stirring occasionally, until the cucumbers are soft on the outside but still have some crunch at the center. Turn out onto a plate. Serve hot or at room temperature.

*Making jao tze in a Kunming market*

# Summer Stir-fry

WE HAD ALWAYS LOVED STIR-FRYING CORN THAT WE CUT FRESH FROM the cob in the middle of the summer, but one particular August, with our two children and their friends enduring a mass exodus of baby front teeth, cutting corn from the cob took on a whole new meaning and sense of urgency. This dish was a savior.

This is also one of many dishes that come to the table to test one's ability with chopsticks. Of course you can use a spoon, but it's much more fun to try to pick up an individual kernel of corn or, better yet, an oiled peanut, with your sticks.

The lion's share of the preparation of this dish is in shaving off the corn kernels with a sharp cleaver, then dicing the zucchini, but once these two things are done, the dish is nearly ready.

2 tablespoons peanut oil or vegetable oil

½ cup raw peanuts

1 tablespoon chopped garlic

2 medium ears of corn, kernels cut from the cobs (1 cup)

2 small zucchini, cut into dice the same size as the corn kernels (1½ cups)

1 tablespoon soy sauce

½ teaspoon sugar

Heat a wok over high heat. When it is hot, add 1 tablespoon of the oil. When the oil is hot, add the peanuts. Stir-fry for 1½ minutes; the peanuts are done when they are quite brown—just before burning. Immediately transfer to a plate.

Add the remaining 1 tablespoon oil to the wok. When it is hot, add the garlic and stir-fry for 30 seconds. Add the corn and zucchini and stir-fry for 1 minute. Add the peanuts and continue stir-frying for another minute. Add the soy sauce and sugar, mix well, and stir-fry for 30 seconds. Transfer to a flat plate and serve.

# Chinese Green Vegetables

One winter's day, in the course of working on this book, we went over to the Chinese grocery store not far from where we live and brought home every green vegetable we could find. Almost all of them were in some way familiar to us, either because we'd eaten them frequently in China or Taiwan or simply because we'd seen them in the produce section day in and day out for years. But for some reason we rarely bought most of them, reaching habitually for the produce we knew more about.

So now we had brought them home—tiny baby *bok choi,* robust *choi sum,* hearty *gai laan*—and we put a big pot of salted water on the stove to boil. One at a time we boiled each vegetable, tasting frequently to determine the cooking time. As each one came out (most took no more than a minute, three minutes at the maximum), we lightly salted them and began eating. It was an earth-shattering discovery: Each one was fabulous! Some had a sweet edge, some were slightly bitter, but all were delicious. And easy. And nutritious.

Ever since, Chinese green vegetables have had a regular home in our kitchen. Some months later, in summer, we went through the same process, and we were thrilled to find a whole new group of green vegetables. And now we are not just converts, we are proselytizing converts.

We know that Chinese green vegetables aren't commonly available across North America, that you have to be lucky enough to live near an Asian grocery with a good produce section to enjoy them year-round, but they should be available. Most are of the cabbage family and grow easily in a wide range of climates. Many, in fact, were native to Europe and North America, yet ended up in Asia.

What we have to do now is nag our supermarket produce buyers, then to buy the vegetables once they are stocked, and cook them, and build them into our kitchen repertoires. It's easy because they're easy, and oh so good.

Here's a list of the ones we've been eating, under their Cantonese names, with a brief description of each. We recommend doing as we did, boiling them one at a time just to get to know the taste. Remember to wash all greens thoroughly before cooking. (Note: Transcriptions of Cantonese vary, so *bok choi* is also *bok choy* sometimes, *gai laan* may be written *guy lan,* and so forth.)

## Winter Greens

In North America, these are available in fall and winter, sometimes into early spring.

**bok choi** Known in English as Chinese white cabbage or as bok choy, it has flat white stems joined tightly at a central stalk and dark green leaves. The wider the white stem in relation to the length of the leaf, the more tender the cabbage. Miniature bok chois are the tenderest of all. Bok choi has a mild taste and is suitable for soups, stir-fries, and casseroles. Cook it with garlic and ginger.

**choi sum** Chinese broccoli, or flowering cabbage, has ridged stalks with four spaced leaves and small yellow flowers just coming out. It is good stir-fried, or parboiled and then stir-fried, with garlic and ginger.

**gai laan** Chinese kale has white flowers and tough, smooth round stalks. It needs good long simmering or parboiling. Dress it with oyster sauce or, after parboiling, stir-fry with beef, garlic, and hot chiles.

**Shanghai bok choi** The same shape as bok choi, but light or bright green all over, it can be used in the same way as bok choi.

**tai gu choi** A variant of bok choi, it is a flat Chinese cabbage about 4 inches tall and 6 inches to 1 foot in diameter, with white stalks and dark green leaves. It is also known as *tatsoi,* its Japanese name. Stir-fry or braise it, like bok choi. To divide, cut it into wedges (rather than pulling off individual leaves).

**wong nga baak** Known as Chinese cabbage, lettuce, or celery, or napa, or Beijing cabbage, it has mild-tasting, long, tightly wrapped pale leaves. It can be eaten raw; often used for making pickles. It is best braised slowly, with garlic and some ginger for warming.

## Spring Greens

These are available in winter in Hong Kong and southern China, but in North America they usually appear in late winter and spring.

**dou miu** Pea shoots or tender pea greens, a luxury vegetable and quite expensive, it is best used as a simple stir-fry with fresh ginger or parboiled in a broth and simply dressed.

**sai yeung choi** With small leaves on thick green stalks, in Asian markets, watercress is usually sold from a large messy-looking pile. In grocery stores, it usually comes in bunches. The tender green tips are best, so look for the finest stalks. It is often served well boiled in a pork broth–based soup, though it is also useful in Thai or Western dishes as a garnish or a salad green.

## Summer Greens

**saang choi** Leaf lettuce, cooling and faintly bitter, *saang choi* is used in congees and stir-fries or as a wrapper for hot and tasty foods.

**een choi** Chinese spinach, a variety of amaranth, is sometimes written *yin choi* or *yin choy.* It is high in protein, calcium, iron, and Vitamin A. Stir-fry it with garlic or garlic shoots, or toss it into a simple pork broth.

**ong choi** *Ong choi* is water spinach, a dryland variety of the water-grown vegetable known as *pak boong* in Thai. Its large heart-shaped leaves on long stalks stay crunchy when cooked. Stir-fry it over very high heat with lots of garlic, some chile paste, and a little fermented shrimp sauce or fermented bean curd or soy sauce.

# Quick and Easy Chinese Greens

*choi sum*

OUR FRIEND RUTH, WHO IS CHINESE FROM SABAH IN MALAYSIA AND WHOSE daughter, Hanna, was in kindergarten with our son Tashi, complains because the only food that Hanna likes is green vegetables. She especially loves stir-fried *choi sum*. "This is a problem?" we ask. "If only we had this problem with our kids!" Ruth smiles gently. She's just rubbing it in.

But even Tashi, who is not the world's most daring eater, enjoys stir-fried *choi sum*. He especially likes it if we don't overcook it, if it is still crisp and a beautiful bright green. As for us, we could happily see it, or a similar stir-fried Chinese green vegetable, on the table every day.

½ cup chicken stock or vegetarian stock, preferably unsalted, or water

1 tablespoon oyster sauce

1 tablespoon Chinese cooking wine (see Glossary) or dry sherry

1 tablespoon soy sauce

¼ teaspoon sugar

1 tablespoon peanut oil or vegetable oil

1 tablespoon minced garlic

3 scallions, cut into 1-inch lengths

½ inch ginger, peeled and minced

1 pound Chinese greens (*choi sum*), cut into 3-inch lengths and thickest stalks cut lengthwise in half

2 teaspoons cornstarch, dissolved in 1 tablespoon cold water

In a small bowl, mix together the stock, oyster sauce, wine, soy sauce, and sugar. Place by your stove, together with all the other ingredients.

Place a wok over high heat. When it is hot, add the oil. Let heat for 20 seconds, then toss in the garlic, scallions, and ginger. Stir-fry for 30 seconds, then add the greens. Stir-fry for 1½ to 2 minutes. Add the sauce mixture and bring to a boil, then cover and simmer for 3 minutes. Stir the cornstarch mixture, then add it to the wok and stir-fry until the sauce thickens, about 15 seconds.

Transfer to a small platter or a large plate and serve hot, with rice.

# Eggplant with Spicy Sesame Sauce

**Serves 4 to 6 as part of a rice-based meal**

THIS EGGPLANT DISH IS RICH IN TASTE AND TEXTURE, COMBINING ALL THE wonderful elements of Sichuanese cooking: garlic, ginger, chiles, and Sichuan pepper, all in generous amounts. It makes a very good centerpiece for a vegetarian meal, as there is nothing mild or shy about its taste. Serve it with rice and with dishes of contrasting textures, such as Summer Stir-fry (page 82) or Everyday Sprouts (page 80).

1½ pounds Asian eggplant (approximately 4 large)

1 tablespoon minced garlic

1 teaspoon minced ginger

½ teaspoon salt

3 tablespoons sesame paste (see Glossary)

¼ cup warm chicken stock, vegetarian stock, or water

3 tablespoons soy sauce

2 tablespoons cider vinegar

1 tablespoon chile oil (see Glossary)

1 tablespoon roasted sesame oil

1½ teaspoons Sichuan pepper (see Glossary), dry-roasted and ground

2 to 3 scallions, minced (about 3 tablespoons)

Place the eggplant in a large steamer over boiling water and steam until well softened, about 15 minutes. (If necessary, cut the eggplant in half to make them fit into the steamer, but steam in one layer only.) Remove from the steamer and lay on a platter to cool slightly.

When the eggplant is cool enough to work with, transfer to a cutting board and cut into slices: Cut lengthwise in half, then cut each half diagonally into slices. If necessary, cut the slices in half so none is more than 3 inches long. Transfer to a shallow bowl.

*If using a mortar and pestle,* place the garlic, ginger, and salt in the mortar and pound to a smooth paste. Place the sesame paste in a medium bowl, then stir in the warm stock or water to blend well. Add the soy sauce, vinegar, and both oils, stirring to blend. Stir in the garlic-ginger paste and the ground Sichuan pepper. *If using a blender or food processor,* combine all of the sauce ingredients in the machine and process thoroughly.

Just before serving, stir the minced scallions into the sauce.

Pour ¾ cup of the sauce over the eggplant and stir gently but thoroughly to distribute the sauce. Serve the remaining sauce on the side.

**Alternatives:** Our friend Cassandra prefers the slightly chewy texture of grilled or broiled eggplant to the softness of steamed eggplant. To make this dish, cut the eggplant lengthwise in half, then make shallow crosshatch pattern cuts on the cut sides and brush with chile oil or sesame oil—a technique she adapted from Barbara Tropp's exhaustive *Modern Art of Chinese Cooking.* The eggplant goes into a 400°F oven on a baking sheet, cut side down, until well softened, about 15 minutes. To cook it on a charcoal grill, turn it partway through cooking.

# Chinese Cabbage with Black Mushrooms

DRIED BLACK MUSHROOMS PACK MORE FLAVOR PER WEIGHT THAN ALMOST ANY other food we know. They also store well, so we try always to have a supply on hand. If we find ourselves close to dinner with little in the kitchen to cook, we can always soak a few black mushrooms in a cup of hot water and we are on our way to a tasty dish to accompany a pot of hot rice.

Here is one example using Chinese cabbage (also known as napa; see Chinese Green Vegetables, page 83).

6 medium dried black mushrooms, rinsed

1 cup warm water

¼ pound lean boneless pork (tenderloin, shoulder, or butt)

1 tablespoon soy sauce

1 tablespoon Chinese cooking wine (see Glossary) or dry sherry

1 pound Chinese (napa) cabbage (3 cups sliced or torn leaves)

1 tablespoon peanut oil or vegetable oil

1 tablespoon minced garlic

½ teaspoon salt

Place the mushrooms and water in a bowl, immerse the mushrooms thoroughly, and let soak for at least 30 minutes.

Meanwhile, thinly slice the pork against the grain. Mix together the soy sauce and wine in a small bowl and add the pork, turning to coat. Let marinate for at least 15 minutes. Prepare the cabbage by separating the leaves, stacking several of them at a time, and cutting them crosswise into 1-inch strips; alternatively, tear them into 1- to 2-inch strips. Set aside.

Drain the mushrooms, reserving the water, and slice into thin strips, discarding any hard bits. Place near your stovetop, together with all the other ingredients.

Heat a wok over high heat. When it is hot, add the oil and swirl it slightly to coat the wok. When the oil is hot, toss in the garlic and stir-fry for 20 seconds. Toss in the pork, mushrooms, and salt and stir-fry for about 1 minute, or until the meat changes color. Add the cabbage and cook, tossing and pressing it against the hot wok to wilt it, for 1 minute. Add the mushroom soaking water and bring to a vigorous boil, then cover and steam for 2 to 3 minutes, until the cabbage is tender. Turn out onto a small platter and serve hot.

# Mr. Wu

I first met Mr. Wu in the Botanical Gardens in Taipei, Taiwan. I was sitting on a bench when he asked if he could bother me for some help with a few words in English that were giving him trouble. Sure, I said. He sat down, opened a book on ornithology, and asked me more than half a dozen words. I had no clue in the world what any of them meant.

But we ended up chatting. He was a mainlander, having arrived in Taiwan in 1951, as a teenage soldier with the retreating army of Chiang Kai-shek. In the late 1940s the Nationalist Army had come through his village looking for "volunteers" and away he was taken, fifteen years old. It was the last time he ever saw his family and friends.

Mr. Wu was a well-educated man, but he had never attended a day of school in his life. We talked about politics, about food, about birds, about the war. He was wonderfully alert and curious and animated, and when he started talking about something for which he had strong feelings, he would stand up and address me straight on with great emotion. But he was missing four or five front teeth, and whenever he smiled, he automatically brought one hand up quickly to cover his mouth. It is how I remember him now, many years later, with his hand up over his mouth, speaking with conviction.

Mr. Wu and I became friends. We would meet for lunch, for steamed dumplings that we would dip in dark rice vinegar and then "chase" with large whole cloves of raw garlic. And he would talk to me about the taoists, about Lao-tzu and Chuang-tzu. Sometimes in the evening we would meet to drink Ng Jia Pi together, a strong medicinal liquor made from millet that we both liked a lot. We'd get pretty drunk, Mr. Wu and I, but even so he would never smile without bringing that hand up to cover his mouth.

Little restaurant near Yangshuo

# Spicy Simmered Tofu

Serves 4 as a main dish with rice

THERE ARE MANY DIFFERENT VERSIONS OF SPICY HOT SIMMERED TOFU IN THE regional cuisines of Sichuan, Hunan, and parts of South China. The soft silky texture of the tofu together with the thick, spicy hot sauce is an unbeatable combination.

This particular version is a regular in our house. Not only is it easy to make, but also, because it is slowly simmered, it can wait to be served while other stir-fried dishes are prepared. Though it is most often made with a little pork, it is equally satisfying and successful without meat. Made with a tablespoon of chile paste, it is medium-hot but not extremely spicy. If you wish to increase the heat, add more chile paste. To make the dish milder, use less ginger and only a teaspoon of chile paste.

About 1 pound squares fresh tofu

2 tablespoons peanut oil
    or vegetable oil

3 scallions, cut into 1½-inch lengths

4 cloves garlic, minced

¼ pound boneless pork, trimmed of fat
    and thinly sliced (optional)

1 tablespoon minced ginger

1 to 2 tablespoons Hot Chile Paste
    (page 76)

3 tablespoons soy sauce

½ cup chicken stock or vegetarian stock,
    preferably unsalted

½ teaspoon salt, or to taste

1 tablespoon cornstarch, dissolved in
    1 tablespoon cold water

Place the tofu squares on a large plate or platter. If they are an inch thick or more, cut in half horizontally. Cut each square into ½-inch cubes. Drain off any water that accumulates as the tofu stands.

Heat the wok over the highest heat. Add the oil and when it's hot, toss in the scallions and garlic. Stir-fry for 30 seconds, then toss in the optional pork slices, the ginger, and chile paste and stir-fry for 30 seconds more, tossing and pressing the mixture against the sides of the wok. Add the soy sauce and continue to cook, scooping and stirring, for another 30 seconds. Add the tofu and stock and bring to a vigorous boil, then lower the heat and simmer for 4 to 5 minutes.

Add the salt and stir well, then taste and adjust the seasonings if you wish. Stir the cornstarch mixture, then add to the wok, raise the heat, and stir-fry for about 20 seconds more, until the sauce thickens and becomes clear. Turn out into a shallow serving bowl and serve. (Because the sauce is soupy, it's easiest to serve with a small ladle.)

# Tofu with Tomatoes and Coriander

Serves 4 to 6 as an accompaniment to rice

WHEN TRAVELING IN ASIA, WE OFTEN MEET PEOPLE WHO DON'T LIKE FRESH coriander, and it seems such a shame. It's as debilitating as not liking chiles, because coriander is used so extensively in Thailand, India, even China. During my very first week in Taipei, I passed a big construction site. There, amid all the concrete and the rubble, was a patch of wild coriander plants, flourishing. "Well," I thought, "I've certainly come to the right place." In Mandarin Chinese, coriander is called *yiang cai,* or "sweet-smelling leaf," which seems a particularly appropriate name.

Coriander is one of our favorite plants to have in the garden, but for years we couldn't understand why it would always flower and go to seed just as it was beginning to mature. We finally learned from a knowledgeable gardener that it has two seasons, spring and fall, and that in the heat of the summer it always goes to seed. So now we enjoy it while we have it, then let it flower and the seeds disperse, and wait for the second season.

This simple stir-fry is light and easy comfort food, and it takes just minutes to prepare.

| | |
|---|---|
| 1 pound tomatoes (2 large or 3 medium) | ½ teaspoon sugar |
| 4 squares fresh tofu (about 1 pound) | 1 teaspoon soy sauce |
| 1 tablespoon peanut oil or vegetable oil | Generous grinding of white or |
| 1 tablespoon minced garlic | black pepper |
| ½ cup chopped scallions | ¼ cup fresh coriander leaves |
| 1 teaspoon salt | |

Cut the tomatoes and tofu into 1-inch squares and set aside in separate bowls. Discard any water that drains from the tofu as it stands.

Heat a large wok or heavy skillet over high heat. Add the oil and swirl to coat the pan. Toss in the garlic and scallions and stir-fry briefly, until the garlic starts to change color. Add the tomatoes and stir-fry until softened, about 1 minute. Add the tofu, salt, sugar, and soy sauce. Stir to blend, bring to a boil, and cook, stirring briefly once, for 30 seconds. Turn out into a shallow serving bowl, top with the pepper and coriander, and serve hot.

# Taipei in January

No one had warned me not to arrive in Taipei in January, in the middle of the winter, two weeks before Chinese New Year. I actually thought it would be a good time to arrive, what with the New Year and the festivities and great food. But that was in 1980, and Taipei was not what I would call a beautiful city. Street after street of twelve-story concrete buildings had been built way too close together, way too cheaply, and way too quickly. The traffic and pollution were a nightmare, second only to Bangkok's, and the city had a climate often likened to the ill temper of an ill-tempered Chinese mother-in-law. To be kind about it, Taipei looked and felt exceedingly dreary.

I had gone there to learn Mandarin, to work, to eat, to travel. But I quickly realized that nothing forward-moving would happen for me until after the two-week-long New Year holiday had passed. At New Year's, everything comes to a dead stop. There would be no work and no school; even food would get hard to come by, and I had very little money. So I got a dorm bed in a worker and student hostel, sharing a tiny room with a student from Thailand, a student from Japan, a worker from Korea, and an old Chinese man (I never figured out why he was there). To save money, I shopped in the market instead of eating in restaurants, but as New Year approached, even the cost of vegetables rose out of sight.

Each day I brought food back to the room to prepare, eating mostly salads, as we didn't have cooking facilities. With all my uncooked vegetables, my diet must have been appalling to the old Chinese man, but I didn't realize it at the time. Whenever I prepared food, he would be standing looking over my shoulder, insisting that I go back to the sink and get every little speck of grit out of the green onions. It was bleak, bleak, bleak.

But time passed. Late one night, I went out with the Korean worker and the Japanese student and we found a noodle shop that also served liquor. They ordered Ng Jia Pi, Mei Gwei Jyou, and Jiu Ye Jing, three Chinese liquors that I would come to love. As we drank, we realized that we could actually piece together a conversation. The more we drank the better the conversation got. We became friends.

Finally, New Year came and went, and for the next nine months life was anything but bleak or dreary. I was very sad to leave Taipei.

The basic equipment of Taipei street vending

# Frozen Tofu with Winter Vegetables

FREEZING TOFU HAS BEEN USED AS A METHOD OF PRESERVATION IN CHINA and Japan for centuries. Tofu is traditionally left outside on cold winter nights, where it not only freezes but also dehydrates, making it "freeze-dried." When cooked, frozen tofu is firm-textured and, unlike fresh tofu, absorbent like a sponge. In slowly simmered dishes, it holds onto all the flavors of the sauce it cooks in, a little bit like the way chunks of eggplant cook in a tomato sauce.

*Selling tofu and wheat gluten in Shangai*

Freezing tofu is also a very practical way of dealing with surplus squares of fresh tofu. Simply cut them into half-inch squares, arrange them on a plate or large plastic lid, and put them in the freezer. The next day you can lift them off the plate or lid, wrap them in a plastic bag, seal it, and store them frozen until you need them. Freezing tofu in a freezer is not quite the same as freezing it outside, where it will dehydrate even more in the fresh air. As frozen tofu from the freezer thaws, it gives off water; just squeeze out the tofu once it has thawed to make it all the more absorbent.

This recipe is for a slowly simmered winter vegetable stew. The chunks of tofu become truly flavor-packed.

2 tablespoons soy sauce

2 tablespoons Chinese cooking wine (see Glossary) or dry sherry

2 cups frozen tofu cubes (see headnote), defrosted and excess water squeezed out

4 cups chicken stock or vegetarian stock, preferably unsalted

2 tablespoons peanut oil or vegetable oil

1 tablespoon minced garlic

4 scallions, cut into 1½-inch lengths

½ pound mushrooms, coarsely chopped

1 teaspoon minced ginger

¾ pound carrots, cut into ½-inch cubes (2 cups)

¾ pound potatoes, peeled and cut into ½-inch cubes (2 cups)

1 teaspoon salt (less if using salted stock)

Generous grinding of black pepper (optional)

In a small bowl, mix together the soy sauce and 1 tablespoon of the wine. Add the tofu cubes and turn to coat. Set aside.

Put the stock in a medium pot and bring to a boil over medium-high heat. Lower the heat to maintain a simmer.

Meanwhile, place all the remaining ingredients near your stovetop. Place a large heavy pot over high heat. When it is hot, add the oil, and heat for 15 seconds. Toss in the garlic and scallions and stir-fry for 30 seconds. Toss in the mushrooms and ginger and stir-fry until the mushrooms begin to soften and to give up some moisture. Add the remaining 1 table-spoon wine, toss, and stir, then add the carrots and potatoes and stir and turn for 2 minutes.

Add the hot stock and bring to a boil. Lower the heat to medium and simmer gently for about 15 minutes. Add the tofu with its marinade and the salt and simmer for another 5 to 10 minutes, until the carrots and potatoes are tender. Serve immediately, or set aside and reheat just before serving. (The stew may be made ahead and frozen, or stored in the refrigerator in well-sealed nonreactive containers for up to 3 days.)

# Steamed Fish Heaped with Scallions and Ginger

**Serves 4 to 6 as the centerpiece of a rice-based meal**

WHEN I WAS LIVING IN DOWNTOWN TAIPEI, ONCE A WEEK FOR NEARLY NINE months I would travel by bus far out into a suburban neighborhood to attend a class in Shanghai cooking. It was held in the basement of a church and attended by thirty to forty women who lived in the neighborhood. I never saw another man in the class, but that didn't seem to matter to anyone there.

The recipes and techniques demonstrated were for the most part quite elaborate. Meats and vegetables would often be lightly steamed or blanched, then deep-fried, and sometimes even stir-fried after that. Dishes would often come to the table glistening with oil, a little too rich for my taste. But the class was always interesting, if only to watch the teacher perform magic with her cleavers.

This dish is one I learned in that class and have been making ever since. It's a classic Chinese technique for steaming fish, first flavoring the fish lightly with salt, ginger, scallions, cooking wine, and, often, a little sesame oil, and then placing it on a plate and steaming it for ten to twenty minutes, depending on the size of the fish. The process is quick, and the cooking time is relatively easy to judge. All you need is good fresh firm-textured fish. Though black sea bass is classic, we also like to use nontraditional freshwater fishes with firm flesh, such as salmon trout or pickerel, as they are often the freshest fish available to us.

Steaming requires no special equipment. The water can boil in a wok or a large pan or pot. The fish is laid on a plate and the plate then sits either in a bamboo steamer over boiling water or on a trivet (to keep it above the water). You'll need a lid or aluminum foil to seal in the steam. Try to come up with a steaming arrangement that has enough room for the size of fish you are cooking; otherwise, you'll have to cut the fish and the presentation won't be as impressive.

One 1½- to 2-pound fish, such as black sea bass, red snapper, salmon trout, or pickerel, cleaned and scaled

1½ teaspoons sea salt, plus a pinch

2 tablespoons minced ginger

2 tablespoons soy sauce

2 tablespoons Chinese cooking wine (see Glossary) or dry sherry

1 teaspoon roasted sesame oil

8 scallions

1 tablespoon peanut oil or vegetable oil

Wash the fish with cold water and wipe dry. Make three parallel diagonal slashes, about 2 inches long, on each side of the fish from the top of the back down, slicing through to the bone. Rub the fish all over with the 1½ teaspoons salt. Lay the fish on a plate large enough to hold its full length (if the plate is not large enough, as a last resort you can cut off the fish head and/or tail to make it fit).

Place the ginger in a mortar or bowl with a pinch of salt and pound with a pestle or mash with the back of a large spoon to a paste. Using about one third of the ginger paste, stuff a little paste into each of the slashes on the fish.

Place the remainder of the paste in a small bowl. Add the soy sauce, wine, and ½ teaspoon of the sesame oil. Stir to mix well. Spoon the mixture into the cavity and over the top of the fish. Let stand for 10 to 20 minutes to marinate. Just before steaming, spoon the marinade liquid on the plate over the top of the fish.

Smash the scallions flat with the side of a cleaver or a large heavy knife, then cut into 1-inch lengths. Pull apart the pieces to make thinner shreds. Place one quarter of the scallion shreds inside the fish and heap the remainder on top.

*If using a bamboo steamer in a wok,* place 3 to 4 cups water in the wok and bring to a boil. Place the plate with the fish in the bamboo steamer and cover with a lid. When the water is boiling vigorously, place the steamer over the water; the water must not touch the plate. *If using a trivet placed in a large pot or pan,* place the trivet in the center of the pot and add enough water so that the trivet is not quite covered. Bring the water to a boil and then place the plate on the trivet (use oven mitts so you don't get burned by the steam) and cover the pot with a tightly fitting lid or aluminum foil.

Let the fish steam for approximately 10 minutes per inch of thickness at its thickest point. Most fish of this size will take 12 to 15 minutes, some as long as 20 minutes. When cooked, the flesh will be opaque and will flake (separate easily) when prodded with a fork.

When the fish is close to done, place the peanut oil and the remaining ½ teaspoon sesame oil in a small skillet and heat until very hot.

Remove the plate with the cooked fish from the steamer. Pour the hot oil over the fish to give it a pleasing glaze (steaming often leaves a dull finish). Serve immediately, directly from the plate. Guests can lift pieces of fish off the plate with chopsticks as they eat, or they can be served formal portions. If you serve individual portions, be sure to spoon a little sauce over each serving. (Any leftovers are very tasty cold.)

# Smoky Red Pepper Chicken

Serves 4 as part of a rice-based meal

DOWN THE STREET FROM US IS A PLEASANT RESTAURANT THAT SERVES good Sichuan and Hunan food. When our oldest son was about three years old, he developed a passion for the "General George Chicken" on the menu, a version of a Sichuan favorite that features seared (and searingly hot) dried red peppers. The waiter would always look worried when we ordered it, but with the peppers and onions moved to one side, Dominic would work his way through a whole plate of spicy chicken. Parents were granted only a meager portion.

Chiles laid out to dry in the sun
in Xingping, Guangxi

This is our own version of that smoky flavorful chicken dish. Once the chicken has marinated, cooking time, as with all stir-fries, is short. Be sure to let the onions soften completely before adding the chicken. In the finished dish, the soft onions and crunchy toasted peanuts are a lovely contrast to the succulent chicken. A tofu dish and a parboiled or stir-fried mild-tasting Chinese green, lightly dressed, make good accompaniments.

¾ pound boneless skinless chicken
breasts, cut into ½- to ¾-inch cubes

### Marinade

2 tablespoons Chinese cooking wine
(see Glossary) or dry sherry

1 teaspoon salt

2 teaspoons cornstarch

6 dried red chiles (see Glossary)

2 tablespoons peanut oil

2 tablespoons minced garlic

1 tablespoon minced ginger

1 large or 2 small onions, cut into large
dice (about 1 cup)

3 tablespoons soy sauce

1 tablespoon Chinese cooking wine
(see Glossary) or dry sherry

1 teaspoon sugar

¼ cup boiling chicken stock or water

1 teaspoon rice vinegar

2 tablespoons dry-roasted peanuts
(see Glossary) or cashew nuts,
coarsely chopped

Place the chicken in a shallow bowl. Mix together the marinade ingredients in a small bowl and pour over the chicken. Toss well to coat. Let stand, covered, for 30 minutes at room temperature, or as long as 12 hours in the refrigerator. Bring to room temperature and stir and mix thoroughly before proceeding.

Place all the remaining ingredients by your stovetop. Heat a wok over high heat. Toss in the dried chiles and dry-fry briefly, pressing them against the hot wok to sear them. Remove from the wok and set aside.

Place the wok back over high heat, add the oil, and when it is very hot, toss in the seared chiles. Let cook for 30 seconds to flavor the oil, then toss in the garlic and ginger and stir-fry for 10 seconds. Add the onion, lower the heat slightly, and stir-fry until translucent and softened, 4 to 5 minutes.

Raise the heat, add the chicken, and stir-fry for about 2 minutes (cook until it has changed color all over, then for another 30 seconds), pressing it against the hot wok and tossing constantly. Add the soy sauce, wine, and sugar and stir. Add the stock or water and bring to a boil. Add the vinegar and let cook for another 15 seconds, stirring, then turn out on a serving platter. Top with the coarsely chopped peanuts or cashews. Serve hot to accompany rice.

**Note:** If your wok is small, cook the chicken in two batches, using half the oil, chiles, garlic, ginger, and onions for each; this will ensure even cooking of the chicken. Cook the first batch until the chicken is just cooked through, then transfer to a bowl and set aside. Repeat with the remaining oil, garlic, onion, ginger, and chicken. Once the second batch of chicken has cooked through, return the first batch to the wok and complete the dish.

# Soupy Chicken with Mushrooms

WHEN YOU ARE EATING RICE AS A STAPLE FOOD, IT IS IMPORTANT TO HAVE contrast in the foods that accompany and bring flavor to the rice. The various dishes you serve can contrast in texture, in color, in temperature—hot versus cold; in "heat"—with chiles or without; and in richness—versus simplicity. Contrast makes for a more interesting meal. It helps keep each flavor or food distinct from the others, while each one helps to highlight the others.

In preparing simple home-style Chinese cooking, it is relatively easy to come up with good-tasting seasonal stir-fries, such as stir-fried leafy greens or sprouts or broccoli, dishes that are essentially dry when they come to the table. Dishes that are slowly simmered and "soupy," on the other hand, can be harder to come up with on a regular basis, though they are just as important as stir-fries in bringing contrast to a meal.

This recipe, which we fondly call Soupy Chicken, is an ideal dish for serving alongside a tasty stir-fry. It has a depth of flavor that you'd think could come only from a good stock and a long simmer, but it needs neither.

Allow thirty minutes for the mushrooms to soak and the chicken to marinate, then just five minutes of cooking, and it's done! Soupy Chicken.

### Marinade

1 tablespoon Chinese cooking wine (see Glossary) or dry sherry

1 teaspoon cornstarch

½ egg white

½ teaspoon salt

6 ounces boneless skinless chicken breast (1 large half-breast), cut into ¼-inch cubes

6 to 8 dried black mushrooms, rinsed

3 cups hot water

2 tablespoons peanut oil or vegetable oil

1 tablespoon minced garlic

¼ pound mushrooms, cut into quarters

1 medium green bell pepper, stem, seeds, and membranes discarded, cut into ½-inch squares

2 tablespoons soy sauce

1 tablespoon Chinese cooking wine (see Glossary) or dry sherry

½ teaspoon salt

½ teaspoon sugar

1 teaspoon roasted sesame oil

1 teaspoon cornstarch, dissolved in 1 tablespoon cold water

Freshly ground white or black pepper (optional)

In a medium bowl, mix together the marinade ingredients. Add the chicken and turn to coat well. Let stand, covered, for 30 minutes (or as long as 8 hours in the refrigerator; bring back to room temperature before proceeding).

Place the dried mushrooms in a medium bowl and pour over 1 cup of the hot water. Press and stir the mushrooms to start them soaking, and let soak for 30 minutes, or until softened.

Remove the mushrooms from the water, reserving the soaking water. Chop off and discard the tough stems, then cut into quarters and set aside.

Place all the ingredients by your stovetop. Place a large wok over high heat. Add the peanut or vegetable oil and when it is hot, add the chicken, reserving the marinade. Stir-fry for 30 seconds, then remove and set aside. Heat the oil again, add the garlic, and stir-fry for 20 to 30 seconds. Add the fresh mushrooms and continue stir-frying for 1 minute, then add the dried mushrooms, green pepper, and the chicken, together with the reserved marinade. Stir-fry for another 30 seconds, then add the reserved mushroom soaking water and the remaining 2 cups hot water, along with the soy sauce, wine, salt, and sugar. Bring to a boil, then add the sesame oil. Stir the cornstarch mixture, add to the wok, and cook for another 30 seconds to 1 minute, until the sauce thickens. Transfer to a shallow serving bowl. Grind white or black pepper over if you like and serve immediately, to accompany rice.

# Winter in Downtown Toronto

We live in downtown Toronto. As I write, it is midwinter here in the city; the days are appallingly short, the air is frigid and dry. Tropical Asia seems far away. But our neighborhood is Chinatown, and just a few short blocks away are Spadina Avenue and Kensington Market. In this one small commercial area there are well over a hundred Asian groceries and restaurants. We think the market is the best of its kind in North America; at least it's the best we've seen so far.

One night I walked over to the market to buy some things for dinner. It was not yet five o'clock, but it was already as dark as midnight. On the sidewalks of Spadina vendors were bundled in winter jackets, hats, and heavy gloves, calling out in Cantonese to advertise their bargain produce: ten limes for a dollar, bunches of fresh coriander two for a dollar, bags of bird chiles fifty cents each. Inside the brightly lit restaurants, there was already a bustle of activity, and the windows were suitably steamy and inviting.

All around me were the smells of tropical food, Asian food, all penetrating the cold night air. It was a battle between hot, spicy food and the cold air, and the food was having its way, melting the dark winter chill, transforming it into soft tropical night. For a moment I almost liked winter.

**left to right**

Rice steamer cooking rice on the street in Kunming

Winter in Toronto

# Snow Peas with a Hint of Pork

Serves 4 as part of a larger rice meal or
2 as a main dish accompanied by rice and a vegetable dish

SNOW PEAS AND SUGAR SNAP PEAS ARE A LUXURY, A WONDERFUL BRIGHT GREEN treat. The tender, slightly sweet pods keep a little crispness when stir-fried. We like to cook them on their own or with a small amount of meat. However tired or out of sorts our children are, they will always happily eat vast quantities of this simple dish.

To prepare the peas, wash thoroughly, then work your way one by one through the pile of pea pods, snapping off the tough stem end and pulling with it the "string" that runs along the pod to the other end. The job always goes more quickly than you think, and it's one chore children find rewarding.

| | |
|---|---|
| 1 tablespoon Chinese cooking wine (see Glossary) or dry sherry | 2 cloves garlic, minced |
| 1 tablespoon soy sauce | 3 scallions, cut into ½-inch lengths |
| ¼ pound lean boneless pork (loin, shoulder, or butt), thinly sliced against the grain | ½ teaspoon salt |
| | ½ teaspoon sugar |
| ½ pound snow peas or sugar snap peas, trimmed | ½ cup mild stock or water |
| | 1 teaspoon cornstarch, dissolved in 1 teaspoon cold water |
| 1 tablespoon peanut oil | |

In a small bowl, mix together the wine and soy sauce for the marinade. Place the pork in the marinade and stir well to coat. Let stand for 30 minutes to 1 hour.

Meanwhile, bring a medium pot of water to a boil. Toss in the snow peas and parboil for 1 minute, then drain, refresh with cold water, drain again, and set aside.

About 8 minutes before you wish to serve the meal, heat a wok and add the oil. When the oil is hot, add the garlic and scallions and stir-fry for 30 seconds. Toss in the pork, with any remaining marinade, and stir-fry for 1 to 2 minutes, until it has changed color. Add the snowpeas and stir-fry for 30 seconds, then add the salt, sugar, and stock or water. Cover and let cook for 1 minute.

Stir the cornstarch mixture, add to the wok, and cook, stirring occasionally, until the sauce thickens, about 1 to 2 minutes. Transfer immediately to a serving platter and serve hot.

# Yunnanese Spicy Ground Pork Sauce

**Serves 6 to 8 with plenty of rice**

YUNNAN IS A LARGE MOUNTAINOUS PROVINCE IN SOUTHWESTERN CHINA. Although it has long been a part of China proper politically speaking, culturally it is very much a part of Southeast Asia. In China there are approximately fifty-four different minority populations, and of these, thirty-five are found in Yunnan Province. People like the Hmong, Lisu, Minchia, Tai, and Dai all live in Yunnan, yet over time they have also come to inhabit remote mountainous regions of Laos, Vietnam, and Thailand. Many of these populations are small, but others, such as the Hmong, number anywhere from five to eight million people. As a result, Yunnan has an incredibly rich interplay of people and culture, and Yunnanese cuisine is as exciting as it is diverse.

A child outside a local restaurant in Dai, Yunnan

In this dish, the rich savory sauce has a taste more Southeast Asian than Chinese. Dried mushrooms, pork, and plenty of shallots are all finely chopped to make a smooth, aromatic sauce or "gravy." There's a hint of anise and of cinnamon as well as a touch of chile heat, but nothing overpowering. The sauce is meant to top a large bowl of rice as a simple one-dish rice meal, sprinkled with some fresh coriander if you wish.

This is quite a meaty sauce and a little goes a long way. We like to make a double quantity, then freeze it in smaller portions to pull out for other meals. Before freezing, take out the star anise.

8 dried black mushrooms, rinsed

3½ cups hot water

1 tablespoon peanut oil or vegetable oil

1 cup finely chopped shallots

1 pound lean ground pork

3 tablespoons soy sauce

1 teaspoon sugar

½ teaspoon salt

⅛ teaspoon ground cinnamon

1 star anise

1 or 2 dried red chiles (see Glossary)

**Optional garnish**

Approximately ½ cup loosely packed
    fresh coriander leaves

Place the mushrooms in a medium bowl with 1 cup of the hot water to soak for 30 minutes, or until well softened.

Remove the mushrooms from the water, reserving it. Chop off and discard any tough stems, then finely chop the mushrooms and set aside.

Place a medium heavy pot or a wok over medium-high heat. Add the oil, and when it is hot, add the shallots. Stir-fry for 3 to 4 minutes, until well softened. Add the meat and mushrooms and stir-fry for another 3 minutes. Add the mushroom soaking water and the remaining 2½ cups hot water and stir well. Add the remaining ingredients and bring to a boil, then lower the heat and simmer gently, uncovered, for 30 minutes.

Serve as a sauce over large bowls of plain rice. Garnish with the fresh coriander if you wish.

# Beef and Lettuce Congee

Serves 4 to 6 as a one-dish meal

THOUGH CONGEE IS MOST OFTEN SERVED AS A SIMPLE UNSEASONED RICE soup, with different flavors added by people as they eat (see Basic Rice Congee, page 65), some congees are flavored during cooking. Yam and pumpkin congees, fish congees, sweet bean congees, and other congees become wonderful collections of contrasting tastes and textures.

We're particularly fond of this beef and lettuce congee, which is very easy to prepare as it needs no broth or long simmering. Flavor and texture are added just after the rice has cooked, in the form of marinated thinly sliced beef, chopped scallion, and strips of crunchy romaine lettuce. We serve it as a hot one-dish meal, like a Vietnamese soup. Once it's served, we like a choice of simple condiments: either Hot Chile Paste (page 76) or Thai Fish Sauce with Hot Chiles (page 124), or simply a grinding of fresh white or black pepper on top.

1 teaspoon cornstarch

1 tablespoon Chinese cooking wine
(see Glossary) or dry sherry

1 tablespoon soy sauce

6 ounces boneless eye-of-round or other
lean fine-grained beef, very thinly
sliced across the grain

1 cup medium- or short-grain rice
(Chinese, Japanese, or Korean)

8 cups cold water

4 scallions, cut into ¼-inch lengths

1 medium head romaine lettuce or
½ pound Chinese leaf lettuce (*saang
choi,* see page 84), cut crosswise into
1-inch strips (about 4 lightly packed
cups)

1 teaspoon salt

Freshly ground white or black pepper
to taste

In a medium bowl, mix together the cornstarch, wine, and soy sauce. Add the sliced meat and turn to coat well. Set aside to marinate.

Wash the rice thoroughly under cold running water until the water runs clear. Place in a large pot and add the cold water. Bring to a vigorous boil, then lower the heat and simmer, uncovered, until the rice is very tender, about 20 minutes. (The dish can be prepared to this point up to 6 hours ahead: Remove the rice from the heat, cover, and refrigerate until ready to proceed. Refrigerate the beef as well.)

To serve the dish, bring the rice and water to a vigorous boil. (If you have let the cooked rice stand for any length of time, it will have absorbed more water; you may have to add up to a cup of water to thin the mixture back to a soupy texture.) Add the meat with any marinade and the chopped scallions, stir well, and remove from the heat. Stir in the lettuce strips and salt. Serve immediately in large bowls and pass the pepper mill.

Note: If you have any leftovers, they will thicken during standing. Before reheating, add some water to restore the soupy texture.

# Egg Fried Rice

THIS ATTRACTIVE FRIED RICE IS A GOOD WAY OF USING LEFTOVER RICE AND odds and ends of vegetables. We've suggested using a little ham and chopped carrot, but if instead you have other strong-tasting cooked or cured salty meat left over, use that instead. If you have neither, then a little finely chopped bacon makes a good substitute. For a vegetarian version, use half a cup of finely chopped fried tofu squares (see Glossary) and increase the salt to one teaspoon, or marinate the tofu for a few minutes in some soy sauce.

This recipe serves two; to double, cook a second batch separately. As with all stir-frying, it's important that you not cook too much at once, or you'll lose the wonderful flavor of wok-seared rice. Serve this with a salad or simply cooked Chinese greens if you wish.

2 large eggs

½ teaspoon salt

1 teaspoon soy sauce

2 tablespoons peanut oil or vegetable oil

¼ cup finely chopped ham or lean bacon (see headnote for vegetarian options)

2 large scallions, finely chopped

¼ cup finely chopped carrots (optional)

3½ cups cooked long- or medium-grain rice, cold or at room temperature

Cucumber slices for garnish (optional)

In a small bowl, whisk the eggs, salt, and soy sauce.

Heat a wok over high heat. When it is hot, add the oil and the bacon, if using. When the oil is hot, add the scallions and optional carrot and stir-fry for 30 seconds. Add the egg mixture and cook for another 30 seconds, using your spatula to break up the egg mixture so it cooks evenly. Add the ham, if using, and the rice, and use the spatula aggressively to break up the rice into the eggs. With the back of the spatula, push the rice against the surface of the wok, making sure that all the rice actually comes into contact with the wok, to sear it. Stir-fry aggressively for 3 minutes. Turn the rice out onto two individual plates and serve, garnished with the cucumber, if you wish.

# Sweet Rice and Pork Dumplings

*Makes 35 to 40 dumplings; serves 8 as a snack or hors d'oeuvre*

EACH WINTER AROUND CHINESE NEW YEAR, OUR NEIGHBOR GRACE, WHO is from Taiwan, holds a large potluck party. The food is always great, ranging from Grace's potluck standby, a slow-simmered braised beef dish, to Beijing-style pot stickers and red-cooked baby eggplant.

Not surprisingly, a lot of the conversation is about food—who contributed what, other versions of the same dish, and so forth. Last year we fell into conversation with two guests from China. When we asked them about their favorite foods, one of them began describing sweet rice and pork dumplings, a version of the Cantonese dim sum classic *siu mai* from his home-town up the Yangtze River from Shanghai. In traditional *siu mai,* seasoned ground pork is the main ingredient, wrapped in wonton skins or dumpling wrappers and steamed, then eaten with a dipping sauce. Here the main ingredient is not meat but sticky rice. The pork and a few black mushrooms are used as flavorings. The rice gives the dumplings body and a more tender bite than *siu mai,* as well as a more subtle flavor.

1½ cups short-grain sticky (sweet) rice

**Dipping sauce**

3 tablespoons soy sauce

2 tablespoons rice vinegar or cider vinegar

½ teaspooon roasted sesame oil

1 tablespoon peanut oil

½ pound lean ground pork

6 dried black mushrooms, soaked in hot water for 30 minutes, drained, and finely chopped

1 tablespoon minced dried shrimp (see Glossary)

2 tablespoons soy sauce

2 tablespoons Chinese cooking wine (see Glossary) or dry sherry

½ teaspooon sugar

¾ teaspooon salt

¼ teaspoon freshly ground black pepper

¼ cup minced scallions

35 to 40 dumpling wrappers or wonton skins

Wash the rice under cold running water until the water runs clear, then soak in warm water for 30 minutes.

Drain the rice thoroughly, then place in a heavy medium pot with 1¼ cups water. Bring to a boil and let boil for 30 seconds to 1 minute, then cover and simmer for 20 minutes. Remove from the heat and let stand, covered, for 10 minutes. *Alternatively,* cook the rice in a rice cooker.

Heat the oil in a wok over high heat. Toss in the pork, mushrooms, and shrimp and stir-fry until the color of the pork changes, breaking up the pork with a spatula so there are no lumps or clumps. Add the soy sauce, wine, sugar, salt, and pepper and stir-fry briefly. Stir in the cooked rice and the scallions and mix well. Remove from the heat and divide between two medium bowls.

*If using wonton skins,* trim to a circular shape. Place a small bowl of water (for moistening your fingers as you shape the dumplings) and a large lightly oiled plate by your work surface. Lightly oil one or two 10-inch or larger steamers.

To shape the dumplings, place 1 generous tablespoon filling in the center of a wrapper skin or wonton and then, with moistened fingers, pull the edges up around the filling and pinch just at the top of the filling to make a pleated "neck" with a "frill" of wrapper above. Repeat to make more dumplings. As you complete each dumpling, place it on the lightly oiled plate and push down gently to flatten the bottom.

When you have made 15 to 20 dumplings, transfer them to a steamer. In a large wok or pot, bring water for steaming to a boil. Place the steamer over boiling water (the water should be no higher than ½ inch below the steamer), cover, and steam the dumplings for 6 minutes.

Continue to shape the remaining dumplings while the first batch cooks, then cook the remaining dumplings.

Mix together the dipping sauce ingredients in a small bowl.

Serve the dumplings hot or at room temperature, either from the steamers or on plates. Accompany with the dipping sauce, served in one or two small bowls.

# Hilary's Sticky Rice Rolls
## nuomi tuan

Serves 6 to 10

OUR FRIEND AND NEIGHBOR HILARY IS AN AVID COOK AS WELL AS A marvelous linguist. A fluent Mandarin speaker, she has explored many Chinese-language cookbooks for us. We were delighted when she came up with a recipe for sticky rice rolls, one of our favorite snack or anytime foods. Now she brings them over fairly often as a contribution to a potluck or simply as a neighborly treat to sustain us.

This recipe is actually an adaptation of several recipes. Having experimented with both short- and long-grain sticky rice, Hilary prefers to use Thai-style long-grain sticky rice. The rice is soaked overnight, then steamed for about twenty-five minutes. It can then be used for many treats, some sweet, some savory, like this one. To make these rolls you'll need the long cruller-like deep-fried Chinese breads called *yu tiao* in Mandarin. They come in pairs, two long sticks stuck together along their length and easily separated. We buy them in Chinatown.

Assembling the rolls is quick once the rice has cooked and the filling is mixed. The rice is wrapped around a length of *yu tiao* bread with a little salty, savory flavoring. The whole roll is wrapped in plastic wrap or, more intriguingly, in a banana leaf (banana leaves are sold, frozen, in many Asian stores and keep indefinitely in the freezer). The rolls should be assembled just before serving so the *yu tiao* has no time to lose its crispness. Serve as a snack or to accompany a simple meal of soup and cooked vegetables or salad.

2 cups short- or medium-grain Chinese
    or Japanese sticky (sweet) rice or long-
    grain Thai sticky rice

### Filling

1 double Chinese cruller (*yu tiao*)
    (see headnote)

1 teaspoon peanut oil or vegetable oil

1½ to 2 tablespoons finely chopped
    pickled Chinese cabbage (*tianjin dong
    cai*) or pickled turnip (see Glossary)

4 to 5 tablespoons shredded cooked pork
    (*rou song*, see Glossary)

¼ teaspoon sugar

Freshly ground white pepper

Wash the rice thoroughly in cold water and drain well. Soak overnight in cold water to cover by several inches; drain.

Line a bamboo steamer or colander with cheesecloth or a wet dishcloth. Put in the rice, spreading it out to make an even layer, then cover. Place the steamer over a pot or wok filled with several inches of hot water and bring the water to a boil. Steam for 20 to 25 minutes, then remove the rice from the heat and set aside, covered, until cool.

Meanwhile, prepare the filling: Preheat the oven to 350°F. Line a baking sheet with a piece of brown paper (to absorb excess oil). Place the *yu tiao* on the baking sheet and heat until crisp, about 10 minutes. Set aside to cool.

In a small nonreactive skillet, heat the oil over medium heat. Add the cabbage, sugar, and pepper to taste. Stir for about 1 minute, until the cabbage has warmed and absorbed the seasonings. Set aside to cool.

To assemble the rice rolls, separate the *yu tiao* and cut into 4-inch lengths. Divide the rice into five portions. Lay a piece of plastic wrap about 10 inches by 12 inches on your work surface and place one portion of rice in the center. Press the rice down with your hand to form a rectangle about 6 inches by 5 inches and ¼ inch thick. Sprinkle 1 to 1½ teaspoons of the cabbage mixture in a line across the center of the rice. Sprinkle a scant tablespoon of the pork fiber over the cabbage. Place one length of *yu tiao* over the flavorings. To roll up, use the plastic wrap to help roll: Grasp it by the two far corners and begin to roll tightly toward you. Stop to press the rice down over the ends of the filling and fold the sides of the plastic wrap over toward the center. Finish rolling and press firmly to seal. Repeat to make 4 more rolls.

To serve, cut each roll in half to make 10 large portions, or into 4 slices each. Remove the plastic and stack on a serving plate.

**Notes:** You will have several lengths of *yu tiao* left; thinly slice and use as croutons in soup or add to fried rice.

To make a sweet version, substitute ground roasted unsalted peanuts mixed with a little sugar for the cabbage-pork mixture.

Rural farm and limestone mountains near
Pangna Bay, in southern Thailand

inset: Farm woman near the Mekong

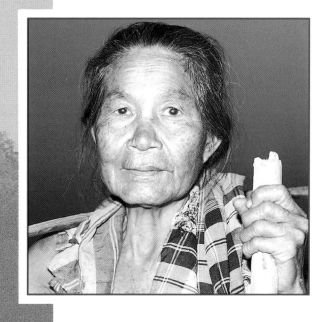

Jasmine,
Sticky Rice,
Thai Red

*T*hai cookery is eclectic: It embraces improvisation and scorns rigidity. We once met a car mechanic in a small village in northeast Thailand who had spent four years cooking for several hundred Thai workers in rural Iraq. He had absolutely no Thai ingredients to work with in Iraq (not even fish sauce), but he had somehow ingeniously managed to create Thai food that was palatable to all. As he described some of the dishes he came up with, there was even a hint of homesickness in his voice for his Iraqi Thai food.

We have been cooking Thai food at home for almost twenty years, and over that time the meals that we prepare have evolved in different ways depending on the ingredients we have available, and on our changing tastes. We like to joke that we are developing our own regional cuisine. Arugula and *shiso* (perilla) from the garden work beautifully in Thai salads, as do habanero chiles from the Caribbean. Julienned strips of carrots make an excellent substitute for green papaya in *som tam,* the popular salad, and so do julienned strips

Woman wearing a traditional Issahn hat

**opposite**

Selling eggplant, herbs, and *nam prik* sauces in Bangkok

of yard-long beans. We also eat a higher proportion of *yams* (Thai salads) than people in Thailand generally do, just because we love them, and we love eating them with sticky rice.

But all of this experimentation feels to us well within the spirit of Thai cooking. Our most emphatic suggestion to people going to Thailand for the first time is to try everything. There will probably be foods you won't like, but there are so many little surprises that it is worth being adventurous. Thais take great pride in the incredible variety of their cuisine, from grilled field rat and fried insects to raw pork with chiles!

To get started cooking Thai food, you need a few basic recipes, a small pantry of essential ingredients, and big bags of Thai jasmine and sticky rices. Use the recipes as a starting point, and soon you will find yourself altering and improvising as the season dictates. If you always have garlic, limes or lemons, shallots, chiles, and Thai fish sauce on hand, you are three quarters of the way toward being well prepared.

When we are planning a Thai meal, or when we enter the kitchen, we first decide which kind of rice we want to eat, Thai sticky or Thai jasmine. Jasmine must be rinsed and then takes about twenty minutes to cook. Sticky rice is soaked before steaming; you can leave it to soak overnight or through the day, then just steam it for twenty minutes before you are ready to eat. We often try to short-cut the soaking time: If you soak the rice in very warm water for two hours, it will still cook in twenty minutes, though the flavor of the rice is better with a long soaking in cold water.

Once the rice is cooking, we start chopping and slicing ingredients for the other dishes. When they're ready, total cooking time is usually short, very much like a Chinese

stir-fry. Always remember to taste as you are cooking, since balance of flavor, hot, sour, salty, sweet, and bitter, is crucial to good Thai food. Each dish should be big on flavor—there is seldom anything shy or restrained about Thai dishes. Also, with savory dishes, try to serve them on leaf lettuce or with a vegetable garnish. The garnish becomes yet another tasty element of the dish.

Preparing most Thai dishes requires very little in terms of specialized kitchen equipment. A good wok is invaluable for stir-fries, and a good heavy pot or a rice cooker for cooking rice is a must. For cooking sticky rice, a Thai or Laotian-style rice basket and steamer pot will make life a lot easier. A grill is handy, but you can always use an oven broiler instead. The one piece of specialized Thai cookware that we do wholeheartedly suggest buying is a Thai

Buddha statue near Bang Saphan being visited by pilgrims

mortar and pestle. The mortar stands about eight to ten inches high and is made of lightly glazed clay, and the pestle is about a foot long and made of wood. Unlike many mortars, the Thai version is large enough to hold a lot of food. It is easy to wash out, cheap to buy, and handsome to look at. Also, there is no way a food processor or spice grinder can totally match the effect of a mortar and pestle in grinding a spice paste.

Ten years ago, putting together a Thai pantry in North America took a lot of luck and effort, but the quantity and quality of Thai ingredients available in Asian groceries and through mail-order sources (see Mail-Order Sources, page 438) now makes the task a relatively easy (and inexpensive) one. When searching, don't overlook your local supermarket; many ingredients such as Thai rices, rice noodles, fish sauce, coconut milk, and a wide range of chiles are now easily found in well-stocked imported foods sections. If fresh ingredients such as lemon grass and lime leaves aren't available, talk to someone in the produce section and see if they can't be ordered.

# Thai Jasmine Rice
*khao plow*

THAI JASMINE RICE IS ONE OF THE BEST KNOWN OF THE AROMATIC RICES and one of our favorite daily rices. It is a long-grain low-amylose indica, a softer rice than basmati or most American long-grain rices. The uncooked grains are translucent. When cooked, they are separate but soft and slightly clingy. We buy our jasmine rice in twenty-pound bags, usually Peacock Brand or another "superior quality" rice from Thailand.

Plain Thai jasmine rice should be thoroughly washed in cold water but needs no preliminary soaking. It is most often cooked the absorption way, with just enough water to boil and steam the rice, as described below. It can also be steam-cooked. Thai jasmine rice is cooked plain, with no salt and no oil. When cooked, it has an aromatic flavor as well as the grain taste of good rice. The dishes served with the rice supply all the seasoning needed.

**3 cups Thai jasmine rice**
**Water**

Wash the rice thoroughly: Place the rice in a heavy medium pot with a tight-fitting lid, add cold water, swirl around several times with your hand, and drain; repeat twice, or until the water runs clear. Add the cooking water: Add enough water to cover the rice to a depth of about ½ inch, most easily measured the traditional way, by placing the tip of your index finger on the surface of the rice and ensuring that the water comes just barely to the first joint.

*Alternatively,* if you prefer measured amounts, place 3 cups rice, washed thoroughly and then drained well in a sieve, in a heavy pot with just over 3½ cups cold water.

With either method, bring the water to a full boil, uncovered, and let boil for about 15 seconds. Cover tightly, lower the heat to the lowest possible, and cook, *without lifting the lid,* for 15 minutes. Remove from the heat and let stand, covered, for another 5 minutes. When you take off the lid, you will see the grains of rice standing up firmly on the top layer. Turn the rice gently, with a rice paddle, then place the lid back on to keep warm. The rice is best served within 1 hour of cooking.

**Rice cooker method:** Rice cookers usually have instructions giving the volume of water to use for a specific amount of rice. The rice should be measured, well washed and drained, and then cooked according to the rice cooker directions. If there are no water to rice proportions marked on your rice cooker, use just a touch less water than described in the method above or the measurements set out above. If you're using a measured amount of water, remember to drain your washed rice well in a colander before placing in the rice cooker and adding water.

# Thai Sticky Rice
*khao neeo*

**Makes approximately 6½ cups rice**

STICKY RICE IS EATEN AS A STAPLE IN NORTHERN AND NORTHEASTERN Thailand. It is long-grain and opaque white in color before cooking. A different variety from jasmine rice, it becomes "sticky" when cooked because its starch component is different (it has very low amylose and a high proportion of amylopectin compared to nonsticky rices; see page 9 for more details). Asian sticky rice is sometimes sold labeled "sweet rice" or "glutinous rice." The rice from Thailand will often be marked *pin kao*, or with the Vietnamese term for sticky rice, *gao nêp*.

Sticky rice is soaked overnight in cold water, then steam-cooked in a basket or steamer over boiling water. The long soaking time gives it a very good flavor, but you can use the short-cut method instead and soak in very warm water for two hours. Many Thais in the north and northeast save a little cooked rice each day to soak with their next batch of raw rice. They say it gives extra depth of flavor.

Sticky rice tends to be a big hit with children and adults alike. It has a slightly sweet grain taste and sticks to itself but not to your hands. You just pick up a small clump from the serving basket and lightly squeeze it into a ball, before dipping it in some sauce or using it to pick up a little grilled meat or piece of salad, rather as you might use a tortilla chip.

*Sticky rice steaming in a traditional basket*

Knowing how much sticky rice to prepare for a meal can be a tricky proposition. We used to buy Thai sticky rice in five-pound packages, the size most commonly available in Asian groceries here in North America. For a dinner for four hungry adults, we would cook one third of a package (or about three cups of uncooked rice). But people tend to eat a lot of sticky rice, or at least we do and so do our friends, so now we prepare four to five cups for four hungry adults and several children. And now we buy our sticky rice in twenty-pound bags.

There are several different options for steaming sticky rice. If you can shop in a Thai, Lao, or Vietnamese grocery, chances are that they will have for sale a conical basket used for cooking sticky rice as well as the lightweight pot the basket rests in as it steams. Otherwise, use a steamer or a large sieve, lined with cheesecloth or muslin and placed over a large pot of water.

**3 cups long-grain Thai sticky rice**

Put the rice in a container that holds at least twice the volume of the rice, cover with 2 to 3 inches of cold water, and soak for 8 to 24 hours. Or, if you need to accelerate the soaking time, soak in warm (about 100°F) water for 2 hours.

Drain the rice and place in a steamer basket or in a steamer or large sieve lined with cheese-cloth or muslin. Set over several inches of boiling water in a large pot or a wok. *The rice must not be touching the boiling water.* Cover and steam for 25 minutes, or until the rice is shiny and tender. Be careful that your pot doesn't run dry; add more water if necessary, making sure to keep it from immersing the rice.

Turn the rice out into a basket or a bowl, break up into smaller lumps, and then cover with a cloth or lid. (In Thailand and Laos, cooked sticky rice is kept warm and moist in covered baskets.) The rice dries out if exposed to the air for long as it cools, so keep covered until serving, then serve directly from the basket or bowl.

# Rice in Thailand

Thailand is part of the Indochinese and Malay peninsulas, stretching almost twelve hundred miles from south to north, all the way from six degrees north of the equator to twenty degrees north. The country is relatively flat except in the north, where mountains and large hills stretch down from Myanmar (Burma) and southwestern China. Rivers flowing down through these mountains eventually empty into the Gulf of Thailand and the South China Sea, along the way providing water for the fertile ricelands of central Thailand.

Thailand is roughly the same size as France, with approximately the same size population. Bangkok is the country's biggest city and its central hub. Outside of Bangkok, Thailand is a primarily agricultural country. From a geographical perspective, as well as from a cultural and linguistic one, the country can be divided into four distinct regions: the center, the north, the northeast, and the south.

The center is Thailand's most fertile region. The Chao Phraya River flows down through central Thailand and empties into the Gulf of Thailand. Here are the ancient capitals of Ayuthuya and Sukothai, as well as present-day Bangkok. Central Thailand has long been the country's major rice-producing region, the region where most long-grain Thai jasmine rice is grown.

Northern Thailand is marked by large mountains and fertile valleys. For centuries it was a separate kingdom, the kingdom of Lanna, and people here still hold on to a great deal of regional pride. Though a variety of different rices grow in the north, it is Thai sticky rice that is predominant.

Northeast Thailand rests on a plateau nearly one thousand feet above sea level. The northeast is the poorest region in the country, with poor soils and unpredictable supplies of water for crops. Culturally and linguistically, the northeast is closely related to neighboring Laos, and, as in Laos, most of the rice grown and consumed is sticky rice.

The south, the long thin arm of Thailand that stretches down the Malay Peninsula, receives the most rainfall of any of the regions and at one time had large tracts of tropical rain forests. Tin mining, rubber, and fishing

Rice vendor in Chiang Mai

**opposite**

Woman harvesting rice outside Chiang Mai

are the south's important industries, together with tourism.

Thailand has long been a major producer of top-quality rices. Until only a few years ago, if you were traveling by train from Thailand to Malaysia, you had to be prepared for a very long wait at the border while Malay customs officials went carefully through each compartment and every bag. What were they searching for? Thai rice!

*Wielding a huge rice basket at harvest near Chiang Mai*

Rice is at the center of virtually every meal in Thailand. In the north and the northeast, where sticky rice is eaten more commonly than jasmine rice, the rice is first soaked in water overnight, then drained and steamed in a basket over a pot of boiling water. In the south and the center, where jasmine rice is more frequently eaten, rice is cooked by the absorption method, these days commonly in a rice cooker; or it may be steam-cooked in individual bowls.

In a sticky rice meal, each person is given a large helping of rice on a plate or in a small basket, and then savory dishes are placed in the middle of the table for everyone to share. You pull off a ball of sticky rice (approximately the size of a Ping-Pong ball) with your hand, then use it to pick up a piece of food from one of the central dishes in the middle of the table or to dip into the sauce. Small portions of food can also be taken from the plates in the middle and put on your individual plate, especially foods like a portion of fish or meat that have bones that will be fingered through.

For a plain jasmine rice meal in the central and southern regions, each person is given a helping of a rice on a plate, and the savory dishes are put into the middle, just as with a

sticky rice meal. It used to be that this kind of rice meal was also eaten by hand, but most people nowadays eat with a spoon and fork, using the spoon to carry the food and the fork simply to help arrange the food on the spoon, much the way Europeans eat using a knife to help gather food onto the fork.

Because of the two different methods of eating rice, the foods commonly served at each type of meal follow slightly different patterns. You will find more *yams* (which are easy to grab onto) and dipping sauces served with sticky rice, while soups, *tom yams*, and curries are more commonly served with plain rice.

# Thai Black Sticky Rice

**Makes about 4 cups rice**

THAI BLACK STICKY RICE IS A BEAUTIFUL UNMILLED RICE. WHEN COOKED, IT'S a little chewy (like brown rice) and not at all sticky, because the black rice bran means the grains stay separate, almost like wild rice in texture. You can cook black sticky rice just as you cook white sticky rice, by soaking and steaming. (See Sweet Black Rice Treat, page 168, for a traditional sweet version of black rice.) Though we have never seen black rice served as a savory dish in Thailand, it is being used this way successfully by inventive chefs in American restaurants. Serve it as you would serve wild rice, to accompany vegetables and meats or added to a soup for extra color, texture, and flavor. (See Thai Sticky Rice, page 116, for a detailed discussion of steaming options.)

**2 cups Thai black sticky rice**

Place the rice in a large pot or bowl, cover with 2 to 3 inches of cold water, and soak for 8 to 24 hours. If you need to hurry things along, soak in warm (about 100°F) water for 2 hours.

Drain the rice and place in a steamer basket or in a Chinese-style steamer or large sieve lined with cheesecloth or muslin. Place over several inches of boiling water in a large pot or a wok. *The rice must not touch the boiling water.* Cover and steam for 35 minutes, or until the rice is cooked through; it will still be chewy, like brown rice. Be careful that your pot doesn't run dry; add more water if necessary, making sure to keep it from touching the rice.

Turn out into a basket or a bowl. Cover with a cloth or lid to keep warm and prevent drying out. Serve the rice directly from the basket or bowl.

# Thai Red Rice

UNTIL RECENTLY, SPECIALISTS WRITING ABOUT THAI RICES AND PROBLEMS involved in increasing exports often talked about the difficulty of ensuring that Thai jasmine rice was not "contaminated" by red rice.

Although it was originally viewed as a problem, rather like a weed, Thai red rice has now become sought after as a novelty food. It is pretty to look at and good to eat, slightly chewy with a grainy nutty flavor. It is available in many Thai groceries and specialty stores (see Mail-Order Sources, page 438). The grains are slender, brittle, and reddish brown. (Some grains will be white because the bran has rubbed off during milling, shipping, or storage.)

Since this is an unmilled rice (like brown rice), it takes longer to cook than polished rices such as Thai jasmine. Because its grains are slender, Thai red rice cooks more quickly than many other unmilled rices and in less water.

**1 cup Thai red rice**
**1½ cups water**

Wash the rice well and drain. Place the rice and the 1½ cups water in a heavy medium pot. Bring to a boil, uncovered, over high heat. Give a brief stir to ensure that the rice is not sticking and let boil for about 1 minute, then cover, lower the heat to very low, and cook for 30 minutes. Let stand, still covered, for 10 to 15 minutes before serving, then stir gently with a fork or turn carefully with a wooden rice paddle. Some of the rice will have split open, some will still be intact. Serve in place of Thai jasmine or other long-grain rices or brown rice.

# Mama's Restaurant

Mama's restaurant looks much like any other small neighborhood restaurant in Bangkok. About the size of a two-car garage, it opens to the front and is floored in concrete. When morning comes and the tin doors roll open, the restaurant spills out onto the street: little boxes of laundry detergent, bags of peanuts, packages of mosquito coils, candles, Mekong whiskey, and whatever else daily life in Bangkok may require. A faded old Marlboro poster and a neon Coca-Cola sign that no longer works help advertise—in case there is any doubt—that food is served inside.

Inside the restaurant there are a couple of tables and five or six chairs. There are two separate cooking areas, one to your right as you enter and one to your left. There are condiments on each table: fish sauce with chopped fiery bird chiles in it, vinegar with sweet green chiles, and bottles of fish sauce. And there is—from morning until night—a wonderful, warm smell of cooking rice, fragrant Thai jasmine rice, my favorite rice in the world.

Twenty years ago, the first time I set foot in Mama's, two large old trees grew up through the middle of the building. The restaurant had been built around the trees, as if

Small restaurant
in northeast Thailand

space weren't already in short supply. The trees extended up through a second floor, the living quarters, a room the same size as the restaurant. At that time, anywhere from twelve to sixteen people called it home. In 1978, Bangkok was still a city living out the end of the Vietnam War. Many of the people Mama looked after were orphans or children who'd been abandoned during the war.

I was in Bangkok to learn how to cook, to travel, to be in Asia for the first time in my life. In Laramie, Wyoming, where I'm from, I'd worked in a restaurant kitchen with Supote, Mama's son. Supote was in Laramie to attend graduate school, but to help pay his way through school he got a job dish washing at a local steakhouse. One night, when a cook didn't show up for work, Supote was asked to fill in, and soon thereafter he was head of the kitchen. He had grown up in a kitchen; he could do the work of five of me and still not look busy. We got to be friends, and one night at work when I said that I would be quitting and heading off to Asia, Supote looked as if he already knew.

"You'll stay with my mother," he said. "She will teach you how to cook."

Mama was not a day over fifty, but she looked sixty-five. She worked harder than any person I had ever met, not in a hurried frantic tired sort of way, just steadily. "Call me Mama," she said in a gravelly, seen-it-all kind of GI English the first time we met. She sat me down beside one of the trees. A cold drink appeared, then a plate of fried rice. "Do you like chiles?" she asked, passing a small bowl of *nam pla prik*. But before I could answer she was off, back to work.

My first few nights I slept on a wooden platform in the back of the kitchen, but on the third evening Mama told me that I would be moving to another house. Kang, a twelve-year-old boy who lived with Mama, would accompany me by local bus so that I wouldn't get lost. I gathered my belongings, and off we went into the night.

For the first hour or so we stood in the jam-packed bus, but as we started to get outside the city we at last got seats. It felt strange to be entirely dependent on a twelve-year-old late at night in a huge city, even stranger to think that he would retrace our path back to Mama's still later that night, but he thought nothing of it.

When we were well outside the city, Kang at last asked the bus driver to stop at the next dirt road, and off we got in the darkness. We walked up a lane to a small compound of dimly lit wooden houses and knocked at a door. An older woman came to greet us, then she and Kang showed me to a room where I would sleep. They showed me where I should bathe and where there was boiled water to drink, and then we all said goodnight and Kang left to catch another bus home.

The house was an old wooden one built high up on stilts set out over a canal. Flat-bottomed motor boats traveled up and down the canal at all hours, night and day, and with each passing boat the house would rock and the wood would creak. There was also a train track nearby, and the trains, too, would send the house aflutter. But the house was peaceful and quiet, and it had a wonderful feel and smell of age, of age in a tropical country.

And so I settled in, finding my way to Mama's restaurant each day and then coming back each night. I stayed five months, and have been going back ever since.

# Fish Sauce with Hot Chiles

*nam pla prik*

**Makes just over 1 cup hot sauce**

YOU MIGHT SAY THAT WE ARE ADDICTED TO *NAM PLA PRIK*. WE DON'T NEED to have it on the table at every meal (though it does end up there most of the time), but it does at least have to be in the refrigerator. For many years we have kept a constant supply on hand in a plastic container with a tight-fitting lid. If we run low on fish sauce, we simply pour more in; and if we run low on chiles, we buy some fresh bird chiles, chop them, and toss them in. (Sometimes we buy serranos or jalapeños, but they aren't as hot as tiny bird chiles. One time we experimented with Scotch bonnets, but they were too hot!)

*Nam pla prik* is as simple as can be: finely chopped chiles in fish sauce (*nam pla* means "fish sauce," *prik* means "chiles"). But what it brings to a meal is something special and unique. It is always served separately at a Thai meal, so you have the choice of just how much to use, bite after bite after bite. You simply take a little on the end of your spoon and include it with what you are about to eat. Unlike a curry or other dish that has overall heat, *nam pla prik* works more like a salsa, and in an even more precise way. We have met many foreigners who come to Thailand not eating chiles and leave loving chiles, all on account of *nam pla prik*.

When you first make up a fresh batch, it will be at its hottest, but as the chiles sit in the fish sauce over a period of a few weeks, it will mellow considerably. Beware when working with the chiles, as they are very hot on your fingers. You may want to protect your hands with rubber gloves. Scrub your hands as well as your cutting surface thoroughly immediately after cutting, and still be aware of not touching your eyes or anywhere on your face for a while.

> 2 ounces (about ½ cup) bird chiles (*prik ee noo*)
>   (see Glossary)
> 1 cup Thai fish sauce

Cut the stems off the chiles. Either by hand or in a food processor, mince the chiles into very small pieces (if using a food processor, be careful not to puree the chiles). Put the chiles (and all the seeds) in a glass jar or other glass container and pour in the fish sauce. Serve in small individual condiment bowls. Store in the refrigerator in a well-sealed nonreactive container; it keeps indefinitely.

# North Thai Sauce for Sticky Rice

*nam prik ong*

*NAM PRIK ONG* IS NOT UNLIKE SPAGHETTI SAUCE, ONLY WITH A THAI SHIFT in flavor. It is from the regional cuisine of north Thailand, where pork and beef have always been much more available than fish and seafood. Eaten with sticky rice, *nam prik ong* is a staple of the north and available freshly made in every market. It is usually sold alongside Grilled Chile Salsa (page 126); you can easily recognize them both whenever you see a deep-red yummy-looking sauce next to a fresh green earthy-looking one. *Nam prik ong* takes no time to make. Serve a Thai salad with the rice and sauce if you like.

1 teaspoon dried shrimps or ½ teaspoon shrimp paste (see Glossary)

2 tablespoons chopped shallots

1 to 2 serrano chiles, chopped

1 teaspoon finely chopped lemon grass (or 1 teaspoon dried lemon grass soaked in water for 30 minutes and drained)

2 teaspoons peanut oil or vegetable oil

1 tablespoon minced garlic

¼ pound lean pork, finely chopped (it should resemble ground pork), or ¼ pound lean ground pork

1 pound ripe tomatoes (about 4 medium), chopped

1 teaspoon sugar

1 tablespoon Thai fish sauce

½ cup water

Salt (optional)

Grind the dried shrimp or shrimp paste, shallots, chiles, and lemon grass together in a mortar with a pestle (or very finely chop with a knife or food processor).

In a heavy medium saucepan, heat the oil over medium-high heat. When the oil is hot, add the garlic and fry until starting to brown. Add the shrimp mixture and cook for 30 seconds. Add the pork and stir until browned, approximately 2 to 3 minutes. Add the tomatoes, sugar, fish sauce, and water, turn the heat to high, and cook for 2 minutes, stirring frequently. Reduce the heat, partially cover, and cook at a low simmer for 15 minutes. The sauce should be of a medium-thick consistency. Taste for seasoning and add salt if you wish. Remove from the heat and pour into an attractive small bowl for serving.

# Grilled Chile Salsa

*nam prik num*

**Makes about 1½ cups sauce; serves 6 to 8 as part of a rice-based meal**

IN THIS CLASSIC NORTH THAI SAUCE, FRESH CHILES, SHALLOTS, TOMATOES, AND garlic are thoroughly softened and blackened in a dry skillet, then chopped and seasoned. It comes out a beautiful rich earthy color and has good chile heat and flavor. The main ingredient is *num,* a long medium-hot pale yellow chile very like the banana chiles available in North America (which we use here). If you want a milder taste, substitute mild Hungarian wax chiles or cubanelles for some or all of the banana chiles. Remember that this salsa is meant to accompany sticky rice, not to be eaten on its own, so the flavors are punchy, with an agreeable taste of the grill.

Serve the salsa in a bowl, from which guests can help themselves. Put out plenty of sticky rice. Place a plate of sliced cucumbers, lettuce leaves, and other greens on the table so guests can use them, as well as the sticky rice, to scoop up the sauce.

| | |
|---|---|
| 4 to 5 banana chiles | 2 to 3 tablespoons fresh coriander leaves, coarsely torn |
| ¼ pound shallots, cut into halves or quarters | 2 tablespoons Thai fish sauce |
| 6 to 8 cloves garlic, left whole or cut in half | 2 tablespoons fresh lime juice |
| ½ pound cherry tomatoes or small plum tomatoes | |

Heat one or two heavy skillets over high heat. If you use only one, the vegetables will have to be cooked in sequence; with two, you can get everything cooked at the same time. In one skillet, place the whole chiles, shallots cut into halves or quarters, and whole or halved garlic cloves. In the other, place the tomatoes. Lower the heat to medium-high under both skillets. Press down gently on the chiles to expose them to the heat, and then as one side blackens, use tongs or a wooden spatula to turn them. Similarly, the shallots and garlic will soon blacken on one side and should then be turned over to cook the other sides. Use tongs to turn the tomatoes and expose the sides as well as the top and bottom to the heat.

Remove the vegetables when they seem well scorched and softened (about 8 to 10 minutes). Place on a cutting board to cool slightly.

Slice off and discard the stem end of the chiles. Slice the chiles lengthwise in half and discard the seeds (unless you want a very hot salsa). Chop finely, then transfer to a medium bowl. Finely chop the remaining vegetables and transfer, together with the juices from the tomatoes, to the bowl. Add the coriander, fish sauce, and lime juice and stir to blend. The sauce will be somewhat chunky and a little bit soupy. (*Alternatively,* all the ingredients can be chopped together in the food processor.)

If you have time, let the sauce stand for half an hour before serving to allow the flavors to blend and mellow. Store in a covered nonreactive container in the refrigerator. This will keep for 4 to 5 days.

**Note:** In Thailand, vegetables are grilled over an open flame in a grilling rack rather like an old-fashioned toasting rack. The method for grilling described above uses a dry-frying technique. You can also grill the vegetables over a gas or charcoal grill, then chop and combine them as directed.

Traditional outdoor kitchen in Mae Sot, northern Thailand

# Three Dipping Sauces and a Condiment

WITH FISH SAUCE, LIME JUICE, SUGAR, AND CHILES TO WORK WITH, THAIS HAVE come up with a fabulous array of dipping sauces. Here are three easy favorites. Use them as sauces for grilled meats or as flavorings for jasmine rice or Thai sticky rice. The condiment is toasted rice powder, a northeast Thai specialty.

## Tangy Lime Sauce

**Makes ⅓ cup sauce**

USE THIS FRESH TART-SWEET-SALTY SAUCE AS A DIPPING SAUCE FOR GRILLED Pork Satay (page 156) or any other grilled meat or vegetable.

2 tablespoons fresh lime juice

1 tablespoon Thai fish sauce

1 tablespoon soy sauce

1 teaspoon cayenne pepper

1 tablespoon palm sugar (see Glossary) or substitute brown sugar

2 tablespoons chopped fresh coriander leaves

Place all the ingredients except the coriander in a small bowl and mix well. If necessary, adjust the balance of lime juice, fish sauce, cayenne, and sugar to taste. Mix in the coriander and serve. To store, remove the coriander leaves and pour into a sealed glass jar. It will keep, refrigerated, for up to one week.

# Hot-and-Sweet Dipping Sauce

*nam jeem gai yang*

**Makes about ½ cup sauce**

WHENEVER YOU STOP AT A THAI STREET STALL TO BUY *GAI YANG* (GRILLED chicken), you will be handed with your chicken a small bag of sticky rice and an even smaller plastic bag of dipping sauce, bright reddish orange with chile peppers and sticky with sugar. The sauce is very easy to make at home and adds a wonderful final touch to grilled chicken, pork, or lamb. Serve in small individual condiment bowls so guests can dip their meat and their sticky rice in it as they eat.

½ cup cider vinegar or white vinegar

½ cup sugar

1 to 2 cloves garlic, finely minced

¼ teaspoon salt

1½ teaspoons chile pepper flakes or
  minced dried red chiles (see Glossary)

Place the vinegar in a small nonreactive saucepan and heat to a boil over high heat. Stir in the sugar, lower the heat to medium-low, and let simmer for 5 minutes.

Meanwhile, using a mortar and pestle or a bowl and the back of a spoon, pound or mash the garlic and salt to a paste, then stir in the pepper flakes and blend well.

Remove the vinegar from the heat and stir in the garlic paste until dissolved. Let cool to room temperature; store in a sealed glass jar. The sauce will keep, refrigerated, for several weeks, but is best used within 5 days.

# Red Curry Sauce

THIS RICH HOT DIPPING SAUCE IS WONDERFUL DRIZZLED OVER GRILLED vegetables. More traditionally, serve it in individual bowls as a dipping sauce for Grilled Pork Satay (page 156) or other grilled meat, for raw vegetables, or as a flavoring for rice.

1 teaspoon peanut oil or vegetable oil

2 tablespoons Red Curry Paste (page 148) or store-bought (see Note)

1½ cups fresh or canned coconut milk (see Glossary)

2 tablespoons palm sugar (see Glossary) or substitute brown sugar

Juice from 1 teaspoon tamarind pulp (see Glossary), soaked in 1 tablespoon warm water and strained

1 tablespoon Thai fish sauce

2 ounces raw peanuts, dry-roasted (see Note) and finely chopped

*If using curry paste,* heat the oil in a heavy medium saucepan over medium-high heat. Add the curry paste and stir for 30 seconds. Add the coconut milk and continue stirring until milk just begins to boil.

Reduce the heat slightly and add the sugar, stirring to dissolve it completely.

Stir in the tamarind juice and fish sauce and cook for 1 more minute. Remove from the heat. Stir in the peanuts. The sauce can be made the day before using but should not be kept longer than one day because of the coconut milk.

Pour the sauce into one medium or several small bowls and serve.

**Notes:** For less heat, reduce the amount of curry paste by half.

To dry-roast, place peanuts in a heavy skillet over medium-high heat and cook, stirring occasionally to prevent sticking and burning, until lightly browned and aromatic, about 5 minutes.

# Roasted Rice Powder
## khao kua

**Makes about ¼ cup rice powder**

ROASTED RICE POWDER, CALLED *KHAO KUA* IN THAI AND *THINH* IN VIETNAMESE, is used in both cuisines almost as a seasoning salt. It is sprinkled on top of or mixed into a dish, adding an easy nutty flavor. In Thai food, you will find it always used in *laap* (Savory Chicken Finely Chopped, page 150) and sometimes in Grilled Beef Salad (page 144).

Roasted rice powder is very easy to make. We like having it around to sprinkle on all sorts of things, especially on rice. Rice on rice—it's good, especially with a little *nam pla prik*.

**¼ cup Thai sticky rice**

Heat a small heavy skillet over medium-high heat. Add the rice and stir constantly as the rice heats. After several minutes, it will have a lightly toasted aroma and will be beginning to turn pale brown. Keep stirring until all the rice has changed to a light tan color, then transfer to a spice grinder or a large mortar and pestle and grind to a fine powder. Roasted rice powder, once completely cooled, keeps well in a sealed glass jar for several weeks.

Leading buffalos home from the fields in Sangkom, northeast Thailand

# Lime Leaf and Oyster Mushroom Soup
*tom yum het*

**Serves 4 as part of a rice-based meal**

THIS CENTRAL THAI DISH IS TRADITIONALLY MADE WITH SHRIMP OR CHICKEN, but we prefer to use oyster mushrooms; they are just as meaty in texture yet more subtle in taste. Although it is served as a soup in North American Thai restaurants, *tom yum* actually falls somewhere between a soup and a curry. In Thailand, it is served as a condiment to rice, just like the other dishes on the table. Dry wild lime leaves can be used instead of fresh leaves, but be sure to soak them in water for twenty to thirty minutes before using them to bring out the flavor (and add the soaking water to the broth). Use fresh leaves whenever available, as they have a wonderful aroma; store any extras in a well-sealed plastic bag in the freezer (their shelf life in the refrigerator is less than a week) to use later for soup.

2 cups chicken stock (use stock from Savory Chicken Finely Chopped, page 150, if you have it)

3 inches lemon grass

2 fresh wild lime leaves (see Glossary), or 1 tablespoon dried leaves, soaked in ¼ cup warm water for 20 to 30 minutes

2 bird chiles or serrano chiles, cut into long thin strips

7 ounces oyster mushrooms, halved lengthwise

3 ounces straw mushrooms, halved lengthwise

3 tablespoons fresh lime juice, or more to taste

3 tablespoons Thai fish sauce, or more to taste

In a large nonreactive saucepan, bring the stock to a boil. Smash the lemon grass with the side of a cleaver or a heavy knife and add to the stock, together with the lime leaves (with the soaking water if using dried leaves), chiles, and mushrooms. Cook until the mushrooms are tender, approximately 5 minutes. Reduce the heat to low, and add the lime juice and fish sauce. Taste and adjust the seasoning accordingly. Serve in small individual bowls to accompany steamed rice.

# Thai Salads

*Yams* for us, more than any other kind of dish, embody the essence of Thai food and cooking. They are usually translated into English as "salads," for the sake of a better word. Like salads, *yams* are often served at room temperature and use garden herbs and raw vegetables to achieve a good fresh taste. But unlike most salads, which we eat to refresh our palates, *yams* are anything but shy in flavor. They are quick and easy to make, absolutely full of flavor, and fun both to prepare and to eat. All we have to do is to put together a couple of different *yams* and a basket of hot freshly steamed sticky rice, and we've instantly created a special occasion.

*Enjoying a traditional sticky rice meal near Chiang Mai*

*Yam* in Thai means to mix, or to blend together. The art of making Thai *yams* is truly one of orchestration, of bringing together flavors, textures, and colors. Dressings for *yams* strike a balance between the salty taste of *nam pla*, the sweetness of palm sugar, the pucker of lime, and the heat of chiles. And while all these strong flavors come together, no taste dominates.

In Thailand, *yams* are often served when people get together for a glass of beer, when they want something to nibble on that is bursting with flavor—and in Thailand this means really bursting! People unaccustomed to chiles will find many *yams* quite hot, but the heat is always balanced by cooling fresh vegetables and the mellowing presence of Thai rice. Garnish each *yam* liberally with lettuce and cabbage leaves, slices of cucumber and tomato, fresh herbs, and whole scallions. The greens add even more texture and contrast to these dishes, already rich in both. Do as many Thais do and pile a separate plate with more greens. All these fresh ingredients have a function, for in addition to being used as garnish, they become eating utensils. When eating *yams,* take a leaf of lettuce or a slice of cucumber and use it as a spoon for gathering up a bite, just as you would do with a ball of sticky rice.

Thai *yams* can be served by themselves as appetizers. You can also present several of them together, along with Thai jasmine rice or sticky rice, to make a larger meal. Most can be made well in advance, and all of them take less than an hour from start to finish.

# Grilled Eggplant Salad

*yam makeua yang*

Serves 6 as part of a rice-based meal

THIS *YAM* CAN BE MADE QUICKLY WHEN GUESTS TURN UP UNEXPECTEDLY; Naomi especially likes it for its soft textures and tart dressing. Long thin Japanese eggplants are sliced and grilled, then tossed with shallots, plenty of Vietnamese coriander, and a dressing that is salty-sour-hot and slightly sweet. After you have made the salad once, you might want to play around with the balance of seasonings, perhaps increasing the chile heat.

1½ pounds Japanese (purple Asian) eggplants (5 to 6 medium)

½ cup finely sliced shallots

½ cup fresh Vietnamese coriander leaves (see Note), coarsely torn (or substitute a mixture of coarsely torn regular coriander and finely chopped fresh mint)

**Dressing**

6 tablespoons fresh lime juice

3 tablespoons Thai fish sauce

¼ teaspoon sugar

½ to 1 bird chile or serrano chile, finely minced

1 small head Bibb or other tender lettuce (optional)

Preheat a broiler or grill.

Slice the eggplants on the diagonal into ⅛- to ¼-inch slices. *If broiling,* arrange the slices on a large lightly oiled baking sheet and place on the top rack of the oven. (If all slices don't fit on one baking sheet, cook in two batches.) *If grilling,* place the slices directly on the grill rack or in a wire-mesh grilling rack. Broil or grill until golden brown on the first side, about 7 to 8 minutes, then turn over and cook until golden brown on the second side. Let cool briefly, then coarsely chop. Transfer to a large bowl.

Separate the shallot slices into rings with your fingers and add to the eggplant. Add the Vietnamese coriander or mixed herbs.

In a small bowl, combine all the dressing ingredients and mix well. Pour over the salad, then toss gently to mix. The salad is best if left to stand for half an hour before serving; this gives the flavors a chance to blend and to soak into the eggplant.

Serve the salad mounded on a decorative colorful plate, or line a large plate with lettuce leaves, then mound the salad on top. Serve with jasmine or sticky rice. Diners can also use the lettuce leaves to pick up a bite of salad.

Note: Vietnamese coriander is known in Vietnamese as *rau ram* and in Thai as *pak chi wietnam;* it is usually sold cellophane-wrapped in Vietnamese and Thai grocery stores. See Glossary.

# Oyster Mushroom Salad
*yam het*

IN THIS RECIPE WE USE FRESH OYSTER MUSHROOMS, COMMON IN THAILAND, and fresh portobellos. Both are available in Asian or gourmet groceries. If you can't find one or both of these mushrooms, substitute regular cultivated mushrooms. The result will still be delicious.

½ pound portobello mushrooms or cultivated mushrooms, cleaned, stems trimmed, and coarsely chopped

½ pound oyster mushrooms or cultivated mushrooms, cleaned, stems trimmed, and coarsely chopped

1 clove garlic

½ teaspoon sugar

1 to 2 teaspoons crumbled dried red chile (see Glossary) or chile pepper flakes

3 tablespoons fresh lime juice

2 tablespoons Thai fish sauce

2 tablespoons finely sliced shallots

1½ cups loosely packed fresh mint leaves, coarsely chopped, or 1 cup fresh mint leaves plus ½ cup Vietnamese coriander leaves (see Glossary), coarsely chopped

Tender Bibb or other lettuce leaves or greens, to line serving dish

Place about 2 inches of water in a large saucepan and bring to a boil. Add the mushrooms, partially cover, and cook until tender but not mushy, about 4 minutes. Drain (reserving the cooking water if you wish for stock) and set aside.

Place the garlic and sugar in a mortar and pound to a paste, then add the dried chiles and pound to combine. Add the lime juice and fish sauce and blend well. *Alternatively*, use a small food processor to make a paste of the garlic, sugar, and chiles, then add the lime juice and fish sauce and pulse to blend.

Place the mushrooms in a bowl, add the shallots, pour the dressing over, and toss gently to coat. Add the chopped mint or mixed herbs and toss to blend well. (The salad may be made up to 2 hours ahead. Once the mushrooms have cooled to room temperature, cover the salad.)

Line a serving platter or a shallow bowl with lettuce or other greens and mound the salad on top. Serve warm or at room temperature.

# Green Papaya Salad
*som tam*

*SOM TAM* IS AS POPULAR IN THAILAND AS GREEN MANGOES AND THAI boxing, and that's popular. It has its roots in the villages of northeast Thailand, where green (unripe) papayas are cheap and abundant, yet it regularly appears on the menus of Bangkok's finest restaurants. It is traditionally pounded in a large Thai mortar to blend it, thus softening the green papaya and tomato and marrying the different textures and flavors, but it works perfectly well when assembled in a large bowl. Green papayas travel well, and as a result they are increasingly available in many Asian groceries. If green papaya is unavailable, julienned carrots make a good substitute.

### Salad

1 tablespoon dried shrimp (see Glossary), or substitute ¼ pound medium shrimp, shelled and deveined

1 large clove garlic

¼ teaspoon salt

1 tablespoon raw peanuts, dry-roasted (see Glossary) and coarsely chopped

2 bird chiles or serrano chiles, finely chopped

½ teaspoon palm sugar (see Glossary), or substitute brown sugar, or to taste

¼ cup fresh lime juice

1 to 2 tablespoons Thai fish sauce

2 plum tomatoes, coarsely chopped

1 medium green papaya (about 2 pounds), peeled and coarsely grated (discard seeds and membrane), or 4 cups coarsely grated carrots (just under 1 pound)

### Accompaniments

½ pound long beans (optional)

Leaf lettuce or romaine, torn into 2-inch pieces

¼ head green cabbage, cored and cut into thin wedges

*If using fresh shrimp instead of dried,* bring 3 cups of water to a boil in a small saucepan. Add the shrimp and cook until just opaque throughout, 2 to 3 minutes. Drain and rinse under cold water. Cut the shrimp into small pieces.

*If using the optional long beans as an accompaniment,* in a large pot of boiling salted water, blanch the beans for about 5 minutes, until tender-crisp. Drain, cut into 3-inch lengths, and set aside.

*If using a mortar and pestle,* place the garlic, salt, peanuts, dried shrimp, if using, chiles, and sugar in the mortar and pound throughly to a paste. Stir in the lime juice and fish sauce, then add the chopped tomatoes, the fresh shrimp, if using, and a generous handful of the papaya or carrots. Pound with the pestle (being careful not to splash yourself) to blend with the dressing. Gradually add the remaining papaya or carrot, pounding and blending as you do so. If your mortar is too small to handle the whole amount at once, prepare in two batches.

*Alternatively,* mince the garlic. Dissolve the sugar in the lime juice and set aside. Place the peanuts in a small food processor. With the processor blade spinning, feed the garlic, the dried shrimp, if using, the chiles, lime juice mixture, and fish sauce through the tube. Process until a coarse paste forms. Turn out into a large deep bowl and add the tomatoes, the fresh shrimp, if using, and a handful of grated papaya or carrots. Using a large flat spoon, press and mash the tomatoes and papaya or carrots into the dressing. Gradually add the remaining papaya or carrots, blending well.

Line a serving plate with lettuce and mound the salad on top. Place the wedges of cabbage and lengths of beans around the edge of the plate. Serve a side platter of more fresh greens and vegetables. Guests can use the beans, cabbage, and other greens to scoop up the salad.

Preparing green papaya for *som tam*

# Fish Farm

Nowadays, our friend Supote lives back in Bangkok. He and his wife, Oie, have three daughters, the oldest of whom has now graduated from college. Supote works in the Ministry of Foreign Affairs and Oie in the Ministry of Education. Their lives are hectic, getting the younger kids to school and themselves to work, and then back again, all in the crazy chaos that is Bangkok traffic. On Saturdays, Supote goes to his mother's restaurant and helps out, doing the books or simply frying up plates of *khao phad* or *guay teeo*.

A few years back, his mother decided to start a fish farm, so she moved out of Bangkok and found herself a lonely piece of land in south Thailand. She built the farm up from scratch, hiring a local person to help. Just as always, she is up well before dawn each day and she works until dusk. "I'm never going back to Bangkok," she told us when we asked about whether she missed the city, the only other place she has ever lived, "except to get a new pacemaker." "Mama" is now on her fifth pacemaker, and she hasn't slowed down an instant in the last two decades.

But whether in Bangkok or rural south Thailand, come evening, it's time to start thinking about food. Oie has been to the local market and unloads piles of fresh produce from the car. Supote deep-fries tiny fish from the farm until they are crunchy and so good. Mama pulls up fresh turmeric and picks lime leaves from the kitchen garden for the curry. Naomi and I collect water from the huge stone jars that store the drinking water from the rainy season. The kids fly kites, out across the beautiful flat marshy grasses of the fish farm.

With so many cooks, dinner is ready in no time; it is eating that will take time. Dinner with Mama, Supote, and Oie is one of the greatest pleasures we know.

"Mama" eating her lunch at the fish farm

# Shrimp, Pork, and Watercress Salad

*yam phaeng phuai*

SHRIMP AND PORK SEEM LIKE AN UNLIKELY COMBINATION, BUT IT IS COMMON in China, Thailand, and Vietnam. We wonder if its origin might have something to do with rice paddies, because of the tiny freshwater shrimp that sometimes live in the flooded paddies. This salad, though it uses saltwater shrimp, might support that idea, for in Thailand it is often made with aquatic leafy greens and herbs that grow on the edge of riverways and rice paddies.

Whatever its origin, the combination of shrimp and pork is a good one, and it's especially good with leafy watercress as in this salad.

| | |
|---|---|
| 1 pound small shrimp, shelled and deveined | ½ cup raw peanuts, dry roasted (see Glossary), and chopped |
| 1 tablespoon peanut oil or vegetable oil | 2 tablespoons Thai fish sauce |
| ¼ cup chopped shallots | 3 tablespoons fresh lime juice |
| 4 garlic cloves, chopped | 1 teaspoon sugar |
| ½ pound lean ground pork | 2 large tomatoes, thinly sliced |
| 1 large bunch watercress, large stems removed | 2 teaspoons crushed dried red chile (see Glossary) or chile pepper flakes |

In a medium saucepan, bring 5 cups of water to a boil. Add the shrimp and cook until opaque throughout, 2 to 3 minutes. Drain and rinse under cold water. Drain well, pat dry, and set aside.

In a heavy skillet or wok, heat the oil over medium heat. Add the shallots and garlic and cook until softened but not browned, about 30 seconds. Add the ground pork and cook, stirring, until no traces of pink remain in the meat, 5 to 6 minutes. Remove from the heat. If there is any excess fat in the skillet or wok, drain it off. Let the pork cool slightly.

In a large bowl, combine the watercress, shrimp, and peanuts. Add the pork mixture and toss well.

In a small bowl, stir together the fish sauce, lime juice, and sugar. Pour the dressing over the salad and toss. Arrange the tomato slices on a serving platter, overlapping them slightly. Spoon the salad on top and garnish with the crushed chile pepper.

# Seafood Salad
## yam thalae

**Serves 4 generously**

YAM THALAE CAN BE A GREAT MANY DIFFERENT THINGS, DEPENDING ON what seafood is chosen—and in Thailand, this can be a mind-boggling choice. The best *yam thalae* we have ever had was one we ate almost daily for an entire month while living outside

*Scraping the beach for clams near Tap Sa Kae*

the town of Tap Sa Kae in southern Thailand. We'd rented a house on a long lonely stretch of beach, and though we had a kitchen, we were in Thailand and not at all prepared to be eating our own cooking when we could be eating at local restaurants.

On our first evening, we climbed into our car and set out looking. The first restaurant we came to, a few miles up the beach in a tiny fishing village, looked good and we stopped. Dominic and Tashi started playing soccer with a few kids from the restaurant, we ordered food and drinks, and for the next month, we looked forward each day to eating there, like children who had never before had ice cream. The woman who managed the restaurant and did most of the cooking was from the village, but she had always loved northeastern Thai food, so she prepared dishes from that cuisine made with seafood and served with sticky rice.

Her *yam thalae* was seldom the same from one day to the next, but for us she always included dried white fungus, which we absolutely loved; it acted just like a little flavor sponge, sopping up the lime juice and fish sauce and all the flavors of the other seafood.

You can find white fungus in well-stocked Chinese groceries. If you find it, soak a quarter cup in warm water until soft, then drain, coarsely chop, and include in the salad.

Begin with already cleaned and filleted fish and seafood, and the preparation of *yam thalae* will be quick and easy. Cut back on the chiles if you don't like hot tastes, or increase them for greater authenticity; in Thailand, *yam thalae* is usually made very hot, with at least double the number of chiles called for here. Serve the salad warm or at room temperature, with jasmine rice or sticky rice and a plate of freshly sliced tomatoes and cucumber.

½ pound cleaned squid

½ pound tiger shrimp or other large
    shrimp

½ pound monkfish, orange roughy, or sea
    bass fillets

### Dressing

3 large cloves garlic

Pinch of salt

2 bird chiles or serrano chiles, finely
    chopped

2 tablespoons chopped coriander root
    (see Note)

3 tablespoons Thai fish sauce

1 tablespoon sugar

¼ cup fresh lime juice

6 shallots, thinly sliced

½ cup packed coarsely chopped fresh
    coriander leaves

2 tablespoons fresh lime juice

Freshly ground black pepper to taste

Slice the squid bodies into ¼-inch rings and chop the tentacles; set aside. Shell and devein the shrimp. Cut the fish into thin slices.

Prepare the dressing by pounding the garlic, salt, chiles, coriander root, fish sauce, and sugar together in a mortar until a paste forms; or process to a paste in a blender. *Alternatively,* very finely chop the garlic, chiles, and coriander root, then place in a small bowl and stir in the sugar and fish sauce.

Transfer the dressing to a large serving bowl and add the ¼ cup lime juice. Separate the shallot slices into rings and add to the bowl, along with the chopped coriander leaves.

In a medium nonreactive saucepan, combine 4 cups salted water and the 2 tablespoons lime juice and bring to a boil over medium-high heat. Toss in the squid and bring back to a boil. After 1 minute, add the shrimp and fish. Bring to a boil, then, using a slotted spoon, transfer the seafood to the serving bowl. Stir well to coat all the seafood with dressing, grind black pepper over, and serve warm or at room temperature.

**Note:** Look for bunches of coriander with the roots still on so you can make this recipe using the roots of one large bunch; the leaves go into the dressing too.

# Grilled Red Snapper Salad with Basil
## yam pla

BLACK PEPPER, THE ONLY "HEAT" AVAILABLE TO THAI COOKS UNTIL THE sixteenth-century arrival of chiles from the New World, is the featured spice in this aromatic fish salad. The unforgettable combination of pepper and basil, set off by the bite of lime juice, makes this *yam* one of our favorites. Serve it as an appetizer accompanied by a plate of fresh greens, or as an accompaniment to Thai jasmine or sticky rice.

3 to 4 small or 2 medium whole red snapper (2½ pounds), cleaned, heads removed, rinsed, and patted dry

¼ cup Thai fish sauce or mild stock (if broiling)

¼ cup white wine or mild stock (if broiling)

**Dressing**

1 clove garlic

1 teaspoon black peppercorns, coarsely ground

½ teaspoon sugar

5 tablespoons fresh lime juice

3 tablespoons Thai fish sauce

½ teaspoon vegetable oil

1 cup fresh Asian basil or sweet basil leaves, coarsely torn or chopped

Tender leaf lettuce to line serving plate

Preheat a broiler or a grill.

*If using a broiler,* position the rack 5 to 6 inches from the broiler element. Place the snapper in a lightly oiled shallow pan. Mix together the fish sauce and wine and/or stock and pour into the pan to prevent the fish from drying out. Place under the broiler for 3 to 4 minutes, then turn the fish over and broil for 3 to 4 minutes on the other side. Remove from the oven and cut deeply into one fish near the backbone to test for doneness; the flesh should be opaque white. If it is still translucent, place the fish back under the broiler for another minute or two.

*If using a grill,* place the snapper on the grill over a low fire and grill until done, about 8 minutes, turning after 4 to 5 minutes. (See the test for doneness, above.)

Transfer the fish to a plate to cool slightly.

Meanwhile, prepare the dressing by combining the garlic, black pepper, and sugar in a mortar and pounding to a paste with a pestle. *Alternatively,* mince the garlic, combine in a small bowl with the pepper and sugar, and mash against the side of the bowl with a spoon. Add the lime juice and fish sauce and stir to blend.

When the fish is cool enough to handle, separate the flesh from the skin and bones. Transfer to a shallow bowl and shred into bite-sized pieces.

Heat a skillet or wok over high heat and add the oil. When it is hot, add the basil, lower the heat to medium, and stir-fry for barely 30 seconds. Add the basil to the fish, then pour the dressing over and toss the salad thoroughly. (The salad can be made up to 2 hours ahead. Once the fish has cooled to room temperature, cover the salad with plastic wrap.)

Line a serving plate with lettuce leaves and mound the salad on the plate. Serve warm or at room temperature.

*Beach restaurant near Tap Sa Kae*

# Grilled Beef Salad

*yam neua*

Serves 6 as part of a rice-based meal, or as an appetizer

WHEN WE'RE AT HOME, BEEF IS NOT SOMETHING WE PREPARE ALL THAT OFTEN. But if we are making food for a party, or for a summer potluck, this grilled beef *yam* is one of our all-time favorite recipes. We'll even splurge and get a very good cut of meat, such as the tenderloin called for in this recipe.

In Thailand, there are probably as many different versions of *yam neua* as there are cooks, each having a different idea about how best to find that perfect balance of hot, sour, and salty. So before serving, be sure to taste for yourself.

1 pound beef tenderloin, at room temperature

About ½ teaspoon freshly ground black pepper

2 tablespoons Thai fish sauce, or more to taste

5 tablespoons fresh lime juice, or more to taste

2 to 3 bird chiles or serrano chiles, minced

½ cup thinly sliced shallots

4 scallions, cut into ½-inch lengths

½ cup packed fresh coriander leaves, plus a few sprigs for garnish

2 tablespoons finely chopped fresh mint

1 European cucumber, scored lengthwise with a fork and thinly sliced

Preheat a grill or broiler. Halve the tenderloin horizontally to form 2 pieces approximately 1 inch thick. Rub both sides of each piece with the pepper, pressing it into the meat.

*To grill*, place the meat on the grill and cook until medium-rare, 5 to 8 minutes on each side.

*To broil*, place the meat on a broiling rack so that the meat is 3 to 5 inches from the broiling element. Broil for 6 to 7 minutes on each side, or until medium-rare.

Let the meat cool for 30 minutes to 1 hour, so that it is easy to slice. (The cooled meat can be put into the refrigerator covered and then sliced several hours later, if more convenient.) Slice the meat as thin as possible with a sharp chef's knife or cleaver, cutting across the grain.

In a large bowl, mix the fish sauce, lime juice, and chiles. Add the meat, shallots, and scallions and turn to coat. Mix in the coriander leaves and mint. Taste for a good balance among the salty fish sauce, the tart lime juice, and the hot chiles, and adjust according to your taste.

Arrange the slices of cucumber around the edge of a decorative plate or platter, then mound the salad in the center. Garnish with coriander sprigs and serve.

# Photographing at Rice Harvest

Early one morning, well before sunrise, I climbed into our old blue pickup truck and headed out of the city of Chiang Mai. It was early November, the middle of sticky rice harvest, and I hoped to be in the fields as the farmers first arrived. It was lovely to be driving, as the roads were almost empty and the air was cool, almost cold.

It was still dark by the time I arrived, but people had already begun to gather in the fields. I parked my truck and walked over to join one small group huddled around a fire, everyone rubbing hands together to stay warm. The day, like every other day this time of year, would be sunny and warm, but for now the fire was a welcome sight.

"Where are you from?" someone asked, "and why are you here?"

"I'm here to take pictures, and to watch," I explained.

"Then you can help harvest!"

"Oh no, oh no," I replied, as everyone laughed, "I can only take pictures."

A man handed me a glass of *lao khao*, a local homemade rice liquor made from sticky rice, poured from a big plastic container. Then everyone began speaking quickly, and in northern dialect, and I couldn't understand a word. But there was a long day's work ahead, and they were ready to begin.

Rice harvest near Chiang Mai

By the time the sky had begun to brighten, rice was already being cut, threshed, and loaded into bags. This time of year, after the fields have been harvested, the straw left in the fields is burned, leaving the land black and filling the sky with smoke and haze. There is also dust from the straw, all of which makes for sunrises and sunsets vibrant with red and orange, and this morning was no exception.

People laughed and joked as they worked, yelling across the fields. The grandparents in the group where I stayed the longest made sure that my glass of *lao khao* remained full, as did their own glasses. They demonstrated several different methods of threshing by hand, and there was a friendly competition to see who could carry the most cut rice into the threshing ground.

By nine o'clock I was exhausted. Taking photographs is such hard work.

# Tofu Fried with Basil

*taohou bai gaprow*

**Serves 4 as part of a rice-based meal**

THAILAND DOESN'T REALLY HAVE A VEGETARIAN TRADITION, APART FROM the very small number of Buddhists who do practice vegetarianism. But it is something that is beginning to catch on, especially among young people. Vegetarian restaurants can now be found in big cities like Bangkok and Chiang Mai, and they tend to serve very good food. When you take fish sauce out of Thai food, you must almost by definition be a creative cook.

If you overlook the fish sauce, Thai cuisine has many delicious meatless dishes. This recipe is a version of the well-known chicken with basil often served in North American Thai restaurants (but too often without the large-quantities-of-basil-and-chiles pizzazz it should have). It takes only minutes to prepare and, together with a plate of plain jasmine rice and a few slices of fresh cucumber, it makes a light, tasty, easy meal.

Holy basil, called *gaprow* in Thai, is a close relative of sweet basil and the more anise-tasting Asian (Thai) basil. It has narrow, sometimes purplish leaves and little taste when raw. Its taste is strong and distinctive only when cooked. *Gaprow* is sometimes available from Asian groceries that carry fresh produce. If you can't find it, substitute Asian or sweet basil, but stir it in just before serving.

1 tablespoon peanut oil or vegetable oil

2 tablespoons finely chopped garlic (4 to 6 cloves)

½ pound long beans or green beans, finely chopped

1 to 2 bird chiles or serrano chiles, finely chopped

4 squares fresh tofu (about 1 pound), cut into 1-inch squares

¼ cup vegetarian stock, chicken stock, or water

1 teaspoon soy sauce

1 tablespoon Thai fish sauce

1 teaspoon sugar

½ cup packed fresh holy basil leaves (or substitute Asian or sweet basil), coarsely chopped (save a few whole leaves for garnish)

Heat a large heavy skillet or wok over high heat. When it is hot, add the oil. When the oil is hot, add garlic and cook until just golden brown. Add the beans and chiles and cook for 1 minute, pressing them against the hot sides of the pan.

Add the tofu and cook for 2 minutes, stirring constantly (the tofu will break apart and look like scrambled eggs; don't be concerned). Stir in the stock or water, then add the soy sauce, fish sauce, and sugar and mix well. Cook until the beans are tender (long beans will cook faster than ordinary green beans), about 5 more minutes. Add the basil leaves, stir-fry for 30 seconds, and remove from the heat. Serve garnished with basil leaves on a platter to accompany rice, and place a small plate of sliced cucumbers alongside.

# Red Chicken Curry

*gaeng ped gai*

PREPARING A THAI CURRY USED TO BE DIFFICULT AND TIME CONSUMING. Now, with good-quality curry paste and coconut milk readily available in the stores, it can be simple and quick.

Even when you are preparing a quick Thai curry, however, there's a distinction between quick and very quick. To please the eye of most Thais, a good coconut curry should have a clearly visible thin layer of coconut oil floating on the surface. This is achieved by heating thick coconut "cream" early on in the cooking so that the oil separates. We're not persuaded that this makes any difference in the taste of the curry, but it does add to the appearance of the dish. This recipe offers the "long" quick version; if you are really in a hurry, don't worry about "thick" and "thin" coconut milk—just add all the coconut milk at once, bring to a boil, and add the chicken. Serve this with fragrant Thai jasmine rice and a small plate of sliced cucumbers.

3 cups canned coconut milk
(see Glossary)

2 tablespoons peanut oil or vegetable oil

2 tablespoons Red Curry Paste (page 148)
or store-bought

1 pound boneless skinless chicken
breasts, cut into ¼-inch slices

5 to 6 fresh wild lime leaves
(see Glossary) (optional)

½ cup fresh Asian basil leaves
(see Glossary)

2 long red chiles (such as cayenne chiles),
or substitute green cayennes or
serranos, cut into long thin strips

Canned coconut milk often has already separated itself into "thick" and "thin" milk, the thick milk having settled on the top. If this hasn't happened, transfer the milk to a glass jar and let it sit in the refrigerator for a while before using; the two milks will separate when cold.

Heat a wok or heavy-bottomed saucepan over medium-high heat. Add the oil. When the oil is hot, add the curry paste. Stir the paste for 1 minute; it will stick a little to the bottom of the pan. Add 1 cup "thick" coconut milk and stir, then cook, stirring, for 5 to 8 minutes, until the oil begins to separate.

Add the chicken pieces and lime leaves, increase the heat to high, and cook, stirring, for about 4 minutes, until the chicken has changed color and become firmer in texture. Add the rest of the coconut milk and bring to a boil. Reduce the heat and simmer for 4 to 5 minutes.

Just before serving, stir in the basil and garnish with the strips of chile.

# Red Curry Paste
## krung gaeng deng

**Makes about 1¼ cups thick paste**

RED CURRY PASTE IS INCREDIBLY HANDY TO HAVE IN YOUR PANTRY. YOU CAN use it not only for making curries (see Red Chicken Curry, page 147) but also for dipping sauces and marinades (see Red Curry Sauce page 130). We like to use it as a flavor paste for Classic Thai Fried Rice (page 158): Put a dab in the hot oil before adding the other ingredients to give the rice great flavor and heat.

Good red curry paste is now available at Thai and other Southeast Asian grocery stores. Sometimes, though, it's a pleasure to assemble your own. Flavors are more vivid, and you come to a better understanding and appreciation of the final taste when you combine the ingredients yourself. We use both a mortar and pestle and a food processor to reduce all the ingredients quickly to a paste. You can also use just a mortar or just a processor. All three options are described below.

Red curry paste relies on dried red chiles, peppercorns, and galangal (or ginger) for heat, and there's a strong citrus element from lemon grass and lime zest. The paste keeps well in a sealed glass container in the refrigerator.

| | |
|---|---|
| 1½ cups (about 1½ ounces) dried red chiles, preferably from Thailand, (see Glossary) | ¼ cup coarsely chopped peeled fresh galangal (see Glossary) or ginger |
| 1½ tablespoons coriander seed | 1 teaspoon minced wild lime zest (see Glossary) or regular lime zest |
| 1 teaspoon cumin seed | ¼ cup coarsely chopped garlic |
| ⅛ teaspoon black peppercorns | ¼ cup coarsely chopped shallots |
| 2 stalks fresh lemon grass | 1 teaspoon salt |
| 1 tablespoon coarsely chopped coriander root | 1½ teaspoons shrimp paste (see Glossary) |

Break off the stem end from each chile, break the chile into two or more pieces and shake out the seeds, and place the chile pieces in a medium bowl. Discard the seeds and stems. Pour hot water over the chile pieces and let soak for at least 30 minutes, or as long as 2 hours.

Meanwhile, dry-roast the coriander and cumin seeds: Heat a small heavy skillet over medium-high heat. Put in the coriander seeds and heat, occasionally shaking the pan or stirring, until aromatic and beginning to change color, about 3 minutes. Transfer to a mortar or a small bowl and repeat with cumin seeds, which will take about 1 minute. Dry-roast the peppercorns just until fragrant, about 1 minute. Using a small mortar and pestle or a spice grinder, pound or grind the spices together to a powder and set aside.

Cut the hard root end off the lemon grass stalks and discard. Cut off the grassy ends, leaving about 3-inch stalks. Peel off the hard outer layer and discard. Smash the stalks with the flat side of a cleaver or heavy knife, then finely chop and cut crosswise to mince.

*If using a large mortar and pestle,* place the ground spices in the mortar. Add the minced lemon grass, galangal or ginger, and coriander root. Pound well to reduce to a paste. Add the lime zest and pound to blend. Add the garlic, shallots, and salt and pound and mash to a smooth paste. (Even if you are using a large mortar, it may be getting full at this point. If it is, transfer the contents to a bowl and set aside.)

Drain the chiles, saving a little soaking water. Place the chiles in the mortar and pound to a paste. (This will take a few minutes.) When the paste is fairly smooth, add the shrimp paste and pound and mash to blend. (If you have set aside the other paste ingredients, stir them into the chile paste, either in the mortar or in a bowl.) If the paste is very dry, add a little of the chile soaking water.

*If using the combination method,* use both a large Thai mortar and pestle and a food processor as we like to. The processor makes quicker and better work of reducing the chiles to a paste. Use the mortar as described above to mash and blend all ingredients except the chiles. Then transfer the paste to a food processor, add the drained chiles plus a little of the chile soaking water, and process to a smooth paste, 45 seconds to 1 minute. You may have to stop partway through and use a spatula to push the paste down the sides of the bowl.

*If using a food processor only,* chop the galangal or ginger, coriander root, garlic, and shallots fairly fine and place in the processor with the reserved ground spices, the minced lemon grass, lime peel, salt, and shrimp paste. Process to a paste. Drain the chiles, reserving the soaking water, and add the chiles and a little soaking water to the processor. Process to a paste. You may need to add a little extra soaking water to help with grinding or to create a paste texture.

Stored in a well-sealed glass container in the refrigerator, this keeps for 3 to 4 months (with a slight loss of intensity over time).

# Savory Chicken Finely Chopped
## laab gai

**Serves 4 to 6 as part of a sticky rice meal**

LAAB GAI IS A QUICKLY PREPARED DISH OF POACHED MINCED CHICKEN tossed with herbs in a lime-based dressing. It is traditionally served with sticky rice. To eat it, you make a small ball of sticky rice with your hand, then use it to scoop up a little *laab*.

*Laab* is a category of dishes from the regional cuisine of the northeast, traditionally made with uncooked pork. What makes it distinctive is the method by which the meat is prepared:

Morning market at Chiang Khan

You begin with an entire cut of meat, then start chopping it with a heavy cleaver. If you have two cleavers, all the better, and a sound will come from the kitchen resembling a tribal drum roll. The effect of using one or two cleavers in this way is that the meat resembles ground meat, but it is much more irregular in texture, and a lot more interesting in the dish. Try it, it's easy and fun.

*Laab gai* differs from the pork version in its use of *rau ram*, or Vietnamese coriander, an herb increasingly available here in Southeast Asian groceries. (It actually doesn't resemble coriander at all, except that it is a strong, distinctive-tasting herb.) In Malaysia and Singapore, it is known as *polygonum;* in Thailand, as *pak chi wietnam.* We have it in our garden in the summer and bring it inside in the fall. It is a perennial, so we stick with it during its straggly dead-looking period (in late winter), and it comes back to life and sprouts new green leaves in the spring. If you can't find *rau ram*, substitute a mixture of fresh regular coriander and mint leaves.

This dish goes well with Lime Leaf and Oyster Mushroom Soup (page 132), as the stock that is made here can be used as the base for the soup.

1 tablespoon Thai sticky rice or
  1 tablespoon Roasted Rice Powder
  (page 131)

1 pound boneless skinless chicken breasts

3 to 4 shallots, thinly sliced

2 dried red chiles, preferably from
  Thailand (see Glossary), chopped

3 to 4 tablespoons fresh lime juice

3 tablespoons Thai fish sauce

1 teaspoon sugar

¼ teaspoon freshly ground black pepper

¼ cup packed fresh Vietnamese
  coriander (*rau ram*) leaves
  (or substitute 2 tablespoons fresh mint
  and 2 tablespoons fresh regular
  coriander leaves), or more to taste,
  coarsely torn

Leaf lettuce for garnish

If using raw rice, dry-roast the rice in a small heavy skillet over medium heat. When the rice has browned, grind it to a fine powder using a blender, a coffee grinder, or a Thai mortar and pestle.

Using a cleaver, pound and chop the chicken until it resembles the consistency of ground beef. In a small saucepan, bring 2½ cups water to a boil. Toss in the chicken and cook until all the chicken has changed color, about 2 minutes. Drain the chicken and save the stock for another use. (The recipe can be prepared ahead to this point and the chicken stored, covered, in the refrigerator for up to 24 hours. Bring to room temperature before proceeding by letting stand or by briefly dipping into boiling water; drain well.)

In a medium bowl, mix the chicken with the shallots, chiles, lime juice, fish sauce, sugar, and black pepper. Mix in the Vietnamese coriander (or mint and coriander) leaves. Set out on a plate lined with leaf lettuce and sprinkle the roasted rice powder on top.

# Thai Grilled Chicken

*gai yang*

**Serves 6 as part of a sticky rice meal**

FOR CONNOISSEURS OF GRILLED CHICKEN, THAILAND IS PARADISE. GRILLED chicken, called *gai yang*, is a common street food and restaurant specialty, and though it is most closely associated with the regional cuisine of the northeast, each region has its own distinctive ways of marinating and grilling chicken.

This recipe is our new favorite version, one we learned while staying in south Thailand near the town of Tap Sa Kae. Coconut milk is added to the marinade, giving the chicken even more succulence and depth of flavor.

### Marinade

2 cloves garlic

Pinch of salt

2 teaspoons black peppercorns

2 tablespoons chopped coriander root, minced (see Note)

3 tablespoons Thai fish sauce

1 cup canned coconut milk (see Glossary)

3 pounds chicken breasts or breasts and legs, chopped into 10 to 12 pieces (see Note)

### Accompaniment

Hot-and-Sweet Dipping Sauce (page 129)

Prepare the marinade using a large mortar and pestle or a small food processor: Combine the garlic, salt, and pepper and pound or process to a smooth paste. Add the coriander root and pound or process to a paste. Transfer to a large bowl and stir in the fish sauce and coconut milk. Place the chicken pieces in marinade and turn to coat well. Let stand at room temperature for about 1 hour.

Preheat a charcoal or gas-fired grill, then place the chicken 4 to 5 inches from the flame, bone side down. Once the bottom side is starting to brown, brush the pieces with some marinade, turn over, and cook on the other side until golden brown and the juices run clear.

*Alternatively,* the chicken can be cooked under a broiler. Preheat the broiler. Lightly oil a broiling pan, add the chicken pieces bone side up, and place 4 to 6 inches from the broiler element. Cook for 8 to 10 minutes, or until the chicken is starting to brown. Turn pieces over and lightly brush with a little of the marinade. Broil for another 8 to 10 minutes, or until the juices run clear.

Transfer to a platter and serve with the dipping sauce and plenty of sticky rice.

**Note:** You will need a cleaver to chop the chicken into smaller pieces: A whole chicken breast, for example, should be split in half, then each half chopped into four pieces. Legs are chopped in two: drumstick and thigh. You can also ask your butcher to cut up the chicken. Remove the skin or leave it on, as you wish.

Because coriander root is so handy to have for preparing many classic Thai dishes, we try to stockpile it. We always buy coriander with the roots on, then, when we've finished with the leaves, we wash the roots, wrap them in foil, and freeze them. Defrost simply by running them under cold water. This marinade can also be used for grilled fish steaks or grilled pork.

Preparing grilled chicken near Tap Sa Kae

# Guk Gai

Ten years ago, we put up a little notice in the main Toronto Library asking if a native Thai speaker would be interested in exchanging English lessons for Thai lessons. Months passed with no replies, so when the phone rang one day, we'd all but forgotten about the notice. "Hello," said a young woman, "do you still want to exchange English for Thai lessons?" "Yes," we replied, thrilled as could be. A few days later we began our lessons, and Saratwadee—Guk, for short—has been our good friend ever since.

Guk eventually ended up moving back to Thailand, to her hometown, Chiang Mai. She decided that there were more opportunities for her there than in Canada, and we thought she made a good decision. We were very sorry when she left, but at least now she is there whenever we go to visit.

The one thing to know about Guk is that she doesn't know how to cook. When we first met, we couldn't believe it: She *really* didn't know how to cook. We used to tease her about it, but she explained it simply: "I buy my food in the market. I buy *nam prik ong* and *nam prik num*, a bag of sticky rice, perhaps a curry or some *gai yang* and *som tam*, and I take it home to eat. Why should I know how to cook? I could never do a better job than the people in the market."

She's right. In Thailand, prepared food in the market, or food made on the street, is immense in its variety and exceptional in its quality. It's also inexpensive. For restaurants that try to charge a lot of money for Thai food, it is a difficult task, difficult to compete with the street vendors and market people. If people in Thailand want to spend money on a meal, they usually go to a fancy Chinese restaurant, or to a restaurant that floats down a river or has a theme park for kids.

A while back, the city of Bangkok elected a new mayor named Chamlong Sri Muang. Chamlong gained enormous popularity, described as the first honest politician in Thai democratic history. He didn't drive a car, he

Picking up street food for breakfast

**opposite top and bottom**

Grilling sausage at a local carnival in southern Thailand

Prepared curries on display on a Bangkok street

lived in a tiny house, and he dressed in the same traditional denim clothing that Thai farmers wear in the fields. He was, to boot, an avid vegetarian, and ran a vegetarian restaurant where people could come and eat cheaply and learn about vegetarianism.

One of the first things Chamlong did in office was to lead a cleanup campaign in the city, and one of his first targets was the street vendors. Chamlong wanted to relieve congestion on the sidewalks by cutting back on street vending. Well, Chamlong may have been immensely popular, but this particular idea was a bust. More than a million people earn at least part of their income every day through street vending in Bangkok. "Bangkok without street vendors," people screamed, "that's like Venice without water." No, it's worse.

Chamlong quickly gave in.

And Guk still hasn't learned how to cook.

# Grilled Pork Satay

*moo ping*

**Serves 4 to 6 as an appetizer, or more as part of a buffet-style rice meal**

THIS IS A THAI VERSION OF A SOUTHEAST ASIAN CLASSIC. MARINATED STRIPS OF lean pork are either grilled on small bamboo skewers or broiled in the oven, then offered with a choice of two delicious sauces. Cold crisp slices of cucumber can be used to scoop up leftover sauce.

Put out a bowl of each sauce on the table, or if you prefer, serve individually in small bowls for each diner, along with individual plates of cucumber slices. For a buffet-style rice meal, serve with a salad such as Grilled Eggplant Salad (page 134), as well as Lime Leaf and Oyster Mushroom Soup (page 132) and Tofu Fried with Basil (page 146).

**Marinade**

2 large cloves garlic, minced

2 tablespoons finely chopped coriander roots and stems

3 tablespoons Thai fish sauce

1 tablespoon palm sugar (see Glossary) or substitute brown sugar

1 tablespoon soy sauce

1 teaspoon freshly ground black pepper

½ cup fresh or canned coconut milk (see Glossary)

1 pound pork loin, thinly sliced into strips approximately 2 to 3 inches long by ¾ inch wide by ¼ inch or less thick

Tangy Lime Sauce (page 128)

Red Curry Sauce (page 130)

Leaf lettuce for serving

Cucumber slices for serving

Combine all of the ingredients for the marinade in a medium bowl and mix thoroughly. Add the pork strips and toss until all the strips are coated with marinade. Let stand at room temperature for 1 hour or more. If using wooden skewers, place skewers in water to soak.

Preheat a grill or broiler. *If grilling*, thread one or two pieces of pork onto each skewer. Grill over a hot fire for 2 to 3 minutes on each side, until the meat is cooked through. *If broiling*, place the meat on a lightly oiled broiling rack and broil about 2 inches from the heat source for approximately 5 minutes, turning once after 3 minutes, until browned and cooked through.

Serve on a platter garnished with leaf lettuce. Put out bowls of the sauces and individual plates of cucumber slices.

# Meeting a Monk at Work

I once had an office job in Bangkok helping to edit an English-language textbook. The job didn't last very long, or rather I didn't last very long in the job. I blame it on a co-worker, a man from Australia who had been working his way around the world for years. In his time in Thailand, he'd become interested in the language, and also in Buddhism, so he had decided to take the simple vows of a novice monk and to live in a monastery. After a year, and in command of fairly good spoken Thai, he left the monastery and proceeded to walk around the country as a monk. He walked all the way from north to south, and from east to west. He even went from island to island. With his alms bowl and black umbrella, the two possessions of a monk, wherever he was he would appear on the street at dawn each morning and be given food, eating only once each day. If he was on a small island where there weren't any monks, he would often be asked to perform ritual services.

He had the greatest stories, and whenever we had time to talk at work we would. Before long, I was convinced that I should do exactly as he had done, but I was too cowardly. Instead, I decided, I would quit work and hitchhike around the country, staying whenever possible in small local monasteries. And so I did. It was a far cry from my friend the monk's experiences, but in a few months I learned a great deal and had a lot of fun.

*Monks on their morning alms round in Chiang Khong*

One evening I was staying in a monastery in Haadyai, a border town in southern Thailand. It was during the rainy season, so the monastery was full of novice monks, young men in their late teens and early twenties from the surrounding countryside who, at least once in their life, become a monk for three months (usually during rainy season), as is the custom in Thailand. I was sitting with a large group, chatting idly, when suddenly I noticed that everyone was staring at my feet and beginning to laugh. So I looked down, thinking that there must be a problem, but I could see only my normal bare feet. Then I looked around at everyone else's feet, and I realized why they were laughing. My toes were long and narrow, while everyone else had short, tough stubs, toes that had spent a lifetime outside and tramping through mud in rice paddies. It's a strange feeling, having your toes tell so much about who you are.

# Classic Thai Fried Rice
### khao pad

**Serves 1**

FRIED RICE IS A THAI CLASSIC. NO MATTER WHERE YOU ARE, NO MATTER what time of day, you can always order fried rice—*khao pad*—and it will almost always be very good. You can order it with chicken, pork, squid, green vegetables, mushrooms, extra garlic, any way you like—something like ordering a pizza here. Our favorite is *khao pad pak sai khai dao*, vegetable fried rice with a fried egg on top (eggs in Thailand are full of flavor).

But *khao pad* is much more than a neighborhood restaurant dish. It is also cooked at home, almost daily, probably the best way of turning leftover Thai jasmine rice into a quick delicious meal. It is versatile and always satisfying, light and nourishing. If your larder is almost bare, make it only with garlic, lots of garlic. If you have a few mushrooms or a little chicken or pork, slice thinly and add to the wok once the garlic is golden. Whatever you might add, be sure to brown the garlic first, to use *nam pla* (fish sauce), and, if possible, to start with fragrant Thai rice—these are the elements that make *khao pad* so uniquely good.

Thai fried rice is ideally accompanied by a squeeze of fresh lime, a sprinkling of fresh coriander leaves, a few slices of cucumber, and *nam pla prik* (fish sauce with hot chiles). We've seen many a chile hater turn into a chile lover all on account of Thai fried rice and *nam pla prik*.

This recipe is for one serving. If you have a large wok, the recipe is easily doubled to serve two; increase your cooking time by about thirty seconds. If you are serving more than two, prepare the additional servings separately. The cooking time is very short, so once all your ingredients are prepared it is easy to go through the same cooking process twice, or more— simply clean out the wok and wipe it dry each time. It is much easier to prepare *khao pad* when your wok isn't overly full.

Total preparation time is about six minutes; cooking time is about four minutes. Street vendors normally prepare *khao pad* one plate at a time, while you wait.

2 tablespoons peanut oil or vegetable oil

4 to 8 cloves garlic, minced (even more if not using optional ingredients)

1 cup sliced oyster mushrooms or other mushrooms (optional)

2 cups cooked rice, cooled (preferably Thai jasmine or American jasmine rice)

2 scallions, cut into ½-inch slivers (optional)

1 medium tomato, finely chopped (optional)

2 teaspoons Thai fish sauce or to taste

1 teaspoon soy sauce

### Garnish and accompaniments

About ¼ cup packed fresh coriander leaves

About 6 thin cucumber slices

1 scallion, trimmed

½ tomato, sliced (optional)

2 to 3 lime wedges

¼ cup Fish Sauce with Hot Chiles (page 124)

Leaf lettuce (optional)

Heat a medium to large wok over high heat. When it is hot, add the oil and heat until very hot. Add the garlic and fry until just golden, about 20 seconds. Add the mushrooms, if using, and cook, stirring constantly, until softened, about 1 minute. Add the rice, breaking it up with your fingers as you toss it into the wok. With your spatula, keep moving the rice around the wok. At first it may stick, but scoop and toss the rice and soon it will be more manageable. Try to visualize "frying" each little bit of rice, sometimes pressing the rice against the wok with the back of your spatula. Good fried rice should have a faint seared-in-the-wok taste. Cook for approximately 1½ minutes. Add the optional scallions and tomato, the fish sauce, and soy sauce. Stir-fry for 30 seconds to 1 minute.

Turn out onto a dinner plate. Garnish with fresh coriander. Around the rice, lay a row of overlapping cucumber slices, a scallion, the optional tomato slices and one or two lettuce leaves, and wedges of lime. The lime should be squeezed onto the rice as you eat it. Serve with the *nam pla prik*—the salty hot taste of the sauce brings out the full flavor of the rice.

**Note:** Once you've tossed the garlic in the hot oil, you can add about ½ teaspoon (or more) of Red Curry Paste (page 148) or store-bought. It adds another layer of flavor and a little heat too.

**Alternative:** Many people (we're among them) like to eat a fried egg (with a soft yolk) on top of their fried rice. Wipe out your wok, heat about 2 teaspoons oil, and quickly fry the egg in the wok, then turn it out onto the rice. It's delicious. Try it!

# Late-Night Chicken Congee
*khao tom*

ALL ACROSS EAST AND SOUTHEAST ASIA, CONGEE IS A POPULAR BREAKFAST food. As a thick hot soup, it is both satisfying and comforting, as any early-morning food should be. There are many different versions of congee, but the main differences lie in the range and variety of tastes and condiments that are used to dress up and enliven an essentially uncomplicated dish.

We like the common Thai version a great deal, with its savory crunch of chopped shallots and fresh taste of coriander leaf. But then we also have very good associations with Thai congee, as it is commonly served in roadside restaurants that cater to long-range buses traveling very late at night. If you are traveling overnight by bus in Thailand, which is common, you will inevitably pull into such a restaurant. Waking up from a deep sleep, you will walk through the warm night into a large room filled with many tables, and on each table will be plates and bowls full of condiments. After you sit down, there will come a large bowl of hot rice congee. It is up to you to mix and match with all the different condiments, a little of this, a little of that.

It is a humorous situation when you see a whole busload of foreign travelers stopping into one of these restaurants late at night, knowing that for many of the people aboard it is their first encounter with Thai congee. Many will shrug their shoulders and climb back on the bus, but for those who try it, it is a great discovery.

We prefer to use long-grain fragrant Thai rice, but you can also use short-grain rice. This version is easy to make and full of flavor, with a wide choice of condiments to spice it up.

### Congee

3 quarts water

About 2 inches ginger, peeled and cut into chunks

2 pounds chicken legs and breasts

2 cups Thai jasmine or American jasmine rice

1 tablespoon Thai fish sauce

½ teaspoon salt

### Condiment possibilities

Small bowls of soy sauce

Condiment bowl of Fish Sauce with Hot Chiles (page 124)

Small bowl of chile paste or hot salsa

3 tablespoons dried shrimp (see Glossary), coarsely chopped (optional)

3 tablespoons Chinese pickled vegetables (see Glossary) (optional)

¼ cup packed fresh coriander leaves

¼ cup slivered ginger

¼ cup finely chopped shallots

8 cloves garlic, minced and fried in peanut oil or vegetable oil until golden brown

¼ cup raw peanuts, dry-roasted (see Glossary) and coarsely chopped

Place the water and ginger in a large pot. Bring to a boil, add the chicken, and boil over medium heat until cooked through, 30 to 40 minutes. Remove the chicken pieces from broth and set aside. Place the broth in a container in the refrigerator to cool.

Pull off the chicken skin, remove the chicken from the bones, shred, and set aside. Discard the skin and bones.

When the broth has cooled, remove it from the refrigerator and skim off the fat. Strain out the ginger pieces.

Return the broth to the large pot and bring to a boil. Add the rice and stir gently until the broth returns to a boil. Add the fish sauce and salt, cover, lower the heat, and simmer until the rice is cooked and very soft, about 25 minutes.

Stir in the chicken. Congee should be somewhat soupy. If the rice has absorbed all the broth, add boiling water a cup at a time until the desired consistency is achieved.

Serve in soup bowls and place a platter of condiments on the table so that guests can help themselves as they eat.

# Rice and Herbs Salad

*yam khao*

Serves 6 to 8

THERE ARE MANY DELICIOUS WAYS OF USING LEFTOVER THAI RICE. THIS south Thai salad is fresh and attractive with its scattering of watercress and herbs and light dressing; extra dressing is served in small bowls on the side, allowing guests to intensify the spicing as they wish.

### Salad

4 cups cooked Thai jasmine or American jasmine rice

2 tablespoons fresh lime juice

1½ cups packed coarsely chopped watercress leaves and fine stems

1½ to 2 cups chopped long beans or green beans (¼-inch lengths)

2 large or 3 medium plum tomatoes, finely chopped

2 tablespoons finely chopped fresh mint

¼ cup packed fresh Asian or sweet basil leaves, coarsely chopped

1 cup loosely packed coarsely chopped or shredded fresh coriander leaves

¼ cup finely sliced shallots, separated into rings

1 teaspoon finely minced lemon grass

1 bird chile or serrano chile, minced

### Dressing

½ cup Thai fish sauce

¼ cup water

1 heaping teaspoon palm sugar (see Glossary) or substitute brown sugar

½ teaspoon minced lemon grass

1 clove garlic, minced

½ teaspoon crumbled dried red chile (see Glossary)

3 tablespoons fresh lime juice

Leaf lettuce leaves to line the serving platter

Place the rice in a large bowl, tossing with wet hands or chopsticks to break up any lumps. Add the lime juice and toss to mix. Add the watercress and toss. Place a large saucepan with 1 inch of water over high heat and bring to a boil. Add the beans, cover, and blanch for 1 minute, or until slightly softened. Drain and add to the rice, tossing to mix well. Add the remaining salad ingredients and toss to mix.

To prepare the dressing, place the fish sauce and water in a small nonreactive saucepan over medium-high heat. Add the sugar, stirring to dissolve thoroughly. Add the lemon grass, garlic, and chile and bring to a boil. Lower the heat and simmer for 5 minutes, stirring occasionally to prevent sticking. Transfer to a small bowl and add the lime juice.

Stir the dressing well, then add 3 tablespoons of the dressing to the salad. Toss and taste. Add another tablespoon of dressing if desired.

Line a large platter with lettuce. Mound the salad on top. Serve with one or two small bowls of the remaining dressing, with small spoons, for drizzling more dressing on. The salad can be eaten with a spoon and fork, the modern Thai way, or scooped up with lettuce leaves.

# Grilled Sticky Rice Balls
*khao neeo yang*

WE FIRST TASTED THESE GRILLED STICKY RICE BALLS IN THE EARLY-MORNING market in Loei, in northeast Thailand. They were so good, so simple, and such a wonderful surprise that we couldn't eat enough. We ended up going back to the market every morning, but in Loei that meant early, as it was all but shutting down come seven-thirty.

The rice balls we ate in the cool of those early mornings were shaped around the end of a wooden skewer, dipped in egg, and then grilled over a small charcoal fire. We find it easier to shape the rice into flat patties and place them straight on the grill, without bothering with skewers.

Serve as an appetizer or as part of a light meal, with a Thai salad or a soup. These are delicious eaten plain or with one or more highly flavored dipping sauces, such as Red Curry Sauce, Thai Fish Sauce with Hot Chiles, Tangy Lime Sauce, or Spicy Thai Salsa.

| | |
|---|---|
| 2 large eggs | **Optional accompaniments** |
| 1 tablespoon Thai fish sauce | Red Curry Sauce (page 130) |
| ½ teaspoon sugar | Fish Sauce with Hot Chiles (page 124) |
| ¼ teaspoon freshly ground black pepper | Tangy Lime Sauce (page 128) |
| About 3 cups hot freshly cooked sticky rice (or 2 cups sticky rice soaked overnight and steamed, see page 116) | Grilled Chile Salsa (page 126) |

Preheat the grill.

Break the eggs into a medium bowl and whisk well. Add the fish sauce, sugar, and pepper and whisk briefly to blend.

Scoop up about ½ cup sticky rice and flatten it between your palms into a round or oval disk about 3 inches in diameter. Set aside and shape the remaining disks.

Place the bowl of egg mixture near the grill. Scoop one disk through the egg mixture to coat, then place immediately on the grill. Repeat with the other shaped disks. Grill until lightly golden on one side, then use tongs to turn and cook the second side. Remove and place on a plate. Serve immediately, with any or all of the optional sauces if you wish.

**Note:** This recipe doubles easily to make more rice balls. Proportions are approximately 1 egg and 1½ teaspoons fish sauce per 1½ cups cooked rice.

# Lisu Village Sticky Rice

We awoke to the noises of a village morning, pigs rooting around and cocks crowing. But there was another less familar sound, a slow, regular, heavy *thunk, thunk, thunk*. We were in a Lisu village for the lunar New Year, late January in the hills of north Thailand. The day before we'd seen young men head out to cut down small trees, one for each family group or household, to be set up in front of each house. The children were already wearing colorful new clothing for the New Year. Later that day we'd see the dancing: a slow hypnotic tune plucked from a simple lute, a circle of children in New Year's finery being drawn in by the music, holding hands as they slowly dance-stepped around the lute player, and finally, as the late-afternoon shadows lengthened, the arrival of the young men and women of marriageable age, gleaming with silver jewelry, wearing rich black jackets and pastel skirts or pantaloons, elaborate bags and ornate head-dresses, who shyly joined the slowly circling, slow-stepping, hand-holding dancers. The children would eventually drop out, leaving the courting young people to dance all night, eyeing each other's finery, while the village elders looked on.

But long before the dancing began, the sticky rice cakes had to be prepared. The sound we'd heard was the thump of an enormous mortar and pestle being used to pound cooked sticky rice for New Year's cakes. Out we went into the morning light and joined a group of children watching as the cooked rice was emptied into a large wooden basin—the mortar—then pounded. The pestle consisted of a thick rounded stick fixed through one end of a heavy pole about twelve feet long. The pole was mounted across a heavy log, like a large asymmetrical seesaw. Three or four young men would step on the shorter end to raise the other, the working end, into the air. Then they'd step off, and the heavier end would come crashing down, the rounded pestle landing on the rice in the basin. As

it bounced heavily back up, the young men would step back onto the pole to raise the pestle end, then hop off, and down would come the pestle again. Soon the mass of rice in the basin had been reduced to a smooth gooey mass.

The women of the household then emptied it out and used it to shape small flat round cakes or dumplings, wrapped in threes in banana leaves. Most of these would be cooked in the fire to a golden brown, but they handed some out right away to greedy bystanders—not just the village children but also the watching adults, including us—for immediate eating. They were gooey, filling, slightly sweet-tasting. Meanwhile, more cooked rice went into the mortar and the pounding continued. Sometimes the cooked rice was white, sometimes a purplish black. The quantities were huge: rice for New Year's, rice for the dancers, rice to sustain the village through many days and nights of festivities.

# Rice Cakes with Palm Sugar

*khao taen*

THESE ARE JEFFREY'S FAVORITE SWEET SNACK, NOT JUST IN THAILAND, BUT possibly anywhere. They are sold by street vendors and in small shops, usually in bunches of five or ten. The basic ingredient is cooked sticky rice, shaped into flat cakes, dried, and then deep-fried until they puff up. The rice cakes are topped with a swirl of melted smoky-tasting palm sugar that hardens as it cools.

We have experimented with making a home-style version, and in the process have come to appreciate the skill needed to make the large (five-inch-wide) cakes we look for in Thailand. Our version is easier, for the smaller-sized rice cakes dry out easily without breaking and puff up evenly when fried.

About 4½ cups hot freshly cooked sticky rice (or 3 cups sticky rice, soaked overnight and then steamed, see page 116)

Peanut oil or vegetable oil for deep-frying

1 cup palm sugar (see Glossary)

2 tablespoons water

The rice should be warm to hot, just cooled enough that you can handle it. Scoop up a heaping tablespoon of rice and shape into a flat round disk, discarding any dry or hardened grains. Work gently, flattening the mound of rice between your palms and also pulling it apart slightly to stretch and flatten it into a disk. Make the rice cake as thin as possible and 2½ to 3 inches across. Don't press down hard and compress the rice; try to keep all grains intact. Once you've shaped the rice into a very thin round, place it on a dry work surface and smooth the edge by curving your index finger along the edge and squeezing lightly. This will help ensure that the thinned-out grains are still sticking together. Repeat with the remaining rice, placing the finished disks on a wire rack or on a nonstick baking sheet.

When all are shaped, place in full sun to dry or, if you live in an iffy climate like ours, place on a nonstick baking sheet in a very low (150°F) oven to dry for 2 to 3 hours (turn over halfway through). Do not let the cakes color; you just want them dried out so they'll keep well and so they'll deep-fry without hissing and sizzling too much.

When the cakes are dry, let cool, then store in a well-sealed plastic bag until ready to use.

To proceed, heat 3 inches of oil in a wok or deep-fryer. You want a temperature of 325° to 350°F; to test the temperature, drop one rice cake or a small clump of sticky rice into the oil. The cake should sink to the bottom and immediately float back to the surface but without burning or crisping immediately. If it burns, the temperature is too high and you need to lower the heat slightly; if the cake doesn't immediately rise back up, the oil is not yet hot enough and you need to wait a little longer before beginning.

When the oil is at the right temperature, add two cakes and watch as the rice grains swell up. Turn over when the first side stops swelling and cook on the other side until well puffed and just starting to brown. Use a slotted spoon to remove immediately to a paper towel–lined platter or wire rack to drain; pat off the oil from each side. Fry the remaining cakes the same way, making sure that the oil temperature is high enough each time.

Prepare the topping by placing the palm sugar in a small saucepan with the water and heat over medium heat, stirring constantly. When the sugar has melted, lower the heat and let simmer until cooked to a medium-brown syrup, about 5 minutes. Let the syrup cool slightly, until lukewarm. This helps it thicken slightly, so it doesn't just get absorbed by the rice cakes but stays on top as a decorative sugar swirl.

Use a spoon to drizzle a spiral of syrup onto each rice cake, starting at the center and spiraling out. Place on a wire rack to dry out and cool until the sugar has set. The cakes may be tempting when hot but have a much better flavor and texture once they've cooled. Store in a well-sealed container in a cool place for up to 10 days.

**Shaping note:** Thickness/thinness is the important measurement, because if the cakes are too thick they won't puff up properly when fried. But if you press and flatten the cakes too energetically, the rice grains get compressed and mushed out of shape. Then they won't puff properly during frying and the rice cakes will be tough. Don't worry if the edges are a little ragged; that's how homemade rice cakes are.

# Sweet Black Rice Treat

*khao neeo see dum*

**Serves 6 to 8 for dessert or as a sweet snack**

FROM THAILAND TO BALI, WHEREVER THERE IS BLACK RICE, IT SEEMS TO BE prepared with coconut milk and palm sugar to make desserts, snacks, and breakfast treats.

This simple treat is easy to prepare and makes a wonderful dessert. Since Thais don't really have a dessert tradition, it is most commonly eaten as a sweet snack or for breakfast. The black rice is mixed with white sticky rice and soaked overnight. It is then quickly steamed before being bathed in coconut milk sweetened with palm sugar. The result is a soft-textured, delicious comfort food. We like to serve it in small portions for dessert and then eat whatever is left over for breakfast the next morning—a wonderful treat. Black rice can be prepared as long as eight hours ahead and kept at room temperature, well covered. *Do not* place it in the refrigerator, as it will dry out and harden.

Bangkok shop front in the evening

Because black glutinous rice is unpolished, it is chewy, like brown rice. This is why Thais generally prepare and serve black rice mixed half-and-half with white sticky rice. While the rices soak together before steaming, the white rice takes on color from the black rice; the finished product is purple-black and very beautiful, especially when served in rich-colored bowls.

1 cup Thai black rice, soaked for 12 to 24 hours in plenty of water

1 cup long-grain Thai sticky rice, soaked with the black rice

2 cups canned coconut milk (see Glossary)

⅓ cup palm sugar (see Glossary) or substitute brown sugar

½ teaspoon salt

**Optional accompaniment**

Slices of fresh peach, mango, starfruit, kiwi, or other soft tart-sweet fruit

Place the rice in a steamer or a large sieve lined with cheesecloth or a tea towel. Place the steamer over a pot of water; the water must not touch the rice. Bring to a vigorous boil. Steam the rice for 35 minutes, stirring gently after 15 minutes, or until the rice is shiny, the white rice dark-colored and soft, the black rice grains soft inside but still a little resistant outside.

While the rice is steaming, prepare the coconut milk dressing. Canned coconut milk usually separates into thick coconut cream and more watery coconut milk. Mix the two together, then transfer to a saucepan and place over low heat. Stir in the sugar and salt; palm sugar may be solid at first but will quickly dissolve. Keep the sauce warm over very low heat, stirring occasionally, until the rice has finished steaming.

Transfer the cooked rice to a serving bowl and immediately pour 1½ cups of the warm coconut sauce over it, reserving the rest of the sauce. Stir gently to mix well, then let stand covered at room temperature for 30 minutes or as long as 3 hours, to allow the flavors to blend and the rice to soften further.

Serve in individual small bowls topped with a little of the reserved sauce or let your guests serve themselves at the table. If serving with sliced fruit, pass separately or arrange several slices over each serving.

Yasuko Kanda (page 182)
working in her garden in Miyama

inset: Kiyomizu Temple in Kyoto

# Gohan, Sushi, Mochi

There is one small well-stocked Japanese grocery store in our neighborhood, an island in a sea of Chinese and Vietnamese shops. When you walk in, a little bell rings and a voice greets you automatically in Japanese, saying hello. Our first time in there long ago is still vivid: so many unfamiliar-looking packages of unfamiliar foods. Where to begin? But it was really just like traveling—the more time we spent looking, the more things came into focus and began to make sense. That first time we bought a few basics: rice, soy sauce, vinegar, nori, pickled ginger. On return trips we branched out, buying bonito flakes, a few small jars of condiments, an assortment of dried seaweeds, some flavored crackers, and a wider range of pickles. We came to value the ease with which we could make a quick stock (*dashi*) to add depth to simmered dishes. Later we learned a recipe for what has become one of our prized kitchen staples, a rich long-keeping stock concentrate (see Mariko's Must-Have Concentrated Stock, page 184).

If you have access to a Japanese grocery store and you want to cook more Japanese food at home, take some time and slowly work your way through the store. On the shelves you'll notice a lot of little jars of prepared condiments for rice and packages of seaweed of many kinds, dried mushrooms, and bonito flakes; in the cooler, you'll see an array of pickles, prepared fish, and fried tofu, as well as many harder-to-identify items. Buy several small packages of pickles, some bonito flakes and dried mushrooms, and perhaps some sesame seeds and sheets of toasted nori (the seaweed used for sushi rolls). Pick up a bottle each of soy sauce, mirin, and rice vinegar and also, of course, a bag of Japanese rice. You now have all the special ingredients you need to embark on making home-style

**left to right**

A knife maker in the Nishiki market in Kyoto

Young women in the Jidai Matsuri procession in Kyoto

Delivering *bento* (lunch boxes) by bicycle in Kyoto

Japanese rice meals. All of them keep well in the pantry, ready when you are. (Many of these items are also available in well-stocked natural foods shops, as well as in Korean groceries.)

We eat a great deal of Japanese rice in our house. Naomi in particular loves it for breakfast or lunch, with several *umeboshi* plums, and perhaps a fried egg on top, or with pickles and a quick-cooked vegetable of some kind. Simple balls of plain rice, lightly salted (*onigiri*, see page 206), make a good lunch-box item for our children. Japanese rice also makes frequent appearances in the form of basic sushi, most often as Brown Bags Sushi (page 222) or Roll-Your-Own Sushi (page 224). Or, if we want to use the rice as the basis for a meal, if we are "cooking Japanese," there are many delicious home-style dishes to choose from. These dishes are simple to prepare and require few ingredients and little special equipment.

Apart from a good rice-cooking pot or rice cooker, you may want a mortar and pestle or spice grinder. If you come across a Japanese mortar, called a *suribachi*, buy it. It's very efficient and pleasant to use. It looks like a ceramic bowl, with thin ridges running up the inside. You use a wooden pestle to grind toasted sesame seeds and other ingredients against the ridges. Any spice grinder or other mortar can be substituted. Another great Japanese utensil is the grater called *oroshi-gane*, used for grating daikon. Heavy pots are used for cooking simmered dishes, sometimes with a smaller lid placed on the food to press it down.

A Japanese meal depends on a good balance of dishes—for example, a soup, perhaps a tofu dish, and a stir-fried vegetable dish or simmered vegetable or meat dish. Pickles, either store-bought or homemade, round out the meal. All the dishes are set out at once, the rice is served in individual bowls, and diners eat their way through the assortment of dishes as they choose. This simplicity means that once the meal is served, the cook can rest rather than worrying about the next course. There is no dessert tradition; the meal usually ends with pickles eaten with more rice, though fresh fruit may be served afterward, with tea. (Japanese sweets are elaborate specialty items, bought from pastry or cake shops, and meant to be eaten as a snack, most often with tea.)

# Basic Japanese Rice

**Makes about 5 cups rice**

JAPANESE RICE IS OF THE JAPONICA TYPE. IT IS A MEDIUM-GRAIN RICE—THAT IS, the grains are about two and a half times as long as they are wide. The "Japanese rice" available in North America is grown in the United States. It is comparable to good Japanese-grown rice. For people used to long-grain rice, Japanese rice looks rounded and relatively short and wide. The raw grains look translucent and slightly glassy, and a few will have a small opaque white patch. Japanese rice used to be coated in talc to prevent the grains from sticking together during storage and to make it look whiter. Nowadays, however, many bags of Japanese rice display the words "no talc," the talc has been replaced by a light coating of cornstarch.

In Japanese, cooked plain rice is known as *gohan* (the more polite term) or *meshi*, both meaning "honorable food."

Japanese rice absorbs less water than most rices. When properly cooked, it tends to be very slightly sticky and to clump together a bit. It is firm to the bite yet tender, and never mushy. Proper cooking involves rinsing the rice thoroughly and then letting it stand or soak for twenty to thirty minutes. Though most Japanese cooks and cookbooks include this step, we had always omitted it, thinking it unnecessary, until one day several years ago when, in a "Why not?" mood, we tried it. A Japanese friend happened to drop by for dinner. She exclaimed over the rice (the first time she'd ever done so), "But this rice is perfectly cooked!" From that uncontrolled experiment, and many tests since, we've concluded that soaking does indeed make a difference.

The rice is then cooked (in a rice cooker or a heavy pot with a tight-fitting lid) in a measured amount of water by the absorption method, without salt or oil.

IN OUR HOUSEHOLD OF BIG RICE EATERS, WE ALLOW ALMOST 1 CUP RICE per adult, and slightly under ½ cup rice per child. Having leftovers is never a problem anyway, since so many delicious things can be done with cold cooked rice. If you're using up to 3 cups rice, the pot should be of 3½ quarts capacity and at least 8 inches in diameter. If you're preparing more than 3 cups raw rice, the pot should be at least 10 inches in diameter and of 4½ quarts capacity.

The water to rice ratio is $1\frac{1}{6}$ cups water to 1 cup dry rice (slightly less when you are cooking more than 3 cups rice or if rice is marked "new crop"). *If using a rice cooker,* add water up to the line (rice cookers have markings to show how much water to add for a given number of cups of rice). *Alternatively,* some traditional cooks, if the pot is wide enough, lay a hand flat on top of the rice; the water should just cover the back of your fingers.

**2 cups Japanese white rice**

**2⅓ cups water**

Place the rice in a bowl and rinse thoroughly: Pour cold water over to cover, then rub and swish the rice vigorously around. Pour off the water, add more cold water and stir gently, and then pour off. Repeat two or three times, until the water is clear. This rinsing process washes off excess starch, both any coating materials (see above) and any starch granules eroded from the rice during milling or transporting. It prevents excess stickiness in the cooked rice.

Transfer the washed rice to a sieve to drain well. You now have two options: Let the rice stand in the sieve for 20 to 30 minutes, soaking in just the water remaining after washing, or place it in the measured amount of water you will be cooking it in and let it soak for 20 minutes before starting the cooking. We usually let the rice stand in the sieve. On the other hand, Japanese cooks who use rice cookers equipped with a timer often find the soaking in water method easier: They place the washed rice in the cooker with the water, then set the timer to start the cooking sometime later. If you are cooking rice labeled "new crop" in the months of November through February, you may get slightly better results with the sieve method because new rice has more moisture and is a little more fragile.

To cook, place the drained rice in either a rice cooker or a heavy medium pot with a tight-fitting lid and add the measured quantity of water.

*If using a rice cooker,* turn it on. Put its lid on, and let it automatically cook the rice for you. *If using a pot,* heat the rice to a vigorous boil, uncovered, then put the lid on and lower the heat to medium-low. Let cook, without raising the lid, for 5 minutes, then turn the heat to very low and cook for another 10 minutes. Without removing the lid, remove from the heat and let stand for another 10 minutes. Gently turn over the rice with a wooden rice paddle or spoon before serving.

# Rice in Japan

Japan is a country of volcanic islands stretching from the temperate climate of Hokkaido in the north to the milder, subtropical climate of Okinawa (a span of about two thousand miles). Its population is over one hundred twenty million people, or almost half the population of the United States in an area only slightly larger than the state of Florida. Much of the country is mountainous and not suited for agriculture. Of the agricultural land that does exist, most of it lies on narrow coastal plains; the most important of these for rice growing is the area around Niigata, to the north and west of Tokyo.

People in Japan still regard rice as their principle food, though per-capita consumption of rice has been declining for decades (from 330 pounds of rice per person in 1940 to 158 pounds in 1990). In Japanese rice shops, we've seen as many as twelve grades of rice being sold. The highest grade, the most expensive rice in Japan, comes from the Niigata area. This rice, unlike most Japanese rice, is not subsidized by the government and as a result, it's very expensive—six to seven times the cost of the Japanese rice sold in the United States. The least expensive and lowest-quality domestic rice in Japan is subsidized by the government, to help keep rice farmers in production. No Japanese rice is exported; Japan does not grow enough rice for its own consumption, let alone enough to export.

Everyday Japanese rice (*okome*) is medium-grain japonica rice. There is also a short- to medium-grain sticky rice (also known as sweet rice), *mochi gome*. It is used primarily for sweets and for making *mochi* (see page 226), though it is also the essential ingredient in Home-Style Red Rice (see page 228).

Traditionally, plain everyday rice was cooked over an open fire in an *okama*, a large round metal pot with a curved bottom and a wooden lid. In the Miyama area, an agricultural valley with several villages high in the mountains north of Kyoto, we were shown several of these pots. The women who told us about them were proud of the tradition. And when we asked which tasted better, rice cooked the old way or rice cooked in an electric rice cooker, the answer was unanimous—the old way. "So why," we asked, "don't you still cook it the old way?" Responses varied a bit, but in essence they all said that once the kitchen in their house was modernized and an electric or gas stove installed, there was no room for the old wood-burning stove, so it was easier, cleaner, and simpler to adapt to electric rice cookers.

Bags of newly harvested rice at a farmhouse in Miyama

**left to right**

A display of menu offerings in a Kyoto restaurant window

Market gardener beside his vegetable stall in Oharano

Rice cooked the old-fashioned way has a crust on the bottom, a little brown and crispy. This crust is a treat in itself, often saved until the end of the meal. Scorched crust, called *koge*, can be rolled into balls and eaten dipped in soy sauce. In rural areas, the tea served at the end of the meal is drunk by each person from his rice bowl, and if there's any *koge*, it's often left in the rice bowl to be softened by the tea. Tea poured over the rice crust takes on a pleasantly nutty taste, a taste now associated with vanishing rural tradition. These days, the taste is more likely to be reproduced in a commercially available tea called *genmai cha*, a mixture of tea leaves, toasted rice, and puffed rice. It's not the same, but it does evoke an earlier and simpler age. (See also Soothing Tea Rice, page 213.)

Nowadays in many Japanese families the traditional breakfast of *okayu*, or rice porridge (like congee), has been supplanted by a more Western breakfast of toast or rolls, often eaten with coffee instead of tea. But most people still eat rice for lunch or supper, or both. A simple rice lunch is often a one-dish meal of rice topped with cooked chicken or meat or fish and vegetables and served in a large bowl, accompanied perhaps by pickles and tea.

In the evening, a home-style or family rice meal consists of a soup, plain rice, and three or four other dishes, cooked in a variety of ways: perhaps a vegetable dish, a fish or meat and vegetable dish, a tofu dish, and pickles, the choice and presentation depending on the season. The meal is served all at once, with everyone having before him or her a bowl for rice on the left, chopsticks on the right, a small bowl for soup, and a small plate onto which to transfer a little of each of the dishes.

# Semi-Milled Japanese Rice Haigamai

THIS WONDERFUL COMPROMISE BETWEEN BROWN RICE AND HIGHLY POLISHED white rice is available in Japan, but we have not yet found it in North America. It is called *haigamai* and is a pale semitransparent beige in color. It cooks much more quickly than brown rice, needing only five to ten minutes more than polished white Japanese rice and the same amount of water. It has a slightly stronger "grain" taste than white rice. If you find it, try it. Prepare it following the instructions for Basic Japanese Rice (page 174), but allow it to cook over very low heat for twenty minutes rather than just ten, and then let stand for another ten to fifteen minutes, covered.

# Brown Japanese Rice

**Makes about 5 cups rice**

OUR RICE-FARMING FRIENDS YASUKO AND KANDA EAT BROWN OR SEMI-MILLED rice perhaps once a day. They like brown rice for its grain taste and nutritional value. It must also taste to them of their labor in the rice field, their ground, their sun, their rain.

Some of our favorite brown rices are the organic rices grown by the Lundberg brothers in California. They grow both long-grain brown and Japanese-style brown rice. Because the bran is left on, brown rice retains more of the residue of any chemicals used in rice production than other rices do. Hence our preference for organically grown brown rice.

2 cups Japanese (short- to medium-grain) brown rice
3 cups water

Wash the rice thoroughly in cold water until the water runs clear. Place in a sieve to drain and let stand for 1 hour.

Place the rice in a heavy medium pot and add the measured water. Bring to a boil, cover tightly, lower the heat to medium-low, and cook for 5 minutes. Lower the heat to very low and cook for 35 minutes. Remove from the heat and let stand for 10 minutes before serving.

# Three Quick Dashi Broths

DASHI IS AN ESSENTIAL IN THE JAPANESE KITCHEN. IT IS USED LIKE CHICKEN broth or other stocks, as a flavored liquid for simmering vegetables or as a base for soups. It should be used immediately after you make it, since the flavorings are at their best then. Each of the following methods of making dashi is quick and easy and produces four cups of broth, with a distinctive color and flavor. Take your pick. (Note: You can also make "instant dashi" by starting with Instant Dashi Powder, available at Japanese and Korean groceries.) Use as directed in individual recipes.

All three recipes call for kombu. Kombu is a form of seaweed—kelp (*Laminaria longi-cruris*) that has been dried. It is very lightweight and is usually sold in cellophane packages, some from Japan, others from Maine. It often has a grayish coating from crystallized salt. Many of the Japanese and Korean brands of kombu have been rinsed and laid out flat, so they are fairly regular rectangular sheets, about six inches long and three to four inches wide. One of these sheets is sufficient for any of the quick dashi recipes.

Our favorite kombu is from Maine and sold mostly in natural foods stores under the label Maine Coast Sea Vegetables. It comes in wrinkled pieces, so size is a little difficult to estimate. If you are concerned about measuring size, just rinse quickly under cold water. The kombu will soften and you will be able to see how large the sheet is. Measurement is not that critical anyhow, since it will merely affect the intensity of what is anyway a subtle flavoring. And different packages of kombu will have slightly different flavorings, so the precise taste of your dashi will vary slightly from batch to batch.

Once you've used kombu to make dashi broth, it will be smooth and soft and flattened. You can discard it (it makes great compost), but why waste all that flavor? If you want to store it, whether to reuse for dashi or to make Black Kombu Relish (page 186), rinse it off with cold water and store in the refrigerator, in a plastic bag. To reuse to make another batch of vegetarian dashi: Score the kombu with a knife. Bring 2 cups water to a boil in a small pan, add the kombu, and simmer gently for 10 minutes.

# Classic Dashi Broth

**Makes about 4 cups broth**

THIS IS OUR FAVORITE ALL-PURPOSE JAPANESE BROTH. IT HAS A WONDERFUL light smoky taste (from the bonito flakes) and a pretty golden amber color. It is best used immediately but can be stored for up to twenty-four hours, no more, in a well-sealed container in the refrigerator.

One 6- by 4-inch piece kombu, lightly rinsed or wiped with a damp cloth

4 cups water
¼ to ⅓ cup bonito flakes (see Glossary)

Place the kombu in a pot with the water. If there's time, let soak for 15 minutes. Bring to a boil, but just before the water boils, remove the kombu. When the water boils, toss in the bonito flakes and remove from the heat. Stir briefly, then let stand until flakes have sunk to the bottom of the pot. Pour through a strainer lined with a tea towel or cheesecloth and discard the bonito flakes.

# Quick Vegetarian Dashi Broth

**Makes about 4 cups broth**

THIS IS THE SIMPLEST BROTH OF ALL. IT IS DELICATELY FLAVORED WITH KOMBU and has a dark amber color (darker than the classic dashi) and a pleasing taste. We like it for its simplicity and mildness; when we need a stock for cooking subtly flavored ingredients, this will not overpower.

One 6- by 4-inch piece kombu, lightly rinsed or wiped with a damp cloth
4 cups water

Place the kombu in a medium pot with the water. If you have the time, let soak for 15 minutes. Bring to a boil and immediately remove the kombu.

# Quick Mushroom Dashi Broth

**Makes about 4 cups broth**

THE DISTINCTIVE AROMATIC TASTE OF SHIITAKES IN THIS VEGETARIAN BROTH makes it a good choice for winter dishes or for combining with other strong-tasting ingredients. Like classic dashi, it makes a rich-tasting base for miso soup. If you prefer a lighter flavor, use three mushrooms; if you want more intensity, use five. The broth is a clear brown tea color.

One 6- by 4-inch piece kombu, lightly rinsed or wiped with a damp cloth

3 to 5 dried shiitake mushrooms, wiped clean

4 cups water

Place the kombu and shiitakes in a medium pot, add the water, and let soak for 10 minutes. Heat the water to a boil, but just before the water boils, remove the kombu. Remove from the heat. Let the mushrooms stand for another 15 minutes in the broth, then remove and reserve for another use. Strain the broth through a sieve lined with a tea towel or cheese-cloth.

Evening offerings at a small restaurant near the Fushimi Inari Shrine in Kyoto

# Yasuko

"I worked on the thirty-sixth floor and wore high heels. The things that earned me the most money were the most foolish." Yasuko paused, then went on, "I used to think that women needed to be independent and that independence meant going out and working to gain economic independence. But then I came to realize that it was another form of dependence, dependence on the system. . . . The best way is to work with your hands to support yourself."

Yasuko and her husband, Hiroshi Kanda, live in a small village in the Miyama ("beautiful mountain") Valley. Their house is a traditional Japanese farmhouse built of wood. It has solar-heated water for the bath and washing and a back-up gas water heater in the kitchen. Waste water drains into the garden. Inside the house, rooms are separated by sliding wood or paper doors and floors are covered with tatami mats. Shoes are left outside or in the cold stone-flagged hall, a hall that cuts through the house and is used for storing rice, sweet potatoes, dried beans, etc. The rest of the house is a steep eighteen-inch step up from the hall, and hence much warmer.

I stayed with the Kandas one October, hoping to learn something about traditional country foods. Through the sliding wood doors of the room I slept in (on a thin futon rolled out on the tatami-lined floor) was a view of the mountains that rim the valley. I could step through the doors onto a wide wooden ledge sheltered by an overhanging roof, a kind of simple porch. At night or when the weather is bad, shutters are slid into place to protect the porch and keep its contents dry. Daybreak and dusk are signaled every day by the sound of wooden shutters sliding open or closed in all the village houses. Here on the porch in late October were spread azuki beans, in their pale pods, drying. A few of the dark red beans had spilled out from split pods and lay richly colored against the aged-wood floor boards.

The hall of the house is lined with huge brown paper bags of rice, most still in the husk, some brown, and some half-milled or white, all grown by Kanda and Yasuko in their half acre of rice field across the valley. In 1994 they produced fifteen hundred pounds of rice. They allow about nine hundred pounds of rice per year for their family of two adults and two small children, plus Kanda's mother in Kyoto and occasional guests that come to visit. They sell the balance (and premium organic sun-dried rice like theirs sells for a good price).

Nowadays in Miyama the rice is planted in May and harvested in October. The cut rice sheaves are then hung to dry on wooden racks in the fields. Most rice grown in Japan is machine-dried, but Kanda prefers to let it dry in the sun and open air the traditional way, even though the process can be unpredictable because of weather. "It tastes better," he says. After drying, the rice is threshed in the field with a portable thresher, which produces rice (still in the husk) and straw. Some of the straw is left in the field; the rest is used for garden mulch. The rice is bagged, then some is taken home and some taken to the mill to be husked and milled.

Although it is now only three to four hours by road from Kyoto, the Miyama Valley still feels very isolated. It used to be cut off by snowstorms in winter, and the steep mountains meant that travel to Kyoto was rare and difficult until the arrival of modern transportation. Until twenty or thirty years ago, the men of the valley worked high in the mountains cutting timber. A manganese mine also employed many of the men until it closed in 1983. The women planted and tended the rice paddies and the extensive vegetable garden each family depended on. "Now there are no more trees," I was told, certainly none for forestry, so the men have no work except in several small factories in the valley. The women still work in the fields. But the younger generation, women in their twenties and thirties, don't want to do the backbreaking farm labor their mothers and mothers-in-law still take for granted. They'd rather work in a small factory or travel out of the valley to a desk or service job in the next town. The older generation of women worries about what the valley will be like in twenty years.

*Mochi displayed on a tray*

**opposite**

*Yasuko's neighbor working in her vegetable garden*

Kanda and Yasuko left office jobs in Tokyo to find independence in self-sufficiency. When they moved to Miyama, the older women were pleased to have a young family move in that wished to continue working the old way. But the Kanda family is not traditional: Kanda, not Yasuko, does the rice growing. When I asked him how he'd learned, he said he had relied on the advice and experience of the older women. Similarly, to cultivate the large garden that supplies almost all the family's needs, Yasuko needed to learn from her neighbors, and they were ready with advice about everything from pest management to the best day for planting.

Her garden is a marvel of diversity. On a south-facing slope around the house there is everything from tea bushes and *sansho* (Japanese pepper) to ginger (dug up every fall before the first frost), cabbages, kale, eggplants, persimmons, and more. In late October, Yasuko was setting out strawberry plants. Several loofah squashes were soaking in a wooden barrel. Nearby, a neighbor was harvesting persimmons, one by one, using a long forked pole to pull them carefully down. Like the neighbor, Yasuko wears traditional countrywoman's clothing: a cotton head covering something like a minimal pinned-back wimple, a blue cotton smock, loose cotton pants, and farmer's shoes, rubber-bottomed, cotton-topped slippers that fasten up the leg and have the big toe separate from the rest. The slippers are worn with wooden clogs and keep her feet dry and warm. She carries her baby on her back.

# Mariko's Must-Have Concentrated Stock

**Makes approximately 4½ cups stock**

THOUGH MOST HOUSEHOLDS IN JAPAN SEEM TO USE QUICK DASHI BROTHS (see page 179) or instant dashi powder, our friend Mariko Doi uses this traditional recipe that she learned from her grandmother in Kobe. It has become a kitchen mainstay for us. It is dense and full of flavor, not at all fishy despite the dried fish that go into it.

Unlike quick dashi or regular meat- or chicken-based stocks, it keeps for three months in the refrigerator. We've now discovered the joy of having a richly flavored, almost nonperishable stock always on hand. To make dashi (broth) from it, we just take a small amount of the concentrate and add four times as much water. If we need a very subtle broth for a mild-tasting dish, we may taste and then dilute the concentrate even more. The concentrate can also be used with little or no dilution as a dipping sauce.

If you are using it diluted as dashi in other recipes, remember that it is already seasoned, so you may want to cut back on the soy sauce and salt called for.

Two 6- by 4-inch pieces kombu (see page 179), lightly rinsed or wiped clean with a damp cloth

12 dried shiitake mushrooms, wiped clean

1½ cups small dried sardines (see Note)

3 cups soy sauce

1 cup mirin

1 cup sake

Combine all the ingredients in a bowl, cover, and let stand at room temperature overnight. Transfer to a heavy pot and bring to a boil over high heat. Let boil for 1 minute, then reduce the heat to low and simmer for 3 minutes. Strain, setting the solids aside for another use if desired (see Second pressing below and Crumbled Grilled Fish, page 185). Rinse a glass jar thoroughly with very hot water. Cool the liquid, then refrigerate in the glass jar, well sealed. This *noshuka* ("strong") dashi will keep in the refrigerator for 2 to 3 months. (We've kept it as long as 5 months.)

To use the concentrate for dashi, dilute with water in a ratio of 4 parts water to 1 part concentrate. Bring to a boil and boil briefly, then lower the heat and simmer for a few minutes before serving.

**Note:** Dried sardines are available in cellophane packages in Japanese and Korean grocery stores. Ask for *niboshi*.

**Alternatives:** The concentrated stock has many other uses: You can serve it as a dipping sauce, perhaps slightly diluted with water, with shredded ginger or scallions mixed in; it makes a great dip for fresh soba noodles or for udon. You can also use it diluted with 1 to 2 parts water per 1 part concentrate, as a stock when stir-frying and simmering Chinese greens in a wok; the dish will need little or no other seasoning.

**Second pressing:** You can make a quick dashi from a second pressing, using the solids set aside after draining the *noshuka* dashi: Soak the kombu in 2 cups water in a small saucepan for 30 minutes. Add the other solids and bring to a boil. Remove the kombu and continue to boil for about 10 minutes, then strain. This broth must be used within 24 hours.

# Three Condiments for Rice

JAPANESE GROCERY STORES STOCK A WONDERFUL ARRAY OF SIMPLE, INTENSELY flavored condiments for rice. *Aonori,* for example, is small flakes of toasted seaweed (nori). There are also dried fish flakes and sticky rich-flavored relish-like pastes as well as toasted sesame seeds. Many of these condiments originated as a practical way of recycling leftovers. They keep well, but that's rarely a problem, as they tend to get eaten quickly.

# Crumbled Grilled Fish

LEFTOVER DRIED SARDINES CAN BE GRILLED AND THEN USED WHOLE OR coarsely chopped as a tasty, calcium-rich condiment for rice. They need to be dried out so they keep well and lightly browned under the broiler.

> **Leftover dried sardines (*niboshi*) from making Mariko's Must-Have Concentrated Stock (page 184), coarsely chopped**

Preheat the broiler. Place the fish on the broiler pan or in a broiler-proof skillet and broil about 6 inches from the broiler element until dried out and beginning to brown, about 5 minutes; turn once after 2 minutes. Watch carefully to prevent burning.

Let cool, then store in a clean dry glass jar with a tight-fitting lid.

To serve, finely chop, and serve in a small shallow bowl as a condiment to be sprinkled on rice or vegetables.

# Black Kombu Relish

LEFTOVER KOMBU CAN BE RINSED AND SAVED IN THE REFRIGERATOR TO MAKE this thick, good-tasting relish, or you may have just used some kombu, but need more to make this recipe. If so, just drop the number of fresh sheets you need into boiling water for twenty seconds, then remove. This is delicious as a condiment for rice.

4 to 6 sheets moist, previously simmered kombu

2 cups water

2 tablespoons rice vinegar

3 tablespoons soy sauce

2 tablespoons sugar

1 tablespoon dry-roasted sesame seeds (see page 187)

Rinse the kombu and squeeze out the excess water. Pull the kombu into a mound and finely chop. You will have about 1 cup kombu shreds.

Place the water and vinegar in a small heavy nonreactive saucepan and bring to a boil. Add the chopped kombu and simmer over low heat for 1 hour, stirring occasionally to prevent burning or sticking. Most of the liquid should have evaporated. Stir in the soy sauce and sugar and cook until the liquid is reduced to several tablespoons, 10 to 15 minutes. Stir in the sesame seeds and store in a glass jar, well sealed.

Note: To double the recipe, increase the water and seasonings by half and double the quantity of kombu and sesame seeds.

# Sesame Sea Salt

*gomasio*

**Makes about ⅓ cup seasoned salt (enough for several meals)**

THE CLASSIC JAPANESE FLAVORING *GOMASIO* IS A VERY USEFUL CONDIMENT. It's a blend of lightly toasted sesame seeds and sea salt, ground together in a Japanese mortar called a *suribashi*, or just mixed in a bowl. This all-around great condiment can be made with black or white sesame seeds (the white seeds have a slightly milder flavor). Proportions vary, from two parts sesame seeds to one part salt to as much as five parts sesame seeds to one part salt. Experiment to find what pleases you.

Make sure your seeds are fresh. Because they are high in oil, sesame seeds should be stored in the refrigerator to prevent them from turning rancid. If you're not sure about their freshness, put them out for the birds and buy a new batch.

Gomasio is wonderful for sprinkling over grilled or fresh vegetables, plain rice, or anything you please. It is best when made fresh (the sesame seeds have such a wonderful freshly roasted taste), but it can be kept stored in a well-sealed glass jar for several weeks.

**⅓ cup black or white sesame seeds**
**2 tablespoons coarse or fine sea salt**

Dry-roast the sesame seeds in a heavy medium skillet over medium-high heat, stirring constantly, until they begin to jump and pop in the heat and to give off a toasted aroma, 3 to 5 minutes. Add the salt and cook and stir for another 30 seconds, then remove from the heat. Transfer to a bowl and let cool completely. Store in a tightly sealed glass jar.

Serve whole or slightly ground. To grind, place in a *suribachi* (a Japanese mortar), and grind until broken but not completely pulverized. *Alternatively,* place in a clean spice mill or coffee grinder and grind very briefly (you don't want a paste). Serve in a small condiment bowl.

# Koji and Miso

The day I arrived at the farm in Miyama, Yasuko walked with me down to a neighbor's house to watch the *koji* making. *Koji* is the fermented-rice culture that is added to rice mash to make sake and mirin, to cooked soybeans and grain to make miso, to soaked soybeans to make *natto*, to leftover rice and water to make *amazake*. . . . It's indispensable in traditional farm communities, though now rarely used in the cities, where manufactured and preserved foods are commercially available. Traditional *koji* making is a trade and a skill passed down in families from generation to generation. The last artisanal *koji* makers in the northern part of Kyoto prefecture are Mr. and Mrs. Hirai, neighbors of the Kandas. Their grown sons and daughters don't want the work, so they may be the last of a long line. *Koji* making is a strenuous fall and winter activity that begins after the rice harvest and brings the family income during the winter months.

To make *koji*, the Hirais use highly polished rice (they say that rice bran interferes with *koji* development and can give it an off taste). After washing, the rice is soaked in water for twenty-four hours and is then drained and steamed. The cooked rice is spread on straw mats in a well-insulated cellar-like room called a *muro*—which translates as "a warm room for *koji*."

When the rice has cooled to body temperature, *koji* mold (soft green powdery *aspergillus* spores that the Hirais buy from a store in Kyoto) is stirred in. The inoculated rice stands overnight and is then put into wooden boxes, *koji buta*. The boxes are stacked in the muro. The rice ferments for two nights and days, with the Hirais moving the heavy boxes around in the *muro* to assure an even temperature. Then it is ready to be stored in a cool place until it's sold.

Miso is a paste made by adding *koji* to soybeans or grain that has been cooked and mashed, together with salt and water. The mixture ferments for as little as two weeks or as long as two years, depending on the ingredients and the maker. In rural communities, traditionally each household made its own miso, and Yasuko maintains the tradition.

*Koji* can be made from rice, barley, or soybeans; different *koji* (and different basic ingredients) result in different misos. There

are a number of misos available in North America, some imported from Japan and some domestic. Some are relatively mild and a little sweet, good for dressings and light flavorings; others are stronger and darker and go well with strong tasting vegetables or as a flavoring in winter soups. The

lighter-colored misos, which are sweeter, are originally from Kyoto and farther south; the darker ones are from Tokyo and the northeast of Japan, and they are saltier and stronger tasting.

Miso can be bought in small plastic packages or in bulk from health food stores. Those made by the most traditional method are generally the most expensive. Once opened, miso should be stored in the refrigerator or a cool pantry.

Miso is an essential ingredient in the Japanese kitchen. It is used as a flavoring, not just for soups but also in cooked dishes (see Grilled Eggplant with Miso, page 195) and to make pickles. See the Glossary for a list of miso pastes.

# Quick Morning Miso Soup

SOUPS IN JAPAN ARE EITHER CLEAR BROTHS, MOST OFTEN MADE FROM DASHI broth or chicken stock, or miso soups, broths flavored with a little miso paste. Miso soup is a traditional breakfast dish, quick to prepare and warming, though it may appear at any meal.

If you want a quick soup to accompany a rice meal, this is it. Yasuko made it for breakfast to accompany hot rice, pickles, and reheated leftovers from the previous night's meal. Use red or light brown miso (*hatcho miso* would be too strong and *shiro miso* too sweet for most people's tastes). The usual proportion is a scant tablespoon of miso for every cup of liquid. It is important to remember that the miso paste should never be boiled, just dissolved in the hot broth at the last minute.

4 cups water or any mild dashi broth (see page 179)

2 squares fresh tofu, cut into ½-inch cubes (optional)

3 to 4 tablespoons red or brown miso paste (see Glossary)

About ¼ cup fresh mitsuba (see Glossary) or flat-leaf parsley, coarsely chopped, or 1 scallion, minced

Bring the water or dashi broth to a boil in a medium pot. Add the optional tofu cubes and lower the heat to a simmer. Use a ladle or large measuring cup to scoop out about 1 cup of the hot liquid. Dissolve 3 tablespoons miso in it, then return it to the pot. Taste and add a little more miso if you wish, again dissolving it in a small quantity of broth. Bring the soup to just under a boil and remove from the heat.

Divide the fresh greens among four small bowls, then pour the broth (and tofu cubes) over them and serve to accompany rice.

**Alternative:** To make a fuller-flavored and even more nutritious version of this simple soup, begin by boiling ½ pound each sliced carrots, and sliced daikon, in 5 cups water for about 15 minutes. Strain the broth and discard the vegetables (or use for another purpose). Use 4 cups warm broth in place of water as directed above.

# Cucumber and Wakame Salad

LONG AGO A FRIEND OF MY MOTHER'S SHOWED HER HOW TO DRAW THE bitterness out of a cucumber: Cut off about an inch of the stem end, rub the cut surfaces together until they foam, then rinse off the foam. Only recently have we learned that this practice, called *aku nuki*, or "removal of bitterness," is a Japanese technique. We still don't know why it works.

The fresh crunch of cucumber is a good contrast to the softness of wakame, and its pale green color sets off wakame's dark green. Serve this salad with any rice-based meal.

1 cup salted wakame (see Note)

1 Japanese cucumber or ½ medium
  European cucumber

1 teaspoon sea salt

**Dressing**

2 tablespoons soy sauce

1 tablespoon rice vinegar

1 teaspoon sake

1 teaspoon water

1 tablespoon sugar

Pinch of sea salt

Place the wakame in a medium bowl with cold water to cover for 30 minutes, then drain and rinse.

Bring 2 to 3 cups water to a boil in a small pot. Add the wakame, stir, and bring back to a boil, then drain thoroughly and squeeze dry.

Meanwhile, wash off the cucumber. Cut off about 1 inch of the stem end and rub the cut surfaces together until they foam a little. Rinse off. Score the cucumber lengthwise with a fork. Cut it lengthwise into quarters, then cut out and discard seeds. Cut into 1-inch lengths and then into thick julienne. You should have about 1½ cups cucumber. Place the cucumber strips in a sieve, sprinkle the salt over, and let drain for 30 minutes.

Rinse the cucumber thoroughly with cold water and squeeze dry. (The wakame and cucumber can be prepared ahead to this point and placed in separate sealed containers in the refrigerator until ready to proceed.)

Chop the wakame into short lengths (1 inch or less), discarding any tough pieces. Place the wakame and cucumber in a bowl. Mix together all the dressing ingredients in a small bowl, stirring until the sugar is dissolved, then pour over the salad. Toss gently to coat. Mound on a plate or in a shallow bowl. Serve at room temperature (or chilled in summer).

**Note:** Salted wakame is available in Japanese and Korean groceries and in well-stocked natural foods shops. See Glossary.

# Salad of Grilled Mushrooms and Fried Tofu

Serves 4

Frying tofu in Arashiyama

THIS WONDERFUL AUTUMN SALAD WAS MY FAVORITE of all the dishes taught at a cooking class I attended in Kyoto. The class was given by an older woman named Mrs. Marayama, a much-respected teacher with a passion for traditional seasonal ingredients. The class was hands-on, so we divided into groups to prepare the dishes. My very easy job for this salad was to place the mushrooms and pieces of tofu over the gas flame, then use long cooking chopsticks to turn them and ensure even grilling. Others then cut them into long slivers, mixed the dressing, and tossed the salad. It was all very straightforward, and delicious.

½ pound shiitake (6 to 8) or portobello (2 large or 3 medium) mushrooms, stems trimmed

2 small rectangles (2 inches by 5 inches) Japanese fried tofu (*abura-age,* see Glossary)

**Dressing**

1 tablespoon soy sauce

1 teaspoon rice vinegar or fresh lemon or lime juice

1 teaspoon sake

¼ teaspoon sugar

Red pepper powder (*togarashi,* see Glossary) (optional)

Grill the mushrooms and tofu squares directly over a gas flame or a grill, turning them with tongs or long chopsticks to ensure that they are golden on all sides. *Alternatively,* place on one or two small baking sheets under the broiler and broil until the mushrooms are tender and the fried tofu is touched with brown.

Slice the mushrooms into narrow strips, discarding any tough sections. Cut the tofu into strips the same length as the mushroom strips. Place in a shallow serving bowl.

In a small nonreactive saucepan, heat the soy sauce, vinegar, and sake. When they are warm, stir in the sugar until dissolved. Let cool slightly, then pour over the mushrooms and tofu and stir gently to coat. Sprinkle lightly with red pepper powder if you wish.

# Intensely Green Spinach with Sesame Seeds

FOOD TRADITIONS IN JAPAN ARE VERY REGIONALLY BASED, A SURPRISE TO MOST outsiders, who think of Japan as a small country. There are variations from north to south because of differences of climate and season. And because until recently the steep mountainous country in the interior made transportation difficult inland, there are very different coastal and inland food traditions. As we were talking about Kyoto food one day, our friend Mariko reminded us that although Kyoto is now only one hour from Osaka and the sea, it has the culinary traditions of a fertile landlocked valley. "Kyoto people eat lots of root vegetables and greens, especially in winter, maybe because they have less access to seafood. They need the fiber and the vitamins and minerals."

This is a classic home-style Japanese vegetable dish, quick, beautiful, and good at any time of year. The spinach is boiled briefly, then lightly dressed with soy and mirin and topped with toasted sesame seeds or gomasio.

½ pound spinach

1 tablespoon soy sauce

1 tablespoon mirin

1 tablespoon dry-roasted sesame seeds (see page 187), coarsely ground (see Note)

1½ teaspoons sea salt

Wash the spinach well in several changes of cold water until all the grit is removed. Trim off the tough stem ends. Place in a large pot and add about 6 inches water. Bring to a boil and cook, covered, for 4 to 5 minutes, until tender. Drain well and rinse the spinach in cold water.

Squeeze out all the water from the spinach, then chop thoroughly and place in a medium bowl. In a small bowl, mix together the soy sauce and mirin. Pour over the spinach and mix well. Sprinkle on the sesame seeds and salt and toss to distribute. Serve on one plate or shaped into a small mound on individual plates.

Note: You can briefly grind the sesame seeds and salt together in a Japanese mortar (*suribachi*) or other mortar or spice grinder to make gomasio if you prefer. Other green vegetables such as broccoli or collards or bitter greens can also be boiled in plenty of salted water, drained, rinsed, and then squeezed out, chopped, and dressed with the same flavorings. Serve warm or at room temperature.

# Winter Stir-fry with Root Vegetables
*kinpira gobo*

Serves 4 to 6

"*Gobo*," said the produce vendor in Kyoto's Nishiki Market when I asked the name of the long thin beige-white roots stacked in front of her. She seemed surprised that I didn't know. So I bought some and took them back to my friend's house, and of course she knew it well.

*Gobo* is a great fall and winter vegetable. It's called burdock in English, and it's available in health food stores that carry produce as well as in Japanese and Korean shops. Traditionally this country dish was made of burdock, or burdock and carrots, together with thinly cut fried tofu (*abura-age* or *age-dofu*), all sprinkled lightly with sesame seeds. Nowadays many Japanese substitute beef for the tofu, cut into slivers just like the winter vegetables it's cooked with. Instructions for both the beef and the meatless versions are set out here.

¼ pound boneless sirloin steak or other lean beef or 2 small rectangles Japanese fried tofu (*abura-age*, see Glossary)

⅔ pound burdock or carrots, or a combination

1 tablespoon vinegar or fresh lemon or lime juice (if using burdock)

1 tablespoon roasted sesame oil (2 tablespoons if using tofu)

2 tablespoons soy sauce

2 tablespoons mirin

¼ teaspoon red pepper powder (*togarashi*, see Glossary) (optional)

½ teaspoon dry-roasted sesame seeds (see page 187) (optional)

*If using meat,* thinly slice it across the grain, then cut the slices lengthwise in half to make narrow strips. *If using tofu,* cut it into very thin strips. Cut the burdock and/or carrots lengthwise into narrow strips. (We find it easiest to cut them into 4-inch lengths first and then cut into very skinny julienne.) Immediately place the burdock in about 2 cups water with the vinegar or lime or lemon juice and let stand for 10 minutes, to prevent discoloration.

Heat a large heavy skillet or a wok over medium-high heat. Add the sesame oil, allow to heat for 20 seconds, and then add the vegetable strips and stir-fry for 2 minutes (1 minute if using only carrots). Add the meat and stir-fry for 1 minute, then lower the heat to medium, cover, and let cook for 3 minutes longer, or until the vegetables are tender. *Alternatively,* if using fried tofu, cook the vegetables for 5 minutes, add the tofu, and cook 1 minute more.

In a small bowl, mix together the soy sauce and mirin. Pour over the stir-fry, stir to coat, and let simmer for less than a minute, then turn out onto a plate and mound. Sprinkle over the red pepper and/or sesame seeds if you wish. Serve warm or at room temperature.

# Grilled Eggplant with Miso

ONE MORNING IN MIYAMA, I CAME INTO THE KITCHEN TO SEE YASUKO SLICING eggplant. She grilled the slices over a gas burner, then laid them on a plate while she made a topping of miso flavored with mirin and sake and enriched with a beaten egg. The whole dish took less than ten minutes to prepare, interspersed with other tasks, and made a satisfying savory accompaniment to our breakfast rice.

Like many Japanese country dishes, these grilled eggplant slices are strong-tasting, not meant to be eaten on their own but rather to accompany cooked white rice. Rice and pickles balance and neutralize the somewhat salt-and-sweet taste of the miso-based topping: Take a slice of eggplant to your plate with your chopsticks, eat it together with some rice, chase with a sliver of pickle, and wash down with tea.

1½ pounds Japanese or Chinese eggplant, cut into ¼-inch-thick diagonal slices

¼ cup mirin

2 tablespoons sake

1 large egg, well whisked

½ cup light miso (pale yellow *shiro miso* Kyoto style if possible, see Glossary)

Grill the eggplant slices over a gas or charcoal grill until golden brown on both sides, about 10 minutes. *Alternatively,* place on a baking sheet under a broiler and broil until browned, turning the slices once halfway through the cooking time, about 10 minutes in all.

Meanwhile, place the mirin and sake in a small nonreactive saucepan and heat to boiling. Lower the heat to medium, stir in the miso and whisked egg, and remove from the heat. Continue stirring until smooth; the texture will be that of a slightly liquid paste.

Place the eggplant slices on a plate and spread the paste on top of each slice, covering it completely. Serve as part of a meal, with rice, pickles, and tea.

Note: Any leftover topping can be transferred to a glass or other nonreactive container and stored, covered, in the refrigerator for up to 2 days. Rewarm gently before using.

# Winter Warmth

In wintertime, the center of the Kanda house (and most other houses in the country) is the *kotaze*, a low table with a futon draped over it. Under the table is a small charcoal heater that keeps one's feet warm. With the futon to hold the heat in, it also makes a warm "cupboard" where yogurt, miso, and *amazake* (fermented rice gruel) can slowly ferment. The *kotaze* is in the living and dining area, just beside the kitchen. Doors lead from it to the bedrooms, but in winter they're kept closed so that no heat will escape. The bedrooms are unheated, and in winter, getting up in the morning from a snug night under a heavy comforter in an icy-cold bedroom takes a certain amount of willpower.

Yasuko says it's part of the choices they've made. Living with the seasons in all their glory—and all their discomfort—is the Kandas' way of staying connected. It's part of the bargain they have struck in deciding on a farm life, to work hard and enjoy the fruits of their labors.

**left to right**

A garden of rocks and raked sand at the
Ryoanji Temple in Kyoto

Millet drying outside a farm house
in the Miyama Valley

# Kyoto Grilled Peppers

YET ANOTHER EXAMPLE OF THE JAPANESE LIGHT DEFT HAND WITH VEGETABLES, these peppers are quick to make and wonderfully complex in flavor. I first ate them in the mountains of Japan, where they were quickly cooked over a gas flame. They've become a classic fallback in our house, one of the simplest vegetable dishes we know. Traditionally a special found-only-in-Kyoto pepper called *shishito* is used. S-shaped and green, most *shishito* are mild, but occasionally, and unexpectedly, you may come on a hotter one. We substitute hot or mild banana chiles or Hungarian wax chiles; if we're using mild chiles, we usually add one hotter chile to give the dish a little heat.

4 to 5 mild or hot banana peppers or Hungarian wax peppers or 4 mild chiles plus 1 hotter long green chile or 1 or 2 jalapeño chiles

1 to 2 tablespoons soy sauce (to taste)

Approximately 1 tablespoon (3 generous pinches) bonito flakes (see Glossary)

Grill the peppers on a charcoal or gas grill or over a gas flame, turning frequently, until well blackened and soft all over. *Alternatively,* heat a cast-iron skillet over medium-high heat and when hot, dry-roast the peppers, pressing them down onto the hot surface and turning them to blacken on all sides and soften.

Let cool slightly, then cut off the stem ends and discard. Remove and discard the seeds and coarse membranes. Coarsely chop the peppers and place on a serving plate. Pour over the soy sauce, then sprinkle the bonito flakes over. Serve warm or at room temperature.

The Japanese Way    197

# Cooling Summer Tofu

**Serves 6**

SILKY JAPANESE TOFU IS FINER-TEXTURED THAN STANDARD CHINESE-STYLE tofu, enjoyed for its texture, smooth and slippery, and its adaptability. It is available packaged in grocery stores as well as in Japanese and Korean groceries. In summer it's often served chilled, simply dressed with lime juice and soy sauce and topped with finely chopped chives or scallions, as in this recipe. In winter it is served in a bowl of warm water, not meant for drinking but just for warming the tofu, with a strongly flavored dipping sauce.

The long tradition of vegetarianism in the Buddhist temples of Japan has produced a wide-ranging vegetarian cuisine. Tofu plays a large role, as it did in earlier, less prosperous times for many Japanese. In winter it can be frozen and then dried, a technique many attribute to Buddhist monks living in the mountains. Freeze-dried tofu is entirely different in texture and taste from fresh. It absorbs flavors beautifully and makes a great addition to winter stews. If you have too much fresh tofu (it only keeps for a few days), cut it into half-inch cubes and freeze them. (See Frozen Tofu with Winter Vegetables, page 92, for detailed instructions.)

But back to summer. This dish is very quick to make. Just make sure that the tofu is well chilled. For a really refreshing-looking presentation, serve it on a plate placed on a bed of shaved ice.

3 squares fresh silky (Japanese-style) tofu

1 teaspoon fresh lime juice (or substitute rice vinegar), or more to taste

2 teaspoons soy sauce

2 teaspoons minced scallion (tender green parts) or chives

¼ teaspoon seven-spice powder (*shchimi togarashi,* see Glossary)

Cut the tofu into ½-inch cubes. If you have the time, refrigerate, covered, for 15 minutes. Drain off any water that has accumulated before proceeding with the recipe.

Transfer the tofu to a flat plate and mound attractively.

In a small bowl, mix together the lime juice (or vinegar) and soy sauce, then pour over the tofu. Taste; we often increase the lime juice to 2 teaspoons to give it a little more tang, but if using vinegar, be restrained. Sprinkle on the minced greens and dust with the spice powder. Serve immediately.

# Mariko's Lotus Root Sandwiches
## hasamiage (tempura)

Makes about 16 sandwiches, plus 4 to 6 green bean bundles; serves 4 to 6

ONE SATURDAY IN KYOTO, MARIKO TAUGHT ME A TEMPURA DISH THAT'S A favorite with her kids. It uses lotus root, a rhizome sold in "links" like sausages, either covered with mud or cleaned so it's white in color and wrapped in plastic wrap. It makes a lacy cross section when sliced. Here the slices are used to make "sandwiches" around a thin layer of flavorful ground pork. The sandwiches are dipped in batter, then deep-fried. During deep-frying, the pork cooks quickly and the lotus root softens slightly but still keeps a definite crunch.

Though deep-frying can seem daunting, the dish is actually easy to prepare, especially if you have a large wok. It's important, whenever you make this or any other tempura, to prepare the rest of the meal ahead, so that the tempura can come hot to the table. Serve the sandwiches with plain rice, soup, and a simple soft-textured vegetable dish, such as Intensely Green Spinach with Sesame Seeds (page 193).

¼ pound ground pork

1 tablespoon soy sauce

1 teaspoon mirin

1 tablespoon finely minced scallion

½ teaspoon cornstarch

1 medium or 2 small fresh lotus roots
(½ pound)

Peanut oil for deep-frying

**Tempura batter**

1 large egg

2 ice cubes

¼ to ½ cup cold water

1½ cups sifted all-purpose flour

About 20 green beans, topped and tailed,
or 5 long beans, cut into 2½-inch
lengths

**Condiments**

Grated daikon, topped with grated ginger
if you like

½ cup Dipping Sauce for Tempura
(page 201)

In a small bowl, mix together pork, soy sauce, mirin, scallion, and cornstarch; set aside.

Wash the lotus root thoroughly and scrape off the toughest outer layer of skin. Cut off and discard the tough ends. Slice crosswise into ⅛-inch to ¼-inch slices. You should have 30 to 34 slices. Place in pairs.

To assemble the "sandwiches," spread a thin layer of pork on one slice of lotus root, then press another slice down firmly on top. Wipe off any pork that falls out the sides. Set the sandwiches on a plate or tray by your stovetop. Place a paper towel–lined rack nearby.

*continued*

Place 2 inches of oil in a large wok or a large deep pot and heat over high heat. (Make sure the wok or pot is stable: If using a wok, use a collar to stabilize it, or turn over the burner on your gas stove so the wok is held firmly.)

In the meantime, in a small bowl, beat the egg. Add the ice cubes and ¼ cup cold water. Place the flour in another bowl and then add the egg mixture. *Do not mix well*, just give a couple of stirs to produce a lumpy, barely moistened batter. As the ice melts, it will moisten the flour further.

Use a thermometer or ½ teaspoon batter (our preference) to check if the oil has reached 375°F: Drop a bit of batter into the oil. It should sink, then immediately rise. If it burns, the oil is too hot; lower the heat slightly and wait 30 seconds before starting to fry (or before testing another blob of tempura). If it fails to rise right back up, wait a minute longer, then test the temperature again. Lift out the test-tempura with a slotted spoon.

When the temperature is right, begin to cook. Use chopsticks or your fingers to dip a sandwich into the batter, then let it slide into the hot oil. Because the batter is lumpy, the sandwich will probably be a little blobby looking. Wait a moment, then, one at a time, add 2 or 3 or even 4 more sandwiches, if there is room in your wok or pot. The sandwiches can touch, but you don't want them pressing together and sticking to one another. Also, remember that each time you add a sandwich to the oil it lowers the temperature, so wait a moment after you add a sandwich to the oil before adding another. The sandwiches will take 4 to 5 minutes to cook. When done, they will be golden brown. Use a slotted spoon to lift the cooked sandwiches out and place on the paper-lined rack to cool a little and crisp up.

To cook the beans, pick up a bundle of 3 or 4 beans in your fingers, drag it through the batter (the coating of batter will hold the beans together as they cook), and drop into the hot oil. The beans will turn bright green. Remove when the batter is golden brown, about 3 minutes, and place on the rack.

When you have finished cooking the sandwiches and beans, you will have a little batter left. (If there is any dry flour remaining, add a little cold water to moisten it.) Drop small blobs of this batter into the oil to cook. Remove when golden, usually less than 1 minute.

Serve the tempura on a platter or place 3 sandwiches and 1 bean bundle on each guest's plate. Place the tempura bits in a small bowl and pass as a condiment. Pass the dipping sauce so each guest can place a little in his or her sauce bowl. The grated daikon can be used on its own as a condiment; guests can stir some into their dipping sauce, as desired.

**Note:** When you have finished making the tempura, place the oil in a safe place to cool, then strain through a cloth into a glass container and store for reuse.

**Alternative:** Instead of or as well as the green beans, when *shiso* (perilla, see Glossary) is available, make *shiso* tempura: Take 4 to 6 green or red *shiso* leaves and drag each across the batter, trying to coat only the underside of the leaves with batter. Float on the surface of the hot oil after all the sandwiches (and beans) are cooked. They will cook in about a minute, the time it takes the batter to turn golden brown. Serve to accompany the sandwiches.

# Dipping Sauce for Tempura

**Makes about ½ cup sauce**

TEMPURA NEEDS A FORCEFUL DIPPING SAUCE. THE EASIEST OPTION IS TO use Mariko's Must-Have Concentrated Stock if you have it in the refrigerator already, possibly very slightly diluted with water. Otherwise, you can quickly assemble a tasty dipping sauce from basic ingredients. Remember when you taste it that the sauce is meant to be strong, almost overpowering, to match the tempura.

⅓ cup any mild dashi broth (see page 179) or ⅓ cup water plus 2 tablespoons bonito flakes (see Glossary)

2 tablespoons mirin

2 tablespoons soy sauce

OR

½ cup Mariko's Must-Have Concentrated Stock (page 184)

*If using mild dashi,* combine all the ingredients in a saucepan and heat until almost boiling. *If using water and bonito flakes,* heat the water to a boil. Toss in the bonito flakes and remove from the heat. When the flakes have sunk to the bottom, strain and discard flakes. Mix the broth with the mirin and soy sauce.

*If using Mariko's stock,* warm in a saucepan, then taste and dilute with a little water if wanted.

Serve the sauce at room temperature in small individual bowls.

Entrance gate to a small, rural Shinto shrine outside Kyoto

# Pickles

*tsukemono*

In Japan, pickles are a food, not just a garnish or optional condiment. Originally devised as a way of preserving vegetables through the winter (as in Persia, northern India, and northern Europe), they are an essential part of most meals, usually eaten near the end of the meal with rice. In earlier, less prosperous times, rice and pickles were a standard lunch in many rural areas.

Pickles are available in a dazzling array of colors, flavors, and shapes not just in Japan but also in any Japanese or Korean grocery store in North America. They keep well in the refrigerator. To serve, cut them into small pieces and serve on a plate; usually two or three kinds of pickle are served at a meal. They are meant to be eaten only in small quantities, though they are so delicious there's a temptation to eat a great many.

Japanese pickles are made with fresh vegetables that are preserved using rice bran (*nuka*), vinegar (*su*), miso paste, or just salt. Almost any vegetable can be pickled; the crisper and denser the vegetable, the longer it takes to cure. In Kyoto's Nishiki market, the small shops selling pickles are loaded with choices and mystery. Vats of rice bran pickles, the vegetables limp and half-coated with wet beige bran, give no hint (if you've never tasted them) of the delights they hold. In contrast, eggplant pickles are as beautiful as they are delicious, some a rich purple-blue hue, others (when blended with *shiso* leaves) a brilliant burgundy. Daikon (white radish) is part of many mixed pickle combos, but it also stands on its own, in long fat gleaming logs, often tinted a brilliant yellow.

In the end, pickles can be a problem, because choosing is so difficult. It's important to buy only a little of several kinds, thus giving yourself an excuse to return soon for more.

Since many of the store-bought pickles available here in North America contain food coloring and preservatives, you may want to try making a few simple "quick" pickles for yourself. If you've never tasted Japanese pickles, you might start by buying small packages of two or three different kinds and serving them as part of a Japanese-style rice meal. Then try either of the recipes for simple home-style pickles that follow.

# Pickled Ginger
## beni shoga

**Makes about 3 cups ginger**

THAT BEAUTIFUL PILE OF TENDER PINKISH PICKLED GINGER THAT ADORNS THE platter of sushi is a simple treat to make. You can also buy pickled ginger, of course, but home-made is easy. Be sure to start with very fresh (firm and unwrinkled) young ginger. It should have pinkish coloring around the stem end and a thin skin. It's easiest to find in the early fall, at Asian groceries.

If you have no red *shiso* (perilla) leaves, the ginger slices will still turn slightly pink, because of the action of the vinegar. The perilla just intensifies the color beautifully.

| | |
|---|---|
| 1 pound young ginger | ¾ cup sugar |
| 2 tablespoons sea salt | 6 to 10 (or more if you'd like) red *shiso* (perilla, see Glossary) leaves, coarsely torn (optional) |
| 2 cups rice vinegar | |

Peel the ginger (set the skin aside for making tea—see the Note below). Use the Japanese tool called a benriner or a cleaver to slice ginger crosswise very thin; the benriner is ideal, but a sharp cleaver works fine. (Set aside any thick slices or awkward knobs for making tea.)

Place the ginger slices in a bowl and add 1 teaspoon of the salt. Toss with your fingers to blend well, and let stand for 10 minutes. Meanwhile, put a small pot of water on to boil. Rinse off the ginger with the boiling water and drain well.

Place the vinegar, sugar, the remaining 1 tablespoon plus 2 teaspoons salt, and the *shiso*, if using, in a small nonreactive pot and heat, stirring, until the sugar has entirely dissolved. Meanwhile, fill a wide-mouthed 1-quart jar with boiling water, then drain it.

Using tongs, place the ginger in the jar, then pour the hot vinegar mixture over. Cover tightly and let pickle overnight before using. The ginger keeps, well sealed in the refrigerator, for 2 months or more.

**Note on ginger tea:** Ginger tea can be bought in individual sachets, but for better flavor, and a more effective way of chasing colds, make your own. Put the ginger peelings plus any knobby awkward pieces of ginger into a nonreactive pot of boiling water. After 10 minutes at a gentle boil, you will have ginger tea, a wonderful restorative on a cold day, especially when sweetened with a little honey. You can also begin with several slices of fresh ginger, slightly crushed. Drop them into the pot of boiling water and boil gently for 10 minutes. Leftover tea can be stored in a nonreactive container in the refrigerator for several days, to be reheated and sweetened when wanted.

# Mariko's Overnight Pickle

**Makes just over 1½ cups pickles**

THIS QUICK PICKLE IS A LITTLE SALTY, A LITTLE HOT, EASY TO MAKE, AND VERY tasty. It's made with daikon, but you can use a mixture of carrot and seeded cucumber instead.

½ pound daikon, preferably the middle or upper section (see Glossary), peeled and finely chopped (about 1½ cups)

Generous pinch of bonito flakes (see Glossary)

1 small piece kombu (see page 179), briefly rinsed and broken into pieces

2 dried red chiles (see Glossary)

1 teaspoon sea salt

Mix all the ingredients together in a bowl. Place a plate or lid on top of the mixture and weight with a heavy jar or pot. Set aside for 24 hours at room temperature.

To serve, rinse off the amount of pickle you need and squeeze out the excess water, discarding the chiles and kombu. The pickle can be kept for 3 days in the refrigerator. (After the first 24-hour pressing, remove the weighted lid and, if you wish, transfer to a nonreactive container.) Do not rinse off until just before serving.

# Umeboshi

The Japanese pickled plums (actually a kind of apricot) called *umeboshi* are a special kind of pickle, preserved only with salt. *Shiso* leaves (perilla, see Glossary) are used for color and flavor. The fruits are picked in June while they are still green and tart, then salted and pressed for several weeks. The salty, sour brine that comes out of them is poured off and used to soak red *shiso* leaves. Meanwhile the fruits are dried out (traditionally in the sun) and then reimmersed in the brine, which is now tinted dark red by the *shiso* leaves. They soak up the flavor and color of the brine.

There's nothing more mouth-puckering and invigorating than a good pinkish-red *umeboshi* eaten with fresh hot rice for breakfast. Tradition holds that for good health one should eat three *umeboshi* each morning, to get the digestion going (they are believed to stimulate the digestive enzymes). It's a good kick-start to the day. They can also be wrapped in rice balls, either round or triangular, called *onigiri* (see page 206). Sometimes the *onigiri* are then coated lightly in sesame seeds, or wrapped with a little seaweed (nori). Three or four of these rice balls are a good contribution to a lunch box.

*Umeboshi* are available at all Japanese grocery stores and at many health food stores, sold either whole or as *umeboshi* paste. They keep almost indefinitely in a well-sealed nonreactive container in the refrigerator.

# Macrobiotics

Though the macrobiotic movement first developed in Japan, vegetarian and macrobiotic principles are followed there only in temples and in a few rare households. In North America, however, the movement has an important following, hence the availability in many natural foods stores of Japanese or Japanese-style products such as fresh and dried seaweed, soba noodles, brown Japanese-style rice, tamari, and tofu. Macrobiotics divides foods into yin and yang, or expansive and contractive; the goal is to eat a diet that will produce a good balance. No eggs or dairy products or meat are eaten, but seafood—fish as well as sea vegetables—is a major source of essential minerals and vitamins. The diet appears to be very close to the traditional eating pattern of the rural Japanese who live near the sea, where important foods are rice, root vegetables, seafoods, and so on, except that most Japanese prefer white polished rice to the brown rice of macrobiotics.

One of the leaders of the macrobiotic movement in North America is Michio Kushi, whose son Dr. Lawrence Kushi is a nutritional epidemiologist, studying the eating patterns and health and disease patterns of large populations.

We spoke to Dr. Kushi at a conference in San Francisco and asked him what rice his parents eat. The answer was organic Japanese rice, grown in California. They buy it in the husk, then use a husking machine to clean it just before cooking, producing an unpolished brown rice. "Rice in the husk is still a living seed," said Dr. Kushi, so the grain has life in it until just before it is cooked.

**above and left**

Man eating from a *bento* before the start of Kyoto's Jidai Matsuri procession.

Gateway to a Buddhist temple outside Oharano

# Easy Rice Balls
## onigiri

**Makes about 20 rice balls**

*ONIGIRI* MEANS "HANDMADE RICE." THEY ARE SO EASY TO EAT THAT CHILDREN love them, and consequently they are a classic school lunch box staple. They're also featured in the Japanese lacquer box lunches called *bento,* one of the big treats of train travel in Japan. *Onigiri* make great finger food at any time of day and they're an easy way of making an interesting and varied meal out of plain rice. They depend on the wonderful slightly sticky quality of Japanese-style rice, which holds together and can consequently be used as a "wrapper."

*Onigiri* are made quickly by wrapping freshly cooked rice around a small flavor hit such as a bit of puckery *umeboshi* plum, some dried bonito flakes, or a piece of savory stewed mushroom. The possibilities are endless, and you can invent new variations to suit yourself and your pantry. The rice balls are usually assembled while the freshly cooked rice is still warm and are eaten at room temperature, once the rice has had time to firm up.

Below is a list of flavorings and proportions. The first time you make *nigiri* rice you might find it reassuring to follow the list fairly closely. Once you get comfortable with the shaping technique, you will be able to improvise and just use your favorite flavorings.

3 cups just-cooked Japanese rice (white or brown), still warm (see pages 174 and 178), or leftover rice

**Flavorings (choose some or all)**

4 medium or 2 large *umeboshi* (see page 204)

¼ cup Black Kombu Relish (page 186)

About 3 tablespoons bonito flakes or store-bought seaweed paste (see Glossary)

Soy sauce

1½ tablespoons minced pickled daikon or other pickle

About 2 tablespoons white or black sesame seeds, dry-roasted (see page 187) and coarsely ground

1 sheet toasted nori (see Glossary and Note, page 219)

Sea salt

Pickled Ginger (page 203) or store-bought (optional)

Wasabi (Japanese horseradish, see Glossary) (optional)

Prepare the fillings while the rice finishes cooking: Pit the *umeboshi* plums and divide each plum in two if using medium plums or into quarters if using larger plums. Set aside. Divide the relish or paste into 8 equal portions and set aside on a plate.

206 SEDUCTIONS OF RICE

In a small bowl, mix 2 tablespoons bonito flakes with 1 teaspoon soy sauce. Heap the remaining bonito on a small plate. Divide the pickle into 4 equal portions and set aside. Place the sesame seeds on another small plate. Cut the nori into narrow strips or into 2-inch squares. Dip briefly in soy sauce, then set aside.

To shape the rice balls, wet both your palms and sprinkle one lightly with salt (or use salted water to wet your palms). Scoop up about 2 tablespoons rice, place in your salted hand (if using salt), and make a hollow in the center. Fill with an *umeboshi* half or quarter, cover it with the rice, and shape into a ball, a cylinder, a flattened round, or a flattened triangle. Place on a platter. Repeat with remaining *umeboshi*. Wrap a soaked nori strip or square around each of the *umeboshi* balls if you wish. (Moisten the overlapping ends to help the nori stick.)

Schoolchildren eating their rice lunch at a public school in Oharano

Use the same technique to make 8 balls (or cylinders, rounds, or triangles) filled with *kombu* relish. Add to the platter.

Repeat the technique to make 4 bonito balls, filling each with one quarter of the bonito mixture and rolling the finished balls in the remaining bonito flakes. Place on the platter.

Shape 4 balls, filled with the pickle. Roll the pickle *onigiri* in the sesame seeds and place on the platter.

If any rice remains, mix with toasted sesame seeds, whole or ground (¼ teaspoon per ball), and shape into balls or triangles. Wrap a nori strip or square around each sesame *onigiri*.

Arrange all the pieces decoratively on the platter and serve, accompanied by pickled ginger if you wish and a dipping sauce of plain soy sauce or soy sauce flavored with a dash of wasabi.

**Alternatives:** You can also grill *onigiri* lightly, until slightly browned and crisp, then brush the grilled balls with a little soy sauce or a very small amount of brown miso. Grilled *onigiri* can make a simple soup more interesting: Place one ball in each soup bowl, top with minced scallions or a little *mitsuba* (see Glossary) or flat-leaf parsley, and then pour hot broth over.

# Rice Meals and Bread Meals

The children flung themselves on me crying, "We miss Toronto. We want to go back there."
After three years in Toronto, the Doi family had returned to Kyoto. The children, aged seven,
nine, and eleven, had spent several years in Canada attending a lively multicultural downtown
school, and now they found themselves back in the serious, demanding atmosphere of their
local Kyoto school. Every morning they headed off with loaded knapsacks, and every evening
they returned with one to three hours of homework. No wonder there was homework: They
were learning Japanese characters, the two Japanese alphabets, and Roman script, as well as the
usual math, history, and geography, among other
subjects.

Yet there was still time for fun, for watching a little
television, for teaching my bumbling fingers some basic
paper folding, for dropping in on their grandparents
nearby for tea and a treat. On Saturday mornings there is

*Saying a prayer of thanks after lunch
in the classroom*

**opposite**

Woman stirring flavoring
into sushi rice

school, but Sundays are free, so there was time to take me for a hike up Daimanji Mountain to look down on the temple-studded low-rise density of Kyoto, snug in its hill-rimmed valley.

Part of the children's daily load in their knapsacks are appropriate eating implements and cloth napkins for lunch. Lunch is provided at school, and at the beginning of every month a list of what will be served is handed out. The pattern is unvarying: on Mondays, Wednesdays, and Fridays there is a "bread meal," and on Tuesdays and Thursdays it is a "rice meal." For bread meals, they each carry a nested set of knife, fork, and spoon, while for rice, they take chopsticks.

One day I visited Toshi's class just before lunch. Twenty-five to thirty lively eleven-year-olds greeted me boisterously; then, with Toshi translating, we talked about this and that until it was time for lunch. It was Tuesday, so there was a rice meal scheduled. The students rearranged all their desks for lunch, fetched their lunch kits, washed their hands, and sat back in their places. Meantime, large pots arrived at the doorway on a cart and were lifted onto a big table in the corner of the classroom. Several of the students, dressed in caps and aprons, had serving duty; they ladled out rice, a tofu stew, and salad and handed out cartons of milk. When everyone sat back down, heads were bowed and a blessing said: "Thankfully, with gratitude, I'll begin eating."

Then it was time to eat, laugh, and chat. There was enough food for seconds for those who wanted more, then a pause for another brief blessing and thanks: "Thank you for the food."

I went around to talk to small groups of kids and each time I asked whether they preferred *gohan*, the rice meals, or *pan*, the bread meals. It was unanimous: They all said "*Gohan*" very firmly. After clattering down the stairs and out into the yard with the class, I headed back to the apartment with questions for Mariko. "Oh, yes," she said. "They prefer rice meals. In the 1950s, there was bread five times a week in the public schools. In some places the bread meals are now down to twice a week."

Several people told me that they thought that after the war the American administration had instituted bread meals as a way of ensuring that children were adequately fed. It also provided a market for American wheat and flour, since Japan grows very little wheat.

Perhaps it was inevitable, as Japan moved out into the modern Western world, that the Japanese would develop a taste for bread, but surely the school lunches played a big part in making bread a familiar, easy alternative to rice. The result is that these days breakfast in many Japanese households is at least as likely to be bread or rolls or toast as it is the traditional rice.

# Hen-and-Egg Rice
*oyako donburi*

Serves 4

THIS IS JAPANESE COMFORT FOOD, EASILY PREPARED AT HOME BUT MOST OFTEN eaten for lunch in small neighborhood restaurants. *Donburi* are one-dish meals in which a topping of well-flavored meat, eggs, tofu, or a combination is served over rice. (The name *donburi* comes from the large bowl of the same name that the dish is served in.)

Kyoto is known for its *oyako don,* or "parent and child *donburi*" (because both chicken and egg are used in the savory topping). The whole dish can be prepared in forty minutes (including soaking time for the mushrooms)—the length of time it takes to prepare the rice properly. It makes a good lunch, with miso soup, or less traditionally, a salad such as Cucumber and Wakame Salad (page 191) or Intensely Green Spinach with Sesame Seeds (page 193).

2 cups Japanese rice

2⅓ cups cold water

4 dried shiitake mushrooms

½ cup warm water

¼ pound boneless skinless chicken breast

### Marinade

2 tablespoons sake

1 tablespoon soy sauce

½ cup any quick dashi broth (page 179) or ½ cup water plus a large pinch of bonito flakes (see Glossary)

2 tablespoons soy sauce

2 tablespoons rice vinegar

1 teaspoon sugar

2 scallions, minced

4 large or extra-large eggs

Pinch of salt

### Optional toppings

Seven-spice powder (*shichimi togarashi,* see Glossary)

4 sprigs *mitsuba* (see Glossary) or flat-leaf parsley, coarsely torn

Wash the rice well in several changes of water until the water runs clear. Let stand in a sieve for 20 to 30 minutes, then place the rice in a heavy medium pot with the cold water. Bring to a boil, cover tightly, and lower the heat to medium-low. Cook for 5 minutes, then reduce the heat to very low and cook for another 10 minutes. Remove from the heat and let stand for 10 minutes, still covered. *Alternatively,* cook the rice in a rice cooker.

Meanwhile, before putting the rice on to cook, begin preparing the other ingredients: Wipe off the mushrooms, place in a small bowl with the warm water, top with a small lid or bowl to press them down, and soak for 30 minutes. When the mushrooms are softened, remove from the water and slice into very thin strips, discarding the hard stems. Set aside both the mushrooms and the soaking water.

Cut the chicken lengthwise into 1-inch strips, then thinly slice across the grain. Place the marinade ingredients in a bowl, add the chicken, and turn to coat. Let stand for 20 to 30 minutes.

*If using water and bonito flakes,* bring the water to a boil, toss in the bonito flakes, and remove from the heat. When the flakes have settled, strain through a cloth and discard the flakes.

Ten minutes before you plan to serve the dish, place the dashi or bonito broth and the mushroom soaking water in a heavy nonreactive saucepan. Add the soy sauce, vinegar, and sugar and heat to a boil, stirring to dissolve the sugar. Add the chicken and mushroom slices and simmer until the chicken has turned white all over. Stir in the scallions. Whisk the eggs with the salt until frothy, pour into the pan, and simmer for 2 minutes, without stirring. Cover and after 20 seconds, turn the heat to very low and let steam until the eggs are cooked but still very soft, 2 to 3 minutes.

Place the rice in four bowls, top each with a quarter of the egg and chicken mixture, and serve, with the optional topping(s) if you wish.

Note: You can also begin with leftover cooked rice. You will need about 5 cups cooked rice.

# Herbed Rice

Serves 3 to 4

IN SUMMERTIME, WHEN FRESH HERBS ARE PLENTIFUL, TRY THIS SIMPLE RECIPE. It can be made with hot freshly cooked rice (white or brown) or with cold leftover plain rice or sushi rice.

1 cup finely shredded red or green *shiso* (perilla) leaves (see Glossary) or substitute other herbs or greens such as flat-leaf parsley, arugula, sorrel, or mint

4 cups cooked Japanese white or brown rice

½ teaspoon salt, or more to taste

**Optional topping**

1 tablespoon black sesame seeds

Combine all the ingredients and serve in a bowl, topped with the black sesame seeds if you like. *Alternatively,* shape into balls (*onigiri*) and roll in black sesame seeds to coat lightly.

# Autumn Rice with Mushrooms

Serves 6

AUTUMN BRINGS MUSHROOMS TO THE MARKETS OF JAPAN, NOT JUST SHIITAKE and portobello, but also the expensive and sought after forest giants, mazutake mushrooms. These days most mazutake sold in Japan are flown in from the western coast of North America. They are sold by the piece and usually displayed in small quantities.

You don't need luxurious mazutake mushrooms to make this dish, though they are classic. Instead, use fresh shiitakes or portobellos, something with distinctive flavor and meatiness to give the rice a wonderful smoky flavor, the mysterious taste of autumn. In Japan, this dish is often decorated with small colorful "autumn leaves" made of flour paste and sold in the markets.

3 cups white or brown Japanese rice

Scant ½ pound mazutake, shiitake, portobello, or button mushrooms, cleaned and cut into ½-inch pieces

2 cups Classic Dashi Broth (page 180)

3 tablespoons sake

3 tablespoons mirin

2 tablespoons soy sauce

### Optional seasoning/garnish

Seven-spice powder (*shichimi togarashi*, see Glossary) or Japanese pepper (*sansho*, see Glossary)

Wash the rice well in several changes of water until the water runs clear. Let stand in a sieve for 20 to 30 minutes.

Place the mushrooms, broth, sake, mirin, and soy sauce in a saucepan, bring to a boil, and simmer for 3 to 4 minutes, or until the mushrooms are tender. Drain, reserving the cooking liquid. Set the mushrooms aside.

Measure the cooking liquid and add enough water to make a total of 3½ cups if using white rice, 4½ cups if using brown. Place in a heavy medium pot and add the rice. Bring to a boil, cover, lower the heat to medium-low and cook for 5 minutes. Lower the heat to very low and cook for 12 minutes for white rice, 25 to 30 minutes for brown rice. Remove from the heat and let stand for 10 minutes.

Add the mushrooms and use a wet wooden rice paddle or spatula to gently stir and turn them into the rice. Serve with spice powder or Japanese pepper if you wish.

**Alternative:** Instead of stirring the cooked mushrooms into the cooked rice, you can use the rice to shape *onigiri* (see Easy Rice Balls, page 206). Place some of the cooked mushrooms in the center of each rice ball. Serve plain or rolled in lightly toasted sesame seeds or gomasio (page 187).

# Soothing Tea Rice
*chazuke*

THIS IS HOMEY COMFORT FOOD. TEA AND A LITTLE FISH ARE USED AS flavorings for a bowl of rice, making a simple country-style meal. Once you've eaten the rice and fish, you finish drinking the tea from your rice bowl, and perhaps have a second cup. The tea will have picked up a subtle rice flavor from the bowl, the taste of the country and of honored tradition. Serve with small amounts of two or three different pickles.

1 cup Japanese green tea per person

1 to 1½ cups freshly cooked or leftover Japanese rice per person

Scant ¼ cup strong-tasting prepared fish per person, such as smoked salmon, plain or lightly grilled; smoked eel, wiped off and flaked (see Notes); or smoked oysters, drained and coarsely chopped (see Notes)

### Optional garnish

Sliced scallion greens or torn *mitsuba* leaves (see Glossary), flat-leaf parsley sprigs, or shreds of toasted nori (see Glossary)

### Accompaniments

Wasabi (Japanese horseradish, see Glossary)

Japanese pickles, chopped small

Make the green tea.

Warm rice bowls by rinsing with hot water and drying. Place the rice in the bowls, top with the fish, and pour the green tea over. Top with the optional garnish and serve, accompanied by wasabi and pickles.

**Notes:** You can also serve this the "instant way" by buying prepared packages of *chazuke* (tea rice) mix. Simply place the rice in a bowl, sprinkle on a package of the mix, and pour hot water over it. It's adequate, but not nearly as interesting as made-from-basics *chazuke*.

Smoked eel and smoked oysters are available, canned or packaged, at Japanese and Korean groceries and at some specialty food shops.

# Sushi Traditions

Preparing *nare zushi* in Miyama

One day several women from the Miyama agricultural cooperative remembered that farther up the valley, at the end of the road,
a group of farm wives was making *nare zushi*. As we piled into a
car to drive up, Yasuko tried to fill me in, "It's too hard to explain
*nare zushi* in English. It's an old tradition. You have to see it."

On our way, we stopped in to watch *mochi* (see page 226)
being made at a traditional *mochi* bakery, then wound past a
hamlet with steep thatched-roof houses and patches of ripening
millet and up a narrow tree-lined road. At last we stopped
outside a low modern building, the community center for this
end of the valley. Inside, several women were fanning huge
wooden tubs of cooked rice. A beautiful fine-boned old woman,
who was clearly in charge of operations, greeted us and then
went on with her work.

*Nare zushi* is an old form of sushi, the original sushi some
would say. It is found in different versions in several isolated (or formerly isolated) parts of
Japan: in Miyama; near Lake Biwa, where a kind of carp is used; and in the mountains near
Fukui, northwest of Kyoto, where it is made only in July, using trout. There are probably others.
For the Miyama version, fresh mackerel fillets are salted, then pressed onto large cakes of
cooked rice that has been seasoned with sake and salt, but not the vinegar or sugar of the
modern sushi we are familiar with. The rice-fish pieces are then tightly wrapped in a long green
leaf called *sasso* and placed in big pail or barrel lined with more leaves. The fish and rice bundles
are layered in the pail, with leaves between each layer, and pressed down. When the pail is full, a
heavy weight is put on top. The fish and rice ferment, giving off a brine that is poured off after a
day. Lightly salted cold water is added and the sushi is left to stand for ten days. Then the pail or
barrel is turned over to let all the liquid drain out, and the sushi is ready to eat.

Traditionally, *nare zushi* was made in the Miyama area for both the mountain (spring)
festivals and the autumn (harvest) festivals. It's ready-made fast food that can be eaten through
planting time and harvest time, when the women are too busy to cook. It's associated, for the
women, with freedom from kitchen duties.

The atmosphere that day at *nare zushi*–making time was joyous and smiling. The others
teased the woman in charge when she wouldn't tell us her age, "Old enough!" she said firmly.

For most Japanese, the fermented taste of *nare zushi* is foreign and disgusting. I tasted
some that had been made a month earlier. It had a definite aged-cheese flavor, familiar and
tasty to someone like me, raised in a dairy-and-cheese culture, but very off-putting to many
Japanese. A forty-something woman I met that day told me her history with *nare zushi:* "I came
here as a young farmer's bride in my late teens. For the first five years I couldn't be in the same
room with it. For the next five, I could help making it, but wouldn't dream of eating it. In the
next five I took an occasional mouthful, but still didn't really like it. Now I've been here over
twenty years and I love it, can't get enough of it."

# Sushi Rice—Master Recipe

**Makes about 10 cups rice**

SUSHI IS EASY TO MAKE. ALL YOU NEED IS WELL-COOKED RICE, GOOD BASIC ingredients, and a little attention. The rice can be prepared up to six hours ahead, then left covered until you are ready to assemble sushi or to serve Roll-Your-Own Sushi (see page 220). This recipe makes a large quantity of rice because, like bread dough, you might as well make plenty while you're making it. In our experience it always gets eaten.

In addition to a rice cooker or a wide heavy pot for cooking rice, you will need a large shallow bowl or platter, a wooden paddle or spatula, a folded up newspaper or a magazine for fanning, and a large cotton cloth.

| | |
|---|---|
| 4 cups Japanese rice | **Seasoning mixture** |
| One 4-inch square kombu (see page 179), briefly rinsed (optional) | ¾ cup rice vinegar |
| | 2 to 3 tablespoons sugar |
| 4 cups cold water | 1½ teaspoons salt |

Begin preparing the rice at least 1½ hours (and as long as 6 hours) before you wish to serve the sushi. Wash the rice well under cold running water until the water runs clear. Transfer to a large sieve and let stand for 30 minutes to 1 hour.

Place the rice in a large heavy pot, with the optional kombu, add the cold water, and bring to a boil. When the rice boils, remove the kombu (see page 179 for uses for boiled kombu). Cover tightly and lower the heat to medium-low. Cook for 5 minutes, then turn the heat to very low and let simmer for 10 minutes. Remove from the heat and let stand for 5 minutes. If using a rice cooker, follow the manufacturer's instructions; the kombu should be removed when the water boils.

Meanwhile, prepare the seasoning mixture: Combine the ingredients in a nonreactive saucepan and heat to a slow boil over medium heat, stirring to dissolve the sugar. Let cool to room temperature.

To flavor the rice: As soon as the rice is cooked, immediately turn it out into a large shallow bowl or onto a platter and spread out gently with a rice paddle or wooden spatula. Begin fanning the rice immediately with a folded newspaper or a magazine to help cool it and dissipate the steam. Pour in half the flavoring mixture and then, while fanning with one hand, use the wooden paddle or spatula to gently expose all the rice to the liquid: This is classically done by making slow figure-eight sweeps of your paddle through the rice. You can also lift sections of the rice and turn them. You will soon find a technique that's comfortable. Once the liquid is absorbed (usually within minutes), add the remaining liquid and continue to stir and turn gently, still fanning. Once the liquid is absorbed, continue to fan until little or no steam rises from the rice. Fanning, by cooling the rice quickly, results in a glossy sheen.

Cover with a well-dampened cotton cloth (*not* plastic wrap, since you want any remaining steam to be absorbed by the cloth) and set aside until ready to use. Sushi rice can wait at room temperature for up to 6 hours, as long as it is covered with the damp cloth to prevent drying out. *Do not refrigerate;* if you do, the rice will become hard and crusty. (The vinegar and salt help preserve the rice and prevent fermentation.) Use in the recipes that follow.

# Basic Handmade Sushi
## *nigiri zushi*

*Nigiri zushi* IS THE DECEPTIVELY SIMPLE SUSHI MADE BY LAYING A PIECE OF fresh fish or other "something special" on a small compact mound of sushi rice. You can make basic *nigiri zushi* at home and delight both your family and friends.

There are a few rules. Buy ultra-fresh fish at a fish shop or specialty market. Tell them you want it for sushi. Buy only a small amount of one or two kinds. Slice the fish across the grain with a very sharp knife into thin slices about 2 inches long and ½ inch wide. Take a small clump of sushi rice in the palm of one hand and use the fingers of your other hand to shape it into a log, approximately 1½ to 2 inches long and ½ inch in diameter. If you wish, dip your index finger into some wasabi (Japanese horseradish) paste and draw a light line down the top of the rice mound. Top with a slice of the fish and press lightly with your cupped hand to press the fish onto the rice. Set on a serving platter. Repeat with the remaining fish and rice.

# Classic Sushi Roll-ups
*futo-maki*

**Makes 4 rolls, each with about 8 slices; serves 6 to 8 as part of a meal**

MY FIRST VISIT TO A SUSHI BAR OVER TWENTY YEARS AGO IS STILL A VERY FRESH memory: perfect fish and seafood, a talented and amiable sushi chef, and good company ready to taste everything and anything. We had salmon roe, *nami* (sea urchin), tuna both dark red and pale, rich mackerel brightened with a leaf of *shiso*. . . . In one evening I added sushi and sashimi to my list of all-time favorite foods, but for years they remained exotic, special restaurant-only treats. Finally, our friend Cassandra, an adventurous cook who is never afraid of doing anything in a kitchen, suggested that we try our hands at *futo-maki*, and so we did.

Because she is third-generation Japanese-Canadian, she knew sushi could be made at home; her mother's *maki* rolls are some of the best we've ever had. But growing up with an expert in the house, she'd never actually made sushi herself. So after cooking the rice, we phoned her mother, Yone, and got detailed instructions on how to fan and cool it. Yone was appalled at how much Cassandra didn't know, and perhaps even more appalled that we were prepared to call her, long distance several times, in the middle of the day to get instructions. We made sixteen rolls of *futo-maki* that day, then cut them into slices and stacked them in overlapping layers on several platters. They made a very impressive display. Word spread quickly, and by late afternoon they were gone.

Tuna for sale

Our *futo-maki* was fairly classic, like this recipe, with strips of dried gourd (*kampyo*) soaked and simmered in soy sauce, as well as strips of omelet, slivers of parboiled carrot, and a little finely slivered cucumber for green. You will need a sushi rolling mat, called a *sudari*, available at Japanese and Korean shops and some kitchenware stores.

*continued*

About 35 inches dried gourd strips
  (*kampyo,* see Glossary)

Salt

4 dried shiitake mushrooms, wiped clean

½ cup any quick dashi broth (page 179)

2 tablespoons soy sauce

1 tablespoon sugar

Sea salt

A 5-inch piece European cucumber

¼ pound carrots, peeled and cut into
  5-inch-long julienne strips, and/or
  2 cups washed and torn spinach leaves

2 large eggs

Pinch of sugar

4 sheets toasted nori (see Note)

5 to 5½ cups prepared Sushi Rice
  (page 215)

## Condiments and accompaniments

3 tablespoons wasabi (Japanese
  horseradish) powder (see Glossary),
  mixed with water into a paste

¼ cup (or more) Pickled Ginger
  (page 203) or store-bought

¼ cup soy sauce

3 tablespoons rice vinegar

Prepare the fillings: Rub the *kampyo* strips lightly with salt. Place them in a medium bowl and pour boiling water over, then drain. Place the *kampyo* and mushrooms in a medium nonreactive saucepan and add the dashi broth, soy sauce, and sugar. Bring to a boil and simmer for 5 minutes. Remove from the heat and let stand for 30 minutes.

Remove the mushrooms from the broth, cut in half, and discard the tough stems. Thinly slice and set aside. Remove the gourd strips and place in a sieve over a bowl to drain and cool to room temperature.

Spread a layer of sea salt on a large plate or cutting board. Roll the cucumber (unpeeled) in the salt, then cut lengthwise into quarters, discard the seeds, and cut into fine julienne strips. Place in a sieve or colander, add 1 teaspoon salt, and toss gently to distribute. Let drain, over the sink or a bowl, for 15 minutes, then rinse thoroughly, gently squeeze out excess water, and set aside.

Bring a large pot of water to a boil. *If using carrots,* parboil them until barely tender. Remove from the water, refresh with cold water, and set aside. *If using spinach,* lightly salt the water, then toss in the spinach and let cook for 2 to 3 minutes, until tender. Drain, refresh with cold water, and squeeze out the excess water. Finely chop and set aside.

Whisk the eggs in a small bowl with the sugar and a pinch of salt. Place a heavy nonstick or lightly oiled 8-inch skillet over medium heat. When it is hot, pour in half the egg mixture and tilt to coat the pan evenly. When the edges of the omelet begin to curl away from the pan, turn it over and cook the other side for 30 seconds. Transfer to a plate. Cook the remaining egg mixture in the same way. Lay the omelets on top of each other and cut into narrow strips.

To assemble the rolls: Place one nori sheet on a rolling mat. Spread about 1¼ cups rice evenly over the nori, leaving a ¼-inch strip bare along the long side nearest you and a 1-inch strip bare along the other long side. About 1 inch from the edge of the rice nearest you, lay a line of mushroom pieces. Cut a length of *kampyo* and place beside the mushrooms, then place beside it some overlapping pieces of cucumber and carrot and/or a thin line of spinach and several overlapping strips of omelet.

Using your index finger or thumb, smear a trail of wasabi all along the edge of the nori nearest you.

Roll up the nori, first rolling the mat over away from you, and pressing to shape the roll, then, without catching the edge of the mat into the roll, rolling it up. Use a fingertip to dampen the bare edge of nori with a little water and press against the roll to seal. Place the roll seam side down on a platter. Roll up remaining rolls the same way, varying the proportions of ingredients as you wish. Include a little pickled ginger in some if you'd like, or omit the mushrooms to give the other more subtle flavors a chance.

Cut the rolls into 6 to 8 pieces each, using a sharp knife and wetting it with cold water before each slice. Place the slices decoratively on individual plates or on a small serving platter, laying some flat and standing others on their sides.

Mix the soy sauce and vinegar for a dipping sauce. Place small piles of wasabi and pickled ginger on the platter or plates. Set out small shallow bowls of the dipping sauce.

If you have any filling ingredients left over, store in the refrigerator and then reheat (all but the cucumber) briefly in a little quick dashi broth (page 179) for a soup the next day.

**Note:** You can buy plain (black-colored) sheets of nori and toast very lightly and quickly over a gas flame to a bright green, or, easier and better, buy specially toasted nori for sushi.

**Alternative:** You can also make smaller roll-ups, using only fresh tuna or cucumber strips as filling, and using half a nori sheet per roll.

Farm woman in Miyama

# Roll-Your-Own Sushi

LONG AGO A FRIEND INVITED ME TO A NEW YEAR'S PARTY. THE HOST WAS originally from Japan, as were about half the guests. Food for the party consisted of an incredible array of sushi-making ingredients, in seemingly inexhaustible supply. We all just kept rolling sushi, eating, rolling, eating. As I remember, I wasn't the only one who never stopped.

Roll-your-own sushi makes for a great party or buffet-style supper. Just make lots of sushi rice and have a good supply of sake or Japanese beer to keep things moving.

The best way of rolling your own sushi (you can demonstrate to any guests unfamiliar with the idea) is to take a quarter of a piece of nori in your hand, lay some sushi rice (about a quarter cup) on it toward one corner, and top the rice with a selection of toppings. Roll the nori in a cone shape around the rice and flavors, dab on a little wasabi or dip in soy sauce if you wish, and eat with pleasure.

Toasted nori sheets (see Note, page 219), cut into quarters (allow about 2 sheets per person)

Plenty of Sushi Rice (page 215; allow 1½ to 2 cups cooked rice per person for a crowd of big eaters, less if you think people will be more restrained)

A selection of some of the following ingredients:

  black sesame seeds

  avocado, sliced and drizzled with fresh lime juice

  Japanese fish cake (*kamaboko*), cut into small pieces

  European cucumber, cut into long strips, salted, rinsed, and squeezed dry (see Classic Sushi Roll-ups, page 217)

  omelets, cut into strips (see Classic Sushi Roll-ups, page 217)

  thin slices of very fresh raw fish, such as tuna or salmon

  scallions, cut into long thin shreds

  snow peas, blanched and cut into strips

  blanched carrot strips

  spinach, blanched, squeezed dry, and finely chopped

  dried shiitake mushrooms, soaked for 30 minutes in warm water, drained, and cut into thin strips (discard hard stems)

## Condiments and flavorings

Pickled Ginger (page 203) or store-bought

Wasabi (Japanese horseradish) powder (see Glossary), mixed with water into a paste

Soy sauce

Place the selection of sushi ingredients on decorative plates or platters. Provide a medium plate and a small sauce bowl for each guest, so they can make up their own dipping sauce.

Train crossing at evening, near the Fushimi Inari Shrine in Kyoto

# Bullet Journey

The bullet train travels from Kyoto to Tokyo, a three-hundred-mile journey, in less than three hours. And perhaps even more amazing, there is a train every ten to fifteen minutes. The ride is smooth, the seats ample with lots of leg room, and as you sit calmly eating a good lunch from an *o-bento* (lunch box), the countryside scrolls by through the train window. Only if you try to look at anything close to the train do you realize how swiftly you are traveling.

In late October, the countryside we sped through was a panorama of agricultural life. It was Sunday, so families were out in their garden plots and rice fields cleaning up, harvesting, tilling. We crossed wide calm rivers with solitary fishermen standing patiently and small boats crowded along the shore. Outside Nagoya were fields of very ripe rice. Some was being cut by hand; in other patches, small machines were doing the harvesting. Farther along there were bare fields smoldering, the last of the rice straw being burned off. Nearby, rice was draped on racks to dry, great sheaves with the golden grain hanging down toward the ground. We saw beautiful stacks of yellow straw tidily piled at the roadside by small threshing machines. Farther north, on steep hillsides, grew small orange trees and tea.

Finally there came the clutter and intensity of Tokyo, a disorienting end to a journey that had given such a sense of order and deliberateness.

# Brown Bag Sushi
*inari zushi*

SHINTO, ONE OF THE MAJOR RELIGIONS IN JAPAN, CELEBRATES THE SPIRITUAL connection to growing things. Every Shinto shrine has a large twisted rope of rice straw over the entrance, replaced each year, and each shrine is associated with a special animal. The Fushimi Inari shrine outside Kyoto has the fox as its animal deity and good luck patron (*inari* means "fox"). The Fushimi Inari shrine is famous in Japan for its many tori gates, orange gateways with prayers painted over the top. They make long, mysterious, winding corridors up the densely treed hillside behind the shrine. In a clearing on the hillside, a patch of rice is cere-monially harvested each October, with prayer and dance, one of the honors and acknowledgments paid to the importance of rice throughout Japan.

We and our friends know *inari zushi* as "brown bags," since that's what they look like—sushi rice stuffed into golden simmered squares of fried tofu. We don't know why they're called *inari*, or fox, *zushi*—but we do know that *inari zushi* is one of the most delicious moist, straight-forward, I-want-more foods we've ever eaten. It is also a very easy way of serving sushi rice or using up extra rice after you've made Basic Handmade Sushi (page 216). Be sure to make plenty so your guests will feel satisfied. Serve as one of several sushi dishes or as part of a meal in place of rice.

| | |
|---|---|
| Twelve 2-by-5-inch rectangles Japanese fried tofu (*abura-age,* see Glossary) | About 3½ cups cooked Sushi Rice (page 215) |
| **Stock** | **Accompaniments** |
| 1½ cups any quick dashi broth (page 179), light vegetable stock, or water | Pickled Ginger (page 203) or store-bought |
| 5 tablespoons mirin | Soy sauce |
| 2 tablespoons sugar | Dry-roasted sesame seeds (see page 187) |
| 5 tablespoons soy sauce | |

Place the tofu pieces in a large bowl or pot and pour boiling water over them. Drain imme-diately and press to squeeze out any excess water. Cut each piece crosswise in half, making 24 almost-square pieces, each with one open side.

Place the stock ingredients in a large nonreactive saucepan and bring to a boil. Add the tofu pieces and stir to moisten. Place a lid (or heatproof dinner plate) just slightly smaller than the diameter of the saucepan on the tofu to press it down into the stock, lower the heat, and simmer very gently for 15 to 20 minutes. Remove the tofu from the stock and place on a plate to cool to room temperature. Before using, gently squeeze out any excess liquid and pat dry with paper towels.

When ready to proceed, shape a scant ¼ cup of sushi rice into a flattened oval and slide into a tofu pocket, just filling it. Repeat with the remaining rice and tofu. Cover with a damp cloth until ready to serve.

Accompany the *inari zushi* with a pile of pickled ginger, small bowls of soy sauce, and a small bowl of sesame seeds, for dipping.

**Alternative:** Tofu pockets can also be filled with *chirashi-zushi*—sushi rice with other ingredients mixed in. We suggest making the above recipe with half the pockets filled with plain sushi rice and half with a few extra flavorings, as follows: Blanch 10 to 12 snow peas (with tough ends and strings removed) in lightly salted water until just tender, then drain and thinly slice on the diagonal. Soak and simmer 2 dried shiitake mushrooms (see Classic Sushi Roll-ups, page 217), then drain, cut in half, discarding the tough stems, and thinly slice. Gently mix the snow peas and mushrooms into 1¾ cups Sushi Rice (page 215) and stuff the tofu pockets.

# Mackerel Sushi

*zaba zushi*

**Makes 16 to 20 slices, plus some small end pieces; allow 2 to 4 slices per person**
ONE FINE DAY DURING MY STAY IN MIYAMA, YASUKO AND I WALKED OVER to the agricultural co-op for a meeting with her English-language group. This handful of women had asked Yasuko, who speaks English well, if she would give them English conversation lessons once a week. Since I was visiting, Yasuko had rescheduled the lesson so they could all have the opportunity to talk with a native speaker.

We sat on tatami mats around a low table in a comfortable square room with large paper-screened windows. After we all introduced ourselves, each of the women, at Yasuko's suggestion, described her favorite rice dish. For several it was red rice (sticky rice with azuki beans, see page 228), for others it was rice balls (*onigiri*, see page 206) wrapped around *umeboshi* plums and other flavors. I asked questions about methods and ingredients and the answers came in a mix of English and Japanese, with great good humor. As always, food was a good way to break the ice.

Then one of the women made tea while several others unpacked the food they had prepared. There were slow-simmered local mushrooms, very simple to make and rich in taste. There was elaborate *nori maki*, large sushi rolls made up of three smaller seaweed rolls. And then there was a seasonal specialty, *zaba zushi*—fillets of mackerel pressed onto a long flat mound of sushi rice. The mackerel skin was a gleaming blue gray, very beautiful. As she laid out the sushi, the woman who had made it smiled with pleasure at my admiring comments, then took a sharp wet knife and cut each length of sushi into three-quarter-inch slices. She set out slivers of pickled ginger in wet clumps, not the regular pinkish pickled ginger, but a wine-red version (colored with the brine from *umeboshi* plums). The ginger was a wonderful color contrast to the silvery fish.

We sipped tea and ate and ate, talking about food, children, farm life, and hopes for the future. Then one of the women said, "Next time you come to Miyama, why don't you bring your husband and children? And could you stay at my house next time?" The others chimed in, "Yes, tell your friends, we'd love to have foreign guests come to stay; we want to meet people from other places." I was a bit cool to the idea at first, reminding them that we foreigners aren't "house-trained" to Japanese standards and are likely to put soap in the bath, to forget to take our shoes off at the door, to pour soy sauce on our rice, etc. "It doesn't matter," they said firmly. "We can be flexible and the foreigners can learn."

You can make this beautiful sushi either quickly with plain raw mackerel or after soaking the mackerel in salt and vinegar. If you want the vinegared mackerel option, begin preparing the fish four hours ahead or the evening before you wish to serve it.

1 mackerel (about 1½ pounds), filleted

2 teaspoons sea salt dissolved in ¼ cup rice vinegar (optional)

3 to 4 cups Sushi Rice (page 215)

**Accompaniments**

Pickled Ginger (page 203) or store-bought

About 6 red *shiso* (perilla) leaves (see Glossary) (optional)

Use tweezers or your fingernails to pull out any bones from the fillets. Lay one fillet, flesh side down, and working from the tail end, remove the skin: Mackerel skin is almost transparent but tough and membranous, and removing it is rather like trying to peel an old piece of tape off a wall. It is most easily done using the blade side of a knife in one hand to separate the skin from the underskin while pulling on the skin with the other hand, maintaining tension. Beneath the tough outer skin is an attractive blue-silver underskin, which should stay intact. Repeat for the other fillet.

If you wish to salt and vinegar the fish, place the fillets side by side, skinned side up, on a plate and pour the vinegar-salt solution over. Let stand, covered, for 4 hours at room temperature, or overnight in the refrigerator. Lift from the marinade and pat dry before proceeding.

Working on a lightly moistened wooden cutting board or other smooth surface and using moistened hands, take half of the sushi rice and shape it into a long rounded mound, about ½ inch thick and as long and nearly as wide as one fillet. Place one fillet on top, skinned side up, and press to shape it onto the rice. Repeat with the other half of the rice and fillet.

Let stand for 5 or 10 minutes, or as long as 4 hours. Cover the sushi with a damp cloth; do not refrigerate. Just before serving, use a wet knife to slice each fillet crosswise into ½- to ¾-inch slices. Place the slices rice side down in a row on a long plate or small platter, in the same order, to recreate the shape of the fillets.

Place a mound of pickled ginger at one end of the serving platter. If using the *shiso* leaves, stack them, then slice very thinly crosswise to make fine strips. Mound on the serving platter and serve.

# Sticky Rice Cakes
*mochi*

In Japan, New Year's rice cakes are known as *mochi*. Like Lisu's New Year's cakes (page 164), they are made from pounded sticky rice. Japanese friends have told us how until recently, just before New Year's Day, you could hear pounding coming from every house as each family prepared its *mochi* in a large mortar with a heavy wooden pestle. Nowadays, with more people living in small apartments, the pounding is heard mostly in the countryside and at ceremonies like those held each year in Tokyo, when famous sumo wrestlers perform the ritual pounding of the rice.

At temple ceremonies, *mochi* is one of the traditional offerings, as is sake, another rice product. At the annual Kyoto pageant and ritual known as Jidai Matsuri, a ceremony of homage to the emperors of Japan from the nineteenth century back to the eighth century, ritual offerings of gleaming *mochi* are made to a representative of the emperor before the procession begins.

*Mochi* is enjoyed in many forms throughout the year. Specialty shops sell it in balls, or rolls, or in thin fine folded sheets that look like elegant pocket handkerchiefs. Often it is lightly colored rather than white because a flavoring has been added—mugwort, for example (a pale green color, often associated with the spring), tea (also green), or millet (pale beige). *Mochi* is eaten as a sweet snack with tea or taken as a present when you go visiting.

In Kyoto, near the Imamiya Shrine, there are two well-known establishments that prepare and serve tea with grilled *mochi*. Here small balls of *mochi* are placed on thin bamboo skewers and roasted over a small fire, then served drizzled with a sweet sauce of soy sauce, bean paste, and sugar. We have also tasted sweet *mochi* balls at a night market in Taipei, Taiwan. They were small smooth flattened balls simmered in sugar syrup, then served on a plate with a drizzling of syrup and a sprinkling of crushed roasted peanuts and sugar.

In North America, *mochi* made from brown rice is sold at many health food stores. It comes dried out and hard, but it quickly softens when heated. The easiest treatment is to cut it into small squares, then toast it under the broiler. As it heats, it puffs up, becoming slightly crisp on the outside and soft and a bit gooey on

**above and right**

Grilling *mochi* near the Imamiya shrine

An offering of *mochi* to the emperor during the Jidai Matsuri procession

the inside. A white rice version is also available in Japanese grocery stores and sometimes in health food stores. Toasted *mochi* (white or brown) is generally eaten dipped in soy sauce or a soy-based dipping sauce, with perhaps some sprinkled sesame seeds. It makes a great breakfast food.

White rice *mochi* is an essential part of a New Year's Day soup called *ozoni*. Squares of *mochi* are lightly grilled, then served in a steaming-hot bowl of chicken soup. Though recipes vary from region to region and family to family, other ingredients usually include bamboo shoots, crysanthemum leaf, and *kamaboko* (fish cake).

The very smooth, perfect *mochi* that is now the standard in Japan is most easily made using sweet rice flour and warm water to make a dough rather than by the traditional method of pounding cooked rice. To make your own *mochi* the traditional way, you need cooked sticky rice (white or brown). Once it has cooled, chop it and then pound it in a large mortar. You might want to try using a food processor to knead and soften it. When you have a fairly even consistency, flatten it onto a nonstick baking sheet, cut it into squares, and place in a very low (150°F) oven to dry out. Let cool. Then store well wrapped in plastic. The squares will keep almost indefinitely, like crackers, until you wish to toast them.

# Home-Style Red Rice
two methods

Serves 4 to 6

IN JAPAN, RED RICE IS BOTH SIMPLE COMFORT FOOD AND FOOD FOR celebrations. Red rice is made by cooking sweet sticky rice with red azuki beans. As they cook the beans stain the rice a pinkish red. There are two methods for cooking it. In the first, the two ingredients cook together in water. In the second, the two are steamed together over boiling water after a long preliminary soaking. The first method is quicker, the second more traditional.

Serve red rice in place of plain rice, accompanied by soup and a salad or a vegetable dish.

1 cup Japanese sticky (sweet) rice
  (*mochi gome*)

1 cup azuki beans, picked over and rinsed

Water

1 teaspoon salt, plus a pinch

2 to 3 tablespoons dry-roasted sesame
  seeds (see page 187)

**Method one: absorption cooking**

Wash the rice well under cold running water, then place in a bowl and soak in 3 cups hot water while you begin preparing the beans.

Place the azuki beans in a large saucepan with 3 cups water and bring to a vigorous boil. Boil for 3 to 5 minutes, then drain. Return the beans to the pot, add 5 cups water, and bring to a boil. Cook at a low boil until tender, about 1¼ hours. Add the 1 teaspoon salt, simmer for another 5 minutes, and drain, reserving the cooking water.

Place 1¼ cups reserved cooking water (add water if necessary) in a heavy medium pot or a rice cooker. Drain the rice. *If using a pot,* bring the liquid to a rapid boil, add the rice and stir, then add the beans and stir. When the liquid is boiling again, cover, lower the heat to medium-low, and let cook for 5 minutes. Lower the heat to very low and cook for 15 minutes. Let stand, covered, for 5 minutes before serving. *If using a rice cooker,* turn on the cooker, add the rice and beans, and stir well. Place the lid on top and leave to cook. Let stand for 5 minutes before serving.

Meanwhile, place the sesame seeds in a *suribachi* or mortar with a pinch of salt and grind lightly.

Serve the rice warm. Sprinkle each serving with a little of the toasted sesame seeds, or alternatively, mix 2 tablespoons toasted sesame seeds into the rice and serve any remaining sesame seeds as a condiment for those who wish to sprinkle it over their rice.

**Method two: steaming**

Soak the rice and azukis separately overnight in 3 cups water each.

Drain the azukis and save the red soaking water. Place the azukis in a large saucepan with 4 cups water, bring to a boil, and cook for 20 minutes. Drain and set aside.

Meanwhile, drain the rice, pour the reserved red water over and let soak while the azukis cook. When ready to proceed, drain the rice and reserve the red water.

Line a bamboo or other large steamer with muslin or cheesecloth. Place the rice in the steamer, then place the azukis on top. Cover with another layer of cloth. Place the steamer over a pot of water and pour the red water over the cloth. Bring the water to a boil and steam for 20 to 25 minutes. (The water should not touch the steamer.) Remove from the heat and stir the rice and beans gently with a wet wooden rice paddle or spatula.

Because there is no salt added to the azukis during cooking, the sesame topping is made with salt: Combine the 1 teaspoon salt and the sesame seeds in a *suribachi* or mortar and grind lightly. Serve as a condiment to be sprinkled over each bowl of red rice.

Early-morning mist cloaking the Taj Mahal in Agra

inset: A Mishin woman and her fishing basket,
near the Brahmaputra River in central Assam

# Basmati, Gobindavog, South Indian Red

Preparing Indian food, at least in our house, is an entirely different process from cooking Thai, Chinese, or Japanese food. For one thing, we end up eating a lot more Indian food in the winter, when the days are short, when by early afternoon we are already thinking about what to make for dinner. Many of our favorite Indian dishes require slow cooking, with a depth of flavor developing over time. As opposed to many East Asian dishes where flavors are often simply assembled and blended, in Indian cooking there is a greater emphasis on cooking and transforming. (Maybe this accounts for why an Indian curry or dal makes for such great leftovers.)

Nevertheless, home-style dishes in all these cuisines do have one essential characteristic in common: They are all excellent with rice! Preparing a delicious, healthful, and easily prepared Indian meal is just the same as it is with Thai, Chinese, and Japanese foods: First thing in the kitchen, put on the rice. Then you can think about what

**clockwise from top**

Tailor at work in Khajuraho, Madya Pradesh

Woman and oxen at a water wheel in rural Madya Pradesh

Vegetable seller at the Palayam market in Trivandrum

Boy in the Brahmaputra River at dawn

else to serve, whether it is as simple as a fast-cooking dal and a salad or as elaborate as a curry with a dal, chapattis, a yogurt dish, a pickle, pappadums. . . .

Rice and dal, the simplest and most common meal eaten in India, is a meal we never tire of eating or preparing. We try never to be out of orange masur dal and yellow split mung dal, because both of these common dals cook quickly, taste great, and can be prepared in many different ways (not to mention that when stored in glass jars on open shelves, they're beautiful to look at). They can be purchased in large quantities and cost very little, either in Indian or Asian groceries or when ordered from a mail-order source (page 418 and Mail-Order Sources, page 438).

Another important way that Indian food figures into what we prepare at home is at just the opposite of a simple meal. If we are cooking for eight to ten people and want to have a dazzling meal for guests, then Indian food is one of our favorite meals to prepare. An Indian feast is always something special, with so many dishes to choose from and so many tastes to combine with one another. Indian feasts, particularly if vegetarian, tend to be high in carbohydrates and relatively low in fats, a little bit like a mezze meal in the Eastern Mediterranean. Everyone can eat to his heart's content, but won't feel so awfully full later.

An Indian feast is also great fun to cook. Many dishes can be prepared ahead of time and served all at once, family style. If you make homemade chapattis, toast some pappadums, and have good rice, you are already well on your way to serving a great Indian meal.

You need no special equipment for cooking Indian food, only several large heavy pots and a good rice-cooking pot. Traditionally in India, most frying is done in a shallow pan somewhat like a wok, called a *kadhai,* but a wide heavy pot or a good wok can be substituted.

There are many, many Indian rices, parboiled and unboiled, long-grain and medium-grain, white, red, and brown. Basmati is ideally suited to flavored rice dishes such as pilafs and *biryanis,* while parboiled rices are more often eaten plain. We have been thrilled in recent years as rices like rosematta and gobindavog have become available in North America, and we hope that in years to come there will be many more varieties of South Asian rices available.

One last word about rice in India, and that has to do with eating it. Most people in India eat rice with their right hand, though there are different styles used. People in the south of India joke about how people in the north eat so politely with the ends of their fingers that they look as if they are afraid of getting a grain of rice up past their second knuckle. People in the north think that the people in the south, who eat their rice fingers, palm, and all, look crude. We think that while people in the north might have a point, they miss out on all the fun.

Eating with your hand takes some getting used to. Like eating rice with chopsticks, it's best if you can eat directly over your bowl or plate or, as it's done in South India, over your banana leaf. This way, any rice that falls simply falls back on your food. The most important thing to remember when eating rice with your hand is to loosen up and have fun. Here you can be a kid again. In southern India, it's perfectly fine to mush your food around, to make piles of rice and add little bits of curry and pickle and crispy chips of pappadum. When you have the tasty pile just the way you want it, pick it up in your palm and shake it back and forth as if you were about to roll dice at a craps table. This helps form the pile into a ball, about the size of a golf ball. And then with a turn of the wrist, pop it into your mouth. This is the way it is done in South India; the secret is in the wrist, in keeping a loose wrist.

# Basmati

The Indian rice most widely known in North America is basmati. It is long-grain and often described as "needle-shaped" because it is so narrow. The most prized basmati is grown in the Himalayan foothills in Northern India and Pakistan and of that, the top quality is known as "Dehra Dun basmati." Another basmati is grown in western Bengal and is known as Patna. It is a very good rice, not as expensive or as aromatic as Dehra Dun basmati, and easily found in Indian groceries.

All basmati is very long grain rice, best when it has been "aged" for several years (some say up to ten years) before being husked. When it cooks, it expands greatly in volume (almost triple), but especially lengthwise, so it gets even more elongated.

Basmati is the ideal rice for Mogul (North Indian) and Persian cooking because its grains stay separate and firm even when cooked and tender. It does not have the clinging quality of Thai jasmine rices. In India, it is most often cooked in pilafs and *biryanis*. You can also cook it as perfectly plain rice. Cooked basmati is wonderfully fragrant.

In North America, the quality of basmati available varies widely. It is often sold in five-, ten-, and twenty-pound burlap or jute bags. Though these are lined with an inner plastic bag, the rice may still smell dusty. If you wash it well, then soak it, that dusty taste should go, but unfortunately this is not always the case. If you have this problem with a new bag of basmati, return it to the store where you bought it.

Basmati rice is generally soaked in cold water, with or without salt, for half an hour or as long as two hours before cooking. This gives the grains a chance to absorb a little water and to soften so that they are less brittle and breakable and can cook more evenly.

There are two basic ways of cooking plain basmati rice. One is by the absorption method (most commonly associated with Chinese and Japanese rice cookery), the other by boiling in plenty of water, the most widespread method in India. Indians seem to have traditionally cooked their rice in plenty of water. A Sanskrit story from the early seventh century by Dandin describes a young woman preparing food: polishing rice in a mortar, cooking it in boiling water, serving the gruel and then the rice, flavored with ghee, condiments, and spices. These days the cooking water is often poured off and discarded, though in some families it is saved for cooking other foods—or for ironing— because of its starch content.

Men eating their rice meals in a local Trivandrum restaurant

# Basmati Rice

*lots-of-water method*

**Makes about 6 cups rice**

IN MANY INDIAN HOUSEHOLDS FROM BENGAL TO TRIVANDRUM, PLAIN RICE IS cooked as we cook pasta, by boiling it in plenty of water. The water is usually not salted. Basmati rice expands greatly during cooking, so two cups raw rice yields about six cups cooked. It is very important that you watch the rice carefully to prevent overcooking; as with pasta, the best way is to test the rice every thirty seconds or so for doneness, beginning at the three-minute mark after it returns to the boil. It should be cooked through, with no solid core, but still firm, not mushy.

2 cups basmati rice

12 cups water

Approximately 2 tablespoons melted ghee or butter

Wash the rice thoroughly until the water runs clear. Place in a bowl and add cold water to cover by at least 2 inches. Let soak for 30 minutes, then drain.

In a large pot, bring the water to a vigorous rolling boil. Add the rice, bring back to the boil, and cook for 3 to 5 minutes, uncovered, until the rice is just tender but not mushy. Drain thoroughly in a sieve. Place back in the pot, set over very low heat, drizzle on some melted ghee or butter, and cover tightly. Let steam-cook for 20 minutes. Serve mounded on a platter, either plain or with a little more melted ghee or butter drizzled over.

# Basmati Rice

*absorption method*

**Makes about 5½ cups rice**

IN THE ABSORPTION METHOD, ALL THE COOKING WATER IS ABSORBED BY THE rice. Basmati is, as always, soaked first. Traditionally the rice is then cooked in its soaking water, as described below.

2 cups basmati rice

2½ cups water

2 tablespoons melted ghee or butter (optional)

Wash the rice thoroughly in several changes of cold water. Let soak in the 2½ cups cold water for 30 minutes, then drain well in a sieve, reserving the water.

Place the rice in a heavy medium pot with the reserved water and bring to a vigorous boil. Stir gently, cover tightly, and turn the heat to low. Cook for 15 minutes. Turn off the heat and let stand, covered, for 10 minutes.

Serve on a platter, drizzled with a little melted ghee or butter if you wish.

# Brown Basmati Rice

BASMATI IS ALSO AVAILABLE UNMILLED, AS BROWN RICE. TO COOK PLAIN brown basmati, follow the directions given for regular basmati, but double the cooking time and water quantity for the absorption method. If using the lots-of-water method (page 236), the boiling rice will take about twice as long to become tender; it should then be steamed for 25 minutes.

# Rice in India

When you're traveling in India by train and it takes several days and nights to go from one end of the country to the other, you know it is a huge country. It also feels huge when you realize that over fourteen major languages are spoken, and that there are altogether over one hundred ten languages and dialects. But India is in area less than one third the size of the United States, roughly the size of the continental United States from the Rocky Mountains west to California.

The north of India is well watered by rivers flowing from the Himalaya through the northern plains to the sea: the Brahamaputra, the Ganges, the Sutlej, and others. Running from the southern edge of the plains all the way to the southern tip of India is a range of hills called the Ghats. They slope steeply down to the sea on the west side of the subcontinent, and more gradually on the eastern side. The south of India is a lusher and more tropical place than the north, with small differences in average seasonal temperatures. On the southwest—or Kerala—side, the monsoon comes from May to September, while on the southeast side, the monsoon period is from October to December.

In the production of rice, India is second only to China, and far ahead of Indonesia, the world's third largest producer. As in China, rice grows in all regions of the country, but in some areas it is only a minor crop compared to other grains. It is grown predominantly in southern India, in the Himalayan foothills, in Bengal, and in Assam, along the Brahmaputra River.

Farmer returning home, near Khajuraho

Rice cultivation in India goes back at least four thousand years, and because rice has been grown in so many different locations under so many different conditions, there is a rich diversity of species. Several hundred varieties are grown and eaten in India, from the long needle-shaped basmati in the northern hills to the plump speckled-red rices of Kerala and Tamil Nadu.

Rice eaters in India, like rice eaters everywhere, have strong likes and dislikes when it comes to what rice they prefer (though economy often has a greater impact on what rice they buy). People make distinctions between a rice that is good for a *pulao*, one that is good as a sweet pudding, and one that they prefer as their daily rice. Parboiling is common, and in a restaurant, you often will be asked if you prefer "boiled," meaning parboiled, or ordinary rice. Outside India, Indian basmati rice is the rice most closely associated with Indian cooking, but in some parts, South India, for example, it is seldom used.

**left to right**

Harvesting rice near Calcutta

Selling puffed rice and roasted chickpeas in Jodhpur

In the regions of India where rice is the staple grain, it is generally eaten in one form or another at every meal. At lunch in South India, which is the main meal of the day, almost every restaurant serves what is called the "standard meal," or "measured meal," or just plain "meal" for short. A sign will often be put outside announcing "meals ready." The measured part of this meal, the standard part, is the amount of rice that each person receives, which is two hundred and fifty grams of cooked rice, approximately half a pound. Curries, yogurt dishes, chutneys, pickles, and poppodums are all served with the rice, and even though you can have second and third helpings of almost all these other foods, people seldom do. It is the rice that is the meal, and the other foods are there mainly to accompany the rice, to flavor it.

Rice cookery in the north of India, particularly in the northwestern states and in Moslem homes, shows its Mogul heritage in its rich rice *pulaos* and other flavored rice dishes. In Bengal and the South, rice is more often kept plain and then served with foods that bring flavor to it.

More so than in many other countries where rice is eaten as a staple food, in India there are a great many different ways in which it is transformed before being eaten. It is often puffed (in a way not unlike our common breakfast cereal), then eaten as a savory snack (see Spicy Puffed Rice Snack, page 276). It can also be smashed flat to make rice flakes, known as *aval* in Kerala (see Alternative, page 279). In the South in particular, wet rice is ground into a paste that is used to make dumplings and flatbreads. Rice flour is also used extensively for other breads and noodles. In a Tamil dish called *puttu*, rice flour is mixed with grated coconut and steamed in long bamboo tubes, coming to the table as cyclinders of rice ready to be eaten with South Indian Lentil Stew (page 264) or even a tiny sweet banana and a pappadum.

# Gobindavog Rice

IN CALCUTTA, WE WERE INTRODUCED TO A PRINCELY RICE KNOWN AS gobindavog. It is a polished white medium-grain rice, but on a miniature scale, like a baby basmati. It has a delicate, very slightly sweet flavor. In Calcutta, we had it cooked the lots-of-water way with a little salt (as described below). Each time, the rice emerged firm yet tender, with beautifully separate grains. It's an expensive rice in Bengal, within reach only of those with some extra money, but for those who can afford it, it's the rice of choice. Gobindavog is also used to make a delicious rice pudding (see page 281).

When we came home from India, one of the rices we went looking for, without much optimism, was this fabulous one. We were delighted to find it at Kalustyan's in New York (see Mail-Order Sources, page 438). It is now being sold more widely, sometimes labeled "Kalijira." If you ever come across it, buy plenty, then use it as a delicious and delicate everyday plain rice as well as an alternative to basmati for pilafs.

2 cups gobindavog rice

Approximately 10 cups water

1 tablespoon salt

2 tablespoons melted butter or ghee (optional)

Wash the rice under cold running water until the water runs clear. Drain in a sieve.

Bring the water to a vigorous boil in a large pot. Add the salt and then sprinkle in the rice. Bring back to a rolling boil, giving the occasional stir with a long-handled wooden spoon to ensure no rice is sticking. Let boil for 6 to 7 minutes, uncovered, until the rice is just cooked through but still firm. (Test a grain of rice every 30 seconds or so from the 5-minute mark onward to see whether it has cooked through; cooking times will vary with the age of the rice and the altitude.)

Drain the rice in a sieve (placed over a large pot if you have another use for the rice cooking water). Immediately return the rice to the pot, place a cotton cloth over the top, and put on a tight-fitting lid. Let stand for 15 minutes to steam and firm up, then stir gently with a rice paddle to break up any clumped-together rice. The rice should be firm but not soggy, with tender separate grains. Transfer to a platter or bowl and serve, either plain or with a little ghee or melted butter drizzled over.

# Bhutanese Red Rice

BHUTAN IS AN INDEPENDENT KINGDOM IN THE HIMALAYA, JUST WEST OF THE Indian region of Assam. Locally grown red rice is the staple grain of most people in Bhutan. It grows in many parts of the country, except in the high-altitude valleys, where only buckwheat and barley can survive. Recently this interesting and very attractive red rice has become available in North America.

Bhutanese red is a medium-grain japonica-type rice that has been semi-milled. The red of the outer layers is still on the rice in patches, but because it is somewhat polished, it cooks more quickly than brown rice. The cooked rice is pale pink, soft and tender, and slightly clingy so it's easy to eat with chopsticks. Its texture most resembles semi-milled Japanese rice. It can be served in place of white or brown rice, accompanied by hearty side dishes such as bean or meat stews, or can be used to make Central Asian *pulaos* (see Uighur Autumn Pulao, page 310). We make it without salt.

2 cups Bhutanese red rice

3 cups water

½ teaspoon salt (optional)

Place the rice in a pot or bowl and cover with cold water. Swish around well and drain. The water will be a little red. Repeat two or three times, until the water runs clear. Drain well in a sieve.

Place the rice in a heavy medium pot with the water and the salt, if using. Bring to a boil and skim off the foam, then cover, lower the heat to low, and cook for 25 minutes. Remove from the heat and let stand for 10 minutes, still with the lid on. Turn gently with a rice paddle and serve.

**Note:** Recently, another red rice from the Himalayas has come on the North American market. It is usually labeled "Himalayan red rice." It looks very like Thai red rice, with long, slender, red-brown grains. Cook it as you would Thai Red Rice (page 121) and serve it in place of brown rice or partnered with a dal or curry.

# Parboiled Rices

Parboiling is an ingenious technique for increasing the nutritional value of polished rices. It dates back many centuries and seems to have been developed in southern India. Many people in Bengal, Bangladesh, southern India, and Sri Lanka prefer parboiled rice.

Rice still in the hull is boiled, then cooled. This has the effect of driving vitamins from the bran into the center of the rice. The rice is then husked (the hulls are removed) and milled (which gives it better storage qualities—no germ or bran to go rancid). Though milled, it retains much of the nutritional value of unpolished (brown) rice.

Because the rice has been heated, the starches in parboiled rice have gelatinized and are harder in texture. Consequently, it takes a little longer to cook than milled rice that has not been parboiled. The grains also have a slightly glassy look to them and tend to be yellowish rather than semitransparent white.

In North America, parboiling was adopted as a means of improving the nutritional value of rice early in the twentieth century. Some parboiled rice is also precooked, at least partly, so that it does not take as long to cook as parboiled rices from India. Many American rices are available in both parboiled and unboiled forms, though sometimes they are not marked as such. You can usually tell if a rice has been parboiled because its grains will be yellowish in color and more glassy than an unboiled rice. When cooked, it will have a slightly bouncy texture; the grains seem to bounce away from one another. Consequently, parboiled rice usually yields a larger volume of cooked rice, just because the cooked grains are more separate.

Preparing parboiled rice in rural Bengal

# Rosematta

*south indian red rice*

ROSEMATTA, A PARBOILED RED RICE FROM SOUTH INDIA, HAS SLIGHTLY FAT, long grains with some flecks of the reddish outer layers (bran) still on, like a semi-milled rice. When it is raw, even the "white" part of the rice is yellowish because of parboiling. The overall look of the raw rice is pinkish bronze to amber. When you wash the rice, the water foams a bit, perhaps because of loose starch, and it runs a reddish brown color. Once the rice comes to a boil, a brownish froth rises to the surface, rather like the foam when you first bring kidney beans or other dried beans to a boil. Skim off and discard the foam, trying not to remove much water. If you feel you've tossed out a fair amount of water while skimming off the foam, add another quarter cup of hot water to the boiling rice.

When cooked, the rice grains almost seem to bounce apart (like many parboiled rices); they never stick together, but always remain separate. They fill out and become quite "fat" or rounded. The cooked rice has a much whiter color than the uncooked, so that the bits of red show up more clearly as a contrasting color. During cooking, the rice has an almost meaty smell, and the taste of the cooked rice is also somewhat smoky-meaty, reminiscent of small red beans or kidney beans. It reminds us a little of the taste of pork cracklings.

Rosematta goes best with strong flavors and leftovers are particularly good when reheated with definite flavors, such as those in the Quick Onion Pilaf (page 278), or treated cross-culturally and fried South Carolina style, in a little bacon drippings flavored with onion (see page 396).

> 2 cups rice
>
> 3 cups water (2¾ if using a rice cooker)

Wash the rice thoroughly under running water. The water will run reddish brown at first. Place in a sieve to drain. Pick through the rice and discard any hard kernels or other irregularities.

Place in a heavy medium pot or in a rice cooker and add the water.

*If using a pot,* bring to vigorous boil, stir briefly, and boil uncovered for 3 to 4 minutes. Stir again, cover, and lower the heat to medium-low. Simmer for 5 minutes, then reduce the heat to very low and cook, still covered, for another 12 to 15 minutes. Let stand for another 10 to 15 minutes, without lifting the lid, to steam, then stir gently with a wooden paddle. The rice should be firm, bouncy even, and cooked through.

*If using a rice cooker,* turn on, cover, and let cook. When the cooker turns off, let stand, covered for 10 to 15 minutes, before stirring.

# Bash Ful

*parboiled bengali rice*

WE'VE SEEN THIS TASTY PARBOILED BANGLADESHI RICE FOR SALE ONLY AT Kalustyan's in New York (see Mail-Order Sources, page 438). It is an overall beige-cream in color and looks like a blend of rices, with some grains having small flecks of red bran on them and others translucent with an opaque white strip (probably from incomplete parboiling). The rice is short- to medium-grain (the grains are not very long and are quite wide in proportion to their length). As it cooks, in plenty of boiling water, a pale pinkish foam rises to the surface. When cooked, the grains are separate, soft, and tender. This rice is an excellent accompaniment to dals of all kinds.

| | |
|---|---|
| 2 cups bash ful rice | 1 tablespoon salt (optional) |
| About 10 cups water | 2 tablespoons melted butter or ghee (optional) |

Wash the rice thoroughly under cold running water until the water runs clear. Place in a sieve to drain. Pick over the rice and discard any stones or imperfect grains.

Bring a large pot of water to a vigorous boil. Add the optional salt. Sprinkle in the rice and stir gently while the water comes back to a boil. Skim off and discard any foam that rises to the surface. Boil uncovered until the rice is cooked through and tender but not mushy, 11 to 12 minutes from when it comes back to the boil. Test a grain every so often to check for doneness.

Drain the rice in a sieve, shaking the sieve gently to drain off excess water. Place the rice in a wide bowl or back in the pot. Drizzle on the melted butter or ghee if you wish. We like to let the rice stand for at least 5 minutes before serving; it has a more pleasant taste after this short rest. Cover with a cotton cloth until ready to serve, then turn out onto a platter or into a serving bowl.

# South Indian Rice Stall

For several days in the city of Trivandrum in South India, I hung out in the local market with two young brothers who ran their family's rice and lentil stall. They'd agreed to teach me about rice, so I sat in a corner of their tiny stall, watching and listening as people came by and purchased rice: two kilos, five kilos, twenty kilos. Occasionally there were disputes—the price was too high, the rice was poor quality, the kilo wasn't quite a kilo—but they were generally good humored. The brothers were exceptionally nice people, and I had the feeling that they had a very dedicated clientele.

"This rice is for making *dosa*," they explained, holding up a handful of rice. "It sells for nine rupees a kilo and it comes from Tamil Nadu. This rice is from Kerala, people cook it for meals, but it doesn't have a good taste. But it is cheap, five rupees a kilo. . . . ." They sold eleven different rices in their stall, and there were several others that they didn't carry but described in detail. All were set out side by side in wooden bins, next to the brilliant reds, greens, and yellows of the lentils and beans. If people wanted large quantities, there were big bags piled high in every corner of the stall.

Evening at the brothers' rice stall in Palayam market

Shoppers would often pick up a little rice and look it over, a little bit like selecting tomatoes. Then they'd bargain, or at least quibble. They'd pick up a little more, then let it fall through their fingers back into the bin. When a price and an amount were settled upon, one of the brothers scooped up the rice and poured it into a paper bag, then packaged it tightly in a sheet of newspaper and tied it with a piece of twine.

I loved it all. I loved the sweet dusty smell of the stall, the sound of the rice being scooped and poured, the rustle of the paper, the mock disputes, the laughter, the background commotion of a busy market. Every once in a while a brother would yell out for "*chai,*" sweet milk tea, and it would miraculously appear moments later at the stall. The brothers talked to me about the price of rice, about who likes what rice and why, about different ways of cooking different varieties. They talked about their father and grandfather, who used to run the stall.

And then, come evening, they lit incense and put it on the altar for Ganesh, the elephant god, who keeps a watchful eye over the store. At night the market glowed with color, quietly lit with dim bare light bulbs and small white candles.

# Hot Spice Powder

*garam masala*

**Makes about 1½ cups spice powder**

ALTHOUGH YOU CAN BUY COMMERCIALLY PREPARED *GARAM MASALA,* MAKING your own yields a better-tasting powder, isn't time-consuming, and can be a lot of fun. This blend is one we particularly like; you may, however, want to play around with the balance of flavors, perhaps increasing the cinnamon or cutting back on the coriander.

Dry-roasting the whole spices before grinding makes them easier to grind and brings out their flavors. *Garam masala* will keep well for several months in a tightly sealed jar, though with some loss of flavor over time. Use it in recipes as directed or sprinkle lightly on freshly cooked corn or hot pappadums just before serving.

½ cup black peppercorns

½ cup coriander seed

½ cup cumin seed

2 tablespoons cloves

1 tablespoon seeds from green cardamom pods

2 inches cinnamon stick, broken into several pieces

Combine all the ingredients in a bowl. Heat a large skillet over medium-high heat. Add all the spices and dry-roast, stirring constantly with a wooden spoon. After 3 to 4 minutes, the spices will start to give off an aroma. Keep heating and stirring for 2 minutes more, then empty into a bowl.

In a clean spice grinder or mortar, grind the roasted spices to a powder. When completely cooled, store in a clean glass jar.

# Ripe Mango Chutney

*Serves 4 to 6 as a salad or condiment*
*accompanying a pulao or a plain rice meal*

THIS SIMPLE FRESH CHUTNEY TAKES JUST MINUTES TO PREPARE, AND LESS time than that to eat (it's so good), so if you are making it for a dinner, be prepared to hide it before kitchen predators decide to take "just a bite." The lime juice brings out all that wonderful mango sweetness, and then there is a little bite of chile. You can still make the chutney even if you don't have curry leaves, either fresh or dried; they just give it an extra savory depth.

This is one Indian dish that also goes well with a non-Indian menu—for example, with Persian or Silk Road rice dishes and grilled meats (see Index).

2 ripe mangoes (about 1 pound), peeled, pitted, and coarsely chopped

2 tablespoons minced green cayenne chiles or 2 to 3 tablespoons minced jalapeño chiles

2 tablespoons minced shallots

1 teaspoon peanut oil or vegetable oil

5 to 6 fresh or dried curry leaves (see Glossary)

½ teaspoon salt, or more to taste

⅓ cup loosely packed fresh coriander leaves

3 tablespoons fresh lime juice, or more to taste

Combine the mangoes, chiles, and shallots in a medium bowl and stir to mix.

Heat the oil in a small heavy skillet. Add the curry leaves and fry, stirring occasionally, for 1 minute. Add to the mangoes. Stir in the salt, coriander, and lime juice. Taste and adjust the balance of salt and lime juice if necessary.

# Fresh Carrot Chutney

**Makes about 1 cup medium-hot chutney;**
**serves 4 to 6 as a chutney or 2 as a salad**

LIKE RIPE MANGO CHUTNEY (PAGE 247), CARROT CHUTNEY CAN BE SERVED with a great many different meals. It is tangy and tart as an intense little salad on its own, yet served with other strong flavors, it becomes a refreshing taste to bring balance to a meal. And carrots are available all year, so you can enjoy this chutney anytime.

| | |
|---|---|
| 1 cup coarsely grated carrots (2 medium) | 3 tablespoons fresh lime juice |
| 2 jalapeño chiles, minced (see Note) | 2 tablespoons chopped fresh coriander leaves |
| ¼ teaspoon salt | |

*If using a food processor,* place the carrot and chiles in the processor and process for 30 seconds. Transfer to a bowl and stir in the salt and lime juice. *If using a large mortar and pestle,* pound the chiles with the salt almost to a paste. Add the grated carrot and pound to soften and blend. Transfer to a bowl and stir in the lime juice.

Just before serving, stir in the coriander.

Serve to accompany pulao or plain rice with other dishes.

Note: In India, this chutney would be made using fresh green cayenne chiles. Use whatever fresh hot chiles you have available or prefer.

# Sultana Chutney

NAOMI ESPECIALLY LOVES SWEET-HOT CHUTNEYS, AND THIS SULTANA CHUTNEY is just that. The raisins are spiced with cumin seed, warmed with ginger, and made hot with fresh chiles. It is an excellent dish to serve on the side with a *pulao,* and perhaps a yogurt dish as well. We also serve it with plain rice and Bengali Potato and Cauliflower Curry (page 271) for a good simple meal.

| | |
|---|---|
| 1 teaspoon cumin seed | 4 serrano chiles, coarsely chopped |
| 1 tablespoon minced ginger | 1 cup sultana (golden) raisins |
| ¼ teaspoon salt | 3 to 4 tablespoons fresh lime juice |

Heat a small heavy skillet over high heat, toss in the cumin seed, and dry-roast, stirring constantly, until the seeds start to change color. Remove from the heat and continue to stir briefly, then transfer to a spice grinder or mortar and pestle and grind to a powder.

*If using a mortar and pestle,* add the ginger and salt and grind to a paste, then add the chiles and pound and grind well. Add half the raisins, and pound until well mashed, then remove the mixture and pound and mash the remaining raisins. Return the spice mixture to the mortar and pound to blend. The texture should be gooey and fairly even. Stir in enough lime juice to make a soft paste.

*If using a food processor,* blend the powdered cumin, the ginger, and salt together in a small bowl, then transfer to the processor. Add the chiles and raisins and process to a paste, about 30 seconds. Add the lime juice and process briefly to blend.

Transfer the chutney to a sealed nonreactive container and store in the refrigerator until ready to use. Serve at room temperature.

# Apple-Cucumber Salad with Split Mung Dal

*kosumbara*

**Serves 4 to 6 as part of a rice-based meal**

WAY DOWN AT THE VERY BOTTOM TIP OF INDIA THERE IS A TOWN/PILGRIMAGE site called Kanyakumari, in the state of Tamil Nadu. It is a delightful place to visit, as it is small and easy to negotiate, and you are always there with pilgrims from all over India. If you arrive on the day of the full moon, it is a particularly auspicious time. You can sit on the beach and watch as the big tropical sun dips down into the water to the west at just the same moment as the moon is coming out of the water to the east, one hundred and eighty degrees away. For the few days I was there, each evening I would walk up the beach until I found a lonely spot and there sleep the night, waking at dawn to see the gorgeous black sails of fishing boats already out in the water, looking like a vast school of treacherous sharks.

Fishing boat heading out from the village in Kerala

But, best of all, the true delight of being in Kanyakumari is a culinary one. With people coming from all over India, there are individual restaurants that specialize in each and every regional cuisine. Within a few short blocks you can choose from among Maharastrian, Orissan, Bengali, Gujarati, Malayli, and Tamil foods, to mention but a few of the choices. And you can people-watch, trying to guess with each little group of pilgrims entering a particular restaurant whether they are searching out their own food or being adventurous and trying something else.

From the regional cuisine of Tamil Nadu and nearby Andra Pradesh, *kosumbara* is a vegetable salad that comes in many guises, all of them delicious. The distinguishing feature about the salad is the use of black mustard seeds for flavor and split mung dal for color and texture. In this particular version, the combination of crunchy apples and cucumber is so refreshing that we find ourselves putting back spoonfuls of the salad before it ever reaches the table. If it does reach the table, it's great paired with a big-flavor curry and rice.

1 tablespoon split mung dal
(see Glossary)

1 large European cucumber

1 Granny Smith apple

1 green cayenne chile or 2 jalapeño
chiles, seeded and finely chopped

¾ cup loosely packed fresh coriander
leaves

2 tablespoons fresh lime juice

½ teaspoon salt, or to taste

### Tempering

1 tablespoon vegetable oil

1 teaspoon mustard seed (see Glossary)

1 teaspoon cumin seed

1 tablespoon dried curry leaves
(see Glossary)

Place the dal in a small bowl with 1 cup water and soak for 1 hour.

Cut the cucumber lengthwise into 4 or 6 wedges. Discard the seeds, then cut crosswise into ¼-inch to ½-inch chunks. Place in a large bowl. Core the apple, but do not peel, then cut into small chunks and add to the cucumber. Add the chile, coriander, soaked dal, and lime juice and toss to blend well.

Heat a small heavy skillet over medium heat. Add the oil and when it is hot, toss in the remaining tempering ingredients. Give a quick stir, then cover to prevent the mustard seeds from popping out. When most of the seeds have popped, about 30 seconds, remove from the heat and pour over the salad. Sprinkle on the salt and toss well. Serve in a shallow bowl.

# Banana Salad

**Serves 4 to 6 as one of several condiments and side dishes**

WHAT MAKES A MEMORY STICK? I'LL NEVER FORGET THE MAN WHO CAME straight up to me early one morning on a railway platform in India and opened his trenchcoat,

Neighborhood stall selling bananas and other daily necessities, in Trivandrum

motioning with a quick serious gesture for me to look down at what he had exposed. And so I did, and there before me I beheld row upon row of mustaches pinned to his shirt and the inside of his coat. Hundreds of mustaches! Thank you, but I don't want a mustache, I nodded back politely.

Some memories stick for a very good reason, like the memory of the first time I ate a banana salad very similar to this one. I was at a local temple festival in Kerala, and when this salad was served on a small section of green banana leaf, the last thing I expected to be tasting with sweet ripe banana was cumin seeds and cayenne. It's a great combo.

| | |
|---|---|
| 2 large ripe bananas | ¼ teaspoon cayenne pepper |
| 1 teaspoon vegetable oil or peanut oil | ¼ teaspoon salt |
| 1 teaspoon cumin seed | ¼ cup plain yogurt (whole-milk or 2%) |

Peel the bananas and coarsely chop. Heat the oil in a heavy skillet over medium heat. When it is hot, add the cumin seed and stir for 20 seconds, then add the bananas, cayenne, and salt. Stir gently, so as not to mash the bananas, for 30 seconds. Remove from the heat and stir in the yogurt. Turn out into a bowl and serve warm or at room temperature to accompany plain rice and rice dishes.

# Assamese Salad with Radishes, Chiles, and Lime

MOST PEOPLE IN ASSAM EAT RICE IN SOME FORM THREE TIMES A DAY. ON our way up the Brahmaputra River valley from Guwahati to Kaziranga, we passed piles of harvested rice spread out on the road to dry. Farther up the valley we started to see tea plantations, vast acreages covered with the low trimmed shapes of tea trees. Every so often we'd see tea workers, mostly women, carrying huge baskets, moving through the shiny green of the tea.

Later, at market day in the small village near our guest house, we came upon a queue of tea workers waiting for their rations. Many of them come from extremely poor rural areas in other poorer states, such as Orissa, and from Bangladesh. In Assam, their pay is low and their working conditions the subject of strikes, protest, and blockades. They are often paid in food rather than in cash. These women were waiting with baskets to pick up their rice rations, local rice, white and long-grain.

This daikon salad is a good example of straightforward Assamese cooking. It makes an easy accompaniment to any meal, a cross between a salad and a fresh chutney. The lime juice and dried chile set off the freshness of the radish and leave a pleasing hot tart tingle in the mouth.

1 cup coarsely grated, peeled daikon radish, preferably from the top or midsection (see Glossary), or icicle radish (about ⅓ pound)

1 dried red chile (see Glossary) or a generous pinch of chile pepper flakes, or more to taste

2 tablespoons fresh lime juice

¼ teaspoon salt

With your hands, squeeze out the excess moisture from the grated radish. Place in a shallow decorative bowl. Finely mince the chile, if using, discarding the stem and seeds, and add to the radish; or add the chile pepper flakes. Mix together the lime juice and salt. Pour over the salad, then toss gently to mix well. Serve at room temperature.

# Kaziranga

Long ago, when I was living in Sri Lanka, I had a roommate who was from the Netherlands. He was the most courageous traveler I had ever met, having no fear of wild animals or snakes or the jungle, all the things that I will never get accustomed to. From where we lived outside the town of Kandy, he would deliberately take a route into town that took him through the jungle, while I would always walk safely on the road. He'd routinely encounter snakes, and if it was one he'd never seen before, I would hear about it at length that night over dinner. Lucky for me, he was as good a storyteller as he was courageous.

I can no longer remember his name, but I do remember his stories. Once he walked from Indonesian Borneo through the jungle and mountains to Malaysian Borneo, a feat that was not only immensely dangerous, but also absolutely illegal. In Tamil Negara National Park in Malaysia, he traveled by boat in the rainy season, pulling or burning off leeches by the hundreds. In Periyar National Park in India (he'd been to every national park in India), he'd camped one night in the jungle only to be awakened by a herd of elephants stampeding through. "I was really scared," he admitted (the only time I ever heard him say it). "Think about it. When it is totally dark in the jungle and you hear a herd of elephants on the run, you have no idea what direction they are running, and no idea how far away they are."

In the middle of our stay in Sri Lanka, he left and walked into Yala National Park in the southeastern corner of the country. He'd read about a tribe of people who lived there who had had very little contact with the outside world, so he'd decided to trek in and meet them. Two weeks later he was back. He'd had a great time, he'd stayed with the tribe and learned a new way of curing snake bite that involved putting a certain kind of porous stone immediately onto the wound. He was thrilled!

Elephant mother and child heading home with their *mahout,* in Kaziranga

Well, somewhere in the course of our stay together, I asked him if he knew of a national park that I might enjoy, one for people who feel more comfortable in restaurants than in jungles.

"Kaziranga," he at last blurted out. "Kaziranga, in Assam. You can enter by elephant. You won't even need to get off the elephant. It's the only way to enter the park."

"Sounds good," I said. "Kaziranga—I'll go."

So for years hence I tried to go to Kaziranga, but what he had neglected to tell me was that I would need a special permit to go, that I would even need a special permit to go to

Mishin woman bringing home fish from the Brahmaputra River

Assam, the long narrow state in the far northeast corner of India where the national park is located. Several times I went to Calcutta specifically to apply for a permit, only to be routinely sent away.

Recently, staying in Calcutta looking for rice, we thought we'd try again. We turned up at the same old government office, Dominic, Tashi, Naomi, and I, and we applied. And then we waited for the same old hours-of-nothing-happening until the official came back into the room. But this time something funny occurred. Dominic, who was sitting quietly on a chair, suddenly screamed and held his hand up over his mouth, blood pouring out. We were all terrified, including the government official, but then we discovered that he'd simply lost his first baby tooth.

The government official gave us a permit.

And Kaziranga National Park was everything my roommate had promised it would be. We went into the park each day by elephant, and we got right up close to one-horned rhinos, wild buffalo, wild deer. In the late afternoon we'd hang out with the *mahouts* (the elephant keepers) as they'd wash down the elephants. Sometimes in the morning while we were riding on the elephant, the *mahout* would take the kids up with him on the elephant's neck and teach them how to steer using their toes to touch behind the elephant's ears. One time I dropped a lens cap from my camera and it fell into the tall wild grass below, but the *mahout* simply spoke to the elephant and the elephant stopped, dropped her enormous trunk down into the tall grass, and then swooped her trunk back up and over at me, handing me my tiny lens cap. Once our elephant stopped in her tracks, lowered her head, and moaned several times, sniffing with the delicate tip of her trunk at a pile of scattered broken bones on the ground. "Elephant graveyard," said the *mahout*. We were there a long silent moment, then she set off again through the grass.

And do you know what else, in Assam, in late November? It was the height of rice harvest!

# Spicy Yogurt Sauce with Ginger
## inji pachadi

**Serves 6 or more as a condiment for plain rice or flavored rice dishes**

PACHADIS FROM SOUTH INDIA ARE NOT TO BE CONFUSED WITH RAITAS FROM North India. While both dishes have yogurt as a base, in a *pachadi* the yogurt is either warmed slightly at the end, or it is beaten into the cooked ingredients right as they come off the flame. *Pachadis* are a kind of cross between a sauce and a salad.

We like this *pachadi*, with its strong flavors of ginger and coconut, almost more the second day, as the coconut recedes just a bit and the ginger comes forward. There is a some chile warmth, but it is not at all hot.

1 cup plain yogurt (whole-milk or 2%)

½ teaspoon salt

¼ teaspoon mustard seed plus a pinch (see Glossary)

Pinch of cumin seed

2 tablespoons fresh, frozen, or dried grated unsweetened coconut (see Glossary)

About 1 tablespoon water

1 teaspoon vegetable oil

1 dried red chile (see Glossary)

1 to 2 dried curry leaves (see Glossary)

3 tablespoons finely minced ginger

Place the yogurt in a medium bowl, stir in the salt, and set aside.

In a spice grinder or mortar, grind the ¼ teaspoon mustard seed to a powder. Add the cumin seed and grind well. Transfer to a small bowl and stir in the coconut. Add enough water to make a paste, and set aside.

Heat the oil in a heavy skillet over medium heat. Toss in the pinch of mustard seed, the dried red chile, and curry leaves and stir briefly. Cover for 15 seconds, or until the mustard seeds stop popping. Add the spice paste and cook, stirring constantly, for 2 minutes. Lower the heat, add the ginger, and cook and stir for 15 seconds. Stir in the yogurt and cook over lowest heat for about 1 minute; do not boil. Remove from the heat. Serve at room temperature in a bowl, or store in the refrigerator in a covered glass jar for up to 5 days.

# Spicy Yogurt Sauce with Banana
## *pazham pachadi*

**Serves 6 or more as a condiment for plain rice or flavored rice dishes**

THIS BANANA *PACHADI* COMES OUT A VERY PRETTY LIGHT GREEN FROM the blend of green chiles and turmeric. Like the ginger *pachadi* on the facing page, it has a bit of chile heat, but the combination of banana and chile is wild and delicious. When you first make the sauce, it may seem a bit watery (and the same is true with the ginger *pachadi*), but it thickens as it cools. Either way, thick or thin, *pachadis* are a great accompaniment to rice—which is what they are designed to be.

½ teaspoon mustard seed plus a pinch (see Glossary)

1 large red or green cayenne chile or 2 jalapeño chiles, minced (about 2½ tablespoons)

2 tablespoons fresh, frozen, or dried grated unsweetened coconut (see Glossary)

½ teaspoon salt

About 1 tablespoon water

1 tablespoon vegetable oil

1 dried curry leaf (see Glossary)

1 large ripe banana, coarsely chopped

Pinch of turmeric

1½ cups plain yogurt (whole-milk or 2%)

In a spice grinder or a mortar, grind the ½ teaspoon mustard seed to a powder. Transfer to a bowl (unless you're using a large mortar). Add the chile, coconut, and salt. Use the back of a spoon (or the pestle) to mash and blend the mixture. Add enough water to form a paste, and set aside.

Heat a heavy skillet over medium heat and add the oil. When it is hot, toss in the pinch of mustard seed and the curry leaf, stir briefly, and cover for 15 seconds, or until the mustard seeds stop popping. Add the chile paste and cook, stirring constantly, for 2 minutes. Stir in the banana and turmeric, lower the heat a little, and cook, stirring and turning, for 30 seconds. Reduce the heat to very low, stir in the yogurt, and cook, stirring constantly, for another minute; the mixture must not boil. Serve warm or at room temperature. The *pachadi* can be stored in the refrigerator in a covered glass container for up to 5 days.

# Gita's Dal

**Serves 4 to 6 as part of a rice-based meal**

OUR SON TASHI'S PLAYSCHOOL WAS THE REASON WE ENDED UP IN CALCUTTA. His friend's mother, Sanjukta, is from Calcutta, and we used to talk together about India while our children, then three years old, would play together in the park after playschool.

"Where would you go in India to learn about rice?" we asked Sanjukta one day.

"To Bengal, to Calcutta," she replied without hesitation. "If you like, you can stay in my mother's apartment, she spends most of the year in Delhi."

And so it happened one year later, there we were, in Sanjukta's mother's apartment, in the heart of Calcutta. At night, sitting on a sofa on the balcony of the apartment, we would look up at a star-filled sky, finding the Big Dipper. We would talk quietly, wondering how, in the center of a city of thirteen million people, it could be so quiet, so peaceful.

In the daytime, like everyone else, we'd hit the street. Amid the beggars and the rickshaw drivers and the thousands of homeless people who call Calcutta home, we'd go to the market, we'd go exploring, we'd go looking for diversions for Dominic and Tashi and

*Gita cutting vegetables in the kitchen*

ourselves. A month is a long time in Calcutta, a lifetime in terms of thoughts and images.

We shared Sanjukta's mother's apartment with three people: Gita, Shanatan, and Joy. Gita was cook, Shanatan looked after things, and Joy was Shanatan's brother. And for a month we were all a family. Gita, never having lived or worked with foreigners before, didn't know what to make of us at first, but she quickly got our number. She taught Dominic to make his own chapattis, and she delighted Tashi with sweet rice pudding and deep-fried puris. She taught us how to use the traditional Bengali mortar and pestle to grind a spice mixture, and how to cut long beans into perfect thin strips using a Bengali kitchen knife, a sharp curved vertical blade attached to a heavy board, which sat on the floor. Everything happened on the floor, in fact, so she taught us all about clean feet.

Gita's life is not an easy one, and probably not a very happy one. But she has a smile that would make us melt. And she cooks with an enormous amount of pride.

Here is Gita's simplest dal, flavored with nigella seed and mustard oil, a unique Bengali blend. Like most dals, it cooks quickly and is an easy dish to make while you are working on something else. If you want the consistency of the dal to be on the soupy side, use six cups of water to start. Serve with plain rice and a salad, or as part of a multidish rice meal, with a yogurt sauce, a cooked green vegetable, a chutney, and a sautéed or grilled meat or vegetable.

| | |
|---|---|
| 1½ cups masur (red) dal (see Glossary) | 1 dried red chile (see Glossary) |
| 5 cups water | 1½ tablespoons mustard oil or vegetable oil |
| ¾ teaspoon turmeric | |
| 1 teaspoon mustard oil (see Glossary) (optional) | 1 tablespoon minced garlic |
| | ½ teaspoon nigella seed (see Glossary) |
| ¼ teaspoon sugar | 1 teaspoon salt |
| 2 green cayenne chiles or 3 jalapeño chiles | ¼ cup packed fresh coriander leaves |

Wash and drain the dal. Place in a large pot with the water, turmeric, and, if you wish, the mustard oil and bring to a boil. Lower the heat to medium-low, skim off the foam, and simmer until the dal is tender, about 30 minutes. Turn the heat to low and stir in the sugar and whole fresh green chiles. Remove from the heat.

Place a heavy pot over medium-high heat. When it is hot, toss in the dried chile and dry-roast, moving and turning it with a wooden spoon, until it is starting to change color. Add the oil and stir to coat the chile, then toss in the garlic and nigella and stir-fry over medium heat, stirring constantly, for 3 minutes. Pour in the cooked dal and stir well. Add the salt, stir, and remove from the heat.

The dal may be left to stand, covered (refrigerated if standing for more than 1 hour), then reheated just before serving. If the consistency is too thick, stir in ½ cup or more of water as you begin reheating. To serve, turn out into a serving bowl and top with the coriander.

# Joy and His Brother

Joy is in his mid-twenties. He is the youngest of a large family and grew up in a small village about five hours southeast of Calcutta. He speaks English beautifully and after coming to Calcutta when he was nineteen or twenty, took some courses and then found a job in an office downtown. He commutes there every morning in the very crowded but surprisingly efficient Calcutta buses and electric trams. In the evening he attends night classes or plays a little cricket; when we were there, he often played with the kids. He loves Calcutta, loves the liveliness and sense of opportunity in the city. "The village is beautiful, but very limited. There's no way to earn money. If we want to get ahead, we have to be in the city. The schools are better here, there's electricity and more choice of food. Life is better here."

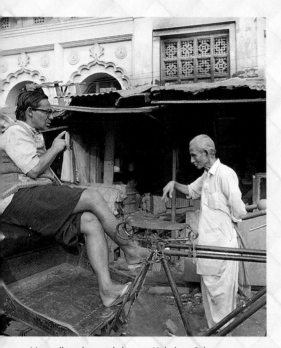

Men talking by a rickshaw in Kalighat, Calcutta

If you ask him about the crowding and dirt of Calcutta, he says, "Yes, but at least there's movement and opportunity. Poor people who come here from Bihar or Bangladesh live on the street and have problems, but most of them gradually do better and get off the street. This is a rich city."

So what are Joy's propects? Does he want to get married and have kids? Does he want to stay in Calcutta? The quick answer is "yes" to all the above, but there are several "buts." The major one is that Joy doesn't see how or when he will ever amass enough money to marry. That concerns him, but not unduly, not yet. He likes his boss and his job, but it doesn't pay enough for him to save much, particularly when a chunk of his earnings gets sent back to his mother in the village.

Joy was just a baby when, twenty-five years ago, his eldest brother, Shanatan, then a scrawny fourteen- or fifteen-year-old, now a compact fortysomething, left the family village and traveled to Calcutta to seek his fortune. Like many young migrants in the city, he hung around the railway station hoping for little jobs doing errands or transporting a load or package. One day he did a small errand for a doctor, a pediatrician, who saw the life and alertness in him and hired him to do odd jobs. Soon Shanatan had joined the household, first running errands, later working as a driver. He learned a little English and a lot of people skills.

After the doctor became ill and died, Shanatan stayed on to help run the household and also took a job working as a driver for another doctor. During all this time he was able to send money back to the village to help support his mother and his younger brothers and sisters. Eventually he was able to marry, to build a house for his family in the village, and to support his wife and two growing children. He sees them every two months or so and though he misses them in between, he is satisfied, like Joy, with his choices. His ambition now is to move his family to the city once the children are teenagers, because the schools are so much better. He wants to give them the chances he had to earn by perseverance and luck.

# Simple Dal

ONE DAY NAOMI WAS IN THE KITCHEN TESTING A RICE THAT WE HAD NEVER cooked before, a rice she had found in New York City called rosematta (see page 243). It's a red firm rice from southern India that gave a good smell to the kitchen as it cooked, a rice we have really come to love. When we sampled a spoonful, our first thought was, where is the dal? A friend was visiting at the time, so we asked her to stay for lunch, and while we chatted we put on a pot of red lentils, seasoned with a stick of cinnamon (the recipe we give here). In half an hour we were eating rice and dal. So good, and so easy.

1 cup masur (red) dal (see Glossary)

4 cups water

1 inch cinnamon stick

1 to 2 bay leaves

1 teaspoon salt

### Seasoning blend

2 tablespoons vegetable oil or ghee

½ teaspoon black mustard seed (see Glossary)

1 teaspoon cumin seed

1 heaped tablespoon dried curry leaf (see Glossary)

1 tablespoon minced garlic

1 cup finely chopped onions (about 2 medium)

Pinch of asafetida powder (see Glossary) (optional)

1 teaspoon cayenne pepper

¼ cup fresh coriander leaves

Place the dal, water, cinnamon, and bay leaf in a medium pot and bring to a boil. Skim off the foam, lower the heat, and simmer, partially covered, for 25 minutes, or until tender; the dal will be thick but still soupy. Stir in the salt, then remove from the heat.

Place a heavy skillet over high heat. Add the oil or ghee and when it is hot, add the mustard seed. Stir constantly until the seeds begin to pop, then add the cumin seed and curry leaf. Continue to stir for about 30 seconds, then add the garlic and onions. Lower the heat to medium and cook, stirring constantly, for 2 to 3 minutes. Add the asafetida and cayenne. Continue to cook for another 2 to 3 minutes, or until the onion is thoroughly softened and beginning to brown. Remove from the heat.

Reheat the dal until very hot, then stir in the seasoning blend. Transfer to a serving bowl and top with the coriander. Serve with rice and a salad or plain yogurt.

# Spinach and Mung Dal

**Serves 6 as part of a rice-based meal**

THIS IS A CLASSIC DAL FROM NORTH INDIA. IT USES YELLOW SPLIT MUNG DAL, spinach, and tomatoes, and with the yellow, green, and red, it is as attractive a dish as you might imagine. The spinach also adds interesting variety in texture.

Split mung dal, together with red lentils (masur dal), are the two legumes we try always to have stocked in our kitchen. Both are versatile, great tasting, and incredibly easy to prepare.

1 pound spinach, trimmed and thoroughly washed

1 cup split mung dal (see Glossary)

4 cups water

1 tablespoon minced garlic

1 teaspoon minced ginger

2 teaspoons salt

### Tadka (tempering)

1 tablespoon vegetable oil

1 teaspoon cumin seed

1 teaspoon cayenne pepper

1 cup finely chopped onions (2 medium)

3 medium tomatoes, coarsely chopped, or 4 canned tomatoes, drained and coarsely chopped

Place the spinach, dal, and water in a large pot. Bring to a boil and toss in the garlic, ginger, and salt, then lower the heat to medium-low and cook, partially covered, for about 25 minutes. When done, the dal will be very tender and the texture thick and stew-like.

Meanwhile, to prepare the *tadka*, heat the oil in a heavy frying pan. When it is hot, add the cumin seed and stir-fry over medium-high heat for about 15 seconds, then toss in the cayenne and onions. Cook over medium-high heat until the onions are well softened, about 5 minutes, stirring frequently, then add the tomatoes and simmer over medium heat for 5 minutes.

Add to the hot dal, stir briefly, and turn out into a serving bowl. Serve hot with rice.

# Massage

In 1977, I lived for half a year in a small yoga ashram in Trivandrum, the capital of Kerala. The guru of the ashram was a doctor of Sidhi medicine, a branch of ayurveda that focuses specifically on massage (it also includes a martial arts form).

Dr. Pillai used a great many different forms of massage. The one I had on two separate occasions is prescribed for general well-being and improved circulation and runs for an hour each day for ten consecutive days. The patient lies on a long wooden table. The masseur holds onto a rope suspended from the ceiling and uses his or her feet to massage, running them up and down the length of the patient's body (which has been oiled with ayurvedic herbal oils), half an hour on the front and half an hour on the back, never stopping. It is pure pleasure for the patient, but, better still, it brings an incredible sense of well-being, of suppleness, of energy. And for ten days, the patient has an appetite that knows no bounds, ideal for Kerala.

We strongly recommend it.

But what does this have to do with rice? One particular massage has all to do with rice. There is a variety of rice grown near Alleppi in Kerala that isn't eaten but is grown entirely for medicinal purposes. The rice is ground with water to make a thick paste, and the paste is then used to cover the patient's body, head to foot. It is an ayurvedic treatment prescribed for arthritic pain, and though I can't attest to its effectiveness firsthand, it is one that is highly regarded locally.

Young women strolling on the beach near Trivandrum

# South Indian Lentil Stew

*sambar*

Serves 4 to 6 as part of a rice-based meal

SAMBAR IS A RICHLY FLAVORED SOUTH INDIAN STEW OF DAL AND VEGETABLES, traditionally soured with tamarind. There are many different versions of *sambar*, because it is made in almost every restaurant and household across the southern part of India. Whenever you sit down to a rice meal, or to eat a *dosa* (a thin rice and lentil flatbread), *sambar* will be served as an accompaniment. It can be thick or thin, tangy and hot or quite mild in taste, but it is almost always there. We try to make a lot at a time because it freezes very well, and there is nothing so luxurious as unfreezing a container of *sambar* and having it there instantly, with rice, for dinner.

½ cup masur (red) dal (see Glossary)

3½ cups water

3 garlic cloves, coarsely chopped

½ teaspoon turmeric

### Masala (spice blend)

1 to 2 dried red chiles (see Glossary)

1 teaspoon cumin seed

½ teaspoon fenugreek seed (see Glossary)

1½ tablespoons coriander seed

1 teaspoon black peppercorns

1 heaping tablespoon tamarind pulp
  (see Glossary)

1 cup hot water

1 teaspoon salt

1 medium potato, peeled and cut into
  chunks

1 medium onion, sliced

1 cup coarsely chopped eggplant or okra

1 or 2 drumsticks (see Glossary), cut into
  1½-inch chunks (optional)

### Tempering

1 tablespoon peanut oil or vegetable oil

1 teaspoon mustard seed (see Glossary)

5 to 6 dried or fresh curry leaves
  (see Glossary)

½ teaspoon asafetida powder
  (see Glossary)

In a large heavy pot, combine the dal, 2 cups of the water, the garlic, and turmeric. Bring to a boil and cook over medium heat until the dal is very tender, about 25 minutes.

While the dal is cooking, in a heavy skillet over medium-high heat, dry-roast all the masala ingredients together, stirring frequently with a wooden spatula to prevent burning. When the chiles and spices are browning noticeably, 2 to 3 minutes, remove from the heat. Grind to a powder in a spice grinder or mortar.

In a small bowl, soak the tamarind in the hot water for 10 to 15 minutes, then strain the liquid through a sieve into another bowl and set aside. Discard the pulp.

When the dal is cooked, add the tamarind water, the remaining 1½ cups water, the salt, and the vegetables. Bring to a boil and then simmer, partially covered, until the vegetables are very tender, about 30 minutes. (At this point, the sambar can be removed from the heat and set aside until about 5 minutes before serving. Reheat, then proceed with the recipe.)

Just before you are ready to serve, heat the oil in a small heavy skillet. When it is hot, add the mustard seed, curry leaves, and asafetida. Stir briefly until the mustard seeds begin to pop, then cover until popping stops. Stir into the hot sambar and serve.

*Dosa stand at night in Kerala*

# Savory Black-eyed Peas

**Serves 6 as part of a rice-based meal**

BLACK-EYED PEAS ARE ESPECIALLY POPULAR IN NORTH INDIA, APPRECIATED for their buttery, tender texture and the tasty broth they create. This dish comes out quite soupy, so that there is lots of broth to enjoy. Serve with rice, plain yogurt or a *raita*, and a fresh tomato salad (or top with a little chopped fresh tomato).

Remember with black-eyed peas (if you are getting accustomed to superfast-cooking red and yellow dal) that they do need to be soaked overnight and that they require a longer cooking time than the split dals.

### Masala paste

2 medium onions, finely chopped

1 tablespoon minced fresh ginger

1 tablespoon minced garlic

2 green cayenne chiles, seeded and minced

### Dal

1 tablespoon vegetable oil or ghee

1 teaspoon cumin seed

1 teaspoon nigella seed (see Glossary)

½ teaspoon turmeric

1 teaspoon ground coriander

¼ cup plain yogurt (whole-milk or 2%)

1 cup black-eyed peas, soaked overnight in 5 cups water and drained

4 cups water

1 teaspoon salt

About ¼ cup chopped fresh coriander leaves

Combine all the *masala* paste ingredients in a food processor or blender or a mortar and grind or pound to a paste. If using a processor or blender, you will have to stop the machine every 5 to 10 seconds and use a spatula to push the paste ingredients back down to the blade. Transfer the paste to a small bowl.

In a large heavy pot, heat the oil or ghee. When it is hot, add the cumin seed and nigella and stir briefly. Add the *masala* paste and fry over medium heat, stirring constantly for 3 to 4 minutes. Add the turmeric and ground coriander and stir well. Add the yogurt, 1 table-spoonful at a time, stirring thoroughly after each addition.

When the yogurt is well blended, add the black-eyed peas, stir to mix well, and add the water. Bring to a boil, then lower the heat and simmer, uncovered, until tender, 1¼ to 1½ hours.

Add the salt and simmer for another 10 minutes. Serve hot in a shallow bowl, sprinkled with the coriander leaves.

Note: The dish reheats very well, so you can make it ahead, then reheat just before serving.

# Green Beans with Coconut Spice

*beans thoran*

THIS IS A CLASSIC *THORAN*, A REGIONAL SPECIALITY OF KERALA IN SOUTH India. What distinguishes a *thoran* is that it is a dry dish with a paste made with coconut (which is what Kerala grows like Wimbledon grows grass), cumin seed, and shallots or garlic. It is also necessary that the yard-long beans or green beans be cut into very small pieces.

Cooking time can vary a little bit depending on the tenderness of the beans. The final texture should be tender rather than crunchy, but the beans should still be bright green.

1 pound long beans or green beans

**Masala**

¼ teaspoon black peppercorns, ground

¼ teaspoon cayenne pepper

½ teaspoon ground cumin

½ cup fresh, frozen, or dried grated unsweetened coconut (see Glossary)

½ cup minced shallots

¼ teaspoon turmeric

**Seasoning**

1 tablespoon vegetable oil

1 dried red chile (see Glossary)

½ teaspoon mustard seed (see Glossary)

Pinch of dried curry leaves (see Glossary)

½ teaspoon split channa dal (see Glossary)

½ teaspoon urad dal (see Glossary)

1 teaspoon raw long-grain rice

1 tablespoon minced shallot

1 cup hot water

1 teaspoon salt

Top and tail the beans and slice into ¼-inch pieces. (You will have about 4 cups.) Set aside.

Place all the *masala* ingredients except the turmeric in a food processor or mortar and process or pound to a dry paste. Turn out into a bowl, stir in the turmeric, and set aside.

Place all the ingredients by your stovetop. Place a large wok or heavy pot over high heat. When it is hot, add the oil and lower the heat slightly. Toss in the dried chile and mustard seeds and stir, then add the curry leaves and cook until the mustard seeds pop. Lower the heat slightly and add the dals, rice, and shallots. Cook, stirring, until the dals and rice change color.

Add the *masala* and stir-fry for 3 minutes, or until golden brown and aromatic. Add the beans and turn and stir for several minutes, mixing well. Add the hot water and salt, bring to a boil, cover, and cook for 3 minutes. Cook, stirring and turning for 1 minute more, then lower the heat to medium, cover, and let cook until the beans are tender but still firm, 10 to 15 minutes. Cook for another 1 or 2 minutes, uncovered, to let the remaining water evaporate, then turn out onto a plate and serve.

In Khajuraho, a grandfather pounding tin while his grandchild sits close by

# Hard and Soft

Naomi likes soft foods, like *har gao* in a dim sum restaurant. I like crisp foods, tortilla chips and toast and that sort of thing. Naomi dislikes crisp foods, particularly the sound they make when people eat them. We also differ in another respect. Naomi cries easily, happy, sad, whatever, tears well up and flow. I seldom cry.

But funny thing, in India I find I cry a lot, happy, sad, whatever. I'll get to laughing and there they'll come, tears. Being in India also has a way of making me think a lot about death and life and the different stages of one's life. It's almost a cliché about foreigners visiting India, but being in India does have the effect of making one ponder life a little more, at least it does for us. One very hot day in Rajasthan I went to a big old cinema to escape the heat. The movie was a typical Hindi one with a famous female star who would pop out from behind a tree and burst into song, and then there were Krishna and Ram. It wasn't a great Hindi film, but at least the cinema was nice and cool.

Anyway, afterward as I was walking down the street I began to cry.

But I will never like soft mushy foods.

# Spicy Cabbage

IN INDIA IN THE WINTER, CABBAGE COMES INTO ITS OWN. HERE IT'S GRATED and slow-cooked until reduced to a tender dense pile, still with a little bite, beautifully tinted with turmeric and flavored with cloves, cardamom, cinnamon, ginger, and mustard oil, with some heat from dried chiles. Gita, who taught us this dish in Calcutta, used shredded (on a coarse grater) green cabbage, then made a fairly dense mound of cabbage on the plate. This version is a little wetter, slightly stew-like, though not soupy. The dish has a good depth of flavor with a slight sweetness very characteristic of Bengali dishes.

1 pound green cabbage

2 tablespoons mustard oil (see Glossary)

2 small dried red chiles (see Glossary), broken into pieces

½ teaspoon cumin seed

1 to 2 small bay leaves

2 cloves

1 inch cinnamon stick, broken into several pieces

2 green cardamom pods, smashed

1 cup thinly sliced shallots

2 medium or 3 small potatoes, peeled and cut into ½-inch cubes

1 large or 2 small plum tomatoes, coarsely chopped

1 teaspoon salt

1 teaspoon sugar

¾ teaspoon turmeric

2 tablespoons minced ginger

½ cup water

Tear the cabbage leaves into 1- to 2-inch squares or grate on a very coarse grater. Set aside.

Place a large pot over medium-high heat. When it is hot, add the oil, then when the oil is hot, toss in the chiles, cumin, bay leaf, cloves, cinnamon stick, and cardamom. Stir briefly and cook for 30 seconds to 1 minute, then add the shallots. Cook over medium heat, stirring occasionally, for 5 minutes.

Stir in the potatoes, tomato, salt, and sugar. Cook for 1 minute, then add the cabbage, turmeric, and ginger and stir and turn to coat the cabbage. Cook for 1 minute, then add the water, bring to a boil, and cook, partially covered, for about 20 minutes, stirring every 5 minutes. The cabbage should be tender and the flavors blended. Remove the lid and cook 5 minutes longer to reduce the liquid, then mound onto a plate and serve.

# Okra with Poppy and Mustard Seed

ONE OF THE PLEASURES OF COOKING IN ANOTHER KITCHEN, ESPECIALLY A kitchen far away from home, is getting acquainted with different tools: pots, utensils, and so on. In Bengal a lot was very new to us, right down to the basic kitchen knife.

This dish shows off the practical simplicity of a Bengali mortar and pestle, though other tools can be substituted. The mortar is a flat block of stone, with a design chiseled into it. The pestle is a heavy lumpy cylinder, also of stone, that is rolled over the top surface of the mortar, most often with a curve of the wrist so it grinds a little as it rolls and crushes. To make this dish, first the mustard seed is ground to a paste with a little water, then the same treatment is given to the poppy seeds. The best substitute for a Bengali mortar and pestle is a Japanese *suribachi* or a spice grinder for grinding the seeds, then a bowl and the back of a spoon to blend the ground seeds into a paste with a little water.

Grinding the mustard seed to a paste to be added as a *masala,* instead of frying it whole, gives the dish an agreeable sharp bite. We've cut back a little on the amount of mustard seed we usually use; if you wish a hotter bite, add two teaspoons rather than one, as Gita did when she taught us the dish.

The chopped okra makes a dense, tender, bright-green pile, held together by its innate stickiness, and flecked with the pale off-white of the ground poppy seeds.

| | |
|---|---|
| 2 tablespoons mustard oil (see Glossary) | 1 teaspoon mustard seed (see Glossary) |
| ½ cup minced onions | 2 to 3 tablespoons water |
| ½ pound okra, cut into ½-inch lengths | ¼ teaspoon cayenne pepper |
| ½ teaspoon anise seed | ½ teaspoon sugar |
| ½ teaspoon salt | |
| 1 tablespoon white poppy seed (see Glossary) | |

Heat the oil in a heavy pot over medium-high heat. When it is hot, add the onions and stir briefly, then add the okra, anise seed, and salt and stir to blend. Cover and lower the heat to medium. Cook for 10 minutes, or until the okra is tender, stirring occasionally to ensure that the okra is not sticking.

Meanwhile, using a mortar and pestle or a spice grinder, grind the poppy seeds and mustard seeds to a powder. Transfer to a small bowl and add enough water to make a paste. Add to the okra, then stir in the cayenne and sugar. Cook for 1 minute, stirring occasionally, then serve.

# Bengali Potato and Cauliflower Curry

*aloo fulkoffi torkarri*

Serves 6 as one of several dishes in a rice-based meal

THIS COMFORT FOOD TASTES GREAT JUST WITH PLAIN RICE AND A SIDE DISH of yogurt, or you may want a dal and a green vegetable as part of a larger meal. Since the flavors take a while to blend, and are harsh and raw until they do, don't taste the stew until it has completely cooked.

Use waxy potatoes, such as Yukon Gold, that will keep their shape, not floury (baking) potatoes.

3 tablespoons mustard oil (see Glossary)

1½ pounds waxy potatoes, peeled and cut into ½-inch or smaller cubes

1 small cauliflower (1 pound), separated into florets, trimmed of tough stems, and cut into 1-inch pieces

2½ cups water

¼ teaspoon anise seed

2 cloves

2 green cardamom pods

2 inches cinnamon stick, broken into 2 or 3 pieces

1 large bay leaf

1 large or 2 small onions, grated (about 1 cup)

1 large plum tomato, coarsely chopped

1 teaspoon salt

¼ teaspoon sugar

2 tablespoons minced ginger

1 tablespoon minced garlic

1½ teaspoons cayenne pepper

½ teaspoon turmeric

In a large heavy pot, heat 2 tablespoons of the mustard oil over medium-high heat. When it is hot, add the potato cubes and stir well to coat with the hot oil. Cook for 2 minutes, stirring and turning frequently, then add the cauliflower, lower the heat to medium, and cook for another 2 minutes, stirring to prevent sticking. Add ½ cup of the water, bring to a boil, and cook, covered, for 3 minutes. Set aside.

In another large heavy pot, heat the remaining 1 tablespoon oil over high heat. Lower the heat to medium and add the anise, cloves, cardamom, cinnamon, and bay leaf. Cook for 1 minute, then add the onion and stir briefly. Add the tomato, salt, and sugar and cook, stirring frequently, until the tomatoes have softened and the onions are translucent, about 7 minutes. Add the ginger and garlic and cook, stirring occasionally, for another minute. Add ½ cup water, bring to a boil, and add the cayenne pepper and turmeric. Stir well to blend and let cook for 3 minutes.

Add the potato and cauliflower mixture and ½ cup water. Stir to coat the vegetables, bring to a boil, and cook over medium-high heat for 3 minutes. Add the remaining 1 cup water (the dish will be quite soupy) and boil hard, uncovered, for 10 minutes, or until the liquid has reduced and the potatoes and cauliflower are very tender. Serve hot.

# Stir-fried Shrimp, Kerala Style

*thoran*

**Serves 4 to 6 as part of a rice-based meal**

DON'T BE SCARED OFF BY THE NUMBER OF INGREDIENTS IN THIS RECIPE FROM Kerala. Almost all are simply seasonings for the shrimp, and if you don't have one or two of them, you'll still be fine (though you should have the coconut). The dish takes only about twenty minutes to prepare, including eight minutes cooking time.

The reason we've included this recipe is because the dish is really good, and because it gives an idea of what happens in a kitchen in South India. There is an infinite number of possibilities for how a seasoning paste or mixture can be put together, and how it can be added to or punctuated further along in the cooking process. It is this kitchen wizardry, kitchen alchemy, that for us makes Indian cooking Indian cooking.

This shrimp *thoran*, like all *thorans*, is deliberately somewhat dry, meant to be eaten with rice and complemented by a moister dish—a *pachadi* or a wet curry.

1½ pounds shrimp, shelled and deveined

½ cup fresh, frozen, or dried grated unsweetened coconut (see Glossary)

1 tablespoon minced garlic

¼ teaspoon dried chile pepper flakes

½ teaspoon turmeric

About ¼ cup water

1 tablespoon rice vinegar or cider vinegar

2 tablespoons vegetable oil

¼ teaspoon mustard seed (see Glossary)

½ teaspoon urad dal (see Glossary)

1 teaspoon raw long-grain white rice

Pinch of fresh or dried curry leaves (see Glossary)

1 teaspoon minced ginger

1 cup minced onions

1 tablespoon minced green chile

¼ teaspoon cayenne pepper

½ teaspoon black peppercorns, coarsely ground

If using large or medium shrimp, cut or tear into approximately ½-inch pieces. Set aside.

Combine the coconut, garlic, chile flakes, and turmeric in a bowl and stir with a large spoon to blend. Add 2 to 3 tablespoons water, or enough to make a crumbly paste. Set aside. In a small bowl, mix 2 tablespoons hot water with the vinegar, and set aside.

Place all the ingredients near your stovetop.

In a heavy pot or deep skillet, heat the oil over high heat until very hot. Add the mustard seed, urad dal, rice, and curry leaves and stir briefly. Lower the heat to medium-high, add the ginger, onions, and green chile and cook, stirring frequently, for 3 to 4 minutes, until the onions are well softened. Keep warm, over low heat.

Heat a lightly oiled wok or heavy pan over medium heat. Add the coconut paste and stir-fry until the color changes. Add the shrimp and stir-fry briefly, then add the water-vinegar mixture, cover, and raise the heat to medium-high. Let steam for 3 minutes. Uncover and stir well over medium heat for 20 seconds.

Add the shrimp mixture to the onion mixture, raise the heat to medium, and cook, stirring frequently, for 1 minute, or until all the shrimp have changed color. Stir in the cayenne and black pepper. Remove from the heat, mound on a plate or in a shallow bowl, and serve.

*Selling dried fish in the Palayam market in Trivandrum*

# Kerala Coconut Chicken Curry

**Serves 6 to 8 as part of a rice-based meal**

THERE IS A FAMILIAR JOKE TOLD IN INDIA ABOUT KERALA, WHERE THIS chicken curry comes from, that Kerala's largest export is people and their brains. Kerala is a unique state. It has the highest population density in India, and it has by far the highest literacy rate, especially for women. It is not unusual to meet Keralese doctors, engineers, and lawyers outside of India, as well as in other parts of the country. There is some truth to the joke.

As you fly into Kerala, the first thing you see from the plane is a huge sea of coconut

An oxcart coming down a city lane in Trivandrum

palms. You don't see paddies, you don't see villages, all you see is coconut trees. Kerala has a lot of coconut trees, and relatively little large-scale agriculture. It's no wonder that so many people must look elsewhere for work.

It is also no accident that Keralese food uses coconut in so many dishes. Coconuts and coconut oil (and palm oil) have had a lot of bad press in the last few years because of their relatively high level of saturated fat, but this bad press has gone a little overboard, fueled in part perhaps by the competitors of these products. Coconut milk curries, whether from South India or Thailand, are some of our favorite foods. If it comes down to a choice between a hunk of cheese or a coconut milk curry, we'll take the curry.

For this curry, the ingredients list is long but the recipe is easy and delicious. The dish is hot, but not burning, with a full-flavored broth that makes a great accompaniment to rice. For less heat, reduce the number of dried chiles to two and the number of green chiles to three.

### Masala paste

4 dried red chiles (see Glossary), each broken into 2 or 3 pieces

1½ tablespoons coriander seed

¼ teaspoon cumin seed

¼ teaspoon anise seed

½ teaspoon white poppy seed (see Glossary)

½ teaspoon black peppercorns

1 inch cinnamon stick, broken into pieces

5 cloves

2 green cardamom pods, smashed

½ teaspoon turmeric

1 to 2 tablespoons water


3 tablespoons vegetable oil or ghee

½ teaspoon mustard seed (see Glossary)

3 to 4 dried curry leaves (see Glossary)

2 onions, thinly sliced

1½ tablespoons minced ginger

6 green cayenne chiles or 8 large jalapeño chiles, cut lengthwise in half and seeded

¾ cup water

2 whole chicken breasts (2 to 2½ pounds)

2 tablespoons rice vinegar or cider vinegar

2 teaspoons salt

2 tablespoons minced garlic

2 cups canned coconut milk, separated into 1 cup thinner and 1 cup creamier milk (see Glossary)

3 to 4 waxy potatoes, peeled and cut into ¾-inch cubes

In a small bowl, combine the dried chiles, the coriander, cumin, anise and poppy seeds, the peppercorns, cinnamon stick, cloves, and cardamom. Heat a heavy skillet over medium-high heat. When it is hot, toss in the spices and dry-roast, stirring constantly with a wooden spatula to prevent burning, for about 1 minute, or until aromatic and starting to brown. Transfer to a spice grinder or mortar and grind to a powder. Return to the small bowl, stir in the turmeric, and add just enough water to form a dry paste. Set aside.

In a large heavy pot, heat the oil or ghee over medium-high heat. Add the mustard seed and curry leaves, stir briefly, then cover until the mustard seeds have popped. Add the onions, ginger, and green chiles and cook over medium heat, stirring occasionally, until the onions soften and become translucent. Add the *masala* paste and stir to distribute well. Add ¼ cup of the water and cook for 3 minutes, stirring frequently.

Meanwhile, with a heavy cleaver, cut each chicken breast in half, then chop each half into 4 pieces.

Add the chicken to the pot and sauté over medium-high heat until it is starting to brown, turning to expose all sides to the heat, about 5 minutes. Add the vinegar, salt, and garlic. Stir and cook for 1 minute longer.

Mix the 1 cup thinner coconut milk with the remaining ½ cup water. Add to the chicken, bring to a boil, and simmer over medium heat for 10 minutes.

Add the potatoes and simmer until tender, another 20 minutes or so. Stir in the remaining (thicker) coconut milk and remove from the heat. Serve hot with plain rice.

# Spicy Puffed Rice Snack

*murree*

### Makes about 3 cups rice snack

THIS EASILY ASSEMBLED SNACK FOOD HAS ONLY ONE PROBLEM: IT'S SO delicious that you and your guests will go through piles of it. It is traditional in Bengal, eaten in handfuls from a large bowl. It has complex flavor as well as fresh crunch from the combination of spicing and finely chopped tomato and cucumber. The puffed rice—available at South Asian grocery stores, sold in large cellophane bags—helps all the flavors blend.

*Murree* is traditionally flavored with *jannachur*, a spicy store-bought mix of dried gram (urad dal), turmeric, cumin, and fried *seva* (vermicelli made of chickpea flour). Since the mixture isn't readily available here, we've adapted the recipe by flavoring the puffed rice with a little spiced oil before tossing it with the remaining ingredients—grated coconut, finely chopped chiles and fresh vegetables, and lime juice. This recipe produces a medium-hot mixture. You can reduce the heat by cutting back on the chiles and cayenne.

2 cups puffed rice

1 teaspoon mustard oil (see Glossary) or peanut oil

½ teaspoon mustard seed (see Glossary)

½ teaspoon cumin seed

¼ teaspoon nigella seed (see Glossary)

Pinch of anise seed

¼ teaspoon turmeric

¼ cup grated unsweetened fresh, frozen, or dried coconut (see Glossary)

½ teaspoon cayenne pepper

2 jalapeño chiles, seeded and finely chopped

1 large shallot, finely chopped

1 small plum tomato, finely chopped

½ cup finely chopped European cucumber

3 tablespoons fresh lime juice

½ teaspoon salt

Place the puffed rice in a large bowl.

In a heavy skillet, heat the oil over medium-high heat. Add the mustard seeds, cumin, nigella, anise, and turmeric, stir briefly, and then cover until the mustard seeds have stopped popping. Pour the oil and seasonings over the puffed rice and stir and toss to coat.

Wash out and dry the skillet, then return to medium-high heat. Add the coconut and stir constantly until the coconut turns a light golden brown. Add to the puffed rice mixture, then add the cayenne and toss to mix well. (The recipe can be made ahead to this point and kept in a covered container in a cool place for several days.)

Shortly before serving (the rice will get soggy if the tomatoes and cucumber are added more than an hour ahead), add the remaining ingredients and toss to blend well.

# Shiva's Pigeons

For years I had a dream about going to India and renting a little apartment with a cozy kitchen, going to the market every day, and having houseplants in my apartment. I'd settle in, learn the local language, find a job. There were several books from my local library, picture books on India, that I would check out and then renew, and renew again, and then finally take back, only to check them out again. I loved to sit at home and go through the books, page after page, trying to envision myself in India, trying to construct the context behind the photographs. My favorite book of all was called *Shiva's Pigeons,* written by Rumer Godden and her sister. The photographs were in black and white, and the text was impressionistic. I loved it. I memorized the photographs, page after page.

Mixing *dosa* in a restaurant near the ashram

Well, eventually there I was, actually in India. After one month I'd lost forty pounds and had chronic diarrhea. I fell asleep one night in a railway station and woke up to an enormous rat chewing on my shoelace. And on my very first day in Delhi, my first week in India, I'd been flimflammed for two hundred and fifty dollars, enough money to last me for months in India. Not everything was going according to plan.

As traveler's luck will usually have it, given enough time to find a way, I ended up finding a place to live, way down at the bottom tip of India in the state of Kerala, in a city called Trivandrum, in a yoga ashram. And while I didn't have a kitchen, or even an apartment, I did have a little room with a bed and a fan. Five or six times each day I'd patronize the local restaurants, if only for a cup of tea and a fried banana. They were heaven, better than anything I could ever have imagined. Some days I would be sitting there eating *wellyappam,* or *uppama,* or *puttu,* or *vada,* or *idyappum,* or wonderful *masala dosas,* and there would be loud movie music on the radio, bare lightbulbs, and cows eating cast-off banana leaves, and how I would wish I could film it all, and send the film to friends back home.

"Eating in South India," I would tell them if I could, "is an immense pleasure, impossible to describe. It has all to do with how you rinse your mouth out with water before and after a meal, with how you wash your right hand and leave it wet as you come back to the table ready to eat. It has to do with a little flick of the wrist you use in gathering up a big ball of rice with your hand before you toss it into your mouth, as if you were eating golf balls. It has to do with a culture where men wear sarongs and tie and untie them all day long, and where women's sarees and skirts burst with the brightest of colors. It has to do with a climate where it never gets cold. . . ."

But sooner or later I'd get back to my meal, content to enjoy it on my own.

I stayed five months at the ashram, and right as I was about to go, I was sitting one hot afternoon in the local library and there I spotted on the shelf *Shiva's Pigeons.* I started going through it page by page. As I looked at all of the pictures I knew so well, there was no longer such mystery, but there was much more meaning.

# Quick Onion Pilaf

**Serves 4 as a main dish, more if part of an elaborate meal**

THIS IS A QUICK WAY OF TURNING YESTERDAY'S RICE INTO A SIMPLE flavored pilaf. It's a little moister than a classic *pulao,* and quite heavily flavored. The recipe starts with plain cooked rice and tosses it with a succulent blend of simmered onions, minced ginger, and fresh jalapeños. The result is an appetizing mound of fragrant, pale-yellow rice dotted with soft tumeric-tinted onions and bright flecks of green chile, and topped with toasted cashews. Serve as a main dish with a yogurt sauce (a *pachadi* or *raita*) and a salad or, more elaborately, with a kebab as well. Total preparation time is twenty minutes.

¼ cup raw cashew nuts or cashew pieces

3 tablespoons vegetable oil or ghee

¼ teaspoon asafetida (see Glossary) (optional)

1 teaspoon mustard seed (see Glossary)

1 teaspoon turmeric

5 fresh or dried curry leaves (see Glossary)

2 tablespoons minced ginger

4 jalapeño chiles or 2 cayenne chiles, minced (see Note)

1 pound onions (3 to 4), thinly sliced into rings or half circles

1½ teaspoons salt

1 teaspoon sugar

4 cups cooked white rice (basmati, American long-grain, or gobindavog)

¼ cup fresh lime juice

Place a heavy skillet over high heat, add the cashews, and dry-roast, stirring constantly, until golden. Remove from the heat and continue stirring for about 15 seconds, then transfer to a plate.

Place all the ingredients beside your stovetop.

Heat the oil or ghee in a large heavy pot over high heat. When it is hot, add the asafetida and stir briefly to dissolve it, then toss in the mustard seeds and stir. Cover the pot as they pop; when they have finished popping, add the turmeric and stir. Toss in the curry leaves, ginger, chiles, and onions and stir to coat with the oil. Lower the heat to medium and cook, stirring frequently, for 7 to 10 minutes, until the onions are softened and starting to brown.

Stir in the salt and sugar, then add the rice, turning and stirring with a spatula to break up any lumps and mix well. Handle the rice gently so the grains stay intact and don't get broken or mushy. Continue turning and stirring until the pilaf is well heated and mixed, 2 to 3 minutes. Add the lime juice and stir and turn for another 30 seconds, then mound on a platter. Top with the cashews and serve.

**Note:** This dish has a mild chile heat. To make it milder, discard the chile seeds; to increase the heat, use more chiles.

**Alternative:** We recently tasted a version of this *pulao* prepared with *aval*, flattened rice, at our friend Molly's house. We'd seen *aval* for sale in Indian groceries, but had never known how straightforward it was to cook with, nor how delicious to eat. Molly, who is a wise woman from Kerala, tells us that *aval* is prepared with parboiled rice that is then crushed or smashed flat and dried to white flakes. To prepare it, rinse well in warm water, then add to the pan instead of cooked rice. It will swell up and become very rice-like as it absorbs water and flavorings.

Produce vendor at a local Calcutta market

# Classic Vegetable Pilaf
## pulao

Serves 6 as part of a multidish meal or 4 as part of a simple vegetarian meal with dal and a salad

INDIAN *PULAOS* ARE CLOSELY RELATED TO THE *PULAOS* (PILAFS) OF CENTRAL Asia, in which rice is cooked and flavored with herbs, spices, vegetables, and sometimes meat. In this vegetable *pulao*, basmati rice is briefly cooked in a spice blend, then the broth and vegetables are added and all the ingredients simmer to a well-blended, soft-textured finished dish; each rice grain is firm and separate and subtly flavored. Serve accompanied by a soupy dal, a drier and spicy meat or vegetable dish, a yogurt sauce, and a chutney.

2 cups basmati rice

½ pound carrots

½ pound green beans

1 tablespoon minced ginger

2 small bay leaves, finely chopped

1 heaping tablespoon finely chopped fresh coriander leaves, plus sprigs for optional garnish

½ teaspoon turmeric

2 tablespoons vegetable oil

1 medium onion, finely chopped

4 cloves garlic, finely chopped

1 teaspoon Hot Spice Powder (*garam masala,* page 246)

2 teaspoons salt

3¼ cups water or vegetarian stock

Approximately 2 tablespoons melted ghee or butter (optional)

Rinse the rice thoroughly under cold running water. Place in a bowl or pot with enough water to cover and soak for 30 thirty minutes, then drain well and set aside.

Slice the carrots lengthwise into thin strips, cut into ½-inch lengths, and set aside. Top and tail the beans, chop into ½-inch lengths, and set aside.

In a mortar or a small bowl, combine the ginger, bay leaves, chopped coriander, and turmeric and pound or grind with a pestle or the back of a spoon to a paste. Set aside.

Place a large heavy pot over medium-high heat and add the oil. Add the onion, garlic, and *garam masala* and cook, stirring frequently, for 10 minutes. Add the ginger paste and the rice, lower the heat to medium, and cook, stirring frequently (and gently so as not to break the rice), until the rice grains become opaque. Add the salt and vegetables and cook and stir for about 5 minutes. Add the water or stock and bring to a vigorous boil, then lower the heat, cover, and simmer until the rice is tender, about 15 minutes. Remove from the heat and let stand for 15 minutes.

Remove the lid and stir gently but thoroughly, then replace the lid. When ready to serve, turn out onto a platter, drizzle with melted ghee or butter, and garnish with sprigs of fresh coriander if you like.

# Aromatic Rice Pudding

*payas*

NEAR THE END OF OUR TIME IN CALCUTTA, THE EVENINGS GREW COOL, AND one day Gita produced this rich-tasting pudding for dessert. It was a huge hit with children and adults alike, a stovetop rice pudding, made with milk that is cooked down and thickened, then sweetened with palm sugar. Gita used gobindavog rice, crushing it to break it slightly before cooking, for a softer texture. You can substitute basmati or long-grain American (non-parboiled) rice.

The pudding is mildly perfumed with spices. Gita used cardamom and dried *taysbatta*, or cassia leaf, available in Korean and Indian groceries. We generally use a stick of cinnamon instead (actually cassia quills, see Glossary), as well as whole green cardamom pods. If you wish, substitute three or four dried cassia leaves for the cinnamon stick. The pudding is rich and sweet, so helpings are small.

½ cup gobindavog or basmati rice

8 cups milk (whole or 2%), plus more if necessary

5 inches cinnamon stick, broken into several pieces

4 green cardamom pods

Generous pinch of salt

6 tablespoons palm sugar (see Glossary) or substitute brown sugar, or more to taste

Wash the rice thoroughly until the water runs clear, then drain in a sieve. Spread on a towel on the counter and use a rolling pin to break the rice into smaller pieces. You do not want a mush, or evenly sized pieces, you just want to break it down a little. Set aside on a plate or in a sieve to dry while the milk reduces.

Place the milk in a large heavy pot and bring to a boil, stirring occasionally with a wooden spoon, then lower the heat until the milk is barely simmering. Add the cinnamon stick and cardamom pods. Cook for 45 minutes, stirring frequently to prevent sticking and to prevent a skin forming on the surface (if a skin does form, stir it back in), or until the milk has reduced to about 6 cups.

Add the rice and salt and continue to cook over low heat, stirring frequently, until the rice is tender, 35 to 40 minutes. As it cooks and absorbs liquid, the mixture will thicken; if necessary (if the rice is not yet cooked and the mixture is very thick), add a little more milk.

When the rice is very soft and tender but not a mush, add the sugar and stir gently to dissolve. Cook for another 5 minutes, then taste for sweetness and add a little more sugar if you wish. Remove the cinnamon stick and cardamom pods. Serve warm or at room temperature.

A Silk Road caravan passing below the Kongur
Massif in the Chinese Pamirs

inset: A traditional housefront in Kuba, Azerbaijan

# Chelo, Polo, Pulao

*I*f the wind, the sun, and the dry desert air all had corresponding flavors, they would be at their best in the cooking of Central Asia and Persia. Rich *pulaos,* savory grilled meats, wintery stews, *tandoor* flatbreads, onions, tomatoes, and whole-milk yogurt: The basic foods of the region are foods we never get tired of eating. At home in our backyard we fire up some charcoal, rub a little freshly ground cumin seed into tiny strips of lamb, prepare some Persian rice, and gather around the grill to cook kebabs and flatbreads. Then we can feast on some of the most straightforward, satisfying foods we know.

Central Asia is the name given to a vaguely defined, mostly landlocked region that stretches from Iran (or Persia) eastward across the mountains, deserts, and high plateaus of Afghanistan, Turkmenistan, Tajikistan, Uzbekistan, and China's Xinjiang Province. It is home to oasis dwellers, with their irrigated gardens and busy bazaars, and nomads alike, who move their flocks of sheep, goats, and camels from grazing ground to grazing ground.

For centuries, caravans carrying silk and spices from China made their way across the empty spaces of Central

**clockwise from top**

Uighur woman at the bazaar in the Kasghar oasis, Xinjiang

Donkey caravan in the Pusa oasis in the southern Takla Makan Desert

Shir Dar Mosque, part of the Registan in Samarkand

Camels waiting at the bazaar in Ashkabad, Turkmenistan

Asia to markets in the west, and over time these routes became known as the Silk Road. These were the routes followed by Marco Polo and other Venetian traders, and by missionaries, explorers, and conquerers. Traders brought goods and ideas and news to and from the cities of China, Persia, and the Mediterranean. Buddhism traveled the Silk Road east from Afghanistan to China, as did Islam. Culinary ideas and new foods also spread along the trade routes. Apricots traveled from Iran to China, and tea came the other way. From India, rice arrived in Central Asia, in the desert oases, and firmly took root.

Nowadays, rice is still much loved in Central Asia, though cherished more as a festive food than as the staff of life. Eaten mostly as pilaf (*pulov* in Uzbek, *pulao* in Uighur), it is served on large platters at wedding feasts or family gatherings or as the equivalent of Sunday dinner. Central Asian pilafs begin with a flavor base of meat and vegetables (lamb, carrots, and onions are constants), then add a layer of rice that absorption-cooks on top of the flavor base.

The pilaf traditions of Central Asia may have come originally from the Persians (Iranians); or perhaps the Persians elaborated on Central Asian rice techniques to come up with their sophisticated rice cuisine. Margaret Shaida, in her definitive cookbook *The Legendary Cuisine of Persia*, tells us that rice for most people in Iran is a dish for special occasions; it is too expensive and precious for everyday eating, except in the north by the Caspian Sea, where it is grown. Consequently, even everyday Persian "plain" rice is a slightly rich and festive dish. There are two versions: one is a more elaborate and richer rice called *chelo,* the other, known as *katteh,* is a simpler dish and the one eaten as daily fare by the rice eaters of northern Iran.

Persian rice is not available in North America. Though Iran still grows rice in the area along the Caspian, as well as in several well-watered valleys in the hills, it does not produce enough for local consumption, let alone for export. The closest approximation to Persian rice is good basmati rice from India—dry, long-grained, and slightly aromatic. The goal in cooking Persian *chelo* or *katteh* is to end up with separate fluffy grains of rice, cooked through but not at all moist or mushy, and basmati is very good in this regard. There should also be a flavorful crust on the bottom of the pot, which is called *tahdig* in Farsi, *kasmag* in Azeri, Uzbek, and Uighur.

In the Persian/Iranian tradition, *chelo* or *katteh* is served with kebabs and a salad or pickles, or with a *khoresh,* a moist stew-like slow-simmered dish, usually made with a little meat and lots of vegetables. Rice is also used as an ingredient in some soups and in simple rice-legume dishes.

When curiosity finally pushed us to try making *chelo,* as with many classics that have stood the test of

Uzbek woman selling peppers at the Tashkent bazaar in Uzbekistan

time, it was a knockout. We love the crust, especially when it's made with yogurt. Recently we tried making *chelo* with a brown basmati grown in California. Though all classic Persian cookbooks stress the need for white and beautiful basmati, the fresh brown basmati made a wonderful *chelo,* flavorful and tender.

Many would say that the *pulao*-pilaf tradition reaches its height in the Persian rice dishes called *polos.* Here rice is soaked and briefly boiled as for *chelo,* then slowly steam-cooked in its own moisture, layered with cooked and subtly spiced meat and vegetable-based flavorings, or with fresh herbs, or legumes, or a combination. The rice absorbs a

little of the flavorings as it steams. After cooking, the *polo* is turned out onto a platter and all the ingredients are well mixed. As with *chelo*, often some of the rice is tinted with saffron and the crust, or *tahdig*, is served on the side or on top as a special treat.

Once you have prepared a simple Persian *chelo* or *katteh*, Grilled Persian or Central Asian kebabs of lamb or chicken, a yogurt-based sauce, and a chopped salad make an easy feast. Most *polos* and Central Asian pilafs are excellent party food, though not our usual everyday fare. The meat and vegetables can be prepared early, then the dish finished just before serving. A platter of hot pilaf makes a dazzling main dish for a large group (see Apricot-Lamb Wedding Polo, page 308). Pilafs and *polos* are best served with a fresh salad of tomatoes or radishes, and perhaps a plate of fresh herbs.

To prepare these dishes, you need no special equipment and few special ingredients. However, life is easier if you have a large wide heavy pot of at least six-quart capacity with a tight-fitting lid. You can use it for Central Asian pilafs, and for Persian *polos* and other rices. You should have good basmati in your cupboard, and also a good medium- or short-grain rice for Silk Road pilafs. Saffron is often called for in Persian dishes, and fresh herbs: parsley, dill, mint. Plain yogurt is another useful staple.

# Special Everyday Persian Rice
*chelo*

Serves 6

As the more elaborate form of everyday Persian rice, *CHELO* is a wonderful treat, usually served with kebabs or with a moist stew-like *khoresh*. The rice is soaked, then briefly cooked in plenty of boiling water. To create a delicious crust and perfectly textured rice, the rice is then returned to the pot and gently steamed for thirty minutes. But first the bottom of the pot is covered with oil or butter with a binder such as egg or yogurt (or both) and a thin layer of rice or some flatbread or thinly sliced potatoes. This bottom layer cooks to a golden crispy crust known as the *tahdig* and is served beside or on top of the finished dish.

Though the instructions may seem elaborate, you'll understand the sequence and be delighted by the perfection of the results after you've made this rice once. Serve it with Persian Lamb Kebabs with Sumac (page 293), Golden Chicken Kebabs (page 296), or Silk Road Kebab (page 294), with a yogurt sauce and sliced ripe tomatoes or cucumbers.

2½ cups basmati rice (see Note)

¼ cup salt

Water

¼ cup vegetable oil or 4 tablespoons butter

2 tablespoons plain yogurt (whole-milk or 2%)

1 large egg

1 teaspoon saffron threads, dry-roasted (see page 431), crumbled to a powder, and dissolved in 3 tablespoons warm water (optional)

Wash the rice thoroughly, then place in a large pot with 3 tablespoons of the salt and enough cold water to cover by 2 inches. Let soak for 2 to 3 hours.

Drain well in a fine sieve. In the same pot, bring 4 quarts of water to a vigorous boil. Add the remaining 1 tablespoon salt, then gradually sprinkle in the rice. Stir gently to prevent sticking, and bring back to the boil. After the rice has been boiling for 2 minutes, test for doneness. The rice is ready when the outside is tender but there remains a slight uncooked resistance at the core of the grain. If the core of the grain is brittle, it's not done enough. Continue to check the rice until done, usually about 4 minutes, then drain in the sieve and rinse with tepid to cool water (to prevent it from cooking any more).

Place the pot back over high heat and add the oil or butter and 1 tablespoon water. In a small bowl, whisk together the yogurt and egg. Stir in about ½ cup of the rice, then place in the sizzling oil and spread over the bottom of the pot. Gradually add the remaining rice, sprinkling it in to form a mound. Use the handle of a wooden spoon to make three or four holes through the mound to the bottom, then cover the pot with a lid wrapped in a tea towel. (The towel helps seal the lid and absorbs moisture from the rising steam.) Heat over medium-high heat until steam builds up, 1 to 2 minutes, then lower the heat to medium-low and cook for about 30 minutes. When it is done, the rice will be tender and fluffy with a flavorful crust, the *tahdig*, on the bottom.

The *tahdig* comes off more easily if, before removing the lid, you place the pot in an inch of cold water (in the sink) for a minute. Then remove the lid and, if you're using saffron, gently spoon about 1 cup rice into the saffron water mixture; stir to blend. Mound the remaining rice on a platter. Sprinkle on the saffron rice, if you have it. Place chunks of the crust on top or on a separate plate; it's a big treat.

**Note:** You can substitute brown basmati for white. Boiling until tender will take 12 to 15 minutes, depending on the rice; begin testing the rice at 11 minutes after it comes back to the boil.

**Herbed rice:** In spring and summer, when fresh herbs are available, you can add to the rice 1 to 2 cups of a mixture of some or all of the following, finely chopped: tarragon, flat-leaf parsley, dill, and/or chives. Add the herbs just before the rice finishes boiling.

**Crust options:** Instead of mixing the rice with the egg and yogurt, you can use pieces of flatbread (split pitas, or flour tortillas, for example) or some grated potato for the crust. Place the oil or butter and water in the pot and heat. Line the bottom of the pot with pieces of flatbread or with the potato. Pour the egg and yogurt mixture over, then mound the rice on top and proceed with the recipe.

**Leftover *chelo*:** Because it has some oil in it, chelo will stay fairly tender for a few days if stored in a sealed container in the refrigerator. It can easily be reheated by tossing it in a lightly oiled skillet or wok. It also makes a filling lunch dish whisked with a little egg, seasoned, and gently cooked in a thin omelette like the classic Spanish tortilla; serve with a green salad.

Uighur men cooking kebabs in western Xinjiang

# Everyday Persian Rice
## katteh

**Makes about 5 cups rice**

THIS SIMPLE ABSORPTION-COOKED RICE IS THE EVERYDAY RICE OF PEOPLE IN the rice-growing region along the Caspian Sea, in the north of Iran. You can vary the amount of salt or butter as you wish. Because the rice is not drained after boiling, the grains stick together a little more than in Special Everyday Persian Rice (*chelo*, page 288). There is a delicious crust, a little less rich tasting than the *tahdig* from *chelo*.

| | |
|---|---|
| 2 cups basmati rice | 1 teaspoon salt |
| 3½ cups water | 2 tablespoons butter |

Wash the rice thoroughly under cold running water until the water runs clear. Place in a heavy medium pot with the water and salt and stir gently to mix. Let soak for at least 30 minutes and up to 2 hours.

Place the pot over high heat and bring to a rapid boil. Lower the heat to maintain a bare simmer and cook for 15 minutes, partially covered. The water will have disappeared from the surface and there will be small steam holes in the rice.

Cut the butter into small pieces and scatter over the top of the rice, then cover the pot with a lid wrapped in a tea towel. (The towel helps seal the lid and absorbs moisture from the rising steam.) Lower the heat to as low as possible and cook for another 30 to 40 minutes. Let stand for 10 minutes before serving.

Mound the rice onto a platter. The bottom layer of rice will have formed a crust. Use a spatula to detach it from the pot and serve pieces of the crust on top of the rice or in a heap to one side.

**Herbed rice:** You can include herbs in this plain rice to make a beautiful green-speckled dish. Use 1 to 1½ cups finely chopped fresh dill or a mix of fresh herbs, as described on page 289, and add to the rice and water when it comes to a boil. You can also cook the rice with caraway or dill seed: Add 2 tablespoons of the seeds, roughly crushed between your fingers, to the water when you begin to soak the rice.

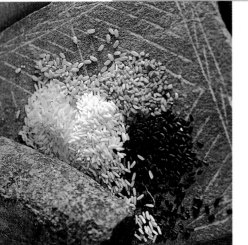

**above**
Freshly cooked Thai Jasmine Rice (page 115)

**left**
Bengali mortar and pestle, with assorted raw rices

Spicy Cucumber Surprise (page 81)

**above**
Sweet Black Rice Treat (page 168)

**left**
Small rice shop in Sapa,
northern Vietnam

**left**
Snow Peas with a Hint of Pork (page 101)

**below**
Thai Sticky Rice (page 116) with North Thai
Sauce for Sticky Rice *(foreground)* (page 125)
and Grilled Chile Salsa (page 126)

**above**
Steamed Fish Heaped with Scallions
and Ginger (page 94)

**left**
Spices at a local market in India

**left**
Senegalese Lamb and Peanut Stew (page 376) over plain rice, with Wolof Hot Chile Paste (page 368)

**below**
Quick and Easy Chinese Greens (page 85)

**above**
Special Everyday Persian Rice (page 288)
with Golden Chicken Kebabs (page 296),
Oasis Salad (page 299), and fresh herbs

**right**
Basic Risotto (page 342)

**clockwise from top**

Sushi, two easy ways: Brown Bag Sushi *(left)* (page 222) and Classic Sushi Roll-ups (page 217), served with Pickled Ginger (page 203)

Indian rice meal: Gobindavog (page 240) with Fresh Carrot Chutney (page 248), Spicy Yogurt Sauce with Ginger (page 256), and Spinach and Mung Dal (page 262)

Dals for sale in an Indian market

# Spring Pilaf with Fresh Greens

*sabzi polo*

A BEAUTIFUL VERSION OF HERBED RICE USING THE FIRST GREENS OF SPRING (*sabzi* means "greens" in Farsi) is traditionally served at Persian New Year, No-Rooz, around the vernal equinox in March. Alongside is presented an herb omelette and, often, fried fish. The rice is prepared as for *chelo*, then it is layered with herbs when it is placed in the pot for steaming. Serve with Golden Chicken Kebabs with Sumac (page 296) and, if you wish, a chopped salad.

### Rice

2½ cups basmati rice

¼ cup salt

Water

¼ cup finely chopped fresh flat-leaf parsley

¼ cup finely chopped fresh dill

¼ cup finely chopped fresh chives

¼ cup vegetable oil or 4 tablespoons butter

2 tablespoons plain yogurt (whole-milk or 2%)

1 large egg

Following the instructions for Special Everyday Persian Rice (page 288), wash and soak the rice, then boil it, drain, rinse, and drain again.

Mix the chopped herbs together and set aside.

If using butter, melt 2 tablespoons in a small saucepan; set aside. In a medium bowl, mix together the yogurt and egg. Add ½ cup of the cooked rice and stir well.

In a large heavy pot, heat 2 tablespoons of the oil or the remaining 2 tablespoons butter with 1 tablespoon water. Place the rice and yogurt mixture into the oil or butter and spread it over the bottom of the pot. Add half the remaining rice, spread on half the herb mixture, and then add another third of the rice, gradually mounding the rice into a cone. Top with the remaining herb mixture and then the remaining rice. Drizzle over the remaining 2 tablespoons oil or the melted butter, cover with a tightly fitting lid wrapped in a cotton cloth, and place over high heat. When steam has built up, after about 2 minutes, reduce the heat to very low and steam for 30 minutes.

Let the rice stand for 10 minutes, then place the pot in 2 inches cold water (in the sink) for a minute or so to help loosen the crust. Remove the cover and turn out onto a platter, mixing the rice and herbs together, and serve the pieces of crust on top.

# Looking for Perfect Persian Rice

A few years ago I was in Baku, Azerbaijan, looking for flatbreads. Staying in my hotel were two businessmen who had come up from Iran, partly for work and partly just to have a look around. We ran into each other in a park not far from the hotel, and as we hit it off (talking mostly about food), we started to hang around together, especially in the evening when it came time to look for a place to eat.

These two men, one from Teheran and the other from a town in southern Iran, were incredibly picky about food, and in Baku, they were never satisfied. The bread was lousy, the meat was lousy, but above all else, it was the rice that was, according to them, almost inedible.

Horsecart transporting people around the Kashgar oasis

It was cooked Azeri-style, which is very much like the Persian tradition. But the rice available (at least in the places we ate) wasn't long-grain fine Persian or basmati style. It was Central Asian medium-grain rice, a little chewier, less delicate, and more sticky than the fluffy rice required by Persian and Azeri tradition. Not having grown up in the demanding Persian tradition, I quite liked the rice dishes. But these men hated them, and when I'd say that I didn't mind them, or even that I liked them, they would look at me as if I'd admitted to liking maggots.

"Are you crazy?" they would ask, and then proceed to tell me about Persian rice dishes, about *sabzi polo* (rice cooked with herbs for the New Year, see page 291), about rice cooked with lamb and apricots, and much more. But I'd remind them that it wasn't worth getting me all excited about all the great Persian rice dishes, as I'm American and traveling in Iran was no longer possible for me. "Right," they'd agree, and back they would go to tearing apart the poor Azeri pilafs.

Though I did notice, they rarely left an empty plate.

# Persian Lamb Kebabs with Sumac

Makes 12 to 15 kebabs; serves 6 to 8 with plenty of rice

THESE SUCCULENT GRILLED KEBABS ARE HALF OF THE CLASSIC COMBINATION *chelo kebab*. Serve them with Special Everyday Persian Rice (page 288), or with any other rice, and a salad. *Chelo kebab* is often served with a raw egg on the side. Guests mix the egg into their hot rice before eating.

Onion juice makes a simple, effective marinade, particularly for lamb. Here strips of lamb are marinated in onion juice, lemon juice, and a little yogurt, then threaded onto skewers for grilling. They are sprinkled with sumac powder just as they are served. Sumac is a dark red spice with a citrus tang to it, available at Middle Eastern groceries and specialty shops. If you can't find sumac, substitute fresh lime or lemon juice.

**Marinade**

1 onion, grated

½ teaspoon salt

2 tablespoons fresh lemon juice

¼ cup plain yogurt (whole-milk or 2%)

1 teaspoon turmeric (optional)

**Kebabs**

2 pounds boneless lean lamb, cut into thin ½- by-2-inch strips

¼ cup melted butter, melted rendered lamb fat, or olive oil

Pinch of saffron threads (optional)

2 tablespoons sumac powder (or juice of 2 limes or lemons)

For the marinade, place the grated onion and salt in a sieve placed over a large shallow bowl and toss to blend. Let stand for 30 minutes.

Meanwhile, pound the meat strips with a wooden mallet or a rolling pin to help tenderize them. Cover and set aside. Press out any liquid remaining in the onion into the bowl. Rinse the onion and set aside for another purpose. Add the lemon juice, yogurt, and optional turmeric to the onion juice and whisk to blend well. Add the meat strips and turn to coat. Cover and set aside in a cool place or the refrigerator to marinate for 3 to 4 hours, or refrigerate overnight; bring back to room temperature before proceeding.

Preheat a charcoal or gas grill or a broiler. Meanwhile, in a small heavy skillet, briefly dry-roast the saffron over medium-low heat, then crumble to a powder in a small bowl. Add 2 tablespoons water and stir to dissolve well. Whisk in the melted butter and set aside.

Thread 3 meat strips each onto metal skewers. Grill or broil 4 to 5 inches from the heat for 3 to 4 minutes, basting frequently with the saffron oil. Turn the skewers and cook for 3 to 4 minutes longer.

Place the skewers on a serving platter and dust the lamb lightly with sumac powder. Serve the kebabs still on the skewers.

# Silk Road Kebab

*barra kabob*

Serves 6 to 8

SHAKRAZABS IS A SMALL TOWN SOUTHEAST OF SAMARKAND IN UZBEKISTAN. At first glance dusty and ordinary, it in fact has a lively market as well as several beautiful remnants of an earlier, glorious era of Uzbek history. Tamerlane the Conquerer built a large caravanserai here at the end of the fourteenth century; its ruins are still awe-inspiring, with their turquoise tiles and soaring flocks of pigeons.

Late one afternoon I arrived in Shakrazabs and hurried out to see the caravanserai. On my way back, I walked through a small square that was filling with people, all of whom were waiting and chatting in the dusk. Small street stands selling grilled kebabs and other snacks did a good business until the reason for the crowd appeared: a troupe of gymnasts and jugglers, acrobats and clowns. They were in town for five days, and this was their opening night. The old-style Central Asian circus kept us all entertained for an hour, with tumbling, swallowing swords and fire, and clowning. Small children squeezed to the front of the standing circle of watchers, or sat on their father's shoulders, staring wide-eyed at the exotically costumed performers. After the last act, the ringmaster sent the children of the troupe around with hats collecting contributions. The show now over, the crowd remained, milling about and reluctant to leave.

Small clusters of people formed around the ice cream sellers and the kebab stands and then some of the women began, impromptu, to dance traditional Uzbek dances, swaying and whirling to the hand-clapped rhythms of the spectators.

Those infamous horsemen, like Tamerlane, sweeping out of the deserts of Central Asia to conquer the rich cities of China or of Europe, are most probably the creators of the meat-cooked-on-a-sword tradition that we know as shish kebab. Kebabs are the most common form of meat preparation all along the Silk Road, from China to Turkey. In every bazaar you will find a few small charcoal grills set up, being tended by men or boys, with spice-dusted skewers of lamb slowly sizzling to doneness.

This Uzbek version of kebab marinates the lamb, a good approach in a region where the herds are well exercised and the meat less than tender. The local tradition generally includes chunks of lamb fat (usually *alya,* or tail fat from the region's fat-tailed sheep). The chunks keep the meat well basted as it cooks. We've left the fat as an option; if you don't use it, brush the kebabs with a little oil or butter as they grill.

Serve the kebabs with Everyday Persian Rice (page 290), Special Everyday Persian Rice (page 288), or Simple Turkish Pilaf (page 322) and a salad or a yogurt sauce.

2 pounds lean lamb, cut into 1-inch cubes

4 ounces lamb fat, cut into small chunks (optional)

1 teaspoon vegetable oil, rendered lamb fat (see Note, page 312), or melted butter (plus extra oil or butter for brushing if not using the optional fat)

2 tablespoons red wine vinegar (see Note)

2 to 3 medium onions, minced

2 teaspoons coriander seed, dry-roasted (see page 148) and ground

1 teaspoon cumin seed, crushed

1 teaspoon freshly ground black or white pepper

### Optional garnish

1 large sweet onion, cut lengthwise in half and thinly sliced

2 ripe tomatoes, sliced

1 European cucumber, thinly sliced

Salt

Chopped fresh mint or crumbled dry mint

Place the pieces of lamb and the optional fat in a large bowl. Whisk together the oil, rendered fat, or butter and the vinegar in a small bowl. Add the onions, coriander and cumin seed, and the pepper to the meat, then pour on the oil and vinegar and toss to blend well. Cover and let stand in a cool place for 4 hours, or refrigerate for up to 24 hours; bring back to room temperature before proceeding.

Preheat a charcoal or gas grill or a broiler. Thread the meat onto metal skewers, inserting a piece of fat (if using) every so often. Make sure the pieces are only lightly touching, not crammed together. Grill or broil about 5 inches from the heat, turning after about 5 minutes, for 7 to 10 minutes. If not using fat, brush with a little oil or butter when you turn the kebabs.

Serve on a large platter, still on the skewers. If desired, top with onion slices, or line the platter with overlapping slices of tomato and/or cucumber, lightly salted and sprinkled with a little mint.

Note: Traditional recipes call for grape vinegar; red wine vinegar is the closest approximation.

# Golden Chicken Kebabs

**Makes 12 to 15 kebabs; serves 6 to 8 with rice**

PERSIAN *CHELO* RICE IS OFTEN EATEN WITH GRILLED LAMB OR CHICKEN KEBABS. These savory chicken kebabs are marinated in a blend of yogurt, garlic, saffron, and dried mint before being grilled over charcoal or broiled. Easy and delicious.

Serve the kebabs with a plate of fresh herbs (basil, tarragon, flat-leaf parsley) and Special Everyday Persian Rice (page 288), Everyday Persian Rice (page 290), or any cooked long-grain rice. You might want to offer Oasis Salad (page 299) as an accompaniment.

2 pounds boneless skinless chicken thighs
   or breasts or a combination

### Marinade

1 cup plain yogurt (whole-milk or 2%)

1 tablespoon minced garlic

⅛ teaspoon saffron threads, dry-roasted
   (see page 431), crushed to a powder,
   and dissolved in 2 tablespoons warm
   water

1 tablespoon crushed dried mint
   (optional)

½ teaspoon salt

½ teaspoon freshly ground black pepper

Cut the chicken into small pieces, ½-inch cubes or smaller, discarding any fat or tough connective tissue.

Combine the yogurt with the remaining marinade ingredients in a small bowl and mix well. Place the chicken pieces in a shallow bowl, pour the marinade over, and stir to ensure that all of the chicken is well coated. Let stand, refrigerated, for at least 3 hours or as long as 24 hours.

Preheat a charcoal or gas grill or a broiler.

Thread the chicken pieces onto metal skewers. Place only a few pieces of chicken on each skewer, and don't cram the pieces together tightly. (If they are packed together, rather than just lightly touching, they will not cook evenly.)

Grill or broil 5 to 6 inches from the heat, turning the skewers after 3 minutes for about 10 minutes, until the chicken is cooked through. Serve hot or at room temperature.

# Rhubarb-Lamb Stew

*khoresh rivas*

RHUBARB IS FOUND IN MANY PARTS OF CENTRAL ASIA AND IS BELIEVED to have originated in the Himalaya. In this stew, its tartness combines well with small slow-cooked chunks of lamb or beef. Although rhubarb is used in Persian and Azeri cooking, other peoples of Central Asia most emphatically do not view it as desirable food. Once while trekking in Zanskar in the Ladakh region of Kashmir, I came across some tender rhubarb on a glacial melt slope. Far from fresh fruits and vegetables, I was delighted, but my Zanskari companion, Dorje, was disdainful. "Cow food," he said as he watched me cook it up with some ginger to make a dipping sauce for fresh chapattis.

Green herbs and vegetables for sale at the Tashkent bazaar

Persian *khoresh* are stew-like sauces that are traditionally eaten over rice. Like Moroccan tagines, *khoresh* slow-cook meat or legumes with spices and are prized for the delicately flavored broth.

In *khoresh rivas*, the meat—either beef or lamb—is first simmered in broth, then the rhubarb, with the role of featured vegetable, is added and simmered until tender. Serve this in bowls, with rice, either *chelo* (Special Everyday Persian Rice, page 288) or *katteh* (Everyday Persian Rice, page 290\).

*continued*

1 tablespoon vegetable oil

3 small or 2 medium onions, finely chopped

1 pound boneless lamb shoulder or eye of round, trimmed of fat and cut into 1-inch cubes

⅛ teaspoon ground cinnamon

Pinch of grated nutmeg

1 cup packed flat-leaf parsley leaves, finely chopped

½ cup packed fresh mint leaves, finely chopped

About 2 cups water

1 pound rhubarb, trimmed, peeled, and cut into 1½-inch lengths (3 cups)

1 teaspoon salt

½ teaspoon freshly ground black pepper

Heat the oil in a large heavy saucepan over medium heat. Add the onions and cook for 5 minutes, until starting to turn translucent. Raise the heat, add the meat, and cook, stirring frequently, until the meat is well browned, about 6 minutes.

Add the cinnamon, nutmeg, parsley, and mint, and stir well. Add the water (the meat should be just covered) and bring to a boil, then lower the heat and simmer gently, covered, for 45 minutes, or until the meat is tender. Check to ensure that the pot isn't running dry; if necessary, add more water. The recipe can be prepared ahead to this point and set aside for several hours or refrigerated overnight (reheat before proceeding).

When the meat is cooked and tender, add the rhubarb and simmer for about 10 minutes, until tender. Serve hot.

# Oasis Salad

COMING INTO AN OASIS FROM THE DESERT CAN BE HALLUCINATORY. ONE moment you're in a vast, open, shadeless space, the sun beating down, the next you've entered the leafy calm of the poplars and cottonwoods that mark the edge of the oasis. Water gurgles in open irrigation ditches, birds sing, and green vegetables thrive in well-tended gardens. Everything smells moist and fresh, and there's a softness to the air. It's tempting to cross back out into the desert just to reexperience the transition, but if you're like us, you're usually too eager for fresh vegetables and a cool drink to take the time.

It's no wonder then that oasis dwellers are famous for their sweet melons, plump red tomatoes, and crisp fresh cucumbers and radishes. These fruits of the desert heat and oasis waters feel like a triumph of human will and effort over nature. And no wonder that most meals along the Silk Road, except in winter, feature at least one salad, very simply dressed. (Wintertime is the season for pickles, a wonderful way to have the crisp bite of radishes and carrots in the cold season.)

When you serve this salad, imagine that you are seated under a canopy of grape vines, sipping hot tea from bowls and eating pilaf and kebabs.

1 cup coarsely chopped red or white (daikon or icicle) radish

1 cup coarsely chopped peeled English cucumber

2 cups ripe tomato chunks

1 teaspoon salt, or to taste

¼ to ½ cup loosely packed fresh coriander leaves, coarsely chopped

Combine all the ingredients in a bowl and toss gently to blend. Serve at room temperature.

# Herat, Afghanistan

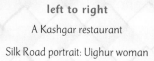
I once worked in a Wyoming restaurant with a young man from Afghanistan named Zia. On my last night there, I told him that I was going traveling to India; he suggested that I go also to Afghanistan. He said that he would give me a letter to deliver to his family, and that I would then be welcome to stay with them. He said to come to his apartment the following day and the letter would be ready.

When I arrived, Zia asked me in to tell me a bit more about his town and family, and also to introduce me to his wife, whom he had met in Wyoming. I asked her if she had been to Afghanistan, and she said no, but that she hoped to be going soon. They bid me farewell and off I went.

Months passed, and eventually I arrived in Herat, Zia's hometown. After traveling across Iran on a succession of local buses, it was the very first town I came to in Afghanistan, just across the border from Iran. At the bus stand, a crowd of kids gathered around me, hoping to make some money taking a foreigner to a hotel, but instead I pulled out my letter, which got passed from hand to hand until someone stepped in who could read it. The letter was read, instructions were given, and then off I went through the narrow, winding, mud-packed laneways, escorted by a dozen little kids.

Fifteen or twenty minutes later, we walked through a gate into a courtyard, and the owner of the house, Zia's father, was summoned. He read the letter and greeted me with a nod of approval, the crowd was dispersed, and I was shown to a room. No one seemed to speak any English, and I spoke no Afghani.

After a few minutes, two young boys came into my room, one carrying a porcelain urn filled with warm scented water, the other carrying a porcelain basin with a clean towel, soap, and a large white linen tablecloth. One boy poured water slowly into the basin as I washed my hands and face, and I used the towel to dry off. After spreading the tablecloth out on the floor, the boys disappeared.

When they reappeared, they carried an unbelievable feast that could feed ten hungry people: stacks of fresh warm *naan*, a plate of lamb kebabs, smaller plates of chickpeas and spinach, and the centerpiece, a huge platter of lamb and nut *pulao*, were all put down on the tablecloth. And then they once again left, and I started to eat, eating rice with my right hand, loving every mouthful.

When I was done, there was tea, served in a tiny glass with lots of sugar, Afghan-style. And after tea, the two young boys, who by this time were feeling more at ease and starting to smile and to laugh, motioned that it was time to leave. So we headed out, walking again through the tiny laneways of a town completely unknown to me. We came to a strange-looking adobe-type building and in we went. It was a bathhouse, and while a few men turned to stare, most people went about their business, getting clean in a large steamy room with wonderful hot water.

When we came out, there was only one more chore to look after: My two companions took me to a tailor. There was conversation with the tailor, a little dispute, they looked me up and down, and then at last there appeared a pair of heavy white cotton, baggy Afghan trousers and a long shirt. They motioned for me to change into my new clothes, which I happily did, and my old clothes were put into a bag, cast off like a worn pair of running shoes.

And finally I was done: fed, bathed, and newly clothed.

I stayed in Herat for six days, and every day, three times a day, a feast appeared in my little room, served on a white tablecloth. A good amount of smiling and laughing took place, but not much spoken language, and no one seemed to care. On my last day, a young man whom I had never seen before appeared, and he spoke in English. He said that he had come on behalf of the family to pass on their good wishes, and to tell me that they were very

Afghan mujahedeen bakery in Peshawar, Pakistan

happy that I had come to visit. He had also come, he said, to introduce me to Zia's wife and Zia's children, and in they came. I was a little surprised, having met Zia's American wife, but I didn't say anything. But the young man speaking English went on to say that everyone was very excited about Zia marrying a second wife, and they were all looking forward to her coming to live there in Herat.

I've never known what happened after that, and I've never forgotten the feasts.

# Pomegranate Onion Salad

In autumn, throughout Central Asia, markets are aglow with beautiful bright stacks of red and yellow pomegranates. And nearby there will usually be piles of onions, the mild sweet yellow onions for which the region is famous. One of the simplest ways in which these two harvests are paired is in this refreshing salad.

The onions are thinly sliced and salted to remove any strong onion tang, then rinsed off after a few minutes. (The juice given off by the salted onions is a favorite ingredient in lamb marinades; see Persian Lamb Kebabs with Sumac, page 293.) They are then dressed with a tart, sweet dressing of lemon juice and pomegranate concentrate and garnished with mint leaves and an attractive sprinkling of pomegranate seeds.

1 large sweet onion (Spanish, Bermuda, or Vidalia), halved lengthwise and thinly sliced crosswise (about 2 cups)

1 tablespoon coarse salt

3 tablespoons fresh lemon juice

1 teaspoon pomegranate concentrate (see Glossary)

½ teaspoon sugar

Pinch of cayenne pepper or dried chile pepper flakes

¼ cup finely chopped fresh mint

½ cup pomegranate seeds (optional)

Place the onion slices in a bowl and add the coarse salt. Toss to ensure the onions are well covered with salt and let stand for 15 to 20 minutes. Rinse thoroughly in cold water and pat dry (or dry in a salad spinner).

In a medium bowl, whisk together the lemon juice, pomegranate concentrate, sugar, and cayenne or chile pepper flakes. Add the onion and mint and toss gently to coat.

Serve mounded on a decorative small plate, topped with the pomegranate seeds if available.

# Yogurt Salad

YOGURT MAY BE YET ANOTHER REMNANT OF THE CENTRAL ASIAN NOMADIC tradition. Certainly it is an essential part of the Silk Road table, as well as the cuisines of Persia and Turkey. Often, as here, it is drained, then whisked with water and seasoned with salt or flavored with fresh herbs. This yogurt salad is colorful with chopped scallions, radishes, cucumbers, and fresh herbs. It's great with *pulao* or kebabs.

2 cups plain yogurt (whole-milk or 2%)

½ cup water

½ European cucumber, peeled and finely chopped

⅓ cup finely chopped radishes (optional)

½ cup chopped fresh coriander leaves, plus 1 or 2 sprigs for optional garnish

2 tablespoons finely chopped fresh dill

1 scallion, minced

1 teaspoon salt, or to taste

¼ teaspoon freshly ground black pepper, or to taste

Place the yogurt in a cheesecloth-lined sieve set in the sink or over a large bowl. Let drain for 1 hour.

Transfer the yogurt to a large bowl and whisk in the water. Add the remaining ingredients and stir to mix. Taste and adjust the seasonings. Transfer to a serving bowl. Serve at room temperature or chilled, garnished with a sprig or two of coriander if you wish.

Selling pomegranates in the Baku market in Azerbaijan

# Central Asian Rice and Bean Stew
*mashkichiri*

THE WORD *MASH* MEANS MUNG BEAN IN FARSI AND FARSI-RELATED LANGUAGES like Azeri and Tajik, as well as in Turkic languages such as Uzbek and Uighur. The word *kichiri* is like the Hindi word *kitchri,* a name for rice dishes made by cooking rice together with other ingredients. (The British took the idea and the name and turned it into "kedgeree.")

We like this satisfying meal-in-one stew we learned in Tajikistan. Potatoes, carrots, and tomatoes give variety of taste and texture to the main event, a spiced combination of mung beans (yellow dal) and long-grain rice. *Mashkichiri* is quick and easy to prepare once the mung beans have soaked, and all too easy to eat in large quantities when accompanied by plenty of yogurt. Serve it as a simple meal in one, or serve with kebabs and a side dish of something crunchy, like sliced cucumbers or radishes, or Persian pickled radish.

The winter version of this dish would have no tomatoes, and would use more carrots and onions instead. Winters in Central Asia are harsh, and there are few fresh vegetables to be had. Root vegetables, which can be stored and used when other vegetables aren't available, are an important part of the winter diet.

3 tablespoons vegetable oil or rendered lamb fat (see Note, page 312)

2 cups coarsely chopped onions (about 3 medium onions)

2 medium potatoes, cubed

2 medium carrots, coarsely chopped

1 pound (about 4 medium) ripe tomatoes, coarsely chopped

1 teaspoon cumin seed, ground

¾ teaspoon dried chile pepper flakes or crumbled dried red chile (see Glossary)

2 teaspoons salt

½ teaspoon freshly ground black pepper

2 to 3 cups boiling water or mild stock

1 cup mung dal (see Glossary), soaked overnight in water to cover

2½ cups cooked long-grain white rice (or 1 cup uncooked rice, cooked while mung beans cook)

## Garnish and accompaniment

Sprigs of mint (optional)

2 to 3 cups plain yogurt

In a large heavy pot, heat the oil or fat until very hot. Add the onions, lower the heat to medium, and cook, stirring occasionally, until lightly golden, about 10 minutes. Add the potatoes and carrots and cook, stirring occasionally, for 10 minutes.

Stir in the tomatoes, then add the cumin, chile, salt, and pepper and stir well. Add 2 cups of the boiling water or stock and bring to a boil. Let boil vigorously for several minutes, then stir in the dal. Once the mixture has again returned to the boil, lower the heat, cover, and simmer until the mung beans are tender, 30 to 40 minutes, stirring every 10 minutes or so to prevent sticking. Add more boiling water or stock if necessary.

When the beans are done, stir in the cooked rice. The mixture should be moist; add a little hot water or stock if necessary. Taste for seasoning. Serve hot, garnished with sprigs of fresh mint (if available) and accompanied by plain yogurt.

**Alternative:** An Uzbek version of this stew includes lamb: Cut ½ pound lean lamb into small cubes. Add the meat several minutes after you begin sautéing the onions. You may wish to increase the salt and pepper.

*Uighur woman selling garlic in the Akmeqit oasis
in the southern Takla Makaun desert*

# Baked Persian Rice with Chicken
## tahchin

**Serves 6 to 8**

THOUGH AROUND THE WORLD MOST RICE IS COOKED IN SOME FORM OF POT OR pan over a flame or other heat, there is a whole category of baked savory rice dishes. These include not only Italian *bomba de riso* and South Carolina baked perloo, but also their probable ancestor, *tahchin,* baked Persian rice. The same principles apply to baked rice as to *katteh* (page 290) and *chelo* (page 288): The goal is fluffy separate grains of rice and a tasty crust, though in this case the bottom layer of rice is thicker and studded with small pieces of chicken.

Sellers of fresh herbs in Tashkent

The chicken is simmered, then placed in a yogurt marinade enlivened with a little dried orange peel (available from Middle Eastern groceries or by mail order; see Mail-Order Sources, page 438) The rice is soaked and boiled, as for *chelo* or *katteh* or *polo,* then placed with the chicken in an ovenproof dish to bake slowly until done. Though this dish was traditionally cooked in a tandoor oven (probably in the waning heat after baking the day's breads), it does very well in a modern electric or gas oven. All you need is a wide heavy ovenproof pot sealed with a tight-fitting lid (or aluminum foil), and several hours cooking time (during which you can forget about it).

The baked rice is a golden round about two inches high. It is inverted onto a large plate, the well-browned crust forming the top surface, then sliced into wedges. Pieces of succulent chicken are buried in the rice and crust. The texture is firm and the slices of the rice hold together well, so they can be eaten as finger food (a pleasure for children especially). Accompany with moist side dishes such as Oasis Salad (page 299), a yogurt sauce, and a plate of greens and fresh herbs such as tarragon, mint, scallions, and salad greens.

### Filling

2 tablespoons butter or vegetable oil

1½ to 1¾ pounds boneless skinless chicken breasts, cut into 1- to 2-inch pieces and trimmed of fat

1 onion, minced

2 tablespoons lemon juice

1 teaspoon salt

Generous teaspoon of dried orange peel (see Glossary)

½ cup plain yogurt (whole-milk or 2%)

2 large eggs

### Rice

3 cups basmati rice

Water

2 tablespoons salt

About 2 tablespoons melted butter

At least 5 hours before you wish to serve the dish, prepare the filling: Heat the butter or oil in a large heavy nonreactive skillet over medium heat. Add the chicken and onion and cook for 10 minutes. Add the lemon juice and salt, cover, and simmer for 40 minutes.

Meanwhile, prepare the orange peel: Bring a small pot of water to a vigorous boil, toss in the peel, and boil for 5 minutes, then drain. In the same pot, bring another 2 cups water to a boil and add the peel, then remove from the heat and let stand for at least 10 minutes. Drain and coarsely chop.

When the chicken is cooked, remove from the heat and stir in the yogurt and orange peel. Cool to room temperature, then cover and place in the refrigerator to marinate for 2 to 24 hours.

Wash the rice thoroughly and put it in a large bowl with 8 cups water mixed with 1 tablespoon of the salt. Let soak for 30 minutes to 3 hours.

When ready to proceed, preheat the oven to 375°F.

Drain the soaked rice, then boil the rice following the directions for Special Everyday Persian Rice on page 288; drain, rinse, and drain again.

Butter or oil a wide (12-inch diameter) casserole or heavy ovenproof pot.

Remove the chicken pieces from the marinade and set aside. Break the eggs into a small bowl and beat well. Stir into the marinade mixture. Mix in 3 cups of the cooked rice. Spread the rice mixture over the bottom and up the sides of the casserole or pot. Distribute the chicken pieces over the rice, then add the remaining rice to cover, smoothing it level. Drizzle on the melted butter.

Bake, tightly covered with a lid or aluminum foil, for 45 minutes. Lower the heat to 350°F and bake for 1¼ hours longer, or until the top of the rice is golden brown.

Just before removing the casserole from the oven, fill your kitchen sink with about 2 inches of cold water.

Remove the casserole from the oven and place in the cold water for several minutes; this will help keep the rice from sticking to the pot. Slide a thin-bladed knife along the sides of the pot to loosen the rice. Place a large plate over the pot and invert; the rice should drop onto the plate (this is easiest with two people). Serve cut into wedges.

# Apricot-Lamb Wedding Polo

**Serves 6**

MANY YEARS AGO WE WERE ASKED TO CATER A WEDDING IN JEFFREY'S hometown in Wyoming. The mother of the bride, who had taken cooking classes from Jeffrey, wanted to make her Lebanese son-in-law-to-be feel welcome. This was especially important since his family would be unable to come to the wedding. They were all in Lebanon, at that time suffering in the depths of civil war. So she asked us to prepare an array of dishes from Persia and the Eastern Mediterranean, serving *mezze* of various kinds and homemade pita breads. For a festive main dish, we proposed this delectable Persian *polo*, with its layers of tender rice and slow-cooked lamb and apricots, a recipe adapted from Claudia Roden's wonderful classic *A Book of Middle Eastern Food.*

At a wedding feast in Samarkand

On the day of the wedding, in early October, the high-altitude weather gods produced a blinding snowstorm. But at the feast there were mountains of food and everything went happily and well, including the wedding *polo.* At one point the groom came into the kitchen with his two close friends, also from Lebanon, to tell us how much he liked the food. "Thank you," he said, "thank you especially for the rice. . . ."

Rice

2 cups basmati rice

¼ cup salt

Water

Lamb and apricot layers

4 tablespoons butter or ¼ cup vegetable oil or olive oil

1 large onion, finely chopped

1 pound boneless lean lamb shoulder or leg, trimmed of fat and cut into ½- to 1-inch cubes

1 teaspoon ground cinnamon

⅛ teaspoon grated nutmeg

½ cup dried apricots, coarsely chopped

3 tablespoons sultana (golden) raisins

Generous grinding of black pepper

¼ cup plain yogurt (whole-milk or 2%)

⅛ teaspoon saffron threads, dry-roasted (see page 431), crumbled to a powder, and dissolved in 2 tablespoons water (optional)

Following the directions for Special Everyday Persian Rice (page 288), wash and soak the rice, then boil it, drain, rinse, and drain again. Set aside.

Meanwhile, heat 2 tablespoons of the butter or oil in a large heavy skillet over medium-high heat. Add the onion and cook until well softened. Add the lamb and cook until the pieces have changed color all over. Add the cinnamon, nutmeg, apricots, and raisins and stir to blend well. Add 1 tablespoon salt and enough water to just cover the mixture and bring to a boil, then lower the heat and simmer until the fruits are well softened and the sauce is very thick, about 20 minutes. Watch carefully to make sure it doesn't stick or burn; add a little extra water if necessary. Stir in the pepper.

Heat the remaining 2 tablespoons oil or butter and 1 tablespoon water in a large heavy pot. In a small bowl, mix the yogurt with ½ cup of the cooked rice. Add to the hot oil or butter and spread it over the bottom of the pot. Spoon over one quarter of the lamb mixture. Top with another layer of rice, gradually shaping a cone or mound as you layer the ingredients, then add another layer of lamb and repeat, alternating the layers and ending with a layer of rice. Use the handle of a wooden spoon to poke about six holes in the mounded rice.

Cover the pot with a tight-fitting lid wrapped in a cotton cloth and place over high heat. When steam has built up, after about 2 minutes, lower the heat to very low and steam for 35 minutes.

Let the rice stand, covered, for 10 minutes before serving. Place the pot in a few inches of cold water (in the sink) for 1 or 2 minutes to help in detaching the crust (page 289).

To serve, mound on a warm platter, mixing the rice and lamb. (If you wish, tint ¼ cup of the cooked rice with saffron, as described in the recipe for Special Everyday Persian Rice, page 288, and sprinkle over the mound.) Top with pieces of the crust.

# Uighur Autumn Pulao
## pulao

THE UIGHURS WHO LIVE IN THE OASES THAT RIM THE TAKLA MAKAN DESERT in the far west of China are cultural cousins of the Uzbeks, who also speak a Turkic language. Uzbeks and Uighurs both have a strong pilaf tradition (in both languages, pilaf is known as *pulao*). *Pulao* is a one-pot dish, cooked in a special pot called a *q'azan* in both Uighur and Uzbek. In both, the flavor base is onions and carrots, and lamb is the meat most commonly used. The *q'azan* is a wide shallow metal pot like a shallow wok, meant to be placed over an open fire (in somewhat the same way as a paella pan). Lacking an open fire and a *q'azan*, it is still possible to make a good *pulao*. We use our large heavy well-seasoned wok on our gas stove, with good results. You can also use a heavy pot, but make sure it is eleven or twelve inches in diameter or more (you want a large cooking surface relative to the depth of the ingredients).

Sunday bazaar in Shakrazabs, Uzbekistan

Like Turkish pilaf and Persian *polo*, *pulao* is a dish of celebration, a festive dish. Consequently, it's traditionally made with plenty of oil, usually a blend of *alya* (rendered fat from the tail of the region's long-tailed sheep) and vegetable oil, and served at weddings, holidays, and other family celebrations. Uzbek *pulao*, like Spanish or Catalan paella, is traditionally made by men over the open fire.

Uighurs and Uzbeks prefer a medium- to short-grain rice for their *pulao*, not the long-grain dry-textured basmati-type rice of Persian tradition. The most highly prized rice in Uzbekistan is known as *devzira*. It's slightly pink and medium-grain, with a firm texture when cooked. The closest approximation we've found is Bhutanese red, though that rice too can be difficult to find. An Italian-style rice such as baldo (often sold as Turkish rice) or arborio or regular medium- to short-grain rice can be substituted.

We had a lesson in Uighur pilaf in Toronto. The tastes and smells transported us back to Kashgar, Aksu, and the other oasis towns of Xinjiang we had visited almost a decade before. Our teacher was a Uighur woman named Bahargul, from Urumchi, the capital of Xinjiang. Bahargul says that to make a Uighur *pulao* in North America, she uses an American medium- or short-grain white rice. The *pulao* she taught us is an autumn *pulao*, with quinces and peppers steam-cooked with the rice. The quinces give a little sweetness to the dish. Bahargul served her *pulao* with a fresh salad of tomatoes and red bell peppers, finely chopped, and sprinkled with a little salt and fresh coriander.

Typically, no individual plates are used when the *pulao* is served. Guests use their right hands or spoons to take rice, meat, and fruit from the platter to their mouths. (The Mandarin Chinese word for *pulao, zhua fan,* means grasp rice.) If eating with your hand, only your fingertips should touch the food.

The proportions below reproduce Bahargul's delicious Uighur *pulao*. For most city-dwelling North Americans, the *pulao* will seem quite oil-laden, and you can reduce the total oil to less than one half cup if you wish. But if you imagine yourself living in Kashgar or Turfan or another Uighur oasis town, eating very little oil or fat, and subsisting mostly on flatbreads and tea, then you can enjoy and appreciate, even luxuriate in, the rich gleaming flavor-laden rice of the *pulao*. Serve it with a simple chopped salad. The salad too is eaten by hand or by guests lifting out small spoonfuls for themselves.

| | |
|---|---|
| 3 cups medium- or short-grain rice | 1 medium tomato, coarsely chopped |
| 5 teaspoons salt | 2 teaspoons sugar |
| 1½ pounds lamb back ribs | 1 large quince, cored and cut into 6 to 8 wedges, or 2 Granny Smith apples, cored and quartered |
| 3 large carrots | |
| Scant ½ cup vegetable oil | |
| ¼ cup rendered lamb fat (see Note) | 1 large red bell pepper, stem, seeds, and membranes discarded, and cut into 8 chunks |
| 1 large or 1½ medium onions, thickly sliced | |

Place the rice in a sieve and rinse three or four times under cold running water. Place in a medium bowl and cover with warm water. Stir in 2 teaspoons of the salt and let soak while you prepare the other ingredients.

Rinse the lamb with cold water. Trim off any excess fat, then cut into 3-inch chunks, leaving it on the bone.

*continued*

Cut the carrots on the diagonal into ¼-inch slices. Stack several of these together at a time and cut crosswise into matchsticks. Set aside.

Heat the oil and fat in a large heavy wok or a large wide heavy pot. When the fat is almost smoking, add 1 teaspoon salt. (Bahargul says this will keep it from igniting.) When the fat is just smoking, slide in the lamb and brown on all sides, about 10 minutes. Add the onions, separating the slices as you add them. Cook for 5 minutes, then add the tomato and stir well. Add the carrots and stir. If they start to stick, lower the heat slightly and use a spatula to lift and turn them as they cook. Let cook for about 8 minutes, then add 1 teaspoon salt and the sugar. Cook for another 5 to 8 minutes, until carrots are very limp and starting to turn a golden brown. If there is excess fat floating in the pan, skim it off.

Add 3½ cups cold water and the remaining 1 teaspoon salt to the pan. Bring to a boil and boil over medium heat for 10 minutes. Taste and adjust the seasonings. Remove the meat and set aside.

Drain the rice and add to the pan. The water should just cover the rice; if necessary, add a little more water. Bring back to a boil and cook for 5 minutes. The water should now be just below the top of the rice; if necessary, add a little more hot water. Place the pieces of quince (or apple) and red pepper evenly over the top of the rice, then top with the chunks of meat.

Cover tightly with a lid or with aluminum foil, lower the heat to very low, and steam for 30 minutes. You should be able to hear a slight sound of simmering; if you don't, raise the heat slightly; do not remove the lid. Remove from the heat and let stand for about 10 minutes to allow the rice to firm up.

To serve, remove the meat and pepper and quince pieces and set aside. Mound the rice on a platter. Place the meat chunks, peppers, and quinces on top of the rice.

Traditionally, at the table the host lifts the lamb chunks off the rice onto a cutting board or other plate. He or she cuts the meat into slices, then places these back on the rice.

Note: Rendering lamb fat is a very easy process: Cut about ½ pound lamb fat into small chunks. Place in a heavy skillet over medium heat. Stir to prevent burning as the fat begins to melt. After about 20 minutes, all the fat will have melted, leaving only small, crisp cracklings. Strain through a paper towel–lined sieve. The rendered fat will be almost odorless and colorless. Half a pound of fat produces about ½ cup liquid rendered fat.

Uzbek pulao: Uzbek *pulaos* are very like Uighur *pulaos*, but in one typically Uzbek variant, a delicious one, a whole head of garlic is buried in the rice when it is added. The garlic boils and steam-cooks, then is served on top of the rice. Guests take individual cloves and squeeze out the mild garlic paste as a condiment.

# Cardamom and Rose Water Rice Pudding

*shir berenj*

LIKE THE SPANISH *ARROZ CON LECHE* (SEE PAGE 353), THIS PERSIAN RICE pudding is made of rice slow-cooked in milk. Flavorings are added near the end of cooking and include aromatic rose water as well as cardamom. Top with a sprinkling of chopped green pistachios if available. If you wish, sweeten the pudding further by drizzling on a little pale honey.

1 cup short-grain rice or broken long-grain rice (see Note, page 416)

4 cups whole milk

2 cups water

1 cup sugar, or more to taste

3 tablespoons rose water

Seeds from 2 green cardamom pods, ground (1 scant teaspoon)

Pale honey (optional)

6 to 8 pistachios, coarsely chopped (optional)

Wash the rice thoroughly. Combine in a large heavy saucepan with the milk and water and bring to a boil. Lower the heat to very low and simmer, stirring occasionally to prevent sticking, for 2 hours, or until most of the liquid has been absorbed; the texture should be slightly soupy.

Stir in the sugar, rose water, and cardamom and cook, stirring, for another 5 minutes. Taste and stir in more sugar if you want. Transfer to a serving dish and let cool to room temperature.

Just before serving, drizzle a little pale honey over the pudding and garnish with the chopped pistachios if you wish.

Istanbul's Blue Mosque courtyard

inset: Italian fisherman

# Pilaf, Paella, Risotto

*P*aella, risotto, and the scrumptious rice puddings of Turkey and Spain, some of the world's best known and favorite rice dishes, all come from the dry rocky shores of the Mediterranean, a region of the world that seems light-years away from the tropical lush-green rice paddies of Asia. But though we may not think of a field of golden rice when we think of the Mediterranean, rice has been grown there for over a thousand years. And even before then, the Greeks knew about red rice from West Africa, and Alexander the Great brought rice back from India, using it for medicinal purposes rather than as a staple food.

Egypt, to this day an important rice producer, was the first significant rice-growing area in the Mediterranean, starting around 500 A.D. The waters of the Nile were used to flood rice fields through the hot dry summers. Later the Arabs carried their love of rice and their knowledge of rice cultivation to Sicily and to Spain. In Spain, rice was grown in deltas and beside rivers near the Mediterranean coast, especially in the Valencia area. In the fifteenth century, rice cultivation began in northern Italy, in the wet marshy lands near the Po River. As marshlands were drained and land reclaimed, in Italy and in Spain, improved water management led to more productive rice growing, and rice became an important supplement to wheat, especially significant in years when the wheat crop was poor.

The rices traditionally grown around the Mediterranean, in Egypt, Turkey, Spain, France, Portugal, Greece, and Italy, are short- to medium-grain japonicas, like Japanese rices, but generally slightly less sticky when cooked. The different varieties have slightly different cooking characteristics, some being more able to absorb liquids, others being softer and creamier. Recently California, with its Mediterranean climate and temperate latitude, has also begun producing Italian-style rice suitable for risottos and paella.

Italy is by far the largest producer of rice in Europe (responsible for two thirds of Europe's total production), and a major exporter. Some of Italy's rice is exported to Turkey. Like their Turkic cousins along the Silk Road in Central Asia, Turks generally prefer to use a short- to medium-grain rice such as baldo or Egyptian rice for pilafs as well as for stuffing vegetables and vine leaves.

In Italy, Spain, and the Camargue region of France, long-grain rices are also being grown, mostly for export to Northern Europe and elsewhere. (The Swedes and the Finns

Making a fish trap in Gallipoli

**opposite left to right**

Spice merchant in the Egyptian bazaar in Istanbul

Outdoor cheese seller at the Monopoli market in Italy

Preparing a field for planting in El Faiyum, Egypt

both have festive Christmas dishes made with long-grain rice, for example, and there is also a growing market in Northern Europe for Asian foods, including rice). These long-grain rices are specially developed new varieties that have the characteristics of long-grain tropical Asian rices but can be grown in the Mediterranean climate, with its hot dry summers. The more traditional short- and medium-grain rices are sold mostly in Italy and Spain, for specialized regional dishes such as risotto and paella.

While Italy and Spain are large producers of rice for domestic consumption, rice eating is a very regional matter within each country. In the rice-producing regions of Spain, such as Valencia and the Ebro Delta, rice consumption is an average of thirty-five pounds per person per year compared with only four pounds in the Bilbao region on the northern coast of Spain. Similarly, in Italy, rice is an important daily food only in the very limited rice-producing regions near the Po. There it is eaten much as the rest of Italy eats pasta, as an important filling course in a larger meal.

For everyday, we like plain Egyptian rice, simple Turkish pilaf, and simple risottos. The more complex flavored rices we usually save for parties or other special occasions. The necessities for making Mediterranean rices are simple. Apart from good rice, you will need good olive oils (a selection so you can try to match the oil with the region the dish comes from), fresh lemons, garlic, onion, tomatoes, flat-leaf parsley, cayenne (or Spanish *pimentón*), saffron, and good fish and chicken stocks.

# Basic Egyptian Rice

EGYPT PRODUCES AN IMPORTANT RICE CROP ON IRRIGATED LANDS IN THE NILE Valley and Delta. The rice is a delicious short- to medium-grain japonica, with smaller grains than Italian or Spanish rices, now available at specialty stores in North America. Traditionally, plain Egyptian rice is cooked with a little oil or butter in salted water, using the absorption method. In her remarkable *Book of Jewish Food,* Claudia Roden recounts that the Jewish community in Egypt uses olive oil, while the Copts and Muslims, with no dietary rules prohibiting the mixing of meat and dairy, use butter. The rice emerges with every grain intact, but with a soft very slightly sticky texture somewhat reminiscent of Japanese rice. It holds its shape well and the coating of oil ensures that the grains do in fact remain separate.

Serve this rice with Savory Fava Bean Stew (page 320), with Slow-Cooked Lamb and Onion Stew (page 321), or with kebabs and a yogurt sauce (see Index).

2 cups Egyptian rice

3 to 4 tablespoons olive oil or butter

Scant ½ teaspoon saffron threads, briefly
   dry-roasted (see page 431) and
   crumbled to a powder (optional)

2½ cups water

1 teaspoon salt

Wash the rice thoroughly under cold running water until the water runs clear. Place in a sieve to drain well. Discard any discolored grains or other impurities.

Place the oil or butter in a heavy medium pot and heat over medium-high heat. Add the rice and the optional saffron and cook for 1 to 2 minutes, stirring gently with a wooden spoon to ensure the rice is well coated with oil. Add the water and bring to a boil. Add the salt and stir gently to ensure no grains are stuck to the bottom. When the water is at a full rolling boil, cover, reduce the heat to very low, and let cook for 20 minutes.

Remove from the heat and lift the lid of the pot briefly to release the steam, then replace and let the rice stand for 10 to 15 minutes before serving.

# Savory Fava Bean Stew

**Serves 2 as a main dish with rice or 4 as part of a larger meal**

FRESHLY COOKED FAVAS ARE WONDERFULLY BUTTERY IN TEXTURE. HERE THEY are simmered with lightly sautéed onion and garlic, as well as freshly ground coriander for an intriguing depth of flavor and a touch of cayenne for pizzazz. This recipe is adapted from Claudia Roden's classic *A Book of Middle Eastern Food*. Once cooked, the beans can be stirred into freshly cooked Egyptian rice and served as a single dish, but we prefer to serve them separately, so that guests can adjust the proportions of beans and rice as they please.

We like to serve fava beans and Basic Egyptian Rice (page 319) with Turkish Yogurt Sauce (page 323) or Central Asian Yogurt Salad (page 303), and perhaps some freshly sliced tomatoes or cucumbers.

1 tablespoon olive oil

1 medium onion, finely chopped

3 to 5 cloves garlic, minced

½ teaspoon coriander seed, ground

2 cups fresh or frozen shelled fava beans (see Note)

Scant ½ cup water (¼ cup if using frozen beans)

½ teaspoon salt, or to taste

¼ teaspoon cayenne pepper or a pinch of dried chile pepper flakes

Generous grinding of black pepper (optional)

**Optional garnish**

About ¼ cup packed coarsely torn fresh flat-leaf parsley

In a large heavy skillet or saucepan, heat the oil over medium-high heat. Add the onion and garlic and cook, stirring frequently, until the onion becomes translucent, about 5 minutes. Stir in the coriander seed and then the favas. Cook, stirring occasionally, for about 1 minute. Add the water, bring to a boil, and simmer until the beans are just tender, 10 to 20 minutes depending on the freshness of the beans. If you want to skin the favas (see Note), remove from the heat and cool slightly, then remove the tough skins and discard. Return the beans to the pan, return to the heat, and proceed with the recipe.

Stir in the salt and cayenne or chile pepper flakes and cook for 2 to 3 minutes longer. Add the optional pepper and turn out into a bowl. Top with the optional parsley and serve warm or at room temperature.

**Note:** If buying fresh favas in the pod, buy 1 to 1¼ pounds to yield 2 cups shelled beans. Frozen favas are available at many Italian and Middle Eastern groceries. If you are using tender young favas or frozen favas, you won't need to skin them, but if you can find only large, very mature beans, then you will probably want to remove the tough outer skin of each bean. This is most easily done after the beans have been cooked.

# Slow-Cooked Lamb and Onion Stew

Serves 6 with rice

THIS IS A SIMPLE WINTER DISH OF NOTHING MORE THAN LAMB AND ONIONS with a few seasonings. The onions give it a slight sweetness; the lamb is meltingly tender. Make it ahead, then reheat just before serving. If you'd rather cook it in the oven, begin by browning the ingredients on the stovetop, then slow-cook the stew in a 300°F oven for two hours. The pepper gives only a mild heat; if you wish more, increase it to two teaspoons.

Serve this with Simple Turkish Pilaf (page 322) or Basic Egyptian Rice (page 319) and Turkish Yogurt Sauce (page 323).

3 tablespoons butter or olive oil

2 pounds lean lamb, cut into 1-inch cubes

6 large yellow onions, coarsely chopped

2 cups water, or more if needed

1 teaspoon ground cinnamon

Sprig of thyme

1½ teaspoons salt, or to taste

1 teaspoon cayenne pepper

Place the butter or oil in a large heavy casserole and heat over high heat. Add the meat and brown, stirring occasionally, about 5 minutes. Lower the heat to medium-high, add the onions, and cook for 10 to 15 minutes, until very soft.

Add the water and bring to a boil. Add the cinnamon, thyme, salt, and pepper, lower the heat, cover, and simmer gently for about 1½ hours, until the lamb is very tender. Check occasionally to make sure the stew is not sticking; add a little more water if necessary.

# Simple Turkish Pilaf

PILAFS ARE FESTIVE FOOD, CELEBRATION FOOD, EVERYWHERE FROM TURKEY and the oases of Central Asia to northern India. But some, like this simple Turkish pilaf, are just easy and delicious ways of making a meal feel like a special occasion. If you can't find Egyptian rice or baldo or arborio, use American CalRiso or American-grown short-grain rice.

| | |
|---|---|
| 2 cups Egyptian rice or baldo or arborio rice | 3 cups mild lamb stock, beef stock, or chicken stock |
| 3 tablespoons butter | 1 teaspoon salt (less if stock is salted) |

Wash the rice well. Put in a large bowl, add cold salted water to cover, and soak for 30 minutes.

In a heavy medium pot, melt the butter over medium heat. Drain the rice thoroughly and add to the pot. Stir for 2 to 3 minutes, then stir in the broth; taste for salt and add as wanted. Bring to a boil, then cover, lower the heat to low, and simmer for 20 minutes.

Remove from the heat, wrap the lid in a cotton cloth or tea towel, replace the lid, and let stand for 20 minutes before serving.

**Festive Turkish pilaf:** For a more festive version of this plain rice, begin by browning 1 onion, finely chopped, and ⅓ cup pine nuts in the butter. Stir in ⅓ cup currants, then add the rice and stir over medium heat for 3 minutes. Add the broth and salt, then add ½ teaspoon freshly ground black pepper. Bring to a boil, then lower the heat, cover, and finish cooking as directed above.

A horsecart pulling a traveling produce market in Istanbul

# Turkish Yogurt Sauce
*cacik*

YOGURT AND LAMB ARE THE TWO FOODS THAT SEEM TO HAVE TRAVELED TO the Eastern Mediterranean with the peoples who invaded the region from Central Asia. Both are originally nomad foods, products of the nomads' herds of sheep and goats. The Turkish method of draining whey from the yogurt and then whisking in a little water intensifies the flavor of the yogurt and somehow makes it sweeter.

Finely chopped cucumber, garlic, and fresh or dried mint give this quickly assembled sauce fresh crunch and good flavor. Use *cacik* as a simple topping or accompaniment to rice dishes, from the plainest to the most elaborately flavored.

1 teaspoon salt, or to taste

2 cups plain yogurt (whole-milk or 2%)

¼ cup cold water

½ teaspoon freshly ground black pepper, or to taste

1 cup finely chopped peeled cucumber, excess water squeezed out

1 to 2 cloves garlic, crushed

¼ cup olive oil

¼ cup minced fresh mint or 2 tablespoons dried mint (optional)

Stir the salt into the yogurt. Place the yogurt in a cheesecloth-lined sieve set over a bowl or in the sink and let drain for 30 minutes to 2 hours.

Transfer the yogurt to a medium bowl, add the water and pepper, and whisk well. Stir in the cucumber. In a small bowl, combine the garlic with 3 tablespoons of the oil and stir into the yogurt.

Place the yogurt in one or more small serving bowls. Drizzle over the remaining 1 tablespoon oil and sprinkle on the optional mint. Serve chilled or at room temperature.

# Rice-Stuffed Grape Leaves
## dolmades

**Makes approximately 40 *dolmades*; serves 10 as an appetizer**

STUFFED VEGETABLES AND LEAVES ARE FOUND ALL OVER THE EASTERN Mediterranean and beyond, from Armenia to Greece to Iraq, all places controlled or influenced at some stage by the Ottoman Empire. The word *dolma* (*dolmades* is the plural) is from the Turkish word meaning "to stuff."

These stuffed grape leaves are easy to make. Rolling up the leaves takes some time, but they can be prepared several days ahead and refrigerated, or frozen, stored in plastic bags. Actually, we think they aren't at their best until at least twelve hours after cooking, when the flavors have had time to blend.

One 1-pound jar grape leaves preserved in brine or 1 pound fresh leaves

¾ cup Turkish baldo, Italian risotto rice, Egyptian rice, or long-grain white rice (see Note)

½ cup finely chopped scallions

1 medium onion, finely chopped

2 large tomatoes, finely chopped

¼ cup lightly packed raisins

3 tablespoons finely chopped fresh flat-leaf parsley

2 tablespoons finely chopped fresh mint or 1 tablespoon dried mint

¼ teaspoon ground cinnamon

Pinch of grated nutmeg

Pinch of ground cloves

½ teaspoon salt

Freshly ground black pepper

5 cloves garlic, quartered

¼ cup fresh lemon juice

2 tablespoons olive oil

1 teaspoon sugar

Approximately 1 cup mild stock or water

Thin lemon wedges for garnish

Grape leaves preserved in brine must be soaked to remove salt, while fresh leaves must be softened. *If using preserved leaves,* drain, place in a large bowl, pour boiling water over, and let stand for 30 minutes. Drain, soak in cold water for 5 minutes, drain, and repeat once more. *If using fresh leaves,* bring a large pot of water to the boil, then drop in the leaves and let boil for 1 to 2 minutes, or until soft. Remove, drain well, and stack flattened and ready for use.

Wash the rice thoroughly, then place in a large bowl and cover with boiling water. Drain immediately. Rinse with cold water then place in a sieve and drain well. Return to the bowl and add the scallions, onion, tomatoes, raisins, parsley, mint, spices, salt, and pepper. Mix well.

In a bowl, mix together the garlic, lemon juice, oil, sugar, and ½ cup of the stock or water; set aside. Line the bottom of a large heavy pot with grape leaves, using those that are torn, imperfect, or very thick.

To assemble, work with one leaf at a time. Trim off the stem, then lay vein side up on a work surface. Place 1 heaping teaspoonful of filling near the stem end, fold the stem end over the filling, fold over both sides, and roll up (as if making an egg roll). The roll should be firm but not tight, as the rice will expand as it cooks. Place, seam side down, in the pot. Fill and roll up the remaining rolls in the same way, laying them side by side and then stacking in two or three layers as necessary to fit.

Stir the garlic and lemon juice mixture well and pour over the rolls. Place a large lid or plate on the top layer to prevent the *dolmades* from being tossed around while cooking. Cover the pot with a tight-fitting lid, bring to a boil over medium heat, and simmer for 1¾ to 2 hours. After 1 hour, add another ½ cup of stock or water; check again at the 1½-hour mark to make sure the pot has not run dry, and add more stock or water if necessary.

Remove from the heat and pick off the garlic pieces and discard. Let the rolls cool in the cooking liquid, with the lid on. The rolls will be soft and shiny. Once cooled, drain well and store in the refrigerator, well covered, or freeze in plastic bags in the freezer.

Serve at room temperature, stacked in layers on a decorative plate. Insert thin lemon wedges among the rolls for garnish.

**Note:** Paula Wolfert, who has spent years studying culinary traditions around the Mediterranean, tells us that in Turkey, medium-grain rice such as Egyptian or baldo is preferred not only for stuffing but also for pilafs, while in Greece, long-grain rice is preferred.

Fresh-grown produce stand at the Mercado Central in Barcelona

# Paella and Other Spanish Arroces

Paella is a country dish in origin, a way of cooking rice in large quantities. Traditionally a large round shallow pan called a paella (from the Latin for pan; *patella*) is used, placed over the coals of a wood fire so that heat is evenly distributed under the entire pan. The rice cooks evenly because it is in a shallow layer. Occasionally the rice is shaken in the pan, but it is not stirred constantly. The rice gradually absorbs the flavored broth it is cooked in and softens. After cooking, it is usually left to stand for five to ten minutes so that the starches firm up, and when served, the rice holds its shape.

Sowing rice in a flooded field in the Ebro Delta

Paella rice is usually cooked in a *sofrito* (*sofregit* in Catalan), the cooked flavor base of oil, garlic or onions, tomato, and, perhaps, other flavorings, before being immersed in the flavored stock to simmer until done. However, some cooks prefer to add the stock to the *sofrito,* then to sprinkle the rice in, without "frying" the rice first. This is the method Puig used for his black rice (see Note, page 332). If you use the cooking-the-rice-first method, heat the stock before adding it to the rice, as instructed in the recipes.

The idea of cooking paella in our own kitchen always felt a little intimidating. How to manage without a paella pan? And even if we did acquire one, how to maintain an even heat under a large paella pan using a domestic stove with small burners?

Then, on a flight back from Spain, we met an American woman who told us that she cooks paella and other Spanish rices all the time. She said that her Venezuelan husband preferred Spanish-style rice dishes, so she had set out to master them. "Now it all seems so easy, I don't know why I was worried," she told us. "You don't need a paella pan; just use a large skillet or if you are making a larger quantity, use two frying pans and divide the recipe."

With that encouragement, we embarked on making paella. Here is what we have discovered. If you want to make a large quantity (for more than eight), you do need a big paella pan (fifteen to eighteen inches in diameter) and an even source of heat. This can be a large fire in your gas or charcoal grill or glowing coals from a wood fire. If you want to make a paella for six to eight, you can do it easily and quickly on your stove (especially if you use gas, but it works fine with electric stoves too). All you need are two heavy frying pans (ours are cast iron)

*Paella pans being sold in the cathedral square in Valencia*

eleven or twelve inches in diameter. Divide a recipe that serves six to eight in two and cook it in two pans at once. Since paella needs very little attention once the broth is added, doing two pans at once is very manageable.

There are many other savory rice dishes from Spain, all often loosely called paella but in fact quite different. Most of these are home-style dishes, slightly moister than paella. Some are cooked in a *cazuela,* a deeper pot than a paella pan; others, called *caldosos,* are like rice stews and are traditionally cooked in a *puchero,* an earthenware pot. Like paella, they depend for their flavor and texture on good rice and a flavorful stock. All begin with the *sofrito,* then the remaining ingredients are added to it, gradually building the wonderful depth of flavor characteristic of Spanish rice dishes.

All of these rice dishes from Spain are easy to make if you have stock on hand. Soon you'll find yourself turning to paella and the other *arroces* (rice dishes) as we do, for a quick meal-in-one when a friend drops by. If you have fish or chicken stock already made, you can have food on the table in half an hour.

Spanish rice can be somewhat difficult to find in North American groceries, but it is available by mail-order (see Mail-Order Sources, page 438). The most outstanding Spanish rice is a variety called bomba; other rices from the Calasparra region are also prized. You may find large Spanish producers including SOS and La Fallera, which sell good medium-grain rices, labeled "Valencia rice" or "rice for paella." Look for the top grade of rice, marked *"extra";* it has fewer broken grains than the next grade, *"categoria 1."* If you can't find Spanish rice, substitute a *superfino*-grade Italian rice such as carnaroli, arborio, or vialone nano.

# Spanish Fish Stock

IF YOU HAVE A GOOD FISH STOCK, LIKE THIS QUICK STRAIGHTFORWARD ONE, you can easily cook most of the Spanish *arroces* from the rice-growing coast.

To make a good fish stock, make a trip to a local fishmonger or a good fish department in a large grocery store. Buy fish trimmings, including heads and necks, shrimp shells, and some bones and tails. Haddock and shellfish trimmings are good; salmon is fine, but don't use more than one third salmon proportionately or its distinctive taste will overpower the other ingredients.

2 tablespoons olive oil

1 Spanish onion, coarsely chopped

1 tomato, coarsely chopped

1 bay leaf

Sprig of thyme (optional)

Several sprigs of flat-leaf parsley (optional)

¼ cup fresh lemon juice (optional)

1 tablespoon salt

About 8 black peppercorns

12 cups water (or up to 4 cups dry white wine plus enough water to make 12 cups total)

4 to 5 pounds fresh fish heads and trimmings and shrimp shells, well rinsed

In a large heavy nonreactive pot, heat the oil over medium heat. Add the onion and cook until well softened, about 10 minutes. Add the tomato and cook until softened. Add the bay leaf, the optional herbs and lemon juice, the salt, and pepper, then add the water (or water and wine mixture) and bring to a boil. Add the fish bones and trimmings and simmer for 40 minutes over medium-low heat, skimming as necessary.

Strain the stock through a large sieve into a bowl and discard the debris. For a much clearer stock, strain a second time, through a sieve lined with several layers of cheesecloth. (We skip this step, because we prefer the extra flavor of the unfiltered stock.)

Let cool, then store in clean nonreactive containers with tight-fitting lids. Fish stock can be stored for 3 days in the refrigerator or frozen for 2 months.

# Garlic and Olive Oil Sauce
*alioli*

**Makes about 1 cup sauce**

IN THE CENTRAL MARKETS OF BARCELONA AND VALENCIA, EACH ON ITS OWN worth a trip to Spain, among all the fish and fresh produce and other wonders, you will come upon stalls selling locally made mortars. They are large and heavy, ceramic, and often a brilliant yellow. The pestle is of wood, about eight inches long. If you don't already own a big mortar, or perhaps even if you do, buy at least one of these for yourself or for a friend. They are made for mashing garlic to a paste with a pinch of salt and, most important, encouraging the mashed garlic to blend with olive oil in the thick, garlicky emulsion called *alioli*. This pungent sauce is a wonderful and necessary partner to many Catalonian rice dishes and is also delicious on meat, especially meat that has been grilled over an open fire.

In French Provence, garlic and olive oil are combined with an egg yolk or two to make *aïoli*. In Catalonia and Valencia, the equivalent dish has even fewer ingredients, for traditionally no egg is used. The sauce is a beautiful creamy yellow and is sharp-tasting and delicious. It makes a wonderful accompaniment to black rice or other rice dishes, dolloped on generously, as well as for grilled meats.

12 large cloves garlic, coarsely chopped

1 teaspoon sea salt, or more to taste

Several drops of water

Scant 1 cup extra-virgin olive oil, preferably Spanish

About 1 tablespoon red wine vinegar or juice of ½ lemon, or more to taste

Mash the garlic to a very smooth paste with the salt in a large ceramic or stone mortar. Add several drops of water, then dribble in a little oil, pounding gently and continuously. Add a little more oil as you pound, and you will see the mixture begin to mound as it forms an emulsion. Continue to add the oil in a thin stream as you pound, until you have about a cup of sauce. Add the vinegar or lemon juice and then a little more oil, pounding it in to blend. Taste and add a little more salt or vinegar if needed; the sauce will have a sharp biting garlic taste. Serve in the mortar or transfer to a serving bowl.

**Note:** If the sauce begins to separate (not a catastrophe, since the taste remains the same, the texture is just not as thick and creamy), you can try to hold it together by pounding in a little bread moistened with vinegar. Even without a separating problem, bread may be added to give the sauce extra body. In *Honey from a Weed*, her extraordinary book of recipes, lore, and wisdom from the rocky Mediterranean shores of Catalonia, Italy, and Greece, Patience Gray says that if bread is added to the sauce, so too is chopped flat-leaf parsley.

# Puig's Black Rice with Alioli
## paella negra

Serves 6 to 8

JOSE PUIG (PRONOUNCED "POOCH") IS A WONDERFUL HOST AND A WARM, welcoming sight at any time. He is also a dedicated maker of wine, vinegar, and olive oil. His vineyards near Vendrell in Catalonia, south of Barcelona, are on a gently south-sloping hillside bordered by a Roman road, a reminder of centuries and peoples long past.

Puig pounding garlic in a mortar

One clear, fine spring Sunday at the vineyard, he prepared a feast for about a dozen hungry and happy guests as we all chatted and sipped his wine. The food was traditional: a black paella, followed by rabbit first coated in salt then grilled. Both were served with a thick yellow *alioli*, the mayonnaise-like Catalan sauce made of garlic and oil (see page 329).

He did the cooking on an open hearth over olive and grapevine clippings. As Puig cooked, I asked him questions about what he was doing and about his views on paella. "Paella is a dish of poverty," he said. "When I was growing up, we ate it every Sunday. If you have only a bit of leftover chicken and other odds and ends, you can make paella. My mother used to make paella every week. We'd really look forward to it. Rice was in other dishes, like chicken stock with rice and *fideos*, but paella was special. Even if it was made with leftovers from the week, she always added something special, something fresh or new. So it was always a festive dish, you could say a special dish of poverty."

Puig thus has an elastic view of what can go into a paella. If you make it with fish, put in a pork rib to enrich the *sofregit* (*sofrito*). You can use any green vegetables, he says, such as artichokes, asparagus, spinach, green beans, or peas, but not carrots: "You can make it with vegetables only if you want, but never use carrots."

"What about dried beans?" I asked.

"They do that in Valencia. I never use them."

The vinegar Puig makes from his Cabernet Sauvignon grapes is quite wonderful, with a rounded, almost sweet taste. He puts a little of his vinegar in the paella as the rice finishes cooking (if you don't have a mellow vinegar, use a little wine). In this recipe, notice that there is no garlic or tomato in the initial *sofrito*. Pounded garlic and a little vinegar are added at the end as a kind of last-minute tempering and flavoring. This is a simple version of a *picada,* pounded flavorings that are added to many Catalan and Valencian rice dishes as they finish cooking, to pull together and heighten flavors.

3 tablespoons olive oil

1 onion, finely chopped

1 large or 2 small bell peppers, stem, seeds, and membranes discarded, and chopped

1½ pounds small squid or cuttlefish, chopped

2 tablespoons squid or cuttlefish ink (see Glossary)

8 cups Spanish Fish Stock (page 328) or mild chicken stock, plus more if needed

3 cups Spanish rice (Valencia or bomba, or substitute an Italian risotto rice such as arborio superfino)

12 stalks asparagus, cut into 1½-inch lengths, or a handful of snow peas, torn across into 1-inch pieces (optional)

8 to 10 cloves garlic, coarsely chopped

Pinch of sea salt

¼ cup Cabernet Sauvignon vinegar or other mellow red wine vinegar, sherry vinegar, or red wine

### Accompaniments

1 cup or more Garlic and Olive Oil Sauce (*alioli*, page 329)

1 to 2 lemons, cut into wedges

In a 15- to 18-inch paella pan or in a large heavy skillet, heat the oil over medium-high heat. Add the onion and peppers and cook for 5 minutes. Add the squid or cuttlefish and cook until the onions and peppers are very tender and softened, 10 minutes or more. Remove from the heat. (The recipe can be prepared ahead to this point and set aside, covered, for an hour or two, until ready to proceed; if making more than 2 hours ahead, cover and refrigerate, then bring back to room temperature before proceeding.)

In the meantime (or about 25 minutes before you wish to serve the dish), place 7 cups of the stock in a medium pot and stir in the black ink. Heat to a gentle simmer. Place the remaining 1 cup of stock in a small bowl.

*If you are cooking on a stove,* heat a second skillet, oil it lightly, and then add half the *sofrito. If you are cooking in one large paella pan over an open flame,* proceed without dividing the *sofrito.* Sprinkle the rice into the *sofrito* (1½ cups in each, if using two pans) and cook over medium-high heat until the rice is translucent, stirring constantly. Add the optional asparagus (not the snow peas) and 6 cups of the hot stock mixture (3 cups to each if using two pans) and bring to a vigorous boil. Give the pan(s) a shake every so often to prevent the rice from sticking as it boils for 4 to 5 minutes over high heat. The rice mixture should be thick and bubbling, with large bubbles dotting the surface like submerged grapes; if using snow peas, place them on top of the rice now.

After 5 minutes, gradually begin lowering the heat. After 10 minutes, the heat should be at medium-low and the rice simmering gently. Shake the pan(s) occasionally to keep the rice from sticking. If the dish seems dry, add a little more warm stock as needed. Gradually reduce the heat a little more as you cook the rice for about 10 minutes longer.

In the meantime, in a mortar or food processor, pound or process the garlic cloves to a paste with a pinch of salt. Stir into the reserved 1 cup broth.

Just before the rice finishes cooking (about 20 minutes after adding the stock), add the garlic-stock mixture and the vinegar or wine. Shake the pan(s) a little to mix and to keep the rice from sticking, then let cook for another 3 minutes or so. Remove from the heat, cover, and let rest for 5 minutes.

Taste, adjust the seasonings, and serve with the *alioli*. Serve your guests directly from the skillets or paella pan. Place a wedge or two of lemon on each plate and invite guests to take a generous spoonful or more of the *alioli*, preferably dolloped on top of their black rice. It makes a beautiful contrast in color.

**Note:** When Puig made this black rice, he did not cook the rice in the *sofrito*. Instead, he added the stock-ink mixture to the *sofrito*, then, once it was boiling, sprinkled in the rice. We have tried both methods, and in our experience, frying the rice in the *sofrito* until it is translucent produces more evenly cooked rice.

Adding rice to the *sofrito* of *paella negra*

# Golden Rice with Shrimp

*arroz a banda en paella*

Serves 2 to 3

AS THE RICE SIMMERS AND ABSORBS THE FLAVORS OF THE SIMPLE *SOFRITO* AND the broth, fresh shrimp are laid on top to cook briefly in the steam. They're also wonderful grilled.

2 cups Spanish Fish Stock (page 328) (2½ cups if using bomba or CalRiso rice)

Pinch of saffron threads

2 tablespoons olive oil

1 medium Spanish onion, minced

4 cloves garlic, minced

1 tomato, peeled and minced

1 cup medium-grain Spanish rice or arborio superfino rice or CalRiso

½ to ¾ pound small or medium shrimp, in their shells or shelled, deveined, rinsed, and patted dry

Garlic and Olive Oil Sauce (*alioli*, page 329)

Place the stock in a small saucepan and heat until simmering; keep hot over low heat until ready to use. Dry-roast the saffron threads in a preheated skillet for 30 seconds, then transfer to a small mortar and grind to a powder. Transfer to a small bowl and pour on ¼ cup of the hot stock. Set aside to steep.

Prepare the *sofrito* by heating the oil in a large cast-iron or other heavy skillet or a 10- to 12-inch paella pan over medium heat. Add the onion and garlic and cook until softened, 5 to 10 minutes. Add the tomato and cook until very soft. Add the rice and cook until translucent, stirring frequently to prevent sticking. Add the hot stock and the saffron with its liquid and bring to a boil. Stir gently once, lower the heat to medium, and cook for 10 minutes. Lower the heat to very low and cook for another 6 to 8 minutes; do not stir. Lay the shrimp on the rice and cook until the color changes on the lower side, 2 to 3 minutes, then turn over to cook the other side. When the rice is cooked through but still firm to the bite, remove from the heat and let stand for several minutes to let the rice set.

Serve with the *alioli*.

**Note:** If you wish to double the recipe, cook in two pans the same size, or in one 15- to 18-inch paella pan over an open fire or other large even source of heat.

**Alternative:** Instead of cooking the shrimp with the rice, grill the shrimp, and perhaps some vegetables, then serve together with the rice.

# Rice Passions

Samuel Monclus Sanchez is the director of Productos la Fallera, a large rice company in Valencia. One afternoon we drove together around the flat green watery spaces of the Albufera, the large freshwater lake just outside Valencia, which was a calming change of pace after the traffic and elegant intensity of the city.

As he drove, Samuel talked passionately about the history of rice in Valencia. He told of the time in the eighteenth century when authorities tried to stop rice cultivation in the Albufera, declaring it unsafe because it was thought to be a breeding ground for malarial mosquitos (in fact, growing rice in fresh water does favor the *anopheles* mosquito, but if the water is brackish or muddy, rice cultivation can reduce malaria). "The local people went on growing rice for themselves," Samuel explained. "They had to eat and rice was what would grow in the wet soil." Rice culture survived, and over time it reestablished itself.

Samuel also told of his own rice research, searching for early references to rice in old Spanish texts. "The earliest mention I have found is from the thirteenth century. As people say, it was the Arabs who first brought rice to Spain, but there is much that we don't know, there is much still to be learned. When I first began working in my job, I had no idea I would get so involved with the story of rice. It's like a drug, wanting to understand all about it. . . ."

**above and right**

Quality-control technician at a rice mill near the Ebro Delta

Bomba rice from Calasparra

# Aromatic Rice and Fish with Two Sauces

*caldero murciano*

**Serves 6**

IN THE PROVINCE OF MURCIA, SOUTH FROM VALENCIA AND SLIGHTLY INLAND, lies Calasparra, the region that produces the most prized Spanish rices. Calasparra is the only rice-growing area with its own "region of origin" (*denominación del origen*) designation. Its most prized rice is called bomba. Bomba costs two to three times what regular Spanish rice costs. It is more difficult to grow and has lower yields per acre, but the rice is wonderful and worth all the trouble. Its rounded grains look like grains of the Italian rice carnaroli, and they also have a white "belly" like many Italian rices.

During cooking, bomba grains expand enormously (to about four times their volume, rather than only two to three times, like most rices), especially lengthwise. They remain firm when fully cooked and seem to absorb flavors even better than other Spanish and Italian rices. The only problem with bomba and other Calasparra rices is that they are difficult to find in Spain, let alone in North America. Recently, bomba has become available by mail order from Williams-Sonoma (see Mail-Order Sources, page 438).

Though this *caldero* from the Murcia region is best made with bomba or another Calasparra rice, it is still excellent when made with regular Spanish rice, or CalRiso, or a good Italian risotto rice such as arborio superfino or carnaroli. It's not a paella and doesn't need to cook in a very shallow pan, but it does require a large heavy-bottomed pot to ensure even cooking. The cooked rice is soft and slightly more liquid than paella rice, and it has a pleasing aroma from the stock.

Mercato Central in Valencia

*continued*

This is a dish for rice lovers and for people who enjoy their garlic. The combination of the sharp-tasting creamy garlic sauce and tender rice is a knockout. Friends who ate this dish the first time we tested it protested that they didn't even need to eat the fish, however good it was. All they wanted was to indulge themselves in rice with garlic sauce. They did admit that the fish was delectable, and its fresh red pepper sauce a pleasure, but the rice was the big hit.

The recipe for this simple country dish is adapted from *El Libro de la Paella y de los Arroces* by Lourdes March. Fish fillets are simmered to make a stock, then set aside while the rice cooks in the stock (a technique very like that used in Senegal to prepare *diebou dien*, page 370). Traditionally the rice is served first, with the creamy garlic sauce, then the fish is served on its own with a mild chile sauce. (Since the mild dried red chile traditionally used for the sauce is not easily available, we have substituted red bell pepper and Spanish *pimentón*.) Rice-impassioned guests may insist that you ignore tradition and leave the rice on the table while you serve the fish, so that they can keep going back to it.

1 red bell pepper

2 tablespoons olive oil

1 head garlic, separated into cloves

3 pounds fresh fish fillets: half hake or haddock and half sea bass

2 medium tomatoes, peeled and chopped

1 tablespoon salt, plus a pinch

7 cups boiling water

1 small potato

Pinch of saffron threads, briefly heated in a dry skillet, then crumbled to a powder

½ teaspoon Spanish *pimentón* (see Glossary) (or a blend of cayenne pepper and paprika)

2 cups bomba rice (or CalRiso or 2¼ cups short- to medium-grain Spanish or Italian rice)

### Garlic sauce for rice

10 small or 5 large cloves garlic, peeled

1 teaspoon salt, plus a pinch

1 small boiled potato (from above)

1 large egg yolk, beaten

½ cup olive oil

½ cup stock (from above)

Generous grinding of black pepper

### Pepper sauce for fish

3 garlic cloves, peeled

¼ teaspoon salt, plus a pinch

¼ red bell pepper (reserved from above)

¼ cup packed fresh flat-leaf parsley leaves, finely chopped

3 tablespoons olive oil

¼ cup reserved stock (from above)

1 to 2 pinches Spanish *pimentón* (see Glossary) (or substitute a blend of cayenne pepper and paprika)

1 to 2 tablespoons fresh lemon juice

Grill the red bell pepper over a charcoal or gas flame or dry-roast in a heavy skillet, turning to expose all sides to the heat. When it is well blackened, place in a paper bag to steam for

10 minutes, then peel and coarsely chop, discarding the core and seeds. Set aside three quarters of the chopped pepper for the fish stock and the remainder for the pepper sauce.

Heat the 2 tablespoons oil in a large heavy pot over medium heat. When hot, add the garlic cloves and sauté for 4 to 5 minutes, stirring occasionally. Add the reserved three quarters of the grilled pepper and stir until very soft. Remove the garlic and pepper from the oil and set aside.

Add the fish to the oil and cook for 5 minutes, turning once. Add the chopped tomatoes and cook for several minutes.

Meanwhile, slide the garlic cloves out of their skins and place in a mortar. Add a pinch of salt and pound the garlic to a paste. Add the cooked pepper and reduce to a paste.

Add the garlic-pepper paste, the boiling water, the 1 tablespoon salt, and the potato to the fish. Cook, uncovered, for 8 to 10 minutes, until the fish is just cooked through. Remove the fish from the broth and set aside, covered, in a warm place.

Several minutes later, the potato should be done. Remove from the stock and set aside. Place a large fine sieve over a large bowl and pour the stock through. Discard the solids. Measure out 5 cups of stock, return to the pot, and bring to a boil over high heat. Place ¼ cup of the remaining stock in a small bowl. Stir in the saffron and the *pimentón*, then add to the pot. Reserve remaining stock.

When the stock comes to a boil, gradually sprinkle in the rice and bring back to a boil, then lower the heat to medium to medium-low and cook gently for 15 minutes. At this point, the stock should be below the top of the rice. If not, continue cooking, uncovered, over low heat, until the liquid is below the top of the rice. When it is, test the rice for doneness; if it is still firm in the center, cover, lower the heat to low if necessary, and simmer for another 10 minutes. Let the rice stand for 5 to 10 minutes before serving to enable it to firm up. The dish should be moist, with the texture of a thick, pourable batter.

Meanwhile, prepare the garlic sauce: Place the garlic in a mortar with a pinch of salt and pound to a smooth paste. Add the boiled potato and pound until smooth. Add the egg yolk and pound until smooth. Add the olive oil in a slow stream (as for making mayonnaise) while continuing to pound with the pestle, to make a smooth emulsion. Stir in ½ cup of the reserved stock, the remaining 1 teaspoon salt, and the pepper. Transfer to a small serving bowl and set aside.

Prepare the pepper sauce: Combine the garlic cloves with a pinch of salt in a mortar. Pound until smooth, then add the reserved chopped red pepper and pound to a smooth paste. Add the parsley and pound to blend, then add the olive oil and finally ¼ cup of the reserved stock. The mixture should be fairly liquid. Season with the remaining 1 teaspoon salt and the *pimentón* or cayenne, then stir in the lemon juice to taste and set aside.

Serve the rice from the cooking pot or a large shallow bowl. Put out the bowl of garlic sauce, with a spoon, to accompany the rice. Serve the fish after the rice: Place the fish on a platter and put out one or more bowls of pepper sauce so guests can serve themselves.

# Rice from the Camargue

The watery open landscape of the Camargue, a region along France's Mediterranean coast (south of Arles and Nîmes and west of Marseilles), has the feel of a Wild West frontier. There are white wild ponies grazing, marshy wetlands, flocks of flamingos, and very few people. The thick walls of old towns, like Aigues Mortes (which means dead water, because the groundwater is very salty here), are a reminder that the area was for centuries a somewhat lawless frontier, known as a place where gypsies and bandits roamed.

Pont du Gard, Roman aqueduct north of the Camargue

Sometime in the fifteenth century, just as in the Po Region in Italy, people realized that the Camargue lands, which had been forever useless agriculturally, could be used for growing rice. Rice tolerates more salt in the soil and in the groundwater than most other food plants, and it also needs a lot of water, so it seemed perfectly suited to the region. But the Camargue is at the northernmost limit of rice growing, so the industry has always been somewhat marginal, with acreage under rice cultivation decreasing through the 1970s. In the early eighties, however, a concerted effort to renew the Camarguais rice industry led to a five-fold increase in rice production.

Today growers are selling their "traditional red rice from the Camargue" and their traditional white rice to chefs in London and Paris, and a small crop of organic rice is also finding a market. New varieties of long-grain rice are also being grown.

At present, it is not possible to find Camargue rices in stores in North America, but all the signs are that this will change as consumer interest in specialty rices continues to grow. The only Camargue rice we have tested in our kitchen is an organic brown rice, a medium-grain japonica, much like its cousins from Italy and Spain.

# Basic Italian Rice

*riso*

Makes about 5 cups rice; serves 2 to 3 as a main dish or
4 to 5 as a pasta course or side dish

ITALIAN RICE CAN NOT ONLY BE EATEN IN PLACE OF PASTA, IT CAN BE cooked and dressed very like pasta. This simple plain rice is best made with a good-tasting superfino grade of Italian rice. As with pasta, you must carefully monitor the boiling rice to make sure that it doesn't overcook. Remember that it will go on cooking a little even after it has been drained, so allow for that when judging whether it is done.

2 cups carnaroli or other Italian rice, or CalRiso

10 to 11 cups water

1 teaspoon salt

3 to 4 tablespoons olive oil

5 to 6 cloves garlic, minced

3 to 4 fresh sage leaves

½ cup freshly grated Parmigiano-Reggiano, or to taste, plus extra for serving

½ cup loosely packed fresh flat-leaf parsley leaves (optional)

Freshly ground black pepper (optional)

Rinse the rice briefly in cold water and drain (optional). Place the water in a large pot and bring to a boil. Add the salt and sprinkle in the rice. Stir gently with a wooden spoon until the water returns to a boil. Cook until just *al dente*, cooked through to the center but still firm-textured, 12 to 15 minutes, depending on the rice.

While the rice is cooking, heat the oil in a heavy skillet over medium-high heat. When hot, add the garlic and sage, lower the heat to medium, and cook until the garlic is just beginning to turn golden. Remove from the heat and set aside.

As soon as the rice is cooked, immediately drain it in a sieve and shake gently to help drain thoroughly. Place in a large bowl and pour the flavored oil mixture over it. Toss gently to blend. Add the cheese, taste, and adjust the seasoning if necessary, then add the optional parsley and pepper and toss again gently. Serve hot, on warmed plates, with extra grated cheese for those who wish it.

**Alternatives:** You can substitute ¼ cup minced onion for the garlic.

You can, if you prefer, wait until the rice is cooked and drained, then immediately use a large deep skillet to heat and flavor the oil. Once the garlic is softened, add the cooked drained rice to the hot oil and toss and turn it briefly to flavor it. Turn out into a shallow bowl, add the cheese and other flavorings, and toss gently.

Flooded rice fields by a manor house near Vercelli

# Po Valley Story

As the train rattled west from Milan it traveled across a tall embankment, and suddenly out my window, I could see miles upon miles of bright green flooded agricultural landscape: European rice paddies. A traveler sitting just behind me on the train turned to her companion and asked: "What is that growing out there? Why is it so wet?"

Well, part of me wanted to leap up, turn around excitedly, and launch right in: "This is the wonderful enchanted land of Italian rice. We're passing through its heart right now. Rice has been cultivated here since before 1475. It was probably first brought here from Spain, where it had previously been introduced by the Arabs. Until only recently the fields were planted and harvested by hand; the *montadini*, or casual laborers from the hills who came in to do that work, led terribly hard lives, immortalized in the 1954 film classic *Bitter Rice*. The fields are still hand-weeded, still home to frogs and to egrets and other birds, still alive with the gurgle of water." But I didn't say anything. Outside the sky looked incredibly big, and the roads and dikes tiny in comparison. It was a calm landscape, timeless.

The lands near the Po and its tributary the Ticino River are lowlying and water is plentiful. Long ago, in the twelfth century, work began to drain swampy areas and organize them into productive agricultural land. Through the centuries water management projects in Piedmont, Romagna, and Lombardy helped keep malaria at bay and control flooding. They also led to the growth of rice cultivation, for with good water management, rice could be grown on wet clay soils not good for any other form of agriculture.

The rice grown here is mostly medium- to short-grain Italian-style rice, such as arborio, vialone nano, carnaroli, baldo, and others, although Italy has recently tried to expand its export markets (particularly to Northern Europe) by growing long-grain Asian-style rices as well. Some growers are also moving into organic (*biológico*) rice cultivation as a way of niche-marketing their grain. Organic production requires more hand labor, part of the reason that organic rice prices are nearly triple those of nonorganic. *Montadini* are still brought in to do much of the work.

Prices for rice are established at the rice exchange, Borsa del Riso, held Tuesdays and Fridays in the Mercato Merci in Vercelli, a small market town in the heart of the rice country. The vendors are the growers, the buyers are industrial distributors, middlemen, and rice merchants. Rice in all its forms is sold here: green, brown, unmilled, rice bran, polished. The terms of contracts are flashed up on an electronic board (a relatively recent innovation).

The spring morning we visited the rice exchange it was not very busy. We were told that in October and November, during and after harvest, the price board up on the wall is contantly flashing and changing. But even on a quiet day, outside the exchange under the high-ceilinged arcade, a small crowd of men with weathered faces and steady eyes stood in small groups talking, talking rice, farming, weather, just as men there have done for centuries. The echos of all those conversations murmured back from the vaulted arcade ceiling like the murmur of irrigation water flowing past the rice fields outside town.

Irrigation stream and rice field near Vercelli

# Basic Risotto

**Serves 4 as a main course or 6 as a pasta course in a larger meal**

RISOTTO IS A PRACTICAL LIGHT-HANDED WAY OF EATING GOOD RICE FLAVORED with simple tastes. This recipe suggests using springtime vegetables, young zucchini and green peas, but you can omit both and just make the dish without them. Alternatively, in fall and winter, instead of using fresh vegetables, you can use two ounces dried shiitake or porcini mushrooms, soaked for thirty minutes in one cup of hot water then chopped (and use the mushroom soaking water as part of your stock). The essentials are good rice, good oil, good stock, good cheese, and a little patience.

There is a mystique about risotto, perhaps because for many years good Italian rice that would hold its shape during cooking was hard to find in North America. Now, with good rice available, risotto is becoming the dish it has always been in Northern Italy, a quickly prepared dish, accessible to all. Make sure your pot has a thick bottom, so the heat is even, and use a wooden spoon for stirring.

Approximately 6 cups lightly salted mild chicken or vegetarian stock

¼ cup olive oil

1 medium yellow onion, minced

2 cups carnaroli, vialone nano, or arborio superfino rice (or substitute Valencia or CalRiso rice)

3 to 4 tiny young zucchini, cut into 1-inch chunks (optional)

Small handful of fresh peas, or 12 snow peas, sliced in half (optional)

⅔ cup freshly grated Parmigiano-Reggiano, plus extra for serving

Freshly ground black pepper

Place the stock in a medium saucepan and bring to a boil, then lower the heat and simmer very gently. Place dinner plates or shallow soup plates in the oven, set to low, to warm.

Heat the oil in a large wide heavy pot. Toss in the onion and cook over medium-high heat, stirring frequently, until softened and translucent, 8 to 10 minutes. Add the rice and cook, stirring, until the grains begin to become translucent, about 5 minutes.

Using a ladle or a cup, add 1 cup of the hot stock and stir gently to prevent sticking. The rice will gradually start absorbing the liquid. Add the vegetables (if using). When the liquid is bubbling and starting to be absorbed, add another ½ cup stock to the rice. Continue stirring every minute or so to prevent sticking and to help distribute the liquid. When the liquid has been mostly absorbed, add another ½ cup stock and repeat. Continue cooking the rice, adding more stock as it is absorbed, until the rice is tender with just a slight firmness at the center, 15 to 20 minutes. The dish should have a creamy texture.

Stir in the grated cheese and let stand 1 minute, then turn out onto the preheated plates. Grind black pepper over each serving. Place a small bowl with extra cheese on the table so guests can sprinkle more on if they like.

**Alternative:** We have also made a delicious basic risotto using an organic *semi-lavorato* (semi-milled) rice of the old rosa marchetti variety, which we bought from Aldo Paravicini at Cascine Orsini, near Bereguardo (see page 346); it's not yet available here. If you do come across *semi-lavorato* Italian rice, follow the instructions above, with the following changes: You will need 1 to 2 cups more stock; cooking time for the rice will be about 40 minutes rather than about 20 minutes; and the vegetables should be added at the 25-minute mark. The dish will be creamy, the rice tender, with a wonderful taste of grain.

Antique rice-sorting machine at a mill near Vercelli

# Risotto alla Birra

**Serves 4 as a main course or 6 as a pasta course in a larger meal**

THE CHEF HAS AN OPEN FACE AND LOTS OF ENERGY. HE AND HIS FAMILY are grabbing a quick bite to eat at the large kitchen table just before the lunch service. He knows he has two to three busy hours ahead, for today is market day in Vercelli, and his restaurant, Vecchia Breuta, is only a few steps from the Piazza Cavour, the heart of the market. His small dining room holds four rows of tables, each covered with a plain white tablecloth. When we come out of the kitchen and sit down, several of the tables are already occupied, mostly by single older men or by men in twos and threes. All are clearly regulars, here to enjoy a warming plate of risotto on a rainy spring day.

We order the chef's specialty, *risotto alla birra,* because it sounds interesting, and soon it arrives, rich in taste and creamy in texture. A good dose of strong dark beer went into the risotto, and cream too. It's luscious.

With few ingredients, most of them easily stored staples, this risotto is a great standby for winter days. The beer disappears into the dish, leaving an intriguing depth of flavor but no "beery" taste. Serve as a main dish with a simple winter greens salad or follow it with some grilled root vegetables or grilled meat.

4 cups lightly salted chicken stock or vegetarian stock

¼ cup extra-virgin olive oil, preferably Ligurian

½ cup minced onion

2 cloves garlic, minced

2 cups carnaroli, vialone nano, or arborio superfino rice

1 cup heavy (whipping) cream

1 cup dark beer

¾ cup finely grated Parmigiano-Reggiano

Freshly ground black pepper

Place the stock in a medium saucepan and bring to a boil, then lower the heat and simmer gently. Place dinner plates or shallow soup plates in a low oven to warm.

Heat the oil in a large wide heavy pot. Toss in the onion and garlic and cook over medium-high heat, stirring frequently, until softened and translucent. Add the rice and cook, stirring, until the grains are well coated with oil, about 1 minute. Add the cream and stir as it heats up to a simmer, then add the beer. Stir occasionally to prevent sticking. The rice will gradually start absorbing the liquid. When the liquid is bubbling and starting to be absorbed, using a cup or a ladle, add about ½ cup hot stock to the rice. Continue stirring every minute or so to prevent sticking and to help distribute the liquid. When the liquid has been mostly absorbed, add another ½ cup stock and repeat. Continue cooking the rice, adding more stock as it is absorbed, until the rice is tender but with a slight firmness at the center, 15 to 20 minutes. The dish should have a creamy texture.

Stir in about ⅓ cup grated cheese. Let stand for 1 minute, then turn out onto the heated plates. Grind black pepper generously over each serving. Place a small bowl with the remaining cheese on the table so guests can sprinkle extra on if they wish.

*Risotto alla birra* cooking in a restaurant kitchen in Vercelli

Springtime in the Vercelli rice fields

# Bio-Dinámico

The integrated organic method known in Italy as *bio-dinámico* is an alternative approach to farming. During our stay in the ricelands near Vercelli, we visited a large bio-dynamic organic farm, Cascine Orsini, run by Aldo Paravicini. On 740 acres of farmland, there were over two hundred dairy cows. The farm sells milk from its dairy herd for the production of yogurt. About 100 acres of land were planted in rice (with an old rice variety called rosa marchetti, as well as with baldo), over 220 acres were being used as pasture, and about 650 acres were kept wooded. There was also land planted in wheat, barley, legumes, and vegetables. Wheat, pearled barley, spelt, rye, corn, and rice are sold directly from the farm as well as through specialty stores in Florence, Venice, and Turin. The rice is milled nearby. Some is kept unmilled (brown rice), some is half-milled to *semi-lavorato* (see page 23), and some is fully milled to white rice.

Production is almost a closed cycle, with the dairy cattle eating hay grown on the farm and providing manure for fertilizer, and crops carefully rotated to maintain soil fertility. As we approached the farm down a quiet road, suddenly the sound of frogs croaking came loudly through the windows of the car and we saw birds in the fields and on the trees. We were out of modern monoculture and into an integrated rural environment.

# Rice Salad

TO MAKE THIS SALAD, COOK YOUR RICE AHEAD, DRESS IT WITH JUST THE LEMON juice, and let stand loosely covered until shortly before you are ready to serve. Then simply add the rest of the ingredients and the olive oil, and serve.

2 cups Italian rice such as arborio or carnaroli, or CalRiso

3 cups water or mild chicken stock or vegetarian stock, preferably unsalted

1 teaspoon salt (omit if stock is salted), or to taste

½ cup minced Spanish onion (optional)

2 tablespoons olive oil

¼ cup capers

3 to 4 ripe tomatoes, peeled and finely chopped

½ cup packed finely torn fresh flat-leaf parsley

Freshly ground black pepper

¼ cup fresh lemon juice

¼ cup extra-virgin olive oil, or to taste

Wash the rice thoroughly, drain well in a sieve, and set aside. Heat the water or stock to a boil in a medium saucepan, then leave simmering until needed.

Place a heavy medium pot over medium-high heat and add the 2 tablespoons oil. When the oil is hot, toss in the minced onion if using and cook, stirring frequently, until soft and translucent. Add the rice and cook, stirring constantly, until the grains become opaque, 4 to 5 minutes. Add the hot water or stock and the 1 teaspoon salt if using and stir gently until the liquid comes to a boil. Cover tightly, lower the heat to very low, and cook for 20 minutes. Remove from the heat and let stand for 15 minutes without stirring.

Turn the rice out into a large bowl to help it cool, gently breaking up any lumps with your fingers or with a wooden spoon. Add the lemon juice and toss gently to mix. Cover with a cotton cloth and let cool.

When ready to serve, add the capers, chopped tomatoes, the optional parsley, and the extra-virgin olive oil to the rice and toss gently to mix. Taste for salt and add as necessary. Transfer to a serving bowl, grind black pepper over, and serve.

Note: You can also use the plenty-of-water cooking method set out in Basic Italian Rice (page 339) to cook the rice for this salad. Drain the cooked rice well, then spread out on a shallow platter to cool slightly. Transfer the rice to a bowl, toss with the lemon juice, and then, just before serving, add the capers, tomato, and parsley. Pour over the extra-virgin olive oil and toss gently to mix. Taste for salt and add if necessary, then grind black pepper over the top.

Alternative: Another take on this salad uses about 3 tablespoons finely chopped anchovy fillets in place of capers (or you could use a combination). If using salted anchovies, soak for 15 minutes in cold water to rinse out the salt, and squeeze well to drain before chopping.

# Risotto with Salami and Red Beans

*panissa*

Serves 4 to 6

THIS HEARTY WINTER DISH IS A SIMPLIFIED ADAPTATION OF THE SOPHISTICATED restaurant version we ate at Osteria Cascine dei Fiori, in the wet green countryside just east of Vercelli, in the heart of Italy's rice country. Originally *panissa* was a practical country dish of rice, beans, and pork, satisfying and filling on a cold damp day.

This version has small pieces of salty salami and soft rich small red beans in the tender flavorful rice. The beans are cooked ahead; the bean cooking liquid is blended with beef stock and used for flavoring and cooking the rice, and a cup of cooked beans goes into the almost-finished dish. The *sofrito* includes onions, tomato, and red wine, with carrots and celery optional.

Approximately 6 cups stock—preferably 5 cups lightly salted homemade beef stock mixed with a cup of bean cooking liquid (see Note)

¼ cup extra-virgin olive oil, preferably Ligurian

½ cup minced yellow onion

1 small carrot, finely diced (optional)

1 stalk celery, finely diced (optional)

1 medium tomato, peeled and minced

1 cup red wine, preferably Barbera or another Northern Italian red

2 cups carnaroli, vialone nano, or arborio superfino rice (or substitute Valencia or CalRiso)

1 cup cooked cranberry beans or small red beans (see Note)

½ pound mild Italian salami, cut into ¼-inch cubes (or use half salami and half culatello)

Place the stock in a large saucepan and heat to boiling, then lower the heat and simmer very gently. Place the beans in a small pan and heat gently; when well heated through, remove from the heat and set aside. Place large shallow soup plates or dinner plates in a warm oven to heat.

In a large wide heavy pot, heat the olive oil. Toss in the onion and stir over medium-high heat for several minutes, then add the carrot and celery if using. Cook until well softened, lowering the heat slightly if necessary to prevent burning. When the onion is soft and translucent, add the tomato and cook until very soft. Add the wine and let cook down for several minutes. Add the rice and stir well to coat.

Using a ladle or a cup, add about 1 cup of the hot stock. Let the stock bubble, then stir gently and frequently over medium-high heat as the rice begins to absorb the liquid. When the liquid is almost all absorbed, add another ½ cup hot stock. Repeat, stirring and adding stock, until the rice is tender but with a slight firmness at the center, 15 to 20 minutes.

About 5 minutes before the rice is finished, gently stir in the reserved beans. Then add two thirds of the salami and stir gently.

After the rice has finished cooking, let stand off the heat without stirring for 5 minutes. Serve on heated plates, each serving topped with a small handful of the remaining salami and a generous grinding of black pepper. (This risotto needs no butter, no grated cheese.)

**Note:** To prepare 2 cups beans, soak 1 cup beans overnight in 4 cups water. Drain, place in a heavy pot with 6 cups water and, if you wish, a 1-inch chunk of pancetta or salami, and bring to a boil. Skim off the foam, then lower the heat and simmer until the beans are very tender, about 1 hour. Just before the beans finish cooking, add 1 teaspoon salt, or to taste. To store, let cool, then divide in half and store in two 1-pint containers in the freezer. You can substitute canned beans and use canned beef broth, though homemade versions (from a handy stash in the freezer, perhaps) produce a fresher flavor.

*Rice farmer bicycling outside Vercelli*

# Rice Croquettes

It's hard to imagine that there would ever be any leftover risotto, but sometimes we overestimate our guests' hunger. This classic method for dealing with leftover risotto also works with leftover paella or other flavored Spanish *arroces*.

To make the croquettes, just shape the leftover rice into small patties and fry them. The rice is usually already so well flavored that it needs nothing more, but if you want, you can put a small piece of mozzarella in the middle of each patty. Traditionally these patties are dipped in beaten egg, then coated in bread crumbs before being fried in olive oil. They emerge warm and tender. We like the softness of a plain egg coating, so we tend to omit the crumbs. Suit yourself, but don't be tempted to omit the egg, for it has the double function of holding the patty together and sealing the moisture in the rice. With no egg, moisture seeps out of the rice and hisses and spits in the hot oil.

1 large egg per cup of risotto (approximately)

Salt and freshly ground black pepper

Bread crumbs for coating (optional)

Olive oil for frying

Leftover risotto, at room temperature

Mozzarella, chopped into small chunks (optional)

Flat-leaf parsley sprigs for garnish (optional)

Beat the egg(s) in a small bowl. Season with salt and pepper to taste. Have ready a plate or shallow bowl of bread crumbs if you want.

Heat 1 inch olive oil in a large heavy frying pan. The oil has reached the correct temperature when a small ball of the rice dropped into the oil floats back up to the surface, without burning. Scoop up a heaping tablespoonful of risotto. Insert a small chunk of mozzarella in the center if using. Use both hands (lightly moistened) to press the patty firmly into a flattened oval 2 to 3 inches long. Dip the patty into the egg, then roll lightly in the bread crumbs if using. Slide the patty into the oil and start shaping the next one. Let the patties cook until well browned, 3 to 4 minutes, then turn over and cook on the other side. As they finish cooking, use a slotted spoon to lift them out, pausing to let excess oil drain off, and then place them on paper towels to drain. Serve hot as an appetizer or snack, sprinkled with parsley if you wish.

# Carlo and Carla

Off in the Marche there is a small field of rice growing on dry unirrigated land. The rice is part of an ongoing experiment by a dedicated pasta maker named Carlo Latini. He has come to rice growing from a continuing passionate interest in wheat, traditional wheat and wheat to make the best pasta. Now, after many years of working with wheats and perfecting his wonderful pasta, he has discovered that approximately a hundred and fifty years ago rice was also grown in the rolling hills and valleys of the Marche. It was cultivated with a dryland technique, not in classic Po Valley–style flooded paddy. Carlo is determined to make a go of dryland rice farming. "If they could do it then, I should be able to do it now," he says firmly. In his first three years of experimenting, he has grown some of all the major Italian varieties, including vialone nano, arborio, even carnaroli, which is notoriously difficult to grow.

Carlo holding a young rice plant

We learned of Carlo's rice experiments from Faith Willinger, a longtime resident of Italy who is consistently generous about sharing her knowledge of Italian food from field to table. She took several of us to meet Carlo at the pasta factory in Francavilla. (Carlo's thoughtful approach to pasta is well described in Burton Anderson's wonderful book of essays *Treasures of the Italian Table,* under "Pasta"). We visited the *pastificio* and then, before heading out to the wheat and the rice fields, we went back to the Latini house for lunch with Carlo and his partner, Carla (after a quick tour of their back room, stacked with boxes of artisanal pasta and bags of rice).

Carlo cooked the pasta until barely done. It was chewy with a wonderful taste of the grain. His approach to rice is similar. The plain risotto he prepared from his own vialone nano was cooked only until very al dente, rather than soft. It was lightly flavored with a little olive oil, scallion, and Parmesan, and cooked not in broth but in hot water. There was nothing to interfere with the fine clear taste of the rice.

Carlo's red hair and smile gleamed with pleasure as we all dug appreciatively into our plates of risotto. Next Carla brought in a platter of *coniglio a la porchetta,* rabbit stuffed with wild fennel, garlic shoots, and rosemary. It was a country feast, a celebration with two people who not only care about food traditions, but also are working to preserve and extend them.

# Rice Pudding with Saffron and Rose Water

*zerde*

THIS AROMATIC RICE PUDDING FROM TURKEY CONTAINS NO MILK OR CREAM or butter. Tinted a pale yellow with saffron and topped with a sprinkling of pine nuts, and gleaming pomegranate seeds, it is a beautiful, delicious, and wonderfully simple dessert for a party. Prepare the pudding ahead and chill it in the refrigerator for several hours, then top it just before serving.

1 teaspoon saffron threads, briefly dry-roasted (see page 431) and ground to a powder

About 6½ cups water

½ cup medium-grain rice, such as baldo, arborio, or CalRiso

1¼ cups sugar

¼ cup rose water (see Glossary)

3 tablespoons cornstarch, rice starch, potato starch, or arrowroot

¼ cup pine nuts, lightly dry-roasted (see peanuts, page 430)

A handful of pomegranate seeds (optional)

Place the saffron in a small bowl. Pour over ½ cup of the water and let soak for 30 minutes, then stir to dissolve the saffron and set aside.

Put the rice and 6 cups water in a large pot. Bring to a boil and boil over medium heat until the rice is very soft, stirring occasionally, about 20 minutes. Stir in the sugar and cook for another 30 minutes over low heat.

Add the rose water and the saffron mixture, bring back to a medium boil, and boil for several minutes. In a small bowl, blend together the starch and 2 tablespoons water. Add to the rice and boil for 1 minute more; the pudding will thicken.

Pour the pudding into small dessert bowls and chill well. Serve garnished with a few pine nuts and the optional pomegranate seeds. Place the remaining pine nuts in a small bowl on the table so guests can add extra as they wish.

# Spanish Rice Pudding
*arroz con leche*

WHEREVER THERE IS RICE, THERE SEEMS TO BE A SIMPLE RICE PUDDING, most often cooked in milk. This classic comfort food from Spain, here presented in its plainest everyday form, is no exception. Be sure to use a very light hand with the sprinkled cinnamon, or you risk overpowering the aromas of the rice.

| | |
|---|---|
| 4½ cups whole milk | 1 tablespoon unsalted butter |
| 2 inches cinnamon stick | ¾ cup sugar |
| Zest of ½ lemon, peeled off in large strips | Pinch of salt |
| ¾ cup Spanish or Italian medium-grain rice, washed and drained | Dusting of ground cinnamon |

Place the milk, cinnamon stick, and lemon zest in a large heavy pot. Bring just to a boil, sprinkle in the rice, and bring back almost to a boil. Stir well, lower the heat to very low, and simmer for 45 to 50 minutes, until the rice is very soft, stirring occasionally to prevent sticking and to break up any lumps. Remove the cinnamon stick. (The recipe can be prepared several hours ahead to this point and set aside until 10 to 15 minutes before serving. Bring the rice just to a simmer before proceeding.)

Stir in the butter, then the sugar and salt. Continue cooking, stirring, for another 5 minutes.

Transfer to a serving bowl or to individual dessert bowls. Serve warm or, our preference, let cool to room temperature. Just before serving, sprinkle on a faint touch of cinnamon.

Egret enjoying a paddy near Marsassoum
in Casamance

inset: Child tending goats on Gorée Island

# Yassa, Mafe, Diebou Dien

went to Senegal, never having been to West Africa, following the trail of rice, wanting to know more about the people and the places from which so many American and Caribbean rice traditions sprang. When I got there, I happily found not only rice, but a whole lot of great food, including several dishes that have become big favorites in our house.

West Africa has an ancient rice-growing tradition. Long before the arrival of Arab or Portuguese traders, the Diola people of the Casamance region of southern Senegal were cultivating rice. The rices they grew were of the African species *Oryza glaberrima*, and they also gathered rice grains from wild species. Archaeologists believe that the Casamance was one of the original rice growing regions of Africa. From here, rice cultivation spread inland as well as northward and southward, establishing itself where there were wet lands or large rivers.

In the Casamance, many households still eat rice two or three times a day. Others, because of the occasional rice scarcity and the growing influence of the millet-eating Mandinka people in the region, eat millet for breakfast and supper and rice for their main meal. The rice or millet is eaten with some form of vegetable stew, often prepared with

**left to right**

Diola woman outside Marsassoum

Eating *diebou dien* on Gorée Island

fish or dried or smoked oysters. The oysters grow on the roots of the mangrove trees that line the wide, slow-flowing rivers of the region. Dried scallops, salted dried fish, fermented dried beans, hibiscus shoots, manioc leaf, and palm oil are important flavorings and ingredients in Casamance.

In the twentieth century, many Senegalese, not just those in Casamance, are rice eaters. Rice is commonly eaten with a stew and the combination is known as *riz sauce*. Similarly in Mali, the Ivory Coast, and Sierra Leone, *riz sauce* or white rice eaten with any one of the many different flavorful stews of the region is a standard lunch-time or main meal.

Diola man paddling a dugout on the Casamance River

In Senegal, rice is usually cooked in a limited amount of liquid, in a version of the absorption technique. Sometimes the cooking liquid is plain water, perhaps with a little salt. The plain rice is then served with a flavorful soupy stew such as peanut-based *mafe* (page 376) or lemony *yassa* (page 364). At other times, especially when the rest of the meal is fish- or vegetable-based, the fish and vegetables are cooked until very tender and then removed from the cooking broth, so it can be used to cook and flavor the rice. The

Across from Marsassoum, a man walking past the stumps of drowned trees

most famous example of this technique is the Senegalese classic *diebou dien* (Senegalese Festive Rice and Fish, page 370), but it is also used for cooking more everyday dishes, especially in Casamance.

Because Senegalese food is new to us, we are just now beginning to develop reflexes and habits with it. We have come to love the easy classics—*mafe* and *yassa*—because their ingredients are very easy to come by and both go so beautifully with plain rice. You can make any plain rice you prefer, as we do. We make the flavored rice dishes such as *diebou dien* when we have guests to dazzle.

You can cook the Senegalese recipes we have selected with no special equipment. We use a large heavy pot for cooking all these dishes, from *diebou dien* to *mafe*. As for a pantry, the list is very short. Senegalese use dried fish and a kind of dried conch or scallop for flavoring. We substitute dried shrimp, easily available in Asian groceries, and salt cod. Palm oil can be found in Latin American and African markets; you will also want a good supply of peanut oil. Since the arrival of the French, Senegalese cooks have come to rely on tomato paste to enrich the flavor of their stews and sauces, so it too should be in your pantry.

Everything else can be bought fresh. Work with the vegetables you have available. Unfortunately, we have never seen African eggplant in North America. We like to use small round green Thai eggplant instead, but if these are hard to come by, don't worry. All these dishes have a well-judged balance of flavors but can always be adapted to the ingredients available.

# Senegalese Plain Rice

SENEGALESE USE WHATEVER RICE THEY HAVE AVAILABLE, MOST OFTEN IMPORTED rice from Thailand, Vietnam, or India. These rices are long-grain but of the lower grades, so there are a lot of broken grains. The rice the Diola grow is long-grain and is cooked right after husking and milling. Because it is cleaned by hand in a mortar and pestle, there are more broken grains than in a store-bought bag of top-quality rice sold in North America. Consequently, whether it's bought or home-grown, the rice cooked in Senegalese homes usually has a high proportion of broken grains and is thus a little more sticky when cooked than top-quality rice. This makes it easy to eat with your hands.

3 cups long-grain rice

6 cups water

1 teaspoon salt (optional)

To reproduce the texture of the rice eaten in most Senegalese homes, take about ½ cup of the rice, place on the counter, and cover with a cotton cloth. Use a heavy rolling pin or bottle to crush the grains a little, then mix them back in with the other rice. Wash the rice briefly in cold water and drain.

In a heavy medium pot, bring the water to a boil, add the rice, and bring back to a vigorous boil. Let boil gently for 5 minutes, uncovered. If any liquid still shows above the rice, use a ladle to scoop out the excess and reserve for another purpose. Cover, lower the heat to very low, and cook for 25 minutes. Let stand for 10 minutes or more, covered, before serving.

# Marsassoum

New landscapes in countries unknown to us can be like dreamscapes. Sometimes, at first, we're so busy deciphering the basic things, or worrying about our relationship to it all, that we don't see much of anything. But then suddenly we'll begin to see. . . .

One morning in southern Senegal, I stood waiting to cross a wide stretch of river to the village of Marsassoum on the opposite bank. The ferry I was waiting for had run aground and couldn't start up again until the tide came back up the river. Waiting with me was a scattering of people. There were two men with their bicycles, a woman with a large basket and a baby, several young boys, two or three pickup trucks, and a tired old car carrying an extended family to a funeral. I'd been dropped off at the ferry landing after a long drive from the town of Bignona. It was hot and there was no shade, no place to sit. The salt-whitened bank of the river was dotted with the stubs of drowned trees.

"Don't worry," I'd been told in Dakar by a friend of a friend, the person who had told me that I should come to Marsassoum, "just ask and people will direct you." A family some-

Selling kola nuts at the Ziguinchor market in Casamance

Buying fish by the river in Marsassoum

where in the village was expecting me to arrive sometime that day. I had the name of the head of the household and the name of the section of the village he lived in.

Eventually the flat-topped ferry creaked its way over to us, and we all made our way aboard. I watched the other shore come nearer over the rumble of the engine. Gradually a small café at the water's edge came into focus, and tall trees, and small fishing boats, and an assortment of people waiting for the ferry, in bright greens and shades of orange and yellow and pink. As we walked off the echoing metal deck, they looked at me closely, a very visible stranger, but no one came forward.

I started up the dirt road into the village under the welcome shade of huge mango trees with hard green fruit. A boy came up to ask where I was going and I told him I was looking for the house of Yatou Guiba in Asourwa Kunda. He smiled and said he'd show me the way.

We walked past the small village market, then took a lane to the right when the path forked. A short way farther, we bore left. The dream-like quality of the morning continued. Though I tried to look back the way I'd come, so I could find my way out if need be, it all seemed utterly unknown yet also somehow familiar. Passing courtyards of bare earth shaded by baobab and mango trees, I saw women standing by tall wooden mortars and pounding with huge long pestles—a hollow syncopated ker-thunk, ker-thunk. Several of them stopped, gave me a look, a smile, and a wave, then went back to their labor. By the path were the dried stalks of the last sorghum and millet crops. There was wood smoke in the air.

Sometime later I was brought back to a fully wakened state by a serious-looking teenager standing in the path. He held out his hand and said, smiling, "My name is Alfou Seni Sane. My uncle went to meet you at the ferry—he must have missed you." He showed me into a large clean-swept courtyard, then presented me to his aunt, Sarta Sane, the mistress of the house and Yatou Guiba's second wife. We sat in the shade under the thatched-roof eaves and sipped cool water dipped from a large earthenware jar inside. Water, dry air, dry earth, blue sky. Africa.

# Senegalese Rice
*steam-and-boil method*

OFTEN RICE IN SENEGAL IS COOKED BY A COMBINATION OF STEAMING AND absorption. The rice is thoroughly washed, then placed in a steamer over a boiling stew or over boiling water for 5 to 7 minutes (in the same way that couscous steams over a flavoring stew). Rice that is steamed over stew (for example, over Sarta's Fish with Lime Juice Sauce, page 366), picks up a little flavor during steaming. The steamed rice is then added to boiling lightly salted water (in a proportion of 1¼ cups water and ½ teaspoon salt to 1 cup raw rice). Once the water comes back to a boil, cover tightly, lower the heat, and cook for 10 to 12 minutes.

The rice-cooking method used in the national dish *diebou dien* (page 370) is a version of this steam-then-absorption-cook technique. In *dieb*, after the rice steams over the stew, it is absorption-cooked in the richly flavored liquid in which the vegetables and fish have slow-simmered.

Sarta milling rice with a mortar and pestle

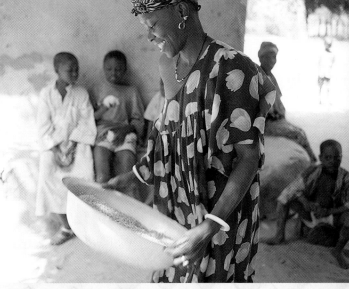

# Daily Labor

After I had stayed for several days in Marsassoum, some of my first dream-like journey through the village began to take on more meaning. I came to know the house where salt was made each day (by rinsing salt-laden riverbank sand with water, then boiling it down until only salt crystals remained) and what the women were pounding in their mortars. I could even find my way to the river on my own. But the sense of wonder, of another world, remained.

The daily household chores alone were humbling. In the mornings, Sarta cleans rice for the noon meal, first taking a sheaf of rice still on the stalk and pounding it in the large mortar, then winnowing away the straw and chaff, then putting the grain back in the mortar to be pounded until polished white, and finally winnowing away the last of the chaff and bran. After the rice comes millet. Starting with whole millet, and often working with her wiry, alert twelve-year-old daughter, also named Sarta, she pounds and pounds with the pestle, raising it high each time. The result after an hour's heavy labor and some winnowing is a pile of millet flour. Later in the day, Sarta will spend another hour tossing and sifting some of the flour into fine millet couscous. The rest she hand-rolls in the evening, by the light of a lantern, into small even balls to be boiled for the morning's breakfast porridge.

All these are everyday chores that can't be avoided or rushed. Friends come by and chat with her as she wields the pestle; my visit also helped break up the routine, but did nothing to lessen the workload. As I stood with Sarta by the mortar letting my pestle drop heavily onto the rice, then lifting it again as hers fell, there was time to smile and laugh, and also time to reflect on the endless labor involved in turning grain into family food. I lasted through the cleaning of the rice, but then only managed ten or fifteen minutes with the millet before Sarta waved me to a shady spot, laughing. I could no longer get my arms to lift the pestle high, was no longer of any help at all. The two Sartas, mother and daughter, strong and sure, then resumed their normal routine, pounding rythmically at the millet until it was fine flour, while I sat watching.

# Lemon Chicken

*yassa*

Serves 6 to 8

*YASSA* IS A FAMILIAR AND MUCH-LOVED DISH ALL ACROSS WEST AFRICA, FOUND on restaurant menus from Bamako to Dakar, usually featuring chicken, or sometimes lamb, and citrus-flavored with lemon or lime. It is often said that *yassa* originated in the Casamance region of southern Senegal, though nowadays in the villages of Casamance, chicken and lamb are luxury foods seldom enjoyed. The only versions of *yassa* I tasted in Casamance homes were made with fish, as were nearly all the home-cooked dishes I ate during my short stay in the region. Families had dried oysters, vegetables, and many kinds of fish to cook with, but never lamb or chicken.

While staying in the village of Marsassoum in Casamance, I was given simple instructions on how to make chicken *yassa*, and later I did manage to sample a particularly delicious version in a tiny eatery in the town of Ziguinchor. When I got back home and tried to reproduce the flavors from the instructions I'd been given, sure enough, it tasted wonderful. The recipe given here has a distinctive citrus tang of fresh lemon or lime juice, balanced by the sweet taste of plenty of slow-cooked onions and a hint of heat from the chile.

When *yassa* is made with chicken, traditionally the whole chicken is used, cut up into pieces with the bone still in. You can begin with a whole chicken the standard West African way, or with a mixture of legs and breasts.

| | |
|---|---|
| One 4-pound chicken or 3½ pounds chicken legs and breasts | 1½ pounds red or yellow onions |
| 1 cup fresh lemon or lime juice | 1 cup water |
| 2 teaspoons salt, or more to taste | 1 or 2 serranos (or substitute 2 dried red chiles) |
| Freshly ground black pepper | ¼ teaspoon dried thyme or 2 sprigs fresh thyme |
| 3 tablespoons peanut oil (more if frying the chicken) | |

Use a cleaver to chop up the chicken (or ask your butcher to do it): The legs should be cut into drumstick and thigh and then each of these chopped in two. Similarly, the whole breast should be chopped in half and then each half into 3 or 4 pieces. If using a whole chicken, chop the back into similar-sized pieces and split the wings. Discard any excess fatty pieces (or set aside for another purpose). The skin is traditionally left on, but you may discard it if you wish.

Place the chicken in a shallow nonreactive bowl. Pour on the lemon juice and turn to coat well. Let marinate, covered, in a cool place for 30 minutes, or refrigerate for up to 8 hours, turning occasionally.

When ready to proceed, remove the chicken from the marinade, strain the marinade, and set the marinade aside.

*If using a grill:* Preheat the grill. If possible, place a shallow pan below the grill rack to catch the juices. Place the chicken pieces on the lightly oiled rack 4 to 6 inches from the coals. Sprinkle on 1 teaspoon salt and a generous grinding of black pepper. Grill until golden, turning to expose all sides to the heat. Remove from the heat and set aside. Save the pan juices.

*If using a broiler:* Preheat the broiler. Place the chicken pieces on a lightly oiled broiling pan and sprinkle on 1 teaspoon salt and a generous grinding of black pepper. Place the chicken 4 to 6 inches from the broiler element and cook until golden, 4 to 5 minutes, then turn the pieces over and cook until golden. Remove from the heat and set aside. Save the pan juices.

*If frying:* Heat ¾ inch of peanut oil in a deep heavy pot. When the oil is hot, add the chicken pieces, being careful not to splash yourself with hot oil. (Depending on the size of your pot, you may have to fry in batches.) Fry until golden, then turn over and repeat on the other side. Remove from the hot oil and let drain on a rack. Drain off all but about 3 tablespoons oil.

While the chicken is cooking, prepare the onions: Cut the onions lengthwise in half, then thinly slice lengthwise. If the onions are large, cut the slices once or twice crosswise.

If you grilled or broiled the chicken, heat the oil in a wide heavy pot. Use your fingers to separate the onion slices as you add them to the oil. Fry over medium heat until soft and translucent, about 10 minutes, stirring frequently to prevent sticking.

Add the chicken pieces, the reserved marinade, and the cooking juices, if any, to the onions, along with the water, chiles, and thyme and bring to a boil. Simmer until the chicken is thoroughly cooked, 15 to 20 minutes. Ten minutes after you begin simmering, add the remaining 1 teaspoon salt and stir and turn to mix well. Just before serving, taste and adjust the seasoning if you wish.

To serve, arrange the chicken pieces in a shallow bowl or on a platter and spoon the onions over. Remove the chiles if you wish. Serve the sauce separately or pour over all. Serve with plenty of white rice.

**Alternative:** You can use this recipe as a guide for making fish *yassa:* Marinate whole fish or fish steaks in the lemon juice marinade; if using whole fish, make several slashes on either side before marinating. Grill or broil the fish until barely done (the flesh will have become opaque). Fry the onions as directed above, add the marinade, water, chiles, thyme, and seasonings, and simmer until very tender. Add the grilled fish and cook for another several minutes, then serve with plain rice.

# Sarta's Fish with Lime Juice Sauce
## *fitouf*

THIS EASY CASAMANCE CLASSIC COOKS VERY FRESH FISH IN A MIXTURE OF palm oil and lime juice. The palm oil tints the sauce a brilliant golden color, the lime juice gives it a strong citrus tang, and the spice blend of dried chiles and black peppercorns adds a little heat. The sauce is traditionally thickened and greened with manioc leaves (available frozen in many African and Caribbean groceries, sometimes labeled "cassava"). Parsley can be substituted for the leaves. The fish is cooked until it is soft and almost falling apart, easy to eat with the fingers.

*Fitouf* is served over plain rice, cooked either the Senegalese Plain Rice way (page 359) or by the Senegalese method of steaming, then boiling (see page 362). Extra sauce, rich and citrusy, a treat on its own over rice, is served on the side. Serve *fitouf* from a large platter; guests can either eat from a central platter the traditional way, or serve themselves onto individual plates.

½ cup palm oil (see Glossary)

1 cup water

1 tablespoon plus 1 teaspoon salt

1¼ cups fresh lime juice (about 6 limes)

2 pounds cleaned, scaled, and headless fish, such as yellowtail snapper (about 3 medium to small)

1 clove garlic

5 dried red chiles (see Glossary)

12 black peppercorns

½ cup chopped frozen manioc (cassava) leaves (see Glossary) or ½ cup packed finely chopped flat-leaf parsley

¼ cup all-purpose flour (see Note)

3 cups raw long-grain rice, cooked (see headnote)

Place the oil and water in a large heavy pot. Bring to a boil and add 1 tablespoon of the salt and ½ cup of the lime juice. Make two or three diagonal slashes on both sides of each fish. Slide the fish gently into the hot liquid, taking care not to splash yourself. Lower the heat and let simmer while you prepare the flavorings.

In a mortar or food processor, pound or process the garlic, the remaining 1 teaspoon salt, the chiles, peppercorns, and manioc or parsley. Add this paste to the pot. Bring back to a rolling boil and add the remaining ¾ cup lime juice. Boil for another 8 to 10 minutes, until fish is very soft but not breaking into pieces.

Use a slotted spoon to lift out the fish and place on a platter. Skim off any foam and add to the fish. Sift the flour into the sauce, whisking well to blend and keep it smooth. Lower the heat slightly and continue to cook gently for 5 minutes, stirring occasionally. Transfer the sauce to a small serving bowl.

Serve the fish and sauce with the rice on a platter: Spread the rice on the platter, arrange the fish on top, then spoon over some sauce. Serve the remaining sauce in a serving bowl, so guests can spoon on extra as they wish. This dish is traditionally eaten from a central platter, with guests eating with their right hands or with spoons. You can also lift portions from the central platter onto individual plates; lift the portions of fish off the bone if serving individually.

**Note:** In Casamance, peanut flour (ground raw peanuts) or millet flour is used for thickening the sauce. If you find either, use it; regular all-purpose flour also serves the purpose.

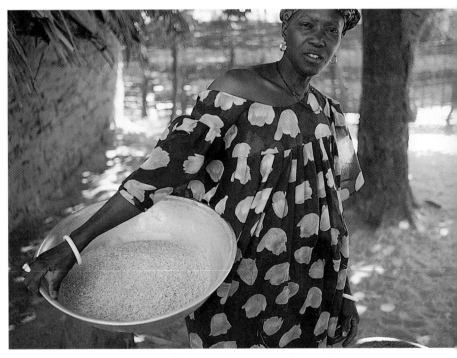

*Sarta with a basin of cleaned rice ready for cooking*

# Wolof Hot Chile Paste

*sauce cany*

**Makes about 1 cup chile paste**

ÎLE DE GORÉE SITS IN THE SHELTERED HARBOR OF DAKAR, A PINK-AND-OCHRE dot when viewed from the ferry that links the island with the city. Gorée was the original toehold in West Africa of the slave-trading European powers and as such is synonymous with the trade. The Maison des Esclaves (Slave House) on the island, built as a kind of intolerable holding tank for people waiting to be shipped out to the Americas, is now a

Stirring a pot of *diebou dien* on Gorée Island

museum. Nowadays, Gorée is a peaceful, beautiful village of fishing people and traders, though on week-ends it gets busy with day-trippers from Dakar who come to eat, shop, or windsurf.

As I was walking down a lane on the island one Sunday afternoon, my eye was caught by a splash of color and light that came out through the half-opened gate of a residential courtyard. The courtyard was dappled with shade from an enormous mango tree, and standing in the shade was a group of women dressed in brilliant silks and satins. One woman was busy using a long wooden pestle, pounding something in a mortar. Another woman was bent over a large fire-blackened pot, stirring with a long-handled spoon while whatever was inside simmered over a hot wood fire.

I put a tentative toe through the gate and said to the person nearest to me, "Excuse me, but I'm interested in traditional Senegalese food. May I have a look at what you're cooking, please?"

"Of course," said a man's voice from just behind me. "They're preparing for my wedding and there's lots of food for you to see." Indeed. One large pot held a bubbling mass of half-made *diebou dien*, the vegetables and fish simmering in an aromatic sauce. On the other fire was the start of a Moroccan-style tajine, and nearby there was couscous being moistened and sorted. The mortar-and-pestle work was for *sauce cany*, a Senegalese cousin of North African harissa. *Cany* means chile pepper in Wolof, and loaded with chiles it definitely was.

Once inside the courtyard I was questioned about my well-being, my family's health, my name, and where I was from—all part of the wonderful sequence of politeness and greetings I encountered in every culture in Senegal. When she heard I was from Toronto, a great smile of amazement spread over the face of the mother of the bride. Her daughter's best friend was coincidentally living in Toronto, less than a mile from my house.

With that, I was truly welcomed in as a guest at the celebration to eat, to photograph, and later on, while the men were at the mosque, to join the women as they danced and danced to the taped music of Youssof N'Dour and other Senegalese greats.

There are many different versions of *sauce cany*. Some have onions and garlic, some have shallots, some brown the onion first, some don't, it's all a matter of individual taste. We particularly like this version. It is quite hot and tasty, very like the one at the wedding.

1 habanero, Scotch bonnet, or other very
   hot chile

1 cup serrano chiles, stems removed

4 cloves garlic

2 shallots, coarsely chopped (optional)

½ teaspoon freshly ground black pepper

1 teaspoon salt, or to taste

½ Maggi cube, crumbled (optional)

About 2 tablespoons peanut oil

*If using a food processor*, process the chiles and garlic to a paste. Add the remaining ingredients and process until smooth. You may need to add a little more oil to make a smooth paste.

*If using a mortar and pestle*, coarsely chop the chiles and garlic, using rubber gloves to protect your hands from the chiles' heat, then transfer the chiles to mortar and pound to a paste with a pinch of salt. Add the garlic, optional shallots, and the remaining salt and pound to a coarse paste. Add the remaining ingredients, and pound and stir, adjusting the quantity of oil as necessary to produce a smooth paste.

Transfer to a serving bowl or to a nonreactive container. Store well sealed in the refrigerator.

# Senegalese Festive Rice and Fish
*diebou dien*

**Serves 8 to 10**

BEFORE LEAVING FOR SENEGAL, I WAS GIVEN ADVICE BY A NUMBER OF PEOPLE. On the subject of *diebou dien,* a friend of a friend, Mamadou Seck, was very explicit: "The best *diebou dien* is made in Saint-Louis—you must go there and learn from a Saint-Louisienne."

So near the end of my stay in Senegal, I took a bush taxi up the road from Dakar to Saint-Louis, a four-hour trip through a hot, spare landscape of red earth and silhouetted baobab and acacia trees. The speed of our passage sent a furnace-dry wind into the car, a numbingly continuous blast of hot air. But as we came round a bend in the road, suddenly there was a gust of cool, miraculously cool, fresh air: We'd arrived at "*le fleuve*" (the Senegal River) and we were finally nearing the colonial capital of Saint-Louis.

Scene at Saint-Louis

The town of Saint-Louis is enchanting. It is built on two long narrow islands (each one is only four blocks wide), which are linked to the left bank of the Senegal River by a long bridge. The town is filled with breezes and light, blowing and reflecting in off the quickly flowing water. Fish is plentiful here, both fresh fish from the sea and the river and dried fish, set out on vast racks on the beach near the fishermen's cemetery. Fresh vegetables, chiles, and local rice arrive in abundance from farther upriver, grown on irrigated lands.

One morning I made my way to the house of Mariam Seck (no relation to Mamadou, above), who had said she would teach me how to make *diebou dien.* We worked outside the cooking shed in the dappled shade of the palm-frond eaves. Mariam's sister Josie helped, not only with the cooking but also with answering my questions and showing me techniques. We prepared *diebou dien,* along with *sauce cany* (page 368) and *sauce pikul* (page 374).

Recipes for *diebou dien* vary with availability of ingredients and money to pay for them, but the basic technique is generally agreed on (at least among the people I spoke with, from Gorée and Dakar to Saint-Louis and Ziguinchor). You must have both fresh fish and dried fish, as well as onions, tomatoes, and as many as possible of the following vegetables: eggplant, African eggplant (see Glossary; we substitute small round green Thai eggplant), manioc, turnips or white radishes, cabbage, and carrots. The fish and vegetables are slow-cooked in liquid, making a well-flavored stock, then removed to a platter. The rice is steamed over the stock, then cooked in it. The cooked rice, fragrant and lightly colored from the stock, is served on a large platter, with the vegetables, fish, and sauce

Mariam with a platter of *diebou dien*

over the center; extra sauce may be served on the side. The crunchy bits of rice that stick to the bottom of the pot are highly prized—like the *tahdig* (rice crust) of Persian tradition—and are served in a pile at the side of the platter. Traditionally, in the center and north of the country at least, men and women eat separately, so two platters are prepared, one for each group.

Once the men's platter had been set before them, we followed Mariam as she placed the women's platter on a mat on the floor in another room. We sat down around it and each of us rinsed our hands with water and wiped them dry. Then it was time to dig in, with the right hand only, assembling a handful of sauce-moistened rice topped with a little fish and a fragment of soft eggplant or tender carrot, squeezing the whole into a rough ball, then flicking it neatly into the mouth. "Ah," I thought, "Mamadou Seck was right—*diebou dien* from Saint-Louis is really the best. . . ."

*continued*

6 medium-small whiting, cleaned, and scaled (about 3 pounds)

About ¼ pound salt cod, soaked for 12 to 24 hours in several changes of cold water and drained

1 large or 2 medium red or yellow onions, coarsely chopped

¾ pound juicy cherry tomatoes or 1½ cups drained canned tomatoes

1 pound carrots

1 pound turnips or white radishes

1 medium or 2 small eggplant (about 1 pound)

½ pound small green Thai eggplant (see Glossary) or tomatillos (optional)

½ pound cabbage, cut into small chunks (optional)

½ pound manioc (see Glossary) (optional)

### Herb paste

3 cloves garlic, coarsely chopped

1 teaspoon salt

1 teaspoon cayenne pepper

1½ cups packed flat-leaf parsley leaves, coarsely chopped

5 scallions, coarsely chopped

½ cup peanut oil

¾ cup tomato paste, diluted with ½ cup water

1 tablespoon tamarind paste (see Glossary), dissolved in 2 tablespoons water, or ½ Maggi cube, crumbled

1 tablespoon salt, or more to taste

2 dried red chiles (see Glossary)

4 cups Thai jasmine or other long-grain rice, well washed and drained

### Optional accompaniment

Wolof Hot Chile Paste (page 368)

Wash and dry the fresh fish. Cut off and discard the heads, fins, and tails. Cut the fish in half crosswise and put into a large bowl of cold water. Coarsely chop the soaked dried fish (discarding any tough bits), and set aside. Coarsely chop the onions, then separate the layers and set aside. Coarsely chop half the tomatoes and set aside. Cut up the remaining vegetables as follows, then place in a bowl of cold water: Quarter the carrots lengthwise and then cut into 4- to 5-inch lengths. Cut the turnips or white radishes into similar shapes. Cut the eggplant lengthwise into quarters or into sixths if large, then cut crosswise into 3- to 4-inch lengths. Cut off the stems of the green Thai eggplant and leave whole; or husk and rinse the tomatillos. Cut the cabbage into small wedges. Cut the manioc in ½-inch julienne.

Prepare the herb paste stuffing: Place the chopped garlic, salt, and cayenne in a mortar and pound to a paste. Add the parsley and scallions and pound until smooth. *Alternatively,* mince the garlic, then place with all the other paste ingredients in a food processor (use a mini-processor if possible) and process to a smooth paste. Set aside.

In a large heavy pot, heat the oil. Add three quarters of the onion and cook for 1 minute, stirring occasionally. Add the tomato paste diluted with water, the tamarind water or the Maggi cube, and salt, then add 2 cups water and the chopped salt cod. Let cook for 20 minutes.

Meanwhile, stuff the seasoning paste into each of the fresh fish pieces down either side of the backbone: Working with one piece of fish at a time, use the tip of your little finger to make a tunnel between flesh and bone along either side of the backbone. Push some herb paste into the tunnels, then set aside and repeat for the remaining fish pieces.

Add the fish to the sauce. Add the chopped tomatoes, then add enough water to cover by 1 inch. Bring to a boil and add the dried chiles, the manioc, and half of each of the remaining vegetables. If necessary, add more water to ensure the vegetables are covered with liquid. Bring to a boil, then simmer, partially covered, for 30 minutes.

Add the remaining vegetables, including the onion and tomatoes, and simmer until all the vegetables are tender, 20 to 30 minutes.

Shortly before the vegetables are cooked, place the rice in a steamer or a sieve or fine colander lined with cheesecloth. Place over the simmering sauce, or alternatively over a pot of boiling water, to steam for 5 to 6 minutes.

When the vegetables are tender, use a slotted spoon to remove all the fish and vegetables from the sauce and set aside on a platter. Taste the sauce and adjust the seasoning if necessary.

Add the rice to the sauce and stir gently to mix thoroughly. The liquid should be at least 1 inch above the surface of the rice; add more water if necessary. Bring to a boil and let cook vigorously for 5 minutes. If the liquid is still above the surface of the rice, use a ladle to remove the excess, until the liquid is just at the surface of the rice, and set aside in a bowl. Cover the pot tightly, lower the heat to medium-low, and cook for 20 minutes. Remove from the heat and let stand for 5 minutes.

*Mariam stuffing fish for diebou dien*

Turn the rice out onto two large platters. Place the crisp crust scrapings in a separate bowl or make a small pile on the side of each platter. Ladle the fish, vegetables, and any extra sauce over the center, distributing them as evenly as possible. Serve hot, with the chile paste on the side if you wish.

**Note:** We find whiting to be an ideal substitute, easily available in North America, for the fish used in Saint-Louis. The fish holds together well during its long simmering and has a very good taste and texture. This method of stuffing the fish with herb paste is a specialty of Saint-Louis. You can omit the herb paste and cook the fish plain if you prefer.

# Tart Vegetable Stew with Fish Balls
## sauce pikul

Serves 4 to 6 with rice

THIS RICHLY FLAVORED VEGETABLE STEW WITH TINY SIMMERED FISH BALLS HAS a mild chile heat, set off by the tart bite of vinegar. You can use leftover ingredients from the preparation of *diebou dien* (see page 370), or you can make and serve the stew on its own as a simple or everyday accompaniment to plain rice.

Josie, the sister of Mariam Seck, who taught me her marvelous version of *diebou dien*, prepared *sauce pikul* as a way of teaching me a simpler fish and vegetable topping for plain rice. She told me that the Maggi cubes or tamarind she uses add a little more depth of flavor. She said one or other was needed now that fish was being stored on ice or refrigerated, which makes it lose flavor.

Though the fish balls may sound elaborate, they are very quick to shape and cook; total preparation time for the dish is less than half an hour.

### Fish ball mixture

3 sprigs flat-leaf parsley, coarsely chopped

1 scallion, coarsely chopped

¼ teaspoon cayenne pepper

1 clove garlic, coarsely chopped

¼ teaspoon salt

⅓ to ½ pound fish fillet (whiting or snapper), skin removed, and coarsely chopped

### Stew

About 1½ cups water

1½ cups white radishes (icicle or daikon), cut into 2-inch-long julienne

1½ cups carrots, cut into 2-inch-long julienne

2 teaspoons salt

½ cup peanut oil

¼ medium yellow onion, cut into long shreds

1 tablespoon tomato paste

2 medium tomatoes or 4 drained canned plum tomatoes, coarsely chopped

1 cup coarsely chopped cabbage (optional)

½ teaspoon cayenne pepper

2 dried red chiles (see Note)

1 clove garlic, minced

⅓ cup cider vinegar

1 teaspoon tamarind paste (see Glossary) or ½ Maggi cube, crumbled

Place all the fish ball ingredients except the fish in a mortar or food processor and pound or process to a paste. Add the fish and pound or process until the paste is very smooth. Remove and discard any bones or pieces of skin or other tough bits you come across. Set aside.

Place a large heavy pot over high heat. Add 1 cup water, the julienned radish and carrots, and 1 teaspoon of the salt. Bring to a boil, cover, and cook over medium-high heat until the vegetables are just tender, about 8 minutes. Remove from the heat and drain, reserving the cooking water. Set aside.

Meanwhile, make the fish balls: Pick up about ¼ teaspoon of the pounded paste with lightly oiled fingers and lightly roll between your thumb and fingertips to form a ball about ½ inch in diameter (not more). Place on a lightly oiled large plate. Repeat with the remaining mixture.

Salt collection at Lac Rose, north of Dakar

Heat the peanut oil in a heavy pot over medium-high heat. When it is hot, add the fish balls and fry until browned and crisp on the outside, turning occasionally, about 8 minutes. Remove the balls from the oil with a slotted spoon and set aside.

Add the onion to the hot oil. Stir the tomato paste into the reserved vegetable cooking water and add to the pot, then stir well. Add the chopped tomatoes, the optional cabbage, and the cayenne and stir. Add the dried chiles, garlic, cider vinegar, tamarind paste or Maggi cube, and the remaining 1 teaspoon salt. Bring to a boil, stirring occasionally, then simmer for several minutes.

Add the steamed carrots and radish to the sauce. Add the fish balls and ½ cup water, or more if necessary to cover the fish balls and vegetables, and simmer over medium heat for about 15 minutes. Remove the hot chiles before serving if you wish, and serve hot over plain rice.

**Notes:** Josie actually used eight tiny dried red chiles grown in the Richard Toll area inland from Saint-Louis. They are medium-hot. We have not seen them here in North America, so have substituted dried red chiles, usually imported from Thailand (see Glossary). The chiles are used whole and then removed either before serving or as people eat the stew; they are not meant to be eaten.

For a simpler, vegetarian accompaniment to rice, omit the fish balls; reduce the oil to ⅓ cup.

# Lamb and Peanut Stew

## *mafe*

**Serves 6 to 8 with rice**

INLAND FROM SAINT-LOUIS, ALL MEMORIES OF COOL OCEAN BREEZES VANISH. The landscape is red sand with the occasional village or herd of cattle. Then a turn north to the Senegal River, and suddenly there are tall grasses and green trees. The river's internal delta of small waterways supports a huge population of migratory birds, especially in and around the Parc National du Djouj, one of the world's greatest bird sanctuaries. With assistance from many countries, Senegal and Mauretania have also established an ambitious irrigation scheme along the river that is meant to support large-scale rice cultivation and market gardening.

Outside a small restaurant in Dakar

Farther inland still is the market town of Richard Toll. In the hard light and unrelenting heat of the early afternoon (and my visit was in mid-March, not yet the really hot season), the main street was almost deserted. My two companions were looking for a little restaurant they knew well, a favorite because of its amiable proprietors and outstanding *mafe*. We drove along until we came to it and then were grateful for the shelter of the thatched roof. There were other customers sitting on the mats on the floor and we joined them. We ordered *mafe* and by the time we'd washed and dried our hands, the platter was ready to be set between us on the mat. The dish was steaming hot, with gleaming reddish brown sauce on pristine, grown-near–Richard Toll rice. The food was delicious as well as extraordinarily satisfying in the dry heat of midday, even though until then I would have thought of lamb and peanut sauce as a rich wintertime dish. We finished the meal with the traditional three glasses of green tea and then sat idly watching the baking street and chatting about this and that until the shadows had lengthened and it was time to go.

The *mafe* I ate that day was a streamlined restaurant version with few vegetables, only a little okra, finely chopped, and some carrots, but no cabbage, turnips, or sweet potato. I was told that farther inland in Senegal, and also in many parts of Mali, *mafe* is made with even fewer vegetables. People work with what is available. Closer to the coast, the other vegetables are more usual and the blend of vegetables begins to resemble the combination found in *diebou dien*. Suit yourself.

2 pounds boneless lamb shoulder

2 large onions

1 large sweet potato, peeled and cut into 1-inch cubes (optional)

2 large carrots, peeled and cut into 1-inch cubes

½ pound okra, chopped into ½-inch lengths

2 tablespoons peanut oil

2 cloves garlic, minced

3 tablespoons tomato paste

4 to 5 cups water

2 large or 4 medium tomatoes or 6 drained canned tomatoes, chopped

2 teaspoons dried shrimp (see Glossary), minced or pounded to a powder (or substitute 2 dried scallops, minced)

2 teaspoons salt, or to taste

⅓ cup natural (unsweetened) peanut butter

2 serrano chiles or dried red chiles

Freshly ground black pepper

Cut the meat into approximately ½-inch cubes, discarding any large chunks of fat. Cut the onions lengthwise in half, then thinly slice lengthwise. If the onions are large, cut the slices once or twice crosswise. Place the sweet potato, carrots, and okra in a bowl of cold water until ready to use.

In a large heavy pot, heat the oil over medium-high heat. Toss in half the onions and half the garlic. Stir briefly, then add the meat. Cook, stirring frequently, until the meat is browned on all sides, about 5 minutes.

In a small bowl, mix together the tomato paste and 1 cup of the water. Add to the meat, together with the chopped tomatoes and dried shrimp or scallops. Add 2 more cups water and bring to a boil. Add the carrots and sweet potatoes, and cook for 5 minutes. Add the okra, along with 1 to 2 cups more water if necessary to cover the vegetables, and bring back to a boil. Add the salt and cook at a strong simmer for 10 minutes.

In a small bowl, blend the peanut butter with 1 cup of the hot broth. Stir into the lamb mixture, then add the chiles, the remaining onion and garlic, and pepper to taste. Simmer over medium-low heat until most of the water has evaporated and the sauce is fairly thick, 15 to 20 minutes. Taste and adjust the seasonings. Serve over plain rice.

**Note:** A young man I met in Saint-Louis talked at length about his favorite version of *mafe*, *mafe aux crabes*, a coastal version of an inland dish. We've never tried to make it, but judging from his pleased expression as he described his mother's crab *mafe*, we'll love it when we do give it a try.

# An Afternoon Walk

One afternoon in Marsassoum, after lunch and a nap, my hostess-teacher Sarta's young nephew Alfo and his friend Bala walked with me to a neighboring village. We set out at about three o'clock. Once out of Marsassoum, the road was a shadeless dirt track through a landscape that seemed dry and uninhabited. But in fact there were human traces everywhere. About two miles out of the village, over to one side were some trees and patches of green, almost a violent color in the dry landscape. "That's rice, a second crop growing near some natural springs," Alfo and Bala explained. "The people who cultivate these fields come from the next village. They're Menjok [a small minority in the Casamance]." As we walked over to see, we passed some dry cultivated earth. "These are rice paddies too, but only in the rainy season. We make small earth walls to hold in the water." There was a patchwork of small tilled areas, each bounded by a two- to three-inch-high earth wall, waiting for the autumn rains to make them fertile.

Meanwhile, in the watered area, women were calf-deep in water, transplanting young rice plants and using buckets to haul springwater to drier areas of the paddy. Here the air was soft and humid. There were egrets standing in the water watching and looking pleased.

Once back on the road, time seemed to stand still as we walked and sweated our way along, until at last we arrived in the village. We headed for the family house of Mamadou Dabo, another of Sarta's nephews and my contact in Dakar. His parents were away, but I met the rest of his family, took lots of pictures of everyone, and gratefully sipped dipperfuls of cool water.

Then we headed back up the road to Marsassoum, but this time the sun was lower in the sky and there was a touch of coolness in the air.

**left and below**

Steaming rice over sauce in Marsassoum

Girl carrying fruit in Casamance

# Rice Pudding

THIS SIMPLE STOVETOP RICE PUDDING, A SENEGALESE ADAPTATION OF WHAT was probably a dish introduced by the French, is delicious comfort food. The pudding cooks to a creamy texture. It can be made ahead, then served chilled or at room temperature. We prefer ours slightly warm, except in the heat of summer. As the pudding cools, it thickens; you can thin it if you wish by stirring in a little warm milk.

1 cup long-grain rice (Thai jasmine or American long-grain, *not* converted or parboiled)

4 cups whole milk

Pinch of salt

One vanilla bean

½ cup sugar

Place the rice on a hard work surface and cover with a cotton cloth. Use a large rolling pin or a bottle to crush and break some of the rice grains.

Rinse the rice with cold water. In a heavy medium pot, bring 4 cups water to a rapid boil. Add the rice, stir gently, bring back to a boil, and let cook for 3 minutes. Drain in a sieve.

Place 3½ cups of the milk in the pot and heat just to a boil. Sprinkle in the rice and add the salt and vanilla bean. Stir well, cover, reduce the heat to low, and let cook for 15 minutes. Remove from the heat and take out the vanilla bean.

In a small bowl, dissolve the sugar in the remaining ½ cup milk. Add little by little to the cooked rice mixture, stirring gently with a fork. Serve the pudding slightly warm or at room temperature, on its own or with slices of ripe mango or other fresh fruit.

**Note:** As the rice pudding stands and cools, it thickens. Consequently, leftover pudding needs to be moistened with a little more milk and warmed to regain its smooth, moist texture. To serve leftover pudding, warm about ½ cup milk in a medium pot until not quite boiling. Lower the heat to very low, add the rice pudding, and stir gently to moisten and warm it.

California rice fields at harvest

Inset: Slave quarters at Mansfield Plantation near
Georgetown, South Carolina

# Hoppin' John, Rice and Peas

In the southern United States, as in Brazil and most of the Caribbean, rice culture has its roots in Africa. As legend has it, rice first came to North America aboard a British sailing ship enroute from Madagascar to England. The ship had taken refuge in Charleston, South Carolina, seeking repair, and after receiving assistance, the ship's captain left behind a bag of Malagasy rice to show his gratitude. The rice, a long-grain Asian rice of the indica type, was then planted, whereupon it flourished, and there began the long and important history of America's first rice, called Carolina Gold.

Carolina Gold came to be highly prized both in the United States and in Europe. Great quantities were sold by the plantation owners, who grew rich on the trade. But it was plantation slaves from West Africa, from what is now Senegal, Gambia, the Ivory Coast, and Nigeria, who had previous knowledge of rice, of how to grow rice and cook it. It was these plantation slaves who made the whole trade possible, and it was their own West African methods of preparing rice that left the longest legacy.

The best-known Carolina rice dish is a version of rice and peas called Hoppin' John, made with long-grain rice and cowpeas or black-eyed peas and flavored with a bit of smoky pork. Jessica Harris, who has explored the history of African-American foods and traced connections back to African sources, points out in *Iron Pots and Wooden Spoons* that this smoky pork flavor probably replaced the smokiness of the dried fish often used

A small eatery (*fonda*) in the old Oaxaca, Mexico, market

Kalustyan's retail and mail-order rice supplier, in New York City

to flavor rice dishes in West Africa. Like many of the rice dishes in the Southern rice kitchen, Hoppin' John makes use of the staples available to laboring people farming the land: rice, pork, beans, and greens.

By the 1930s, rice cultivation had died out along the Carolina and Georgia coasts. There were no slaves to work the fields and the wet ground that had been ideal for intensive cultivation using manual labor was too boggy and difficult for machine farming. Rice could be produced more profitably elsewhere. Rice cultivation moved inland to Texas, Louisiana, Arkansas, Missouri, and also to Northern California. Although enormous quantities of rice are grown in all these states, most of it is for export or for distribution throughout North America. Of all the rice-growing states, only in Louisiana, in the Cajun and Creole kitchens, is there a strong culinary rice tradition.

In Mexico, fairly soon after the Spanish Conquest (and before large-scale cultivation of Carolina Gold began in Georgia and South Carolina), the Spanish introduced rice, and it soon became a staple grain. The rice was not Spanish-style short- or medium-grain rice, but long-grain Asian rice imported from the Philippines, Spain's principal Asian colony. The trade was an important one for Spain. Later, rice was also cultivated in Mexico.

Perhaps because the rice the Mexicans were first introduced to was very different (long-grain and drier) from Spanish rice, the rice dishes traditionally prepared and eaten in Mexico are very unlike *los arroces* of Spain. The rice is first fried in oil and then cooked in flavored broth, but the texture of the finished dish is quite different from Spanish rice, and so is its place in the meal. Mexican rice dishes resemble in texture more the flavored rices of Persia (Iran). They are eaten either as a *sopa seca* (literally, "dry soup," a kind of pasta course that comes after the soup and before the main dish) or as a side to accompany a main dish. Rick Bayless, passionate explorer and practitioner of traditional Mexican cuisine, tells us that in most Mexican households, rice dishes are made with medium-grain rice, though long-grain rice may also be used.

In the Caribbean and South America, the history of rice is mixed. Some islands, such as Cuba, were Spanish-controlled and participated in the Mexico-Philippine trade, while at the same time having a strong connection to the mother country. Consequently, *los arroces* in

*Zapotec woman in Ocotlán*

Cuba, rice-combo dishes influenced by the Spanish rice tradition, may be cooked using medium- to short-grained japonica rices, just as rice dishes are prepared in Spain. However, plain white rice, the essential food in many meals, eaten with beans, or a *picadillo* or meat stew, is always made with long-grain rice, white and fluffy, like Carolina-style rice. Other Caribbean islands were part of the Carolina-Georgia rice sphere and developed pilaf-style rice habits, using long-grain rice. Throughout the Caribbean, the best-known everyday rice dish is a version of rice and peas, in some places known as peas and rice. In Cuba, the dish is made with black turtle beans and is known as *moros y christianos*, a reference to the history of the Arab conquest of Spain and their eventual expulsion in 1492.

Rice is grown in many countries of Central and South America, most important, in Brazil, as well as in Peru, Colombia, Venezuela, Argentina, and Costa Rica. In Brazil, an African-style rice culture took root, adapting to the ingredients available in the New World.

Wild rice is not a rice in the botanical sense (it is the seed of a wild grass called *Zizania aquatica*). It has been gathered and eaten by the Chippewa, Ojibway, and other Native American peoples for over a thousand years. Until well after the arrival of the Europeans, which was followed by the introduction of wheat and wheat flour, wild rice, together with corn and beans, was a vital staple for the people living near the Great Lakes.

Wild rice can be eaten as an accompaniment to stews or to roasted or grilled meats or vegetables. Traditionally at the beginning of harvest it is eaten with wild duck or woodcock. It can also be combined with brown rice and flavorings and used as a stuffing, or sweetened with maple syrup as a dessert.

# Plain Long-Grain Rice

**Makes about 5½ cups rice**

IN THE CAROLINAS AND IN CUBA, PLAIN RICE IS ALWAYS WHITE AND fluffy, the standard most Americans still follow for rice cooking. That texture depends on a good long-grain rice, cooked with a little salt and coated with a little oil of some kind after cooking. Even if you are in a hurry, take the time to let the rice stand for ten minutes after cooking to "steam" (in South Carolina parlance), then add butter, oil, or drippings, stir or fluff gently, and serve. The resting time gives the starches in the grain time to firm up so that it emerges fluffy and with each grain separate.

2 cups Carolina or other American long-grain rice

2½ cups water

½ teaspoon salt

1 to 2 tablespoons melted butter, bacon drippings, or olive oil

Wash the rice thoroughly and drain in a sieve. Place in a heavy medium pot with the water and salt and bring to a boil. Cover tightly, lower the heat to medium-low, and cook for 15 minutes.

Remove the rice from the heat, wrap the lid in a cotton cloth or tea towel, place on the pot (to absorb the steam), and let stand for 10 to 20 minutes. Remove the lid, add the butter, drippings, or oil, and stir gently with a fork to mix. Replace the cloth-wrapped lid and let stand for another 10 to 20 minutes before serving.

**Alternative:** The same fluffy result can be achieved by cooking the rice following the directions in *The Carolina Rice Kitchen*: Place a large pot of water on to boil. Sprinkle in the rice and salt and bring back to a boil. Cook until just tender, then drain the rice in a sieve, place it back in the pot, and cover tightly with a lid wrapped in a cotton cloth. Place over low heat to steam for 30 minutes. Drizzle on a little butter, or melted drippings, or oil and fluff gently with a fork before serving. This is very like the method used for gobindavog (see page 240).

# Long-Grain Brown Rice

**Makes 5 cups rice**

THERE ARE A NUMBER OF LONG-GRAIN BROWN RICES AVAILABLE. THEY TAKE longer to cook than their milled and polished cousins, but they also have a more satisfying grain flavor, particularly suited for partnering strong flavors such as those of hearty stews. We cook long-grain brown rice by the absorption method. If you are preparing the rice to accompany dishes from the New World, cook it in salted water and drizzle on a little oil or melted butter or bacon drippings after the cooking is completed if you wish. If you are using the rice to accompany East Asian dishes, then cook it plain, without salt or fat.

Ripe Carolina Gold rice photographed at Mansfield Plantation

Brown rice uses more cooking water than long-grain white rice and as it comes to a boil may give off a little bran, creating a pale brown foam. Just skim this off, as directed below, and proceed.

> 2 cups long-grain brown rice (see Note)
> 4 cups water

Wash the rice thoroughly under cold running water until the water runs clear. Drain in a sieve (and let stand for 15 minutes if you have time).

Place the rice in a heavy medium pot with a tight-fitting lid. Add the 4 cups water and place over high heat. Bring to a boil, stir gently with a wooden spoon, and let boil, uncovered, for about 1 minute. As the rice boils, use a wooden spoon to skim off and discard any foam. Cover, lower the heat to a bare simmer, and cook for 40 minutes, without lifting the lid. Test for doneness: The grains will still be a little firm but should be softened and cooked through. Remove from the heat and let stand, covered, for 15 to 20 minutes. Turn gently with a wooden rice paddle or flat wooden spoon before serving.

**Note:** We prefer to use organically grown rice when preparing brown (unmilled) rices, since we've been told that residues from pesticides can remain in the bran layer (which is milled off to produce white rice). Organic brown rices are available in natural foods stores and some specialty stores.

# Parboiled Long-Grain White Rice

Much of the plain white rice sold in the United States is parboiled rice. You may find, in a specialty store or in your local grocery store, converted rice that has not been precooked. Regular parboiled rice generally requires a longer cooking time than nonparboiled rice because the starches in the grain gelatinize and harden when the rice is heated and then cooled during the parboiling process. See page 242 for a detailed discussion of parboiled rices, and see Index for other parboiled rices.

2 cups parboiled long-grain white rice      ½ teaspoon salt (optional)
2½ cups water

If you wish, wash the rice well under cold running water until the water runs clear and drain well in a sieve.

Place the rice in a heavy medium pot with the water and optional salt. Bring to a vigorous boil, then cover tightly and lower the heat to a simmer. Let cook for 20 minutes, then remove from heat and let stand for 10 to 15 minutes before fluffing with a fork or a wooden paddle and serving.

# Parboiled Long-Grain Brown Rice

**Makes 8 cups rice**

MOST PARBOILED RICE IS SOLD MILLED AND POLISHED, BUT IN SPECIALTY stores you can find parboiled brown rice. For parboiling, after the harvest, rice is left in its tough outer husk and boiled briefly, often under pressure, then dried. The husk is then removed. The brown rice that results has a different appearance and nutritional profile from non-parboiled brown rice, and slightly different cooking characteristics.

During parboiling, B vitamins and other nutrients move from the bran layer into the center or endosperm of the rice, while oils move out into the bran layer. Consequently, parboiled brown rice is somewhat oily. (If stored in a paper bag, it leaves a noticeable oily trace on the paper.) Since oils don't keep well, this rice should be stored in a very cool place, or even in the refrigerator, and in any case not kept for long.

When cooked, grains of parboiled brown rice are bouncy and separate, tender yet firm. They have none of the chewiness we normally associate with cooked brown rice. The parboiled brown rices we have tried are a pretty pale yellow beige color when cooked. The grains fatten as they cook, so they look wider rather than longer after cooking. We like the taste and texture of this rice very much.

2 cups parboiled long-grain brown rice          1 teaspoon salt (optional)
4 cups water

Rinse the rice well in cold water and drain; repeat until the water runs clear.

Place the rice in a large wide heavy pot with the water and optional salt. Bring to a vigorous boil. After 30 seconds, cover and lower the heat to low. Cook, covered, for 45 minutes; after 35 to 40 minutes, remove the lid, stir very briefly to bring the bottom grains to the top, then cover again and continue cooking. Let stand for 10 minutes before serving.

**Note:** This rice makes very good Thai-style fried rice. Because the grains stay separate, they are easy to stir-fry—there's no need to break up clumps of cold rice as there is with Thai jasmine. The rice holds its shape well during the stir-frying required for fried rice. It is also good in Quick Onion Pilaf (page 278) or as a substitute for long-grain brown rice in any recipe not requiring the grains to stick together or be compressed.

# Louisiana Pecan and Popcorn Rice

*Makes over 8 cups rice*

WE HAD LONG HEARD OF LOUISIANA PECAN RICE AND WONDERED WHERE THE pecans came into it. Now we know—they're in the aroma as it cooks and very subtly in the pleasing flavor of the cooked grain. Similarly, popcorn rice has nothing to do with puffed grains and everything to do with the sweet nutty, buttery aroma of the rice.

Louisiana pecan and popcorn rices are available from specialty stores and by mail order (see Mail-Order Sources, page 438). They are closely related aromatic long-grain rices, which we have found only parboiled, never plain. Parboiled Louisiana pecan and Louisiana popcorn rices have pale yellow grains when raw. When cooked, the grains butterfly, or split open, and become fatter and very bouncy. They don't stick to each other at all.

2 cups Louisiana pecan rice or
   popcorn rice

2½ cups water

1 teaspoon salt (optional)

If you wish, wash the rice well in cold water until the water runs clear, and drain well in a sieve.

Place the rice in a heavy medium pot with the water and optional salt. Bring to a vigorous boil, then cover and lower the heat to a simmer. Let cook for 20 minutes, then remove from the heat and let stand for 15 minutes before fluffing with a fork or a wooden paddle and serving.

**Note:** If you find a nonparboiled version of either rice, you should cook it like Plain Long-Grain Rice (page 385).

# Hoppin' John with a Side of Peas

IF YOU ARE FROM THE SOUTH CAROLINA COAST, CHANCES ARE THAT ON NEW Year's Day you eat Hoppin' John and collards. The rice and beans bring good luck and the collards bring "greenbacks." Even if you're far from the beauty and mystery of coastal South Carolina, Hoppin' John is a pleasure to make and an even greater pleasure to eat, especially on a damp or chilly day.

Hoppin' John is yet another version of rice and legumes or "peas and rice," this time flavored with smoked pork. Black-eyed peas or the traditional Carolina coast cowpeas (sometimes called red peas) are cooked with pork hocks or bacon in water. The pork gives the peas a rich smoky flavor. Then rice is added and cooked with the peas to make the simple "purloo" called Hoppin' John.

Cowpeas are native to West Africa and are still grown and eaten there. They traveled to North America during the slave trade. Because the peas are so moist and flavorful (whether you use cowpeas or black-eyed peas), we like to cook extra. We serve the extra on the side with the Hoppin' John. To make only the Hoppin' John, reduce the quantity of peas to 1 cup, and halve the quantities given for onion, chiles, meat, and water.

2 cups black-eyed peas or cowpeas, soaked in cold water for at least 4 hours, or overnight, and drained

1 large onion, finely chopped

1 to 2 fresh or dried hot chiles (see Glossary) or 1 teaspoon cayenne pepper

2 to 3 (1 to 1½ pounds) pork hocks or ½ pound Canadian bacon, in one piece

Water

Salt (optional)

1 cup long-grain rice, washed well in cold water and drained

Place the peas, onion, chiles or cayenne, and hocks or bacon in a large heavy pot and add 8 cups water. Bring to a boil and skim off and discard any foam. Boil gently, uncovered, for 1 to 1½ hours, until the peas are very tender but not mushy. Check occasionally to ensure that there is enough water and that the peas are not sticking; add more hot water if necessary. When the peas are done, taste for salt and add if you wish.

Transfer half the peas and liquid and one pork hock (if using) to a large heavy saucepan with a tight-fitting lid and set the remaining peas aside. Add the rice to the saucepan and if necessary add a little water so the rice is covered by ½ inch of liquid (place the tip of your index finger on top of the rice and peas; the water should come up to the first joint).

Bring to a boil, stirring occasionally to prevent sticking or burning, then cover and lower the heat to medium-low. Cook for 20 minutes, without lifting the lid, or until the rice is tender, with dry and separate grains. Let stand, covered, for 10 minutes.

Slice the meat from the hocks or slice the Canadian bacon. Heat the remaining peas. Transfer the Hoppin' John to a serving bowl and serve with the extra peas in another serving dish, topped with the sliced hock meat or bacon.

Hoppin' John's in Charleston, South Carolina

# Collard Greens

WHEN WE VISITED SOUTH CAROLINA, IT WAS WINTERTIME, AND BY THE SIDE of the small roads between the highway and our rented house on Edisto Island, there were vegetable stands loaded with stacks of dark green collards. One day, on the advice of Hoppin' John (John Martin Taylor of Charleston), we turned down a small dirt lane off the Edisto road to find Pink's. Pink is an institution around Edisto. She has a small produce shop beside her house, full of ultrafresh seasonal fruits and vegetables. A few days later, just before New Year's, we stopped in again at Pink's for a huge armload of crisp collards, then rushed home to cook them.

Sign for George & Pink's vegetable stand on Edisto Island

Collards are tough-stemmed vigorous greens with smooth leaves. They belong to the *brassica* family and are related to kale. Collards grow in a bunch from a central stalk. In the South, bunches are tied in groups of four to eight and sold in big bundles. Allow half a bunch of collards per person, or a little more, since by the time the greens are cleaned and the leaves stripped from their tough central stalks, quantities shrink. And anyway, leftovers are delicious.

½ pound smoked pork, ham, or
    Canadian bacon, in one piece
8 cups water
4 bunches collards

1 or 2 hot chiles
Salt and freshly ground pepper to taste

### Accompaniment
Sliced Chiles in Vinegar (recipe follows)

Place the pork and water in a large nonreactive pot and bring to a vigorous boil. Lower the heat and let simmer, uncovered, for 30 minutes, while you prepare the greens.

Fill a large sink with cold water. Pull the stalks off each bunch of collards, then, one by one, strip the collard leaves off the tough stalks and discard the stalks. Place the leaves in the cold water and swish around well, then remove from the water. Tear each leaf into 4 to 5 pieces, or slice as follows: Make a stack of about 6 leaves, roll up tightly, and slice across the roll into 1-inch strips.

Transfer the sliced greens to the pot and stir and turn to wet and compress them. Raise the heat and bring back to a boil, then lower the heat to medium and cook, uncovered, at a medium boil for 15 minutes, or until tender. You can serve the greens, once they are tender, by draining them, or you can follow tradition and continue to simmer them, over medium-low heat, until almost all the liquid has evaporated and the collards are a very cooked dark green. (We have prepared and eaten collards both ways. Not having been raised with long-cooked greens, we prefer them cooked until just tender. However, the long-cooked tradition produces an intensely flavored dish that is ideal with plain rice.)

Season the cooked greens with salt and pepper. (The length of cooking time affects the intensity of the flavor from the meat and hence the amount of salt needed.) Slice the meat and serve beside or mixed into the collards. Pass the chiles in vinegar so guests can drizzle them on as they wish.

Note: Leftover collards are delicious. Heat a little bacon fat or olive or peanut oil in a heavy skillet, lightly brown some minced garlic, and then stir-fry the collards to reheat and flavor. You can also, as John Martin Taylor suggests in his classic *Low-Country Cooking*, toss in a minced hot chile to spice things up. Serve for breakfast with a fried egg or two and biscuits or toast.

# Sliced Chiles in Vinegar

Makes about ¾ cup chiles

¾ cup white or cider vinegar

1 teaspoon sugar

Pinch of salt

1 or 2 Hungarian wax or other large mildly hot chiles

Place the vinegar in a small nonreactive saucepan and heat gently. Stir in the sugar and salt until well dissolved. Set aside.

Cut off and discard the chile stems. Cut the chiles lengthwise in half and discard the membranes and seeds. Finely slice. You should have about ½ cup chopped chiles.

Place the chiles in a medium bowl and pour over the warm vinegar mixture. If you have the time, let stand for 30 minutes before serving to allow the flavors to blend. The chiles can be prepared ahead and store in a well-sealed nonreactive container in the refrigerator.

# Shrimp Gumbo

GUMBO IS A SLOW-SIMMERED STOVETOP DISH, A CROSS BETWEEN THICK SOUP and stew, that is traditionally served over plain white rice in Louisiana. It is a close cousin to the *callaloo* of Trinidad (usually made with okra and crab or chicken). In some ways it is most like the *sauce* dishes served over rice in West Africa, with their combinations of vegetables, a little meat or fish or smoked oysters, and lots of flavorful sauce to help the rice go down.

The word *gumbo* comes from *gombo,* a West African word for "okra." A classic gumbo starts with fat (chicken fat, pork lard, or bacon drippings) and some flour to make a roux. Once the roux has browned, celery, green peppers, and onions are added and cooked (like a Spanish *sofrito*) until soft. From there, methods vary. Often, as here, okra is added and slow cooked with very little or no extra liquid until well softened and starting to brown. If chicken or sausage (*andouille*) are used, they go in early; when there's only shrimp, as here, it is added near the end of cooking. The dish cooks and simmers until done, the okra helping to thicken the sauce and the slow-simmering giving the flavors time to blend.

In this shrimp gumbo, the okra is cooked down, then the broth is added and flavored with wine or lemon juice, and the shrimp briefly boiled until cooked. Serve hot over Plain Long-Grain Rice (page 385) or Plain Cuban Rice (page 408).

3 tablespoons chicken fat or bacon fat (or substitute olive oil)

2 tablespoons all-purpose flour

2 medium onions, minced

1 green bell pepper, stem, seeds, and membranes discarded, and cut into small dice

1 cup finely chopped celery

1 teaspoon cayenne pepper

1 pound okra, stems and any tough tips removed, and sliced into ¼-inch lengths

3 cups mild fish stock or chicken stock or water

¼ cup dry white wine or fresh lemon juice

1 pound shrimp, peeled or unpeeled, deveined if you wish

¼ cup chopped fresh flat-leaf parsley

1½ teaspoons salt, or to taste

Generous grinding of black pepper

In a large heavy pot, heat the fat over medium heat. Stir in the flour and cook, stirring, until well browned. Add the onions, bell pepper, and celery and cook, stirring, until well softened, 10 to 15 minutes. Add the cayenne, okra, and ½ cup of the stock or water and cook, stirring frequently, over medium-low heat until the okra is completely softened and shapeless, about 30 minutes. If the okra begins to stick before it is completely cooked, add a little more liquid.

Add the remaining stock or water a cup at a time, stirring to blend in the okra. Bring to a boil, add the wine or lemon juice, and simmer for 10 minutes. Bring to a vigorous boil and add the shrimp, parsley, and seasonings. Cook the shrimp until its color changes completely, about 3 minutes. Taste and adjust the seasonings if necessary. Serve hot over rice.

Note: This version of gumbo is mildly chile hot. To increase the heat, add 1 or more minced serranos, or increase the cayenne to 1½ teaspoons or more.

Okra for sale in South Carolina

# Leftover Long-Grain Rice, Carolina Style

**Serves 2**

IN *THE CAROLINA RICE COOKBOOK,* REPRODUCED IN FACSIMILE IN KAREN Hess's *The Carolina Rice Kitchen,* there's a short recipe for reheating rice that tells us to "take any cold dinner rice and fry in butter until brown." If you're starting with an already flavored

Roadside produce stand south of Charleston

rice such as the Mexican rices or the *pulaos* in this chapter, then simply heating the rice briefly in oil or butter is one option.

But if the leftover rice you're starting with is plain or minimally flavored, you will find this quick rice fry-up a pleasure. It uses the ingredients and flavors of traditional Carolina *pulaos*—bacon, onion, green pepper, and tomato—to transform leftover plain rice into an almost-*pulao.* This technique is especially appropriate for dry, fluffy long-grain rices such as Carolina, basmati, and Texmati, or for parboiled rices

like rosematta, Louisiana pecan or popcorn, or parboiled brown rice. If you use butter or olive oil instead of bacon drippings, the flavor will be less smoky but the dish will still be successful.

2 to 3 tablespoons bacon drippings (or substitute olive oil or butter)

1 medium onion, finely chopped

2 to 3 scallions, cut into ¼-inch lengths (optional)

½ green bell pepper, cut into small dice

1 to 2 fresh or canned medium tomatoes, chopped, with juices (optional)

1 teaspoon salt

Generous grinding of black pepper

3 cups cooked long-grain rice (see headnote)

### Optional garnish

½ cup fresh flat-leaf parsley leaves, coarsely torn

2 fried eggs

Heat the bacon fat (or butter or oil) in a large heavy skillet or a large wok over medium heat. Add the onion and cook, stirring frequently, until well softened and starting to brown, about 10 minutes. Add the scallions and cook for 1 minute. Add the bell pepper, stir well, and cook until softened, 5 to 7 minutes. Add the optional tomatoes, with their juices, and stir until completely blended in, then stir in the salt and black pepper.

Add the rice and stir and turn gently until the flavorings are well distributed and the rice is warmed through, about 1 minute, or longer if the rice has come straight from the refrigerator. Turn out onto two plates and serve, topped with flat-leaf parsley and the fried eggs if you wish. This is also good accompanied by a fresh green salad.

Note: To double the recipe to serve four, double all the ingredients, but sauté the onions and other vegetables in only three quarters of the drippings (or oil or butter). Sauté the vegetable flavor base completely, then remove half from the skillet and set aside. Add half the rice to the skillet, heat through, and transfer to two plates. Heat the remaining fat in the skillet, add the reserved vegetables, and when they are hot, stir in the remaining rice and repeat.

# Classic Low-Country Pulao with Chicken and Bacon

**Serves 6 to 8 as a main dish**

THIS EASY CLASSIC SOUTH CAROLINA *PULAO* RECIPE YIELDS A HUGE PLATTER of flavored rice topped with tender pieces of chicken and bacon that easily feeds eight, with a vegetable or salad on the side. The rice is rich with the flavors of simmered chicken and bacon, and made more aromatic with a little bay leaf, parsley, and thyme.

The recipe is an adaptation from several recipes for Carolina *pulao* that appear in Karen Hess's facsimile edition of *The Carolina Rice Cookbook* (see page 396). Rather than using a whole chicken, as some of the recipes suggest, we use the breasts, legs, and thighs from a large chicken, chopped with a cleaver into smaller pieces. This makes serving easier and also allows the rice to cook more evenly.

The dish begins by frying onions and bacon (mostly lean Canadian bacon, with a little regular bacon for its fat), then sautéing the chicken pieces before adding water, seasonings, and the rice. Several of the original recipes call for boiling the bacon and chicken, then cooking the rice with them in the flavored broth; others start by browning the chicken. We prefer the texture of meat that has been skillet-cooked first, before being simmered in water with the rice. Although traditional recipes that use this method tell us to "brown" the chicken, if you remove the skin, as we like to, chicken does not brown but instead lightens to become almost white.

We like to buy a whole free-range organic chicken, cut off the legs and breasts, and use the rest for making stock. You can also buy just legs and breasts if you wish, then chop them up (or have your butcher chop the chicken pieces). The dish takes about an hour from start to finish, but more than half of that is simmering and standing time. Serve it with one or more salads or with cooked vegetable dishes such as Collard Greens (page 392) or okra.

3 cups long-grain rice

3 pounds chicken parts or breasts and legs from one 4½- to 5-pound chicken, cut up

1 strip bacon, cut in half

About ¼ pound Canadian bacon, cut into 2 pieces

1 large onion, finely chopped

4 cups water

1 bay leaf

1 large sprig parsley

1 sprig thyme

1½ teaspoons salt

⅛ teaspoon freshly ground black pepper

Wash the rice throughly under cold running water until the water runs clear. Drain in a sieve and set aside.

Rinse the chicken, pat dry, and remove and discard the skin if you wish. Use a cleaver to separate the legs and thighs and chop each drumstick and thigh in half. Chop the whole breasts into quarters.

For the browning stage, it's easier to use two pans. We suggest that you use a large heavy skillet and the large heavy pot you will be using to cook the whole dish. Put both pans over medium heat and when they are hot, place half the bacon, including a little fat, if any, from the Canadian bacon, in each. When each pan is well greased with melted fat, add half the onion to each pan and fry for 2 to 3 minutes. Add the remaining Canadian bacon and the chicken pieces, dividing them between the two pans, and fry until the color of the chicken has changed, 8 to 10 minutes, turning the chicken and bacon as necessary.

Transfer the skillet contents to the large pot, then add the water, herbs, salt, and pepper. Bring to a vigorous boil. Skim off and discard any foam. Sprinkle in the rice, bring back to a boil, and stir briefly. Cover, lower the heat to medium-low, and cook for 20 minutes.

Lift off the lid, wrap it in a tea towel or cotton cloth, and replace it. Remove from the heat. Let stand, covered, for 15 to 20 minutes before serving.

Serve on a platter the traditional way, with the rice on the bottom and the chicken and bacon (cut into smaller pieces if you wish) on top. Discard the bay leaf and herb sprigs if you wish.

Historic threshing shed at Mansfield Plantation

# Wehani Rice

Makes about 3 cups rice

WEHANI IS A DESIGNER RICE, DEVELOPED BY THE LUNDBERG BROTHERS IN Northern California. The Lundbergs have become famous for their organically grown rice, for their rices are good-quality rices and free from chemical contamination.

Wehani is a beautiful red-colored rice with long grains. In the bin at the store, it looks very like red Thai rice, though not as fine. Wehani has bigger grains, both fatter and longer. When cooked, it loses a little redness and looks more like a red-tinted brown rice. It then resembles some of the good red rices we've seen in southern India. Because it is sold as whole-grain (unmilled) rice, like other brown rices it has a longer cooking time than white rices. It is also chewier and more filling than white rice, so that if served with side dishes, one cup of raw rice cooks up into enough rice for three or four people.

Rice storage and farm buildings at Lundberg Farms in the Sacramento Valley

Because of its distinctive fresh grain taste, Wehani pairs well with strong and hearty flavors, such as those of grilled mushrooms, meat, and slow-simmered stews.

Although the cooking instructions given by the growers call for two and a half cups water per cup of raw rice, we have found that two and a quarter cups water produce more reliable results. Extra water just makes the rice at the bottom of the pot somewhat soupy, though it still tastes fine. Because the rice is unpolished, it holds its shape well during cooking; on the other hand, it also needs to stand, untouched, in its heavy rice pot, for about thirty minutes after cooking to give the starches time to firm up. This is rather like the cooling time needed after bread comes out of the oven, before it can be sliced successfully.

During cooking, Wehani rice fills the house with a wonderful aromatic smell, slightly buttery and very mouthwatering. The taste is nutty and slightly sweet, the texture chewy but moist and tender; our children love it. We cook it without salt, the same way we cook Asian rices. Side dishes usually supply enough salty flavor, or your guests can salt it when eating if they wish.

1 cup Wehani rice

2¼ cups water or light stock

½ teaspoon salt (optional)

Rinse the rice well under cold running water until the water runs clear. Place in a sieve to drain thoroughly.

Transfer the rice to a heavy medium pot with a tight-fitting lid. Add the water or stock, bring to a boil over high heat, then cover and lower the heat to a simmer. Let cook for 45 minutes, then remove from the heat and let stand, still covered, for 30 minutes before serving.

**Note:** Leftovers are delicious reheated in chicken stock or broth; the rice keeps its shape and slight chewiness even when heated in plenty of liquid. We have also been known to eat leftover Wehani in the morning for breakfast, almost like porridge.

**Wehani stuffing for birds:** Wehani is very good when mixed with a plainer rice to stuff a turkey: We mix it with Thai jasmine rice about one to one. Sauté some chopped leeks and onions in olive oil, add some finely chopped mushrooms, and cook over medium-high heat until softened. Stir in the raw rice and cook over low heat for 2 minutes. Add water to not quite cover, bring to a boil, then simmer for 5 minutes. Season with a dash of soy sauce and some salt and pepper. Let cool completely, then transfer this mixture to the cavity of the turkey, leaving plenty of room for the rice to expand.

# Midwinter Soup with Wehani

Makes approximately 8 cups thick soup;
serves 6 as a soup course or 3 to 4 as a main course

WE HAVE BEEN ENJOYING THIS SOUP FOR YEARS, THOUGH UNTIL RECENTLY we always made it with barley. One day we decided to substitute Wehani for the barley, and it worked perfectly. It is an easy soup to make, thick and satisfying, great on a cold winter night. You can serve it as a soup course or make it the centerpiece of a meal.

½ cup dried porcini mushrooms, washed

2 cups boiling water

2 tablespoons olive oil

1 medium onion, diced

2 bay leaves

¼ teaspoon freshly ground black pepper

4 cups water or mild stock

1 cup Wehani rice or Black Japonica rice

1½ cups diced carrots (about ½ pound)

3 cups diced potatoes (about 1 pound)

1½ teaspoons salt

### Optional accompaniments

½ cup freshly grated Parmigiano-Reggiano or Pecorino

¼ cup chopped fresh flat-leaf parsley

Place the porcini in a medium bowl and pour the boiling water over. Let soak until softened, 20 to 30 minutes. Drain, reserving the soaking water. Coarsely chop the mushrooms and set aside.

In a large heavy pot, heat the oil over medium-high heat. Add the onion and cook until softened, 5 to 7 minutes. Add the mushrooms and stir briefly, then add the bay leaves, pepper, the reserved mushroom soaking water, the water or stock, and rice. Raise the heat and bring to a boil. Partially cover, lower the heat to medium-low, and simmer for 10 minutes.

Add the carrots and potatoes and bring back to a boil, then simmer, partially covered, over medium-low heat for 30 minutes, or until tender. If the liquid looks low, add ½ to 1 cup hot water. Add the salt and let simmer for another few minutes. Serve topped, if you wish, with a little grated cheese and/or fresh parsley, and place extra accompaniments on the table so guests can garnish their soup as they wish.

Note: You can also use leftover cooked Wehani or black Thai sticky rice or any of the parboiled rices, Black Japonica, or brown rice in this soup; use 2 to 3 cups cooked rice. Follow the instructions above (omitting the raw rice), and once the carrots and potatoes are cooked, stir in the rice and heat through. Soup made with leftover rice will be a little less thick.

# Black Japonica Rice

THIS IS ANOTHER SPECIALTY RICE DEVELOPED BY THE LUNDBERG BROTHERS of California. It is a mix of two rices: about 75 percent mahogany-red medium-grain rice and 25 percent black short-grain japonica-type rice. Neither rice is milled, so the mixture has the cooking characteristics of brown rice. The grains of Black Japonica gleam beautifully against the red when you see the raw grain in bulk. After thorough washing, some of the coating on the red rice comes off and the grain looks more mottled in color.   Because the rice is whole-grain, it, like brown rice, needs more water and a longer cooking time than white (milled) rice. There is not much aroma as the rice cooks. When done, it has a grainy, slightly nutty aroma and its taste, too, is grain-like rather than aromatic; it almost tastes like wheat berries. During cooking, the grains burst open as they absorb water, exposing the tender, almost-white grain inside. The cooked rice is reddish brown; it clumps together somewhat, but is less sticky than cooked Japanese-style white rice. The texture is somewhat chewy yet not tough.

If you plan to serve this rice to accompany Japanese or other East or Southeast Asian flavors, do not salt it. If you are using it as plain rice to accompany Western-style dishes, then do use salt during cooking if you wish.

Because of its slight chewiness and firm grains, this rice lends itself to reheating or to use in soups and stews. Because of its distinctive grain flavor, it's not a rice to serve plain with subtle tastes and textures; conversely, it stands up well to strong, meaty flavors (rich stocks, for example). It can be substituted in most recipes for brown rice or for Wehani. Serve as an attractive accompaniment to almost any savory dish. Alternatively, use to make Multicolored Black Rice Salad (page 404).

2 cups Black Japonica rice

4 cups water

1 teaspoon salt (optional, see headnote)

Wash the rice thoroughly under cold running water until the water runs clear. Place in a sieve to drain, then transfer to a heavy medium pot with a tight-fitting lid. Add the water and, if you want, the salt. Bring to a boil, uncovered, stir briefly, and cover. Lower the heat to medium-low, cover, and cook for 45 minutes.

Remove the rice from the heat and let stand for 30 to 45 minutes to firm up. Stir gently with a wooden paddle, then turn out onto a platter and serve.

# Multicolored Black Rice Salad

THE RICH WARM REDDISH BROWN OF COOKED BLACK JAPONICA MAKES A beautiful backdrop to the brilliant color of cooked bell peppers and fresh herbs. The rice stands up well to strong flavors. Its good grain taste is well complemented by the slight sweetness of the cooked peppers. This makes a great dish for a picnic or a potluck because it can be made ahead and keeps its flavor and texture while waiting.

6 cups cooked Black Japonica Rice
   (page 403)

¼ cup olive oil

1 small onion or 2 shallots, thinly sliced

3 cloves garlic, thinly sliced

2 bell peppers (one red and one yellow,
   or as available), stem, seeds, and
   membranes discarded, and cut into
   ½-inch squares

3 scallions, cut into ¼-inch lengths

1 tablespoon dry white wine

1 teaspoon soy sauce

½ teaspoon sugar

1 teaspoon salt, or to taste

About 8 chives, cut into 1½-inch lengths
   (optional)

Several leaves *shiso* (perilla, see
   Glossary) or sorrel, finely chopped
   (optional)

1 cup loosely packed fresh basil leaves or
   flat-leaf parsley leaves, or a mixture

2 tablespoons fresh lime or lemon juice

2 tablespoons cider vinegar

Japanese pepper (*sansho*, see Glossary)
   or freshly ground black pepper
   (optional)

Place the rice in a large serving bowl, breaking up any lumps with your fingers.

In a large heavy skillet, heat 2 tablespoons of the oil over medium-high heat. Add the onion or shallots and garlic and stir-fry until softened and starting to brown. Add the bell peppers and scallions and cook until softened. Add the wine, soy sauce, sugar, and salt. Cook 1 minute longer and remove from the heat. Add to the rice, together with the optional herbs, and turn gently to blend well.

Coarsely tear the basil or parsley leaves. In a small bowl, mix together the lime or lemon juice, vinegar, and the remaining 2 tablespoons olive oil. Add the fresh herbs and press and stir to release and blend the flavors.

Pour the dressing over the salad. Turn to mix well. Sprinkle on the optional Japanese pepper or black pepper, then taste and adjust the seasonings if you wish. Serve at room temperature. The salad may be made up to 2 hours ahead and stored covered at room temperature; this gives the flavors time to blend.

# Plain Wild Rice
## manohmin

**Makes 3 to 4 cups rice**

TRADITIONAL WILD RICE HARVESTING STILL GOES ON EVERY AUTUMN IN small lakes from Ontario to Minnesota. Two people in a canoe go out among the rice plants, one poling, the other using a double pole arrangement called "knockers" to bend the rice stalks over the canoe and then to slap the ripe rice off the stalks into the canoe. The work is hard and slow but still, on a good day two people can fill a canoe, bringing in about three hundred pounds of wild rice. The rice must then be dried so that it will keep. After a preliminary drying in the sun or over a slow fire, it is parched in a metal tub over a fire, to help loosen the husks. After an hour's parching and stirring, the husks have loos-

Wild rice with a grain of bomba (*left*) and Japanese (*right*) rice

ened. The parched rice is then milled by light pounding in a large barrel-shaped wooden mortar, and the husks are winnowed away.

In native tradition, wild rice—*manohmin*—and the wild rice harvest have great significance, not just as food but as an expression of the connection between the people and the land. On her wild rice home page on the Internet, Paula Giese talks of the importance of eating "first rice," the first wild rice harvested each year, with cooked wild fowl, offering and eating the rice with "peace and gratitude."

Traditionally harvested wild rice is very long (up to four inches) and a mix of colors, from blond to black. It cooks fairly quickly, with a smoky taste from the parching. Commercially grown and harvested "wild" rice has shorter grains, usually more broken grains, and a fairly uniform brown to black color. It lacks the smoky taste of the traditional rice and takes a little longer to cook. It is also less expensive than traditional wild rice. Commercial wild rice is often available in supermarkets.

Traditional wild rice can be mail-ordered (see Mail-Order Sources, page 438) or occasionally found in specialty stores. If you feel strongly, as we do, that wild rice traditions should be preserved and encouraged, take the trouble to find traditionally harvested wild rice and pay the extra. It's well worth it.

Since the wild rices you can buy differ greatly, we give the following recipe as a guideline, to be used together with the cooking instructions given by the grower on the package.

2 cups wild rice
8 cups water

Rinse the rice under cold running water. Place in a large heavy pot with the water. Bring to a boil, then cook, uncovered, at a low boil for about 35 minutes. Cover, lower the heat, and cook for 10 minutes longer, or until the rice is soft but not mushy. (If you want to add salt or oil, add only after cooking.)

Serve plain to accompany any vegetables or meat or use instead of brown rice in most recipes.

Note: If your raw rice is black, it has been sun-dried and will take about 15 minutes longer to cook.

# Anasazi Beans

ANASAZI BEANS ARE NATIVE TO THE AMERICAN SOUTHWEST. THEY'RE A VERY attractive mottled dark red and cream, and fortunately they are becoming more available in grocery stores across the country. They lose color when they're cooked, turning a pale pinkish color while holding on to a dark red patch around the seed hollow. If you can't find Anasazi beans, substitute kidney beans (similar cooking time) or small red beans (slightly shorter cooking time).

2 cups Anasazi beans, soaked overnight
   in two changes of water and drained

3 to 4 fresh sage leaves

2 teaspoons salt

2 tablespoons bacon drippings or butter

2 medium onions, minced

1 teaspoon dried chile pepper flakes, or
   to taste

2 tablespoons cider vinegar

4 cups cooked Plain Wild Rice (page 405)

## Optional garnish

Fresh flat-leaf parsley leaves, coarsely
   torn, or ¼ cup chopped fresh chives

Place the beans in a large heavy pot with the sage leaves and 8 cups of water. Bring to a rapid boil and let boil vigorously, uncovered, for about 5 minutes. Skim off and discard any foam that rises to the surface. Lower the heat to medium-low and simmer, partially covered, for 1 to 1½ hours (depending on the freshness of the beans), or until the beans are very tender.

Stir in the salt and cook for another 5 minutes. (The beans can be prepared ahead to this point and stored in a well-sealed container in the refrigerator or freezer. When ready to proceed, place the beans in a large pot and reheat gently.)

Meanwhile, heat the drippings or butter in a heavy medium skillet over medium heat. Add the onions and fry until well softened, about 12 minutes. Add the chile flakes and cider vinegar, stir well, and add to the beans.

Cook the beans for another minute, then serve hot, over the wild rice, topped with the optional herbs if you wish. The strong green of the herbs is beautiful against the pink of the cooked beans.

# Plain Cuban Rice

**Makes about 5½ cups rice**

THE GOAL IN COOKING PLAIN CUBAN RICE IS TO PRODUCE A LIGHT, WHITE, fluffy dish of rice, very like Carolina-style Plain Long-Grain Rice (page 385). The cooking method resembles the Persian *chelo* technique: The rice is cooked in plenty of water and thoroughly drained, then put back in the pot and tossed with a little oil or melted lard or butter to coat the grains. The rice then slow-steams until ready to be served, the bottom layer forming a delicious crust, here called the *raspa*, prized for its taste and chewiness just like the *tahdig* in *chelo*. Serve with Cuban Black Beans (page 409) or in place of any plain non–East Asian white rice.

2 cups American long-grain white rice

10 cups water

1 tablespoon salt

2 to 3 tablespoons melted butter or lard or warm olive oil

Wash the rice thoroughly in cold running water until the water runs clear. Drain well in a sieve. Place the water and salt in a large heavy pot and bring to a rapid boil. Sprinkle in the rice and bring back to a boil. Use a long-handled spoon to gently lift any rice off the bottom of the pot. Cook until just tender but still firm, about 5 minutes, then drain immediately in a sieve.

Put the rice back in the pot, drizzle with the butter, lard, or oil, and toss gently to coat. Shape into a gentle mound. Wrap the lid in a cotton cloth and cover the pot tightly. Place over medium heat and steam for 3 minutes, then reduce the heat to very low and steam for another 15 minutes. Set aside, covered, until ready to serve. Serve, together with the bottom crust, in a large shallow bowl or on a platter.

Ripe rice ready for harvest

# Cuban Black Beans
*frijoles negros*

Serves 6 with rice

THIS RICH-TASTING BEAN DISH IS MEANT TO BE SERVED OVER A MOUND OF white long-grain rice, preferably rice cooked Cuban-style (see page 408).

As with many bean dishes, we like to cook twice as many beans as we need, then freeze half. Cooked beans are always handy to have around. To thaw, just place in a pot with a little hot water over medium heat. If you're making this dish, put some rice on to cook and then prepare the sofrito while the frozen beans are warming. In less than thirty minutes, supper can be on the table.

2 cups small black beans, soaked overnight in water to cover by 2 inches and drained, or 6 cups cooked black beans

Approximately 7 cups water

2 bay leaves

1 lime, cut in half

### Sofrito

2 tablespoons bacon drippings, lard, or olive oil

About 2 ounces Canadian bacon, cut into small cubes (optional)

4 cloves garlic, minced

2 onions, minced

¼ teaspoon ground cumin

Sprig of oregano (optional)

1½ teaspoons salt

*If using dried beans,* place the soaked beans in a large heavy pot with 7 cups water and the bay leaves and bring to a boil. Cook until the beans are tender, 1½ to 2 hours, depending on your beans. Check occasionally to make sure the beans are not running dry, and add more water if necessary. Remove from the heat and add the lime halves. *If using cooked beans,* place in a pot and add the lime halves and enough water to moisten well.

In a heavy skillet, heat the drippings, lard, or oil over medium heat. Add the optional bacon, the garlic, and onions and cook until very soft, about 12 minutes. Stir in the cumin, the optional oregano, and the salt, then transfer this *sofrito* to the pot of beans.

Place the beans over medium-high heat, bring to a boil, and simmer for 15 minutes. Add more water if necessary to prevent sticking. Taste and adjust the seasonings. Serve hot over plain white rice.

**Alternative:** You can include bell peppers if you wish. Add 2 to 3 diced bell peppers (an assortment of colors is more interesting) to the bacon and onion sofrito.

# Jamaican Rice and Peas

VERSIONS OF THIS CLASSIC, A FIRST COUSIN OF HOPPIN' JOHN WITH A SIDE OF Peas (page 390), are made all around the Caribbean. As a satisfying one-dish meal, rice and peas is easy to prepare but subtle and distinctive in its taste. (The legumes we know as beans are called peas in the Caribbean.) You can eat it with pleasure over and over again. No wonder it holds claim to "national dish" status in Jamaica.

Basic ingredients are long-grain rice, kidney beans, and usually coconut milk; the rest are a combination of whatever else a particular cook likes to include in her or his rice and peas. We like this version, but you can leave out any or all of the optional ingredients (tomato, bell pepper, hot chile) if you wish. Serve this with guacamole or salsa and a green salad.

Because large legumes like kidney beans and chickpeas take a long time to cook, we like to cook them in large batches, unseasoned, and then freeze them in two-cup portions. If you're starting with precooked or canned kidney beans (or using a pressure cooker for your beans), this recipe takes less than half an hour.

1 cup kidney beans, soaked overnight in water to cover and drained, or 2½ cups cooked or canned kidney beans

6 cups water (1 cup if using canned or cooked beans)

2½ teaspoons salt (less if using salted canned beans)

1 tablespoon olive oil, vegetable oil, or bacon drippings

2 cloves garlic, minced

1 small onion, finely chopped

1¾ cups canned or fresh coconut milk (see Glossary)

1 large tomato, finely chopped (optional)

1 red bell pepper, stem, seeds, and membranes discarded, and chopped (optional)

2 to 3 sprigs thyme

1 Scotch bonnet or habanero chile (optional)

2 cups long-grain white rice, thoroughly washed and drained

Freshly ground black pepper

*If using soaked and drained kidney beans,* place the beans and water in a large heavy pot, bring to a boil, and boil until tender, about 2 hours. Add 1 teaspoon of the salt just as the cooking is completed. *If using canned or cooked beans,* place the beans and 1 cup water in a large heavy pot over medium heat and simmer until well warmed. If the beans are unsalted, stir in 1 teaspoon salt. Remove the beans from the heat.

Heat the oil or drippings in a heavy skillet over medium-high heat and add the garlic. When the garlic begins to change color, add the onion. Fry, stirring constantly, until the onion is translucent, about 5 minutes. Add the coconut milk, the optional tomato and red pepper, and the thyme. Bring almost to the boil, stir well, and add to the cooked beans.

Mix in the optional chile pepper and the drained rice and add enough water so that the rice is covered by ¾ inch. Add the remaining 1½ teaspoons salt and black pepper to taste. Bring to a full boil, stirring occasionally to keep the rice from sticking, cover, and reduce the heat to low. Let cook for 20 minutes, then remove from the heat and let stand for 10 minutes. Discard the chile and stir the rice and beans gently before serving.

The annual Caribana parade in Toronto

# Mexican Red Rice

Serves 4 as a main dish
or 6 as part of a larger meal

IN MEXICO, RICE MEANS MEDIUM-GRAIN ASIAN-STYLE RICE, NOT SPANISH-style rice. Rice was first brought to Mexico by the Spanish from their colony in the Philippines. Though some rice is cultivated in Mexico, the country still imports its rice.

Chiles and tomatoes for sale in the Oaxaca Valley

The goal when cooking Mexican rice is to end up with a light, fluffy dish in which the grain is imbued with flavor but still perfectly dry—not soupy or gooey. The technique used to achieve this result is not difficult, though it does call for a little of the cook's attention at the start.

Mexican cooks work with rice in a very special way, first cooking the rice in oil until golden, then simmering it in broth with other flavorings. The three main rice dishes in Mexico are red, green, and white rice, red being most common in restaurants and daily life. Though many red rice recipes just add raw tomato and onion to help flavor the cooking liquid, this one starts with grilling the vegetables, much as they are treated in rural Mexico. The smoky flavor they pick up from grilling gives the rice a subtle perfume. If you have a charcoal or gas grill or a gas stove, grill the vegetables; otherwise, reproduce the charred flavor by using a heavy cast-iron skillet to cook the vegetable flavorings.

2 cups medium-grain or long-grain rice

2 medium to large tomatoes

1 small white onion, cut into quarters, or ½ large white onion, cut in half

2 cloves garlic

3 tablespoons vegetable oil

3 cups unsalted chicken stock or vegetarian stock or water

2 teaspoons salt

1 medium carrot, cut lengthwise in half and thinly sliced, or 1 ear corn, kernels cut from the cob (optional)

### Optional garnish

½ cup loosely packed fresh coriander leaves or flat-leaf parsley leaves

Wash the rice thoroughly under cold running water until the water runs clear. Let drain in a sieve for 10 minutes.

In the meantime, grill the tomatoes, onion, and garlic over a grill or gas flame or dry-fry them in a large heavy skillet over high heat. *If grilling or cooking over a gas flame,* turn the vegetables frequently so all surfaces are exposed to the heat (tongs are the best tool for turning them). *If using a skillet,* place all the vegetables in the hot skillet and turn to scorch all over until blackened.

Transfer the vegetables to a food processor, blender, or large mortar and pestle (if using a mortar, coarsely chop the vegetables first). Process or pound to a smooth puree and transfer to a large measuring cup. You should have about 2 cups puree; if you have less, add water to bring to 2 cups, and set aside.

Heat the oil over high heat in a heavy medium pot with a tight-fitting lid. Lower the heat to medium-high and add the rice. Stir well to coat with oil, then cook, stirring occasionally, until the rice is a light golden brown, 10 to 12 minutes.

Meanwhile, place the stock or water in a pot and bring to a boil, then lower the heat to maintain a bare simmer.

When the rice is golden, add the vegetable puree and stir as it comes to a boil. Add the hot stock or water and stir gently as the mixture comes to a vigorous boil. Let boil for 4 to 5 minutes, stirring gently once or twice, then add the salt and optional carrot or corn, stir well, cover, and lower the heat to medium-low. Simmer, covered, for 10 minutes, then remove from the heat and let stand, still covered, for 15 to 20 minutes.

Use a wooden spoon to stir and turn the rice, then transfer to a platter and serve, garnished, if you wish, with the fresh herbs. A fresh green salad is a good accompaniment.

# Mexican Green Rice

THIS IS ONE OF THE SIMPLEST AND BEST FLAVORED RICES WE KNOW, GREAT on its own or accompanied by grilled meats or vegetables, or fresh salsas. It has a delicious, slightly smoky taste and beautiful, soft green color. In Mexico, rice is traditionally served as a *sopa seca,* a pasta-style course that follows the soup course in a full meal. Though red rice is the most common *sopa seca* in restaurants, I tasted both a green and a white rice several years ago at a home-style restaurant in Oaxaca called Dona Elpidia. The green rice was a knockout, especially with a little fresh salsa on the side.

This recipe is adapted from a recipe in Diana Kennedy's wonderful classic *Regional Cuisines of Mexico.* Though poblanos are standard, you can use any mild green or yellow-green chiles: cubanelle, Anaheim, poblano, Hungarian wax. When you scorch them, you want the skins well blackened almost all over. Instead of peeling off the skin, leave it on to help flavor and color the rice.

2 cups medium-grain or long-grain rice

½ pound mild green or yellow-green chiles, such as poblano, cubanelle, or Hungarian wax

1 small or ½ large white onion, coarsely chopped

1 clove garlic, minced

2 cups loosely packed torn romaine lettuce leaves

½ cup loosely packed fresh flat-leaf parsley leaves

3 cups chicken stock or vegetarian stock, preferably unsalted, or water

3 tablespoons vegetable oil

2 teaspoons salt (less if stock is salted)

½ cup loosely packed fresh coriander leaves

Wash the rice thoroughly under cold running water until the water runs clear. Place in a sieve to drain for 10 minutes.

Meanwhile, roast or grill the chiles over a gas or charcoal flame, under a broiler, or in a heavy skillet, turning them to expose all sides to the heat, until the skins are well blackened. Let stand for a moment or so to cool slightly, then discard the stems, seeds, and membranes. Transfer the chiles to a food processor or blender, together with the onion, garlic, lettuce, and parsley. Process to a smooth puree. (If necessary, add a little stock or water to help with the processing.) *Alternatively,* finely chop the peppers, onion, garlic, lettuce, and parsley, then place in a large mortar and pound to a puree. You may find it easier to begin with half the lettuce or less and then gradually add remaining lettuce as a puree forms.

Transfer the puree to a large measuring cup. You should have about 2 cups puree; if you have less, add water to equal 2 cups. If you have noticeably more than 2 cups, decrease the stock or water by an equivalent amount, so the total stock (or water) plus puree amount is 5 cups.

Heat the oil over medium-high heat in a heavy medium pot with a tight-fitting lid. Add the rice, stir well to coat with oil, and cook, stirring occasionally, until the rice is a light golden brown, 10 to 12 minutes.

Meanwhile, place the stock or water in a pot and bring to a boil, then lower the heat to maintain a bare simmer.

When the rice is golden, add the chile puree and stir as it heats to a boil. Add the hot stock or water and stir gently as the mixture comes to a vigorous boil. Let boil steadily for 4 to 5 minutes, stirring gently once or twice, then add the salt, stir once more gently, cover, and lower the heat to medium-low. Simmer, covered, for 10 minutes, then remove from the heat and let stand, covered, for 15 to 20 minutes.

Use a wooden spoon to stir in the coriander. Transfer the rice to a platter and serve.

Note: We love having leftovers of this rice or Mexican Red Rice (page 412). Both are delicious reheated in a little olive oil, and topped with a fried egg, accompanied by fresh tomatoes or a green salad.

The weekly Zimatlán market

# Oaxacan Rice Pudding

*arroz con leche oaxacana*

ALL FLAVORS SEEM MORE INTENSE AND COMPLEX IN OAXACA, FROM THE chocolate *atole* to the *mole* sauces. This rice pudding, so like the Spanish rice pudding (page 353), packs a pleasant extra bit of flavor from the ginger that simmers with the rice.

6 cups whole milk

½ cup medium or long-grain rice, broken (see Note)

2 inches cinnamon stick

½-inch ginger

2 small strips lime zest

¼ teaspoon salt

½ cup sugar

3 large egg yolks

¼ cup raisins

Place the milk, rice, cinnamon stick, ginger, lime zest, salt, and sugar in a large heavy nonreactive pot. Bring almost to a boil, then lower the heat and simmer, stirring occasionally, for 1 hour. Remove the cinnamon stick, ginger, and zest.

Preheat the oven to 350°F. In a medium bowl, beat the egg yolks. Stir in about ½ cup of the rice, then mix back into the rice in the pot. Add the raisins, reserving a few for garnish. Transfer to a large shallow ovenproof dish and bake for 10 to 20 minutes, until the eggs have set. Let stand at room temperature for 10 minutes before serving. Serve warm or at room temperature, in individual bowls, garnished with the reserved raisins.

Note: To break rice, pound briefly in a large mortar, or place on a countertop, cover with a tea towel, and roll briskly with a heavy rolling pin, pressing firmly as you do so.

A small shrine in Oaxaca's main market

# Memories of Childhood Rice Pudding

I CAN'T FIND MY MOTHER'S RICE PUDDING RECIPE. IT WAS WONDERFUL, A baked rice pudding with a golden brown skin that we'd all argue over. The best bits of skin were those that had stuck onto the sides of the aging oval Pyrex dish she baked the pudding in. Because she never included raisins, my idea of rice pudding is very plain. This recipe is our closest approximation of that long ago pleasure, a treat at any time, but especially for dessert on a cold winter night after a long tiring day at school. My father's idea of perfection was this pudding with a little cream, chilled and thick, poured over for extra richness.

6 cups whole milk

½ cup rice (preferably pudding rice or jasmine or Japanese rice)

½ cup sugar

½ teaspoon salt

1 vanilla bean or ½ teaspoon vanilla extract (preferably Mexican)

2 pinches grated nutmeg (optional)

Place the milk and rice in a heavy medium pot or in a double boiler over medium-high heat. If using a pot, bring almost to a boil, stirring occasionally to prevent sticking, then simmer over low heat, stirring occasionally, until the rice is well softened, about 35 minutes. If using a double boiler, cook, stirring occasionally, until the rice is softened.

Preheat the oven to 300°F. Transfer the rice and milk mixture to a 2-quart ovenproof casserole and stir in the sugar and salt. Bake in the center of the oven, uncovered, for 30 minutes.

Stir the pudding with a wooden spoon, stirring in any crust that has formed, then stir in the vanilla and the optional nutmeg. Continue to bake for another 45 minutes, without stirring. A golden brown crust will form. Turn off the heat and let the pudding stand in the oven for another 15 minutes. Serve warm, or at room temperature, plain or with a little cream.

**Alternative:** For a touch of color and tartness, toss in a small handful of dried sour cherries or cranberries when you add the vanilla.

# Glossary

**African eggplant**   *See* eggplant.

**amazake**   Fermented rice gruel from Japan, *amazake* is made from rice, water, and *koji*.

**asafetida powder**   Usually sold as a pale green powder, this Indian flavoring (*hing* in Hindi) comes from the rhizomes of a species of giant fennel. It is used in Indian recipes and is available from South Asian groceries, either as the powder or as an odorless blackish lump. The powder has an unpleasant smell on its own but adds an appetizing lightly oniony aroma and taste when fried in oil. It is especially common in dishes where no onion or garlic is used. It keeps indefinitely in a well-sealed container.

**basil (Asian, holy, sweet)**   *Asian basil*, sometimes called Thai basil (*bai horapha* in Thai), is now widely available, sold in bunches, in Asian and specialty groceries. It is a tropical variety of sweet basil (*Ocimum basilicum*), with pointed dark green leaves and a strong sharp anise aroma and taste. It is widely used in Thai, Lao, and Vietnamese cuisine, raw in salads or added to soups at the last moment. *Holy basil* (*Ocimum sanctum*), known as *bai gaprow* in Thai, is sometimes available in Thai groceries. It has narrower leaves than Asian basil, and the leaves are sometimes tinged with purple. If you crush it or bite it, you'll get little taste, for holy basil must be cooked to release its distinctive flavor. See the recipe for Tofu Fried with Basil (page 146). There are many varieties of *sweet (Italian) basil* available in grocery stores, for Italian and other dishes. They can be substituted for Asian basil, though the taste is not quite as sharp.

**black-eyed peas**   *See* dals.

**black gram dal**   *See* urad dal, under dals.

**black mustard seed**   See mustard seed.

**bonito flakes**   Bonito, a form of tuna, is sold in large dried mahogany-brown blocks in Japanese markets. You can buy a block or instead ask for freshly shaved flakes. Traditionally in Japanese households, fine slices or shavings of dried bonito would be shaved off the block as needed, using a special blade set into a box, a tool called a *katsuo-kezuri-ki*. In North America, the shavings are easier to find prepared in cellophane packages, though in some Japanese shops you can get freshly shaved bonito flakes. They are a pale-to-medium rosy pink in color. Store in a tightly sealed plastic bag in the refrigerator, where they will keep for several months. Use for making quick dashi broth (page 179) or as a sprinkled flavoring (see Kyoto Grilled Peppers, page 197, for example).

**cardamom**  Cardamom is a spice used in making sweets, baked goods, and many Indian savory dishes. Cardamom seeds, freshly ground, are an important ingredient in many *masala* (or curry powder) blends. The cardamom called for in the recipes in this book is green cardamom, either whole pods or seeds. There are a few black seeds in each small pod. White cardamom is a bleached version of green cardamom; if you have a choice, buy the green, since it is generally more aromatic. Do not buy ground cardamom, since it often has very little flavor. Cardamom is available in many large grocery stores, as well as from South Asian shops and well-stocked specialty stores. (Black cardamom is a different spice, also used in India; brown cardamom is used in Ethiopian cuisine.)

**cassava**  *See* manioc.

**cassia bark**  The bark of the cassia tree, a relative of cinnamon (both are members of the laurel family) is old in long sticks. Most of the cinnamon sold in North America is in fact cassia bark. Cassia gives a strong cinnamon taste; it is the cinnamon used in Indian and Vietnamese cooking. *See* cinnamon.

**cassia leaf**  The leaf of the cassia tree, this is also known as Indian bay leaf, *taysbatta* in Bengali. The fresh leaves are long (five to seven inches) and matte green, with a spicy aroma and pleasing sweet taste. We have encountered them only as a flavoring in Bengali rice pudding. It is difficult to find fresh cassia leaves in North America; the dried leaves are sold in small plastic bags in Indian groceries.

**chile oil**  Chile oil is made by infusing chile flakes in vegetable oil. It is used as a condiment and flavoring in Chinese cuisine. Available, in small jars, at Chinese groceries and some supermarkets.

**chile paste**  Used as a condiment and as an ingredient in many East and Southeast Asian cuisines, chile paste, also known as hot pepper paste, is a blend of red chiles, salt, vinegar, and sometimes garlic. We prefer those without the garlic. Our favorite when cooking Chinese food is Koon Yick Wah Kee brand, made in Hong Kong; it has a very smooth texture and good flavor. Sriracha is a common Thai chile paste, used as a condiment and sometimes as a flavoring. It is chile-hot, and widely available from Southeast Asian groceries. Indonesian versions of chile paste are called *sambal oelek;* Vietnamese versions are called *tuong ot tuoi.*

**chiles**  Chiles are native to the Americas but have spread all over the world since 1492 to become a staple in many cuisines. They are an important source of vitamin C. Chiles come in many varieties and may be used fresh or dried for longer-term storage and used that way. Chiles vary greatly in taste and "heat"; even chiles of the same variety will vary, depending on where they were grown and on other unpredictable factors. The heat is greatest in the membranes and seeds. Unless otherwise stated, all the recipes in this book assume that you will leave the seeds in. The heat in chiles can irritate your hands; many people use rubber gloves when handling hot chiles. Be sure not to touch your face or your eyes while handling chiles; if you don't wear gloves, wash your hands thoroughly with soap and water afterward.

### Fresh chiles

**banana chiles**   These five- to eight-inch-long pale green-yellow chiles look very like yellow Hungarian wax peppers. They are two inches wide at the top and taper to a point. They are mild to mildly hot and available in large supermarkets as well as in Asian groceries.

**bird chiles**   These small (less than an inch long) multicolored chiles from Thailand are incredibly hot and delicious. In Thai, they are called *prik kee noo*. Available, usually in cellophane packages, in Southeast Asian groceries. You can substitute serrano chiles.

**cayenne chiles**   Also referred to as fresh red or fresh green chiles, cayennes, red or green, are four to eight inches long, slender, tapering to a point, and hot. You can substitute serranos.

**habanero chiles**   Lantern-shaped habaneros (meaning "from Havana") are among the hottest chiles around. Known as Scotch bonnet chiles in Jamaica, they have a slightly sweet flavor and may be bright green to yellow to orange-red. They are sold in Mexican and Caribbean markets and in some grocery stores.

**jalapeño chiles**   These bright green, medium-shiny hot chiles are one and a half to two inches long with a rounded or blunt tip. They are widely available in supermarkets.

**serrano chiles**   These are one and a half to three inches long, slender, and pointed. They come in dark green or red and are very hot. They are commonly available in supermarkets.

### Dried chiles

**chile pepper flakes**   Made of crumbled dried red chiles, these are readily available in sealed spice jars and can be substituted for dried red chiles in many recipes.

*See also pimentón and togarashi.*

**dried red chiles**   Known in Thai as *prik haeng,* dried red chiles are dried cayennes. They are a versatile pantry item for preparation of Chinese, Thai, and Indian dishes especially. They add a smoky hot flavor to many dishes. Dark-red dried red chiles are available at Southeast and South Asian groceries, usually in small cellophane bags. They keep almost indefinitely.

You can substitute one teaspoon of dried chile pepper flakes for each dried pepper called for.

**Chinese cooking wine**   This rice wine is sold in Chinese grocery stores and well-stocked liquor stores. If it's sold in a grocery store, it will be marked "contains salt" or "not to be used or sold as beverage" in order to enable it to be sold as an ingredient rather than as a liquor. Look for bottles labeled "Shao Xing wine." It is from

15 percent to 18 percent alcohol, keeps indefinitely, and is a staple of the Chinese pantry. You can substitute a dry medium-dry sherry.

**Chinese green vegetables**   *See* the lengthy discussion starting on page 83.

**Chinese pickled vegetables**   *Tianjin* (also sometimes spelled *Tientsin*) cabbage is the easiest-to-find Chinese pickled vegetable. It is sold in plastic packages or small ceramic pots in well-stocked Chinese groceries. It keeps well if tightly sealed in the refrigerator.

**cinnamon**   Cinnamon is the aromatic bark of the cinnamon tree. It comes in smooth medium-brown sticks that can be easily broken or shredded. It has a complex smell with a distinctive, almost sharp edge. A closely related plant, cassia, provides most of the "cinnamon" sold in North America. The sticks, also known as quills, from cassia bark are tougher and thicker and often slightly darker in color than those of true cinnamon. Cassia also has a stronger, less subtle flavor. The cinnamon used in India is also cassia, sometimes known as false cinnamon; for Spanish and Mexican rice puddings, try to find true cinnamon, though cassia quills can be substituted.

## Coconut

**coconut milk**   Coconut milk is made by soaking freshly grated coconut in water and then squeezing the liquid ("milk") out of it. Although you can try buying a coconut, scraping out the meat in shreds, and then extracting the milk, it is simpler (and more reliable, given the difficulty of finding good coconuts in North America) to buy prepared coconut milk. It is sold in cans and in frozen blocks in Southeast Asian and South Asian groceries. We find canned coconut milk most reliable. Be sure to buy *unsweetened* coconut milk. If using canned, try to find a brand made in Thailand, such as Pearl or Aroy. It will be somewhat thick, with the "cream" settled on the top. After you open the can, stir the milk and cream together before using (unless the recipe calls for using the milk and cream separately). If you have any left over, pour it out into a glass container, cover, and refrigerate; use it within three days. Canned coconut milk keeps indefinitely and is a good pantry staple, handy to have in the cupboard for use in a Thai or South Indian curry or a dessert.

   If you wish to make coconut milk from either freshly grated coconut or frozen shredded coconut (see below), proceed as follows: Place 2 cups grated coconut, or thawed frozen grated coconut, in a large bowl with 1 to 1½ cups warm water and stir (the smaller quantity of water will yield a thicker coconut milk). Use your hand to massage and squeeze the coconut shreds thoroughly for about 1 minute. Place a fine sieve (or a colander lined with cheesecloth or muslin) over a bowl and pour in the liquid and coconut. Squeeze the coconut shreds to extract as much liquid as possible. The liquid in the bowl is called thick coconut milk or "first extraction" coconut milk. The coconut dregs can be reused, using the same method and 1½ cups hot water, to yield a second, thinner coconut milk.

**shredded/grated coconut**   Because it's difficult to get good coconuts in North America, we recommend that you use unsweetened frozen grated or shredded coconut: Look in the freezer section of Asian or Mexican groceries. Once frozen shredded coconut has thawed, it can be easily dry-roasted in a skillet to bring out its flavor. It can also be used to make coconut milk (see above). Dried shredded coconut can be reconstituted and used as a substitute *only if it has not been sweetened during processing*. Soak in a little warm water until it softens, then chop to a finer texture and proceed to dry-roast as directed in the individual recipe.

**coriander**   Coriander leaves are used as a flavoring and as a garnish from Mexico to Thailand and China, from Vietnam to India. If possible, buy fresh coriander with its roots still on. You can find it in many grocery stores. Store in a water-filled jar or other container in the refrigerator, with the water coming up to the top of the roots and the leaves loosely covered with a plastic bag. The leaves should stay fresh for at least a week, enabling you to use them bit by bit; discard any yellow leaves. The roots are an essential ingredient in many Thai curry pastes and marinades. We make a habit of cutting the roots off bunches once we've used the leaves and storing them in the freezer (where they keep indefinitely, wrapped in a plastic bag), for use in Thai marinades, curry pastes, and salads. Coriander seed is a widely available spice. For Vietnamese coriander, *see* polygonum.

**cowpeas**   Cowpeas are legumes, whole peas, eaten both fresh and dried in India, Africa, Europe, and the Americas. They originated in Africa, traveled early to India and Europe, and then came to North America with the African slave traffic, and also probably with immigrants from the Mediterranean. They are very like black-eyed peas, but slightly smaller.

**curry leaves**   Fresh or dried curry leaves are used in many Indian dishes, usually to flavor the cooking oil in which other ingredients will be fried, most often near the start of cooking. Curry leaves are of South Indian origin. In Hindi they are called *kari patta*. Dried curry leaves are always available in Indian grocery stores and specialty shops; these days, often the fresh leaves, dark green and glossy, are also available. Use them whenever possible. Stored in a dry place, the dry leaves keep well; use the fresh leaves within a few days of purchase.

**curry paste (Thai)**   Thai curry pastes are a pounded blend of chiles and other spices, not to be confused with Indian curry powders. Thai curry pastes (red, green, yellow, and Mussamen) are now widely available in Thai and Laotian groceries in North America. Look for the Mae Ploy brand, or any other foil-packaged Thai curry paste, as long as it's labeled "Product of Thailand." Keeps indefinitely unopened; once the package is open, store well covered in the refrigerator.

**curry powder (Indian)**   The term used for the blend of powdered spices used to flavor Anglo-Indian curries. In Indian cookbooks, more often the same flavoring is achieved with a freshly made *masala*, or spice blend (see page 246).

**cuttlefish ink**   *See* squid ink.

**daikon**   The Japanese name for the long white radish widely used in Japan is daikon. It is very like the radish known in North America as icicle radish. It is also closely related to the white radishes of India (known as *mooli* in Hindi) and of Central Asia. Daikon can be eaten raw or cooked and is very commonly used as a pickle. It keeps well in the refrigerator. In Japan, it grows in both summer and winter; it is hot (spicy) in the summer, sweet in the winter. The tip of a daikon radish (one third to one quarter of its length) is spicier-tasting than the rest, almost hot: Use it in soups and stir-fries, and use the milder midsection and top for grating and pickles. (Sometimes you can buy daikon in sections, especially in Chinese and Japanese shops.) For a simple condiment, finely grate daikon, and drizzle soy sauce over it.

**dals**   In India, the word *dal* refers to any legume: dried beans, dried peas, and lentils, though used precisely the term means only dried split peas. Dals are sold whole or split; split dals cook more quickly and generally do not require a preliminary soaking. Dals may be sold hulled (skinned) or unhulled; if possible, buy hulled (skinned) dal, also known as washed dal, as it cooks more quickly.

## Split dals

**channa dal**   The split version of dried Indian chickpeas (*channa*, see below), this dal takes longer to cook than most split dals.

**masur (red) dal**   Also known as red split lentils, these small, attractive, quick-cooking lentils are a soft orange color when raw and pale yellow when cooked.

**mung (moong) dal**   A strong golden yellow all over, this quick-cooking dal is from mung beans that have been hulled and split. (See below for a description of the whole unhulled mung bean.) It is a staple in our pantry. Mung dal turns a slightly duller yellow when cooked.

**toovar dal**   Also known as toor dal, these skinned and split yellow lentils are golden straw to ocher in color. They often come oiled (with castor oil, to preserve them), and look a little like small split peanuts. Oiled toovar dal should be rinsed off in hot water before using. Toovar dal takes longer to cook than masur dal or mung dal.

**urad dal**   Also known as black gram or Bengal gram, this useful split bean is available in Indian groceries and occasionally in natural foods stores. The unhulled bean is black to gray; buy the more commonly available hulled urad dal, which is off-white, since it cooks more quickly.

## Whole beans and peas

**black-eyed peas**   Large and oval/kidney-shaped, black-eyed peas are cream-colored with a black spot. They are known in Hindi as *lobhia dal*. Black-eyed peas can be found dried or precooked in cans in most grocery stores. They have a creamy texture when cooked. The dried peas must be soaked overnight before cooking.

**channa**  This is the Hindi word for dried Indian chickpeas (garbanzos). Indian channa is usually slightly smaller than American chickpeas. Dried channa must be soaked overnight before cooking. Cooked canned chickpeas are widely available in grocery stores.

**kidney beans**  Widely available in grocery stores, dried or precooked and canned, these beans are dark red, large, and, yes, kidney-shaped. Called *rajma* in Hindi, they sometimes have a slightly mealy texture when first cooked. Dried kidney beans must be soaked overnight before cooking.

**whole mung**  These small, dull green, and almost round beans, also known as green gram, are good for sprouting or for cooking as a dal. (When skinned and split, they are yellow all over—see Split mung dal, above.) Like all whole (unsplit) dried beans, they need an overnight soaking to shorten the cooking time.

**dashi**  This Japanese broth is made from bonito flakes, or dried mushrooms, or kombu, or a combination, briefly simmered in hot water. It is used as a simple basic ingredient in many recipes. You can make your own from basic ingredients (see page 179) or mix up some instant dashi powder (see below).

**dashi powder**  Sold in Japanese and Korean shops, this is an instant broth mix for use in Japanese recipes. Use only if you have no kombu or bonito to make your own fresh broth.

**dried mushrooms (Chinese black, porcini, shiitake)**  Dried shiitakes are used as a flavoring in Japanese dishes, particularly in colder weather. Dried black mushrooms are also used in Chinese cooking and are believed to strengthen the blood. Buy dried shiitakes at a Japanese or Korean grocery and dried Chinese mushrooms in large clear cellophane bags at a Chinese grocery. The ones with a light-colored pattern of cracks on their caps are most prized, though the darker ones also have good flavor. Italian cuisine makes use of dried porcini, since, like other dried mushrooms, they keep well and are strongly flavored. Soak in warm water before using and use the soaking water to add extra flavor to a broth or other dish.

**dried orange peel**  *See* orange peel.

**dried red chiles**  *See* chiles, dried.

**dried shrimp**  Used in Thai, Vietnamese, and Chinese cooking as a flavoring and widely available in Chinese and Southeast Asian grocery stores, dried shrimp are small and pinkish orange. Buy firm-looking shrimp in well-sealed plastic packages. After opening, seal well and store in the refrigerator; they keep for a month or two. If they start to smell strong, throw them out.

**drumsticks**  An Indian vegetable, available in South Asian groceries, these are usually cut into lengths and simmered until tender. They are medium to dark green, very long (twelve to eighteen inches) cylinders with ridges (the reference is not to turkey legs but to the wooden sticks for playing drums). They look like a cross between cucumber and okra. They are eaten with the fingers; the inner flesh is sucked out and the rest discarded.

**eggplant (African, Asian, green Thai)** *African eggplant* are used in slow-cooked dishes in Senegal. Called *diakatou* in Wolof, these green firm vegetables look a little like a green tomato with tight pleats or wrinkles radiating down from the stem end. They have an agreeably bitter taste. Substitute green Thai eggplant, green tomatoes, or tomatillos. *Asian eggplants* are long (six to twelve inches), narrow, and pale violet or dark purple. They are used in Chinese, Japanese, Thai, and other East Asian cooking and can be found in East Asian groceries and in well-stocked produce sections of large grocery stores. Unlike Mediterranean eggplant, they need no preliminary salting to draw out bitterness. Small *green Thai eggplant* are one of many varieties used in Thai cooking. Pale green and the size of a large cherry tomato, they may be slow-cooked or used raw. They are available in Southeast Asian groceries.

**fagara** See Sichuan pepper.

**fava beans** Often called broad beans, these are available fresh (in springtime) or dried. The fresh beans come in a large flat bean pod and, unless they are very young and tender, must be shelled like peas. The individual beans look like large fat lima beans. They have an outer skin which is tough in very mature beans; if you have beans with tough skins, blanch them and slip off their skins, or wait until they are cooked to slip off the skins. Dried favas are available in Italian and Middle Eastern grocery stores. Try to find split and skinned dried favas; they cook more quickly.

**fenugreek** Fenugreek seeds are used as a spice in many regional Indian cuisines as well as in Ethiopia and Yemen. The seeds are actually legumes, small, irregularly shaped, and yellowish brown in color. They are very hard and have little aroma until dry-roasted and ground, when they smell somewhat of maple sugar. Fenugreek seed is available in specialty stores and in Indian groceries. Fenugreek leaves (*methi* in Hindi) are used both as an herb and as a green in many Indian dishes. They are available dried (and very occasionally fresh) in Indian groceries.

**fish sauce** An essential flavoring ingredient in many parts of Southeast Asia, fish sauce is known in Thai as *nam pla* and in Vietnamese as *nuoc mam*. Thai fish sauce is a light amber color and has a salty, somewhat pungent taste (milder than its strong smell). Fish sauce is available from Southeast Asian and Chinese groceries. Try to find a pale-colored (which equates with higher quality) Thai brand, such as Flying Lion Brand or the fairly common Squid Brand made by the Thai Fishsauce Company. Fish sauce keeps indefinitely in the cupboard.

**galangal** Known in Indonesia as *laos* and in Thailand as *kha*, this is a close cousin of ginger and looks very like it. It is a pinkish or creamy white rhizome with concentric rings of fine dark lines. Not as firm as gingerroot, it is used widely in Thai, Lao, Cambodian, Malay, and Nyonya cooking. It has a fresh, lemon-sharp hot taste. Many Southeast Asian groceries stock it. Ginger can be substituted, decreasing the quantity called for by about one third.

**ghee**  *Ghee* is the generic Hindi word for fats, but in this book it is used to refer only to *usli ghee*, the Indian clarified butter that is widely used in Indian cuisine. You can substitute melted butter, or you can clarify butter—or you can buy *usli ghee* from Indian groceries. Indian clarified butter is made in the same way as French clarified butter, except that it is then strained to eliminate any brown specks. Because all milk solds have been eliminated, ghee keeps well at room temperature. If you are buying ghee, remember that much commercial ghee is made from vegetable oils; read the label carefully to be sure you have found purely dairy ghee.

**ginger**  Fresh ginger is believed in many parts of the world to have medicinal properties as a diuretic and a "heating" food. It also adds incomparable depth and flavor to chicken broths and Sichuanese and Hunanese dishes. Asian markets are a good source of high-quality ginger, since it is an important ingredient in both South Asian and East Asian cuisines. Buy large pieces of ginger if possible, and choose those with smooth firm skin. A wrinkled skin or softened texture tells you that the ginger is old and will be fibrous; sometimes that's all you can find—just make sure that you mince it very finely so that the fibers are broken up. Unless it's being tossed into a broth for flavoring or used to make ginger tea (see page 203), ginger should always be peeled. Store ginger in the refrigerator, loosely wrapped in plastic.

**green cardamom**  *See* cardamom.

**kaffir lime**  *See* limes.

**kamaboko**  Available in Japanese and Korean shops, this firm processed-fish product is precooked and ready to eat. It is usually shaped like a long flattened mound and comes on a piece of wood. It may be golden to white, or it may be colored pink or bright green with food coloring. To use, first cut it into thin slices and then run a knife between the *kamaboko* and the board it comes on to detach the slices. Serve arranged attractively on a small plate, as an accompaniment to rice or sushi, or use as an ingredient in sushi rolls (see Roll-Your-Own Sushi, page 220, and Classic Sushi Roll-ups, page 217).

**kampyo**  This Japanese product, dried gourd strips, is sold packaged in Japanese and Korean groceries. To use, measure off the length you need, then boil and soak in flavorings as instructed (see Classic Sushi Roll-Ups, page 217) before placing in *futo-maki* rolls. It adds texture and a little color and flavor to the rolls.

**kapi**  *See* shrimp paste.

**kelp**  *See* seaweed.

**koji**  A culture made of *aspergillus*-fermented rice or other grains, *koji* is used in the production of miso, sake, *amazake*, *natto*, and other Japanese products. See page 188.

**kombu**  *See* seaweed.

**legumes**  *See* dals.

**lemon grass**   This aromatic dry-looking stalk, known as *takrai* in Thai, is used widely in Southeast Asian cooking. It is available fresh in Asian groceries, usually sold in small bundles. Dried lemon grass may be substituted, but it must be soaked for thirty minutes before using; it has less flavor, so use it only as a fallback. Substitute approximately one tablespoon dried lemon grass for each stalk of fresh called for. Stalks of fresh lemon grass look like dried-out sticks, but when sliced or crushed are very aromatic. Only two to three inches of the bulbous end are used, sometimes in large chunks, not meant to be eaten, or sometimes finely minced and pounded to a paste for curry paste. Fresh lemon grass is very easy to store: It keeps for several weeks in the refrigerator, drying out over time but not going bad. Lemon grass also roots easily, and it is fun to have in a kitchen garden in the summer, or growing inside in a pot in winter.

**limes (domestic and wild)**   Freshly squeezed lime juice is an ingredient or condiment in many Thai dishes and it is also widely used in India and Mexico. In Thailand, lime wedges are always placed beside Thai fried rice so guests can squeeze on a little fresh juice as they eat. We like to keep a supply of limes on hand at all times. Lemon juice can be substituted in most recipes if necessary. Wild limes are the fruit of the wild lime tree, also known as the kaffir lime (*see* wild lime leaves). They are a rich green in color, the size of a domestic lime, with a knobby bumpy skin. The pulp is not eaten; the zest and sometimes the peel of wild limes are used as ingredients in Thai and Cambodian curry pastes.

**long beans**   Widely used in Asia, long beans (also called yard-long beans) look like very elongated green (snap) beans and taste quite like them, but are actually more closely related to black-eyed peas and cowpeas. They cook a little more quickly than most snap beans. They are used both raw and cooked in Southeast Asian cuisines.

**lotus root**   Lotus root is the rhizome of the flowering lotus. It is pale beige to ocher in color and smooth, with a beautiful lattice-like cross section with lacy openings. It is sold in Asian markets, sometimes with traces of mud still on it. It has a fresh taste like young Jerusalem artichokes and a crunchy texture even when cooked. It may be stuffed and deep-fried, or used in soups, whole or sliced. (See Mariko's Lotus Root Sandwiches, page 199.)

**manioc**   The tuber of the manioc plant (also known as cassava) is widely used in Caribbean, West African, and Brazilian cuisines. Sweet manioc may be eaten after a simple boiling; bitter manioc is poisonous and must be processed carefully in order to wash out the poison. Manioc is available in tropical groceries. Manioc leaves are used in West African cooking to flavor the sauces that are eaten over rice (see the recipe for *fitouf*, page 366). Spinach or other leafy greens may be substituted. You may find manioc leaves dried or frozen (the better choice) in Caribbean, African, and Brazilian groceries.

**masur dal**   *See* dals.

**mirin**    Mirin is Japanese cooking wine, sweet-tasting and a staple in the Japanese pantry. Mirin, which contains 14 percent alcohol, is used for flavoring many dishes, often briefly cooked first to boil off the alcohol. It is available in Japanese and Korean groceries and in specialty stores. It keeps indefinitely. You can substitute sake sweetened with sugar.

## Miso pastes

A nutritious flavor paste most often made from soybeans fermented with a rice-based culture (see *koji*, above) started with lactic acid–producing bacteria. Miso may also be made from brown rice or barley or a blend of these with soybeans (see below and Koji and Miso, page 188). Miso pastes are available in most health food stores as well as in Japanese and Korean groceries. These are the types you will find:

*aka miso* (or *inaka miso*)    Called red miso, this has a reddish-brown color and a salty medium-strong taste. It is made using a rice-based *koji* and is good for miso soup.

*genmai miso*    Known as brown miso, *genmai miso* is made of brown rice and has a medium-strong taste.

*hatcho miso*    Very dark colored and strong tasting, with a dry texture, *hatcho miso* is made of soybeans only, with no grain. It is used only in soups.

*mugi miso*    Barley miso, this is usually medium to dark brown in color and medium-strong tasting. Both the *koji* used and the miso itself are barley-based.

*shinshu miso*    Widely available, this has a salty taste and medium yellow to light brown color. Less sweet than *shiro miso*, it is used similarly for toppings, dips, and soups.

*shiro miso*    Known as sweet miso or white miso, *shiro miso* is pale yellow to almost white in color. It is made with a higher proportion of *koji* to soybeans; the *koji* is rice-based. It is relatively low in salt and mild-tasting.

**mitsuba**    Often referred to as Japanese parsley or as trefoil, this green herb is available in Japanese and Korean groceries. It has dark green stalks and bright green serrated leaves, three on each stem. It has a fresh slightly celery taste and is used as a garnish and flavoring in Japanese cooking, very much as Italians use flat-leaf parsley. Flat-leaf parsley may be substituted. Like parsley, mitsuba grows well in North American gardens if given a moist soil.

**mung dal, split mung dal**    *See* dals.

**mustard oil**    A staple of the Bengali kitchen, mustard oil is used for sautéing and frying, and as a flavoring. It gives a pleasing sharp distinctive taste to dishes and is available in many Indian grocery stores.

**mustard seed**   Tiny round reddish-brown to black mustard seeds are used widely in Indian cooking. They may be used whole, to flavor cooking oil when frying (they give it a nutty taste), or ground to make a spice paste (with a sharp hot mustard taste). They are available at South Asian groceries and at well-stocked specialty shops.

***natto***   A Japanese specialty, eaten as a condiment/accompaniment for rice, *natto* is made of soybeans fermented with *koji*. The texture is slippery to slimy and the taste somewhat fermented, so *natto* is loved by some and disliked by others. It is available in Japanese groceries.

**nigella**   Also known as black onion seed, or as *kalonji* (the Hindi name), these small teardrop-shaped black seeds have a tangy oniony taste. They are the seeds of the nigella flower, a garden plant related to baby's breath and to Queen Anne's Lace. Nigella is used often in Bengali cooking and also in other parts of northern India and Central Asia.

**nori**   *See* seaweed.

***okara***   *See* tofu and tofu products.

**olive oil**   Widely used in Mediterranean cooking, olive oil comes in many qualities and is produced in many places. Try to use oil from the country or region whose dish you are preparing: For example, use Italian extra-virgin oil for Italian dishes (or even more precisely, use a regionally produced oil for dishes from a particular region) and Spanish olive oil for paella and other Spanish dishes.

**orange peel**   Dried strips of sour orange peel or tangerine peel are used for flavoring and garnish in Persian, Chinese, and other cuisines. Dried orange peel is available from Persian grocery stores and by mail order (see Mail-Order Sources, page 438). It keeps indefinitely in a dry place. To use, boil for several minutes in water, discard the bitter water, and bring to the boil in fresh water, then set aside to steep for 10 minutes. Small strips of fresh orange zest can be substituted.

**oyster sauce**   A Chinese condiment and flavoring ingredient made originally from oysters, oyster sauce these days is largely made of artificial flavors, often with too much caramel flavoring. Good oyster sauce is dark colored and ideal as a light flavoring for plain cooked greens. Lee Kum Kee brand has a fuller flavor than many; experiment to find one you like.

**palm oil**   Oil palms originated in Africa but are now cultivated in tropical areas of Central and South America and in Asia. Their nuts yield two oils, one a reddish oil from the whole nuts, the other an uncolored oil from the kernels of the nuts. The reddish oil, often extracted by hand in individual households, is traditionally used in parts of West Africa and in Brazil for cooking (see *fitouf* recipe, page 366). It is available from many South American and Caribbean stores. The colorless oil is industrially extracted for use in processed foods.

**palm sugar**   Palm sugar is refined from the sap of the sugar palm and is produced and widely used in India, Thailand, Malaysia, Indonesia, and other parts of Southeast Asia. It is available in South and Southeast Asian groceries, often sold in round disks about half an inch thick and three inches across. You may also find it in cellophane-wrapped blocks (looking rather like maple sugar). In either case, the lumps of sugar are very hard, and we have found the easiest way to handle it is to use a sharp knife to scrape off shavings of sugar. These are easy to measure and also dissolve more quickly than lumps do. Palm sugar has a delightful, slightly smoky taste; brown sugar may be substituted.

**peanut oil**    This widely available oil handles high temperatures well without breaking down, so it is ideal for deep-frying. We buy it in large containers from a Chinese grocery. Although we like peanut oil for deep-frying and for stir-frying many Chinese and Thai dishes (except where ingredients' tastes are delicate and we don't want to taste the "peanut" in the oil), it is important to remember that some people have moderate to severe allergies to peanuts and peanut products. If you are ever serving fried foods and are asked whether there are peanuts in the dish, remember whether or not you used peanut oil for frying. You can substitute canola oil for peanut oil.

**peanuts, dry-roasted peanuts**    Peanuts originated in the Americas; traces of peanuts have been found in archaeological digs in Peru. Portuguese traders took them from South America to Africa, where they soon became an important staple, and to Asia. Peanuts were reintroduced to the southern United States by slaves from Africa. (*Goober,* a southern term for peanuts, is related to the African word *nguba*.) They are an important element in many Asian cuisines as well as in Africa and the Americas. Peanuts, also known as ground nuts, are in fact legumes. The peanut plant sends shoots down into the earth on which the peanuts develop. Their harvest is like potato harvest: The whole plant is pulled up and the peanuts removed.

Raw peanuts are sold in South Asian and East Asian groceries and throughout the southern United States. Locally grown peanuts are also sold boiled in corner groceries in the South and are a passion for many people, especially at harvest time in the fall. Similarly, in China, especially in the southern provinces, boiled peanuts are often sold as a street-food snack. Most of the recipes in this book call for dry-roasting the peanuts: Heat a cast-iron or other heavy skillet over medium-high heat. When it is hot, add the nuts. Stir constantly with a wooden spatula to prevent scorching. The nuts will start to turn brown in less than 1 minute. Lower the heat slightly and continue cooking and stirring until all the nuts are colored with gold and brown. Remove from the heat and keep stirring for 15 seconds, then transfer to a bowl. The roasted nuts can be coarsely chopped using a knife or more finely chopped in a food processor.

**perilla**    *See* shiso.

**pickled Chinese cabbage**    *See* Chinese pickled vegetables.

**pickled ginger**    Available in Japanese and Korean grocery stores, this beautiful pinkish condiment of finely sliced salted ginger is usually sold in clear plastic containers. Once opened, it should be stored, well sealed, in the refrigerator, where it will keep for several months. You can also make your own (see Pickled Ginger, page 203). Serve it to accompany sushi or other flavored rice dishes.

**pimentón**    This Spanish red pepper powder, used to add heat and a wonderful smoky flavor to Spanish dishes, is available by mail order (see Mail-Order Sources, page 438) and from well-stocked specialty stores. It looks like cayenne, with a dark orange color. Store it in a well-sealed container, like any other spice.

**polygonum**    Known as *rau ram* in Vietnam, *pak chi wietnam* in Thailand, Vietnamese coriander in North America, and Vietnamese mint in Australia, this delightful strong-tasting herb can be replaced by fresh basil or mint, but the tastes are not the same. It can often be found fresh in Southeast Asian grocery stores and can also be grown in summer gardens in North America and indoors through the winter; it is a perennial. The leaves are soft, smooth, and dark green (sometimes with a darker blotch), up to one inch long, and sharply pointed, on fleshy stems.

**pomegranate concentrate**    Also known as pomegranate molasses, this is made from sour pomegranate juice cooked down with a little sugar. It is used to give a slightly sour tang to many savory dishes. It is sold in bottles in Middle Eastern and Iranian shops and, once opened, should be kept in the refrigerator. The most commonly available brand is from Lebanon and called Cedar's; 1 plus 1, from Iran, is comparable.

**pomegranates**    Sweet pomegranates, rosy red and firm, are available from late August until February in well-stocked produce sections and in specialty stores. Sour pomegranates are usually yellow, sometimes tinged with pink, and are smaller than sweet pomegranates. They are widely grown throughout the Eastern Mediterranean, Iran, and Iraq and used as a sour flavoring in savory dishes. Sour pomegranates are not generally available in North America, but many products made from them are available at Arab, Iraqi, and Iranian groceries (*see* pomegranate concentrate).

**poppy seeds**    Poppy seeds are tiny and most often, in the European tradition, they are black and used as a filling or topping in baking. In Bengal and other parts of India, white poppy seeds are used in savory cooked dishes as a flavoring, often first ground to a paste. White poppy seeds are available from Indian groceries.

**rice vinegar**    *See* vinegar.

**roasted sesame oil**    *See* sesame oil.

**rose water**    This aromatic water is used to scent desserts, especially in Arab, Turkish, Persian, and Mogul traditional cooking. It is available from Arab, Iranian, and South Asian groceries and from some natural foods stores.

**saffron**    Saffron threads are the pistils of a crocus (*Crocus sativa*), gathered by hand in the spring. Spain produces most saffron; Kashmir is also known for its saffron. Saffron is used for its color and delicate flavor. Because it is rare and expensive, as well as giving food a beautiful color, it is associated with festive dishes. Available in specialty stores and by mail order (see Mail-Order Sources, page 438), saffron should be bought as threads, rather than powdered, and stored in a cool, dry place. Before using, heat the saffron threads gently in a dry skillet to dry them out thoroughly, then reduce them to a powder in a mortar. Dissolve the powder in a little water before adding it to dishes.

**sake**   A mild-tasting Japanese alcohol derived from highly milled rice, sake is used as a drink (drunk warmed, chilled, or at room temperature) as well as an ingredient. It is available in liquor stores.

**salt**   *See* sea salt.

**sansho**   Also known as Japanese pepper and usually sold powdered in small containers in Japanese shops, *sansho* is a mildly hot, aromatic brown spice, related to Sichuan pepper.

**sea salt**   We prefer using sea salt whenever salt is called for in a recipe, because it tastes better to us than iodized salt and is more traditional in most places. (In some parts of the world, rock salt, extracted from the ground, is traditional.) Use fine sea salt unless coarse salt is specified.

### Seaweed

**kombu (kelp)**   Kombu is a form of seaweed, giant sea kelp (*Laminaria*) that is a deep green in color and is sold in twelve-inch-long pieces, dried out and folded. It is very lightweight and is usually sold in cellophane packages, some from Japan or Korea, others from Maine. It often has a grayish coating, from crystallized salt. It is available in Japanese and Korean groceries, as well as in natural foods and specialty shops. (For more information, see page 179.)

**nori**   Sold in flat or folded dry sheets, sometimes pretoasted (and then labeled *yaki-nori* in Japanese), nori is made from laver, marine algae that is dried into thin sheets. It varies in color from a dark green to purple to shiny black. It is most commonly used for wrapping sushi rice and is also used in shreds or powdered flakes as a condiment for rice. It should be toasted before being used for wrapping sushi; for toasting instructions, see Note, page 219.

**wakame**   Sold dried in plastic packages in Japanese and Korean groceries, wakame can be deep green to brown, with curly edges. The green-colored wakame is preferable, because it has a more delicate flavor. Wakame must be soaked in cold to lukewarm water for twenty to thirty minutes, until soft, before using. It makes a good salad ingredient, dressed with vinegar, and is also used in simmered soups and stews in China, Korea, and Japan.

**sesame oil**   This brown-colored oil is made from roasted sesame seeds. The clear sesame oil sold in health food stores should not be substituted. Our favorite brand is the easy-to-find Japanese brand Kadoya, in a dark bottle. Sometimes referred to as Asian sesame oil or roasted sesame oil, sesame oil is most often used to flavor dishes, rather than for cooking.

**sesame paste**   Used as a condiment and flavoring in Chinese cooking, sesame paste is available from Chinese groceries. The sesame seeds in Chinese sesame paste are roasted before being ground to a paste. Consequently, Chinese sesame paste is a dun-brown color, not as pale as the sesame paste made from unroasted seeds, called *tahini*, that is used in the Eastern Mediterranean. The oil and the paste solids separate as the paste stands (as they do with unpasteurized peanut butter); stir them together before using. You can substitute the natural roasted sesame butter sold in some natural foods stores alongside peanut butter.

**sesame seeds (white and black)**   Sesame seeds are available both hulled and unhulled and white (more common) and black (most often available in Japanese groceries). The black seeds have a stronger, earthier taste than the white. Because they are rich in oil, sesame seeds do not keep well. They are best stored in the refrigerator or alternatively bought in small quantities. They are most often dry-roasted before being used as an flavoring or condiment; the toasting brings out their flavor (see page 187 for dry-roasting instructions).

**seven-spice powder**   *See* shichimi.

**shallots**   First cousin to onions and garlic, shallots at their best are small, reddish or purplish, and delicate in flavor. Peel off the outer skin, as you would with an onion, and cut off the tough stem end. If you can't find shallots or if the only ones available are soft and sprouting, substitute mild or sweet onion. Shallots are a staple in the Thai kitchen and in parts of India.

**shichimi**   Japanese seven-spice, or seven-flavors, powder, is sometimes sold as *shichimi togarashi* if it includes hot chile pepper flakes (*togarashi*). It consists of tiny flakes or powder of seven of the following: green seaweed (*ao nori*), powdered dried red chile (*togarashi*), untoasted white sesame seed (*goma*), white poppy seed, dried Japanese pepper (*sansho*), dried orange peel, green perilla (*shiso*), black sesame seed, and flaxseed (*assa*).

**shiso**   This is the Japanese name, now widely used in English, for an herb also known as perilla, or beefsteak plant. *Shiso* can be red- (actually a deep maroon) or green-leafed. It grows well in many parts of North America in the summer, as long as there is some good warm weather, and will reseed itself from year to year. *Shiso* is sold in Japanese and Korean stores, usually in small rather expensive plastic packages, though in summer you may also find it sold in bunches in Asian produce sections. It is related to mint and has a strong distinctive taste and large curved strongly veined leaves. It is used to flavor and color *umeboshi* as well as other pickles, and it is widely used in Japanese cuisine (often shredded) as a flavoring and garnish.

**shoyu**   *Shoya* is the Japanese name for soy sauce. *See* soy sauce.

**shredded cooked pork**    Known in Mandarin as *rou song*, this long-keeping pantry item is used for flavoring and texture and is available in Chinese and Vietnamese groceries.

**shrimp paste**    Known as *kapi* in Thai, *belacan* in Malay, and *trassi* in Bahasa Indonesia, shrimp paste can be bought in small containers or packages in Southeast Asian groceries. It is beige-pink or purple-gray in color. Look for dry shrimp paste, rather than paste stored in oil. Once opened, store it well sealed in the refrigerator, where it will keep well indefinitely. Before using, wrap in foil and dry-roast, either directly over an open flame or by heating in a dry skillet for 5 minutes. Cooking eliminates any fishy taste and makes the shrimp paste more powdery and easier to blend with other ingredients. It is an essential ingredient in Thai curry pastes.

**Sichuan pepper**    Sometimes called fagara, this aromatic spice has been known since earliest times in China. It is available in small packages from Chinese groceries and other supermarkets and well-stocked spice stores. The small brown husks are where the sharp distinctive peppery taste is, more aromatic than black pepper and almost medicinal tasting. Inside the husks are often small black seeds, bitter-tasting and to be discarded. Fagara is botanically related to *sansho* (Japanese pepper).

**silky tofu**    *See* tofu and tofu products.

**soy sauce**    Soy sauce is used for its salty depth of flavor, and sometimes for its color too, in China and Japan and in many Thai dishes of Chinese origin. It is made from soybeans mixed with a roasted grain, wheat or barley or rice, wheat being the most common. The mix is fermented (with a yeast mold and *lactobacillus*) and salted, then left to stand for up to a year before being filtered. The traditional version of soy sauce had small bits of beans still floating in it, but modern commercial soy sauce is strained. There are many brands and styles of soy sauce. For all the recipes given here, use a medium soy, such as regular Kikkoman or reduced-sodium Kikkoman, widely available in grocery stores, or Pearl River brand soy sauce, available in Chinese groceries. (Do not use China Lily or any of the blackish and bad-tasting products that give soy sauce a bad name.) We like the Kikkoman reduced-sodium sauce when making dipping sauces, for it has a lighter, clearer taste than regular soy sauce. We buy regular Kikkoman in half-gallon containers, decant some into a small pouring bottle for daily use, and store the rest in a cool place. *Black soy sauce*, or *dark soy sauce*, is a category of Chinese soy sauce with a darker color and often a stronger flavor, used for the color it gives; it is not called for in any of the recipes in this book. Sweeter and saltier versions of soy sauce are used in Indonesia and Malaysia: *kecap asin*, *kecap manis*, and others. *Thick soy sauce* is a Taiwanese-made specialty, thick, very dark brown, and sweet, that we like to drizzle over fresh tofu. It can be hard to find. Do not use it in these recipes in place of regular soy sauce.

**squid ink**    Both squid and cuttlefish have small sacs filled with a thick blackish ink–like liquid. Before the days of modern processing, if you wanted squid or cuttle-fish ink, you had to buy enough of the seafood and then squeeze out the ink from each sac. These days the sacs are usually cleaned off before the squid and cuttlefish get to market. You therefore have to find a separate supply of ink if you wish to make *paella negra* or a black risotto. In Italy and Spain, and in some specialty stores in North America, the ink is sold in small packages, each containing about one tablespoon. We have found it for sale at a large fishmonger's, where we can buy it in small half-cup sealed containers. It keeps almost indefinitely in the refrigerator.

**tamarind paste or pulp**    Tamarind paste or pulp comes from the pods of the tamarind tree and is used in Indian, Malay, Senegalese, Georgian, Vietnamese, Thai, and other cuisines to add a sour taste. It is sold in Asian groceries, most often in cellophane-wrapped squares that look black and moist. If you buy the pulp, it will have bits of seed and fibers in it; when a measured amount of tamarind paste, say one tablespoon, is called for, begin with one and a half tablespoons pulp. Both paste and pulp must be dissolved in a little warm water before use. In the case of pulp, the liquid must then be strained through a sieve before it is added to other ingredients. Tamarind paste and pulp keep almost indefinitely if tightly wrapped in plastic wrap in the refrigerator.

## Tea

**black tea**    The most commonly available teas around the world, except in Japan, are black teas. The leaves have been fermented, changing their color in the process from green to black.

**genmai cha**    A flavored tea, popular in Japan, consisting of green tea leaves, bits of rice cracker, and puffed rice, *genmai cha* is sold in packages in Japanese and Korean shops.

**ginger tea**    Ginger has diuretic and "heating" properties and is used in most traditional Asian medical systems as a treatment for colds, often in the form of tea. To prepare it, see page 203.

**green tea**    The preferred tea in Japan and in much of China, green tea has been dried and cured but not fermented. Green tea has just as much caffeine as black tea. The most tender young leaves, picked in spring, are used to make the powdered bright green tea used in Japanese tea ceremonies. (Whole books have been written on tea traditions in China and Japan.)

**mugi cha**    Roasted buckwheat tea, a good accompaniment to Japanese food, is available in Japanese and Korean groceries. It is also good cold.

**Thai eggplant**    *See* eggplant.

**Thai fish sauce**    *See* fish sauce.

## Tofu and tofu products

**fresh tofu**    Fresh tofu comes in two basic textures: firm and silky. Firm tofu, the Chinese-style, is more widely available. It can be easily cut into cubes and even gently stir-fried without breaking up. Silky tofu, used in some Japanese dishes and available mainly from Japanese grocery stores, is softer-textured and slippery.

**fried tofu**    Japanese-style fried tofu comes in firm golden-brown rectangles and is called *abura-age* or *age tofu*. The most common size is about two by five inches. It is sold in Japanese and Korean shops, usually in plastic bags holding twelve or twenty-four rectangles. There is no substitute. Chinese-style fried tofu, also golden brown, is often available in Chinese groceries. It comes in a variety of shapes and textures, from small one-inch cubes, fairly firm and dry, to two- by four-inch rectangles, either soft or firm and dry-textured. Chinese-style fried tofu is cut up and used as an ingredient in stir-fries and soups. Sometimes it is quite oily; you can rinse it off briefly in hot water and wipe dry, or just wipe off the excess oil with paper towels.

**frozen tofu**    When fresh tofu cubes are cut into smaller cubes, then frozen and rethawed, the excess water drains away and what results is a dense sponge-textured tofu that is very resilient and very absorbent, ideal for soups and stir-fries. Frozen tofu is most often found in Chinese and Japanese cooking, especially in the vegetarian repertoire.

*okara*    The pulp remaining after cooked soybeans have been pressed to make tofu, *okara* has little flavor but an agreeable texture. It absorbs flavors well so is used in Japan in stir-fries, flavored by other ingredients and seasonings. *Okara* is available from Japanese groceries. It is high in fiber and protein.

**pressed tofu**    When fresh tofu cubes are pressed under a weight to force out some water, the result is a firm, denser-textured tofu that holds together when sliced. It is a common ingredient in Chinese, Japanese, and Thai cooking. Pressed tofu may also be slow-simmered in a dark broth flavored with soy sauce, star anise, and other flavorings.

**tofu sheets**    These thin, tough sheets are sold in cellophane-wrapped packages in many East Asian stores. The sheets are produced during tofu making, when the top layer is skimmed off the tofu milk as it is firming up (rather as cream is skimmed off milk during cheese making). The skimmings are then dried out. They can be soaked and then used as wrappers, or, more commonly, cut into smaller pieces and used as an ingredient in soups, stir-fries, and stews, especially in the vegetarian cooking of China and Japan.

*togarashi*    This is the Japanese word for Japanese hot chile peppers, usually sold dried and powdered, and available in Japanese and Korean groceries. The powder is used on its own and is also an ingredient in the spicy version of Japanese seven-spice powder, *shichimi togarashi*.

*umeboshi*    Usually translated as Japanese pickled plums, these are actually a kind of apricot. *Umeboshi,* available in Japanese groceries, are pink-red and very sour, believed to be good for stimulating gastric juices. They are a traditional accompaniment for rice, especially in the morning. (For more details, see page 204.)

**vanilla bean**    Vanilla is a native of Mexico and is still produced there, though the vanilla most renowned these days comes from the island of Madagascar. The flavor is in the vanilla beans, the long (four inches or more), very slender pods of the vanilla tree. They are usually sold in cellophane packages, often only three or four at a time. Try placing one in a jar of sugar; it will perfume it delightfully. Once used in cooking (for example, to make rice pudding), a bean can be rinsed off and then reused several times. For stronger flavor, slice the bean lengthwise before using.

**vegetable oil**    When we want a neutral taste for frying or deep-frying, we use canola oil. It is a monounsaturated oil extracted from the rape plant.

**Vietnamese coriander**    *See* polygonum.

**vinegar (cider vinegar, rice vinegar)**    Vinegar is a common ingredient in Chinese and Japanese cooking; in Thai cuisine, its place is more often taken by lime juice. We use both *rice vinegar* and *cider vinegar* in Chinese recipes; the cider vinegar has a more robust flavor, so it goes into strong-tasting or spicy dishes. (Chinese groceries also sell a wide range of dark vinegars; these are not called for in this book.) Rice vinegar is used in Japanese recipes, most notably perhaps as part of the flavoring for sushi rice, and also in salads. Japanese rice vinegar has 4 to 5 percent acidity and is made by fermenting rice wine. We usually use Marukan or Mitsukan brand, available at Japanese and Korean shops and at some natural foods stores. Be sure to buy an *unseasoned* vinegar; seasoned rice vinegar is made for flavoring sushi rice and contains sugar. We also enjoy a wonderful Japanese brown rice vinegar (*genmai su*) made by Koyo that can be substituted for cider vinegar and also used in salads. If you don't have any rice vinegar, you can substitute cider vinegar for it, by diluting two parts vinegar in one part water.

**wakame**    *See* seaweed.

**wasabi**    Commonly known as Japanese horseradish, wasabi is the root of a mountain hollyhock. The root is sometimes available in Japanese groceries; it is five to eight inches long, rough-surfaced, and pale brown with green showing through. Inside, it is bright green. If you find the root, grate it and use it fresh. In both North America and Japan, wasabi is commmonly sold dried and powdered in a blend with hot mustard, to be mixed with a little water and reconstituted into a paste. The paste has a sharp hot taste and is used as a condiment, especially with sashimi.

**wild lime leaves**    Also known as kaffir lime leaves, these citrus-scented leaves (*bai makrut* in Thai) are available both fresh and dried in Southeast Asian groceries. They are dark green, shiny, double-lobed, and wonderfully aromatic; even through a well-sealed plastic bag, you'll be able to smell their citrus-lime aroma. Like bay leaves, they are used for flavoring and are not eaten. Dried lime leaves keep indefinitely and are a useful substitute when fresh leaves are unavailable. Store fresh leaves in the refrigerator, where they will keep for no more than a week. For longer-term storage, wrap them in plastic and freeze them. *See also* limes.

**yard-long beans**    *See* long beans.

# Mail-Order Sources

### Anzen Importers
736 Martin Luther King Boulevard
Portland, OR 97232
tel: (503) 233–5111  fax: (503) 233–7208
*Product list; Japanese, Chinese, and Thai dried and canned ingredients*

### Balducci's
tel: (800) BALDUCCIS  (212) 673–2600
*Catalog; mostly Italian*

### Dean & DeLuca
560 Broadway
New York, NY 10012
tel: (800) 221–7714  (212) 431–1691
*Catalog*

### Gold Mine Natural Food Company
3419 Hancock Street
San Diego, CA 92110-4307
tel: (800) 475–FOOD  fax: (619) 296–9756
customer service: 619–296–8536
*Catalog; mainly Japanese, macrobiotic, and organic; rices, beans, pickles, etc.*

### Indian Harvest
P.O. Box 428
Bemidji, MN 56619
tel: (800) 346-7032
     (218) 751–8500  fax: (218) 751–8519
*Catalog; specialty rices, beans, etc.*

### Kalustyan's
123 Lexington Avenue
New York, NY 10016
tel: (212) 685–3451  fax: (212) 683–8458
*Catalog; very complete rice selection; most spices, legumes, and condiments for all but Japanese*

### The Mushroom Man
625 Barrington #19
Los Angeles, CA 90047
tel: (800) WILD404
*Catalog*

### Pacific Gourmet
tel: (415) 641–8400
*WHOLESALE ONLY: catalog; many rices, spices, etc.*

### Penzey's Ltd.
P.O. Box 933
Muskego, WI 53150
tel: (414) 679–7207  fax: (414) 679–7878
website: http://www.penzeys.com
*Catalog; whole and ground spices, herbs, and seasonings*

### Spanish Table
1427 Western Avenue
Seattle, WA 98101
tel: (206) 682–2827  fax: (206) 682–2814
e-mail: tablespan@aol.com
*Catalog; Spanish rices, olive oils,* pimentón, *squid ink, etc.*

### Spice Merchant
P.O. Box 524
Jackson Hole, WY 83001
tel: (800) 551–5999
     (307) 733–7811 fax:  (307) 733–6343
*Catalog; condiments, spices, rices, legumes, and cookbooks*

### Vivande Porta Via
2125 Fillmore Street
San Francisco, CA 94115
tel: (415) 346–4430  fax: (415) 346–2877
*Italian specialties: rices, oils, etc.*

### Williams-Sonoma
P.O. Box 7456
San Francisco, CA 94120
tel: (800) 541-2233

### Zingerman's
422 Detroit Street
Ann Arbor, MI 48104
tel: (888) 636–8162 (toll free)
     (313) 769–1625  fax: (313) 769–1260
*Catalog; Mediterranean products, including rices, oils, etc.*

# Bibliography

Agricultural Research Service, U.S. Department of Agriculture. *Rice in the United States: Varieties and Production.* Washington, D.C.: U.S. Government Printing Office, 1966.

Amma, P. Lakshmikutty. *Mama's Treasure Chest.* Trivandrum, India: St. Joseph's, 1972.

Anderson, Burton. *Treasures of the Italian Table.* New York: Hearst, 1994.

Anderson, E. N. *The Food of China.* New Haven: Yale University Press, 1988.

Andoh, Elizabeth. *An American Taste of Japan.* New York: Morrow, 1985.

———. *At Home with Japanese Cookery.* New York: Knopf, 1980.

Association of Japanese Agricultural Scientific Societies. *Rice in Asia.* Tokyo: University of Tokyo Press, 1975.

Banerji, Chichita. *Bengal.* Calcutta: Ruta, 1993.

Barker, Randolf. *The Rice Economy of Asia.* Washington, D.C.: Resources for the Future, 1985.

Basham, A. L. *The Wonder That Was India.* Calcutta: Rupa/Fontana, 1967.

Batmanglij, Najmieh. *Food of Life.* Washington, D.C.: Mage, 1986.

Bayless, Rick, with Bayless, Deann Groen. *Authentic Mexican.* New York: Morrow, 1987.

——— and Brownson, JeanMarie. *Rick Bayless's Mexican Kitchen.* New York: Scribner, 1996.

Belleme, John, and Belleme, Jan. *Cooking with Japanese Foods.* Brookline, Mass.: East-West Health Books, 1986.

———. *Culinary Treasures of Japan.* Garden City, N.Y.: Avery, 1992.

Ben Yahmed, Danielle. *Les Merveilles de la Cuisine Africaine.* 4th ed. Paris: Editions j.a., 1988.

Bonnemaison, Joel. *Tsarahonenana: Des Riziculteurs de Montagne dans L'Ankaratra.* Paris: Orstom, 1976.

Braudel, Fernand. *The Mediterranean.* Vol. 1. London: Collins, 1972.

———. *The Structures of Everyday Life.* Vol. 1. New York: Harper & Row, 1981.

Bremzen, Anya von, and Welchman, John. *Please to the Table.* New York: Workman, 1990.

Brydson, Sherry. *Thai Sensations.* Toronto: Macmillan Canada, 1995.

Buddenhagen, I. W. *Rice in Africa.* New York: Academic Press, 1978.

Bumgarner, Marlene Anne. *The Book of Whole Grains.* New York: St. Martin's Press, 1978.

Burn, Billie. *Stirrin' the Pots on Daufuskie.* Spartanburg, S.C.: Reprint Company, 1993.

Carter, Danella. *Down-Home Wholesome.* New York: Dutton, 1995.

Chandler, Robert, Jr. *Rice in the Tropics: A Guide to the Development of National Programs.* Boulder: Westview, 1979.

Chang, K. C., ed. *Food in Chinese Culture.* New Haven: Yale University Press, 1977.

Chirinian, Linda. *Secrets of Cooking Armenian, Lebanese, Persian.* New Canaan, Conn.: Lionhart, 1987.

Cost, Bruce. *Foods from the Far East.* London: Century, 1990.

Dahlen, Martha. *A Cook's Guide to Chinese Vegetables.* Hong Kong: Guidebook Company, 1995.

De Gale, Laurice. *Down to Earth Jamaican Cooking.* Toronto: Sister Vision, 1996.

Diop, Saurele. *Cuisine Senegalaise d'Hier et d'Aujourd'hui.* Saint-Louis de Senegal: Papeterie Wakhatilene, 1989.

Dupont, Jacqueline, and Osman, Elizabeth M. *Cereals and Legumes in the Food Supply*. Ames, Iowa: Iowa State University Press, 1987.

Eiseman, Fred B., Jr. *Bali: Sekala & Niskala*. Vol. II: *Essays on Society, Tradition, and Craft*. Berkeley: Periplus Editions, 1990.

Fanelli, Eurosia Zuccolo, ed. *Rice and Restaurants*. Rome: Ente Nazionale Risi, n.d.

Ferguson, Clare. *Rice: From Risotto to Sushi*. Vancouver: Raincoast, 1997.

Fernandez, Adela. *Traditional Mexican Cooking and Its Best Recipes*. Mexico City, Mexico: Panorama, 1985.

Fletcher, Lehman B., ed. *Egypt's Agriculture in a Reform Era*. Ames, Iowa: Iowa State University Press, 1996.

Freeman, J. D. *Iban Agriculture*. London: HMSO, 1955.

Fretz, Sada. *Pilaf, Risotto, and Other Ways with Rice*. Boston: Little, Brown, 1995.

*A Guide to the Georgia Coast*. Savannah: Georgia Conservancy, 1988.

Ghanoonparvar, M. R. *Persian Cuisine, Book One: Traditional Foods*. Lexington, Ken.: Mazda, 1982.

———. *Persian Cuisine, Book Two: Regional and Modern Foods*. Costa Mesa, Calif.: Mazda, 1984.

Gourou, Pierre. *Riz et Civilisation*. Paris: Fayard, 1984.

Grant, Michael. *The Ancient Mediterranean*. London: Weidenfeld and Nicolson, 1969.

Grant, Rosamund. *Caribbean & African Cookery*. London: Virago, 1989.

Gray, Patience. *Honey from a Weed*. London: Prospect, 1986.

Greene, Bert. *The Grains Cookbook*. New York: Workman, 1988.

Grist, D. H. *Rice*. 4th ed. London: Longman, 1975.

Hanks, Lucien. *Rice and Man*. New York: Aldine, 1972.

Harris, Jessica. *Iron Pots and Wooden Spoons*. New York: Ballantine, 1989.

Hekmat, Forough. *The Art of Persian Cooking*. New York: Hippocrene, 1961, 1994.

Hess, Karen. *The Carolina Rice Kitchen: The African Connection*. Columbia, S.C.: University of South Carolina Press, 1992.

Heyward, Duncan Clinch. *Seed from Madagascar*. Columbia, S.C.: University of South Carolina Press, 1937, 1993.

Houston, D. F. *Rice Chemistry and Technology*. St. Paul, Minn.: American Association of Cereal Chemists, 1972.

Hultman, Tami, ed. *The Africa News Cookbook: African Cooking for Western Kitchens*. New York: Penguin, 1985.

Hurmence, Belinda, ed. *Before Freedom, When I Just Can Remember*. Winston-Salem, N.C.: John F. Blair, 1989, 1994.

Iggers, Jeremy. "Rice." *Martha Stewart Living*, September 1994.

Iny, Daisy. *The Best of Baghdad Cooking, with Treats from Teheran*. New York: Saturday Review Press, 1976.

Ishii, Yoneo, ed. *Thailand: A Rice-Growing Society*. Honolulu: University Press of Hawaii, 1978.

Jaffrey, Madhur. *Eastern Vegetarian Cooking*. London: Arrow, 1990.

———. *A Taste of India*. London: Pan, 1992.

Jenkins, Nancy Harmon. *The Mediterranean Diet Cookbook*. New York: Bantam, 1994.

Juliano, Bienvenido. *Rice in Human Nutrition*. Rome: FAO, 1993.

Kahn, E. J. *The Staffs of Life*. Boston: Little, Brown, 1984.

Kahrs, Kurt. *Thai Cooking*. New York: Quintet, 1990.

Kemble, Frances Anne. *Journal of a Residence on a Georgian Plantation in 1838–1839*. Edited by John A. Scott. Athens, Ga.: University of Georgia Press, 1984.

Kennedy, Diana. *The Cuisines of Mexico*. rev. ed. New York: Harper & Row, 1989.

———. *Mexican Regional Cooking*. New York: Harper Perennial, 1978, 1990.

Kritakara, M. L. Taw, and Amranand, M. R. Pimsai. *Modern Thai Cooking*. Bangkok: Duang Kamol, 1977.

Kumar, Tuk-Tuk. *History of Rice in India: Mythology, Culture, and Agriculture*. Delhi: Gian Publishing House, 1988.

Kuper, Jessica, ed. *The Anthropologists' Cookbook*. London: Routledge & Kegan Paul, 1977.

Lal, Premila. *Vegetable Dishes*. Bombay: IBH Publishing, 1970, 1980.

Latham, Michael. *Human Nutrition in Tropical Africa*. Rome: FAO, 1965.

Lewis, Edna. *In Pursuit of Flavor*. New York: Knopf, 1988.

Linares, Olga F. *Power, Prayer, and Production: The Jola of Casamance, Senegal*. Cambridge: Cambridge University Press, 1992.

Littlefield, Daniel C. *Rice and Slaves: Ethnicity and the Slave Trade in Colonial South Carolina*. Urbana, Ill.: University of Illinois Press, 1991.

Lluria de O'Higgins, Maria Josefa. *A Taste of Old Cuba*. New York: HarperCollins, 1994.

Loomis, Susan Herrmann. *The Great American Seafood Cookbook*. New York: Workman, 1988.

Lu, Henry C. *Chinese System of Food Cures*. Petaling Jaya, Malaysia: Pelanduk, 1990.

Lucas, Chin. *Cultural Heritage of Sarawak*. Kuching, Malaysia: Museum of Sarawak, 1980.

Luh, Bor S., ed. *Rice: Production*. vol. 1. 2nd ed. New York: Van Nostrand Reinhold, 1991.

———. *Rice: Utilization*. vol 2. 2nd ed. New York: Van Nostrand Reinhold, 1991.

McDermott, Nancie. *Real Thai*. San Francisco: Chronicle, 1992.

McGee, Harold. *On Food and Cooking: The Science and Lore of the Kitchen*. New York: Collier, 1984.

———. *The Curious Cook*. San Francisco: North Point Press, 1990.

March, Lourdes. *El Libro de la Paella y de los Arroces*. Madrid: Alianza Editorial, 1985, 1994.

Martin, Peter, and Martin, Joan. *Japanese Cooking*. New York: Signet, 1972.

Mateu Tortosa, Enric. *Arroz y Paludismo: Riqueza y Conflictos en la Sociedad Valenciana del Siglo XVlll*. Valencia: Edicions Alfons el Magnanim, 1987.

Mathew, K. M. *Kerala Cookery*. Kottayam, India: Manorama Publishing, n.d.

Mazda, Maideh. *In a Persian Kitchen*. Rutland, Vt.: Charles Tuttle, 1960.

Mojtahedi, A. "Rice Growing in Northern Iran." Department of Geography Occasional Publications (New Series), no. 15. Durham, England: University of Durham, 1980.

"The New Rice Crisis." *Asia Week*, 26 May 1993, pp. 45–50.

Norman, Jill. *The Complete Book of Spices*. London: Dorling Kindersley, 1990.

Ohnuki-Tierney, Emiko. *Rice as Self*. Princeton: Princeton University Press, 1993.

Oka, H. I. *Origin of Cultivated Rice*. Tokyo: Japan Scientific Societies Press, 1988.

Owen, Sri. *The Rice Book*. New York: St. Martin's, 1994.

*Oxford Book of Food Plants*. London: Oxford University Press, 1969.

Padmanabhan, Chandra. *Dakshin: Vegetarian Cuisine from South India*. San Francisco: Thorsons, 1994.

Passmore, Jackie. *The Encyclopedia of Asian Food and Cooking*. New York: Hearst, 1991.

Perry, Charles. "The Soul of Pilaf." *Los Angeles Times,* December 9, 1993.

Philips, Roger, and Rix, Martyn. *The Random House Book of Vegetables*. New York: Random House, 1993.

Piper, Jacqueline M. *Rice in South-East Asia*. Oxford: Oxford University Press, 1993.

Pruthi, J. S. *Spices and Condiments*. New Delhi: National Book Trust, 1976.

Randolph, Mary. *The Virginia Housewife*. Facsimile, ed. Karen Hess. Columbia, S.C.: University of South Carolina Press.

Richie, Donald. *A Taste of Japan*. Tokyo: Kodansha, 1985.

Roden, Claudia. *A Book of Middle-Eastern Food*. London: Penguin, 1986.

———. *The Book of Jewish Food*. New York: Knopf, 1996.

Rudzinski, Russ. *Japanese Country Cookbook*. San Francisco: Nitty Gritty Productions, 1969.

Sahni, Julie. *Classic Indian Cooking*. New York: Morrow, 1980.

———. *Classic Indian Vegetarian and Grain Cooking*. New York: Morrow, 1985.

Salikhov, S. G. *Blyuda, Uzbekskoi Kukhny* [Uzbek Cuisine]. Tashkent, Uzbek: 1991.

Santa Maria, Jack. *Indian Vegetarian Cookery*. Bombay: B. I. Publications, 1973.

Seetharam, A. *Small Millets in Global Agriculture*. New Delhi: Mohan Primlani, 1989.

Shaida, Margaret. *The Legendary Cuisine of Persia*. London: Penguin, 1992.

Shephard, Sigrid M. *Natural Food Feasts*. New York: Arco, 1979.

Shurtleff, William, and Aoyagi, Akiko. *The Book of Tofu*. Brookline, Mass.: Autumn Press, 1975.

Simmons, Marie. *Rice, the Amazing Grain*. New York: Holt, 1991, 1993.

Simmons, Shirin. *Entertaining the Persian Way*. Luton, England: Lennard Publishing, 1988.

Smart-Grosvenor, Vertamae. *Vibration Cooking or the Travel Notes of a Geechee Girl*. New York: Ballantine, 1992.

Southern Rice Industry. *Rice: 200 Delightful Ways to Serve It*. New Orleans, 1935.

Stover, Dawn. "The Coming Food Crisis." *Popular Science,* August 1996.

Tanaka, Heihachi, with Nicholas, Betty A. *The Pleasures of Japanese Cooking*. New York: Cornerstone, 1969.

Tannahill, Reay. *Food in History*. 2nd ed. New York: Crown, 1988.

Taylor, John Martin. *Hoppin' John's Low-Country Cooking*. New York: Bantam, 1992.

Tropp, Barbara. *The Modern Art of Chinese Cooking*. New York: Morrow, 1982.

Vernon, Amelia Wallace. *African Americans at Mars Bluff, South Carolina*. Baton Rouge: Louisiana State University Press, 1993.

Villiers, A., and Delaroziere, M.-F. *Cuisines d'Afrique*. Aix-en-Provence, France: Edisud, 1995.

Visser, Margaret. *Much Depends on Dinner*. Toronto: McLelland and Stewart, 1987.

Williams, Susan, ed. *The McLellanville Coast Cookbook*. McLellanville, S.C.: McLellanville Arts Council, 1992.

Whyte, Robert. *Rural Nutrition in Monsoon Asia*. London: Oxford University Press, 1974.

Wolfert, Paula. *The Cooking of the Eastern Mediterranean*. New York: HarperCollins, 1994.

Yoneda, Soei. *The Heart of Zen Cuisine*. Tokyo: Kodansha, 1982.

# Index

*We have learned so much over the years* from people we've met traveling: countless street vendors, strangers chance-met in the street or on trains or busses, farmers, market people, and more. We don't know your names, as you don't know ours, but you tolerated our questions and photographs with good-humored patience and we are very grateful. Thank you.

This book probably wouldn't be a book if it were not for the Isarankura family, who twenty years ago first took Jeffrey into their home and restaurant in Bangkok and introduced him to the pleasures of eating rice three times a day. There are many ingredients used in Thai cooking, but *lots of love* is one that is always added and never written down. Huge thanks too to Saratwadee Asasupakit of Chiang Mai.

In Japan, we are deeply indebted to the Doi family of Kyoto and to the Kanda family of Miyama for introducing us to the world of Japanese home cooking and rural tradition. Thanks also to the women of the Miyama Rural Cooperative, to Mrs. Sunaho Ogasawara, Mr. and Mrs. Saito of Oharano, Charles Roche, Abby Shweber, and Muraji Noriko and Riu Noriko.

In Calcutta, special thanks to Gita for your teaching and your food, and to Joy and Shanatan. Many thanks to Suneeta and Daniel, to Basu, to Nicholas Cohen, and to Sanjukta Roy. In Assam, thanks to the staff at Wild Grass. In Sri Lanka, thank you to the Munasinghe family, who gave Jeffrey his own kitchen and taught him to pick stones from rice and dal. In Trivandrum, thanks to everyone at the Ajanta Bhavan and the Hole in the Wall.

In Senegal, warm thanks to Sarta Sane of Marsassoum, and also to Yatou Guiba, young Sarta, and Alfo Sane and Bala Moussa Mane. We thank Mamadou Dabo Sane of Dakar and Marsassoum for making it all possible. Thanks to Hamed Bachir Diop and Ousseynou Sarr and to Ousseynou's mother in Kagnoute. In Dakar, many thanks to Eric M'Backe and to Kine M'Baye and her family and friends. Our thanks to Mariam Seck and her sister Josie of Saint-Louis de Senegal, and also to the Belgian consul in Saint-Louis, Aboubakar Diop, and his wife. Here in Toronto, before leaving for Senegal, we were given guidance and advice by Mamadou Seck and by Professor Martin Klein of the University of Toronto. Thank you.

We are grateful for help, advice, and information from many people during our travels in the Mediterranean region, including Carlo and Carla Latini, Faith Willinger, Marina Colonna, Aldo Paraviccini, and Piero Vercellese in Italy and, in Spain, Jose Puig, Isidro and Montsi Girones, Akthem Hababa, Francisco Margadejf, Cristina Villo, and Samuel Monclus' San'chez.

In the world of food, we are grateful for the work we could draw on from many scholars, researchers, cooks, and writers. For specific information, advice, and encouragement we thank Paula Wolfert, Nancy Harmon Jenkins, the late Arlene Wanderman, Nach Waxman, Alison Fryer and Jennifer Grange, Tina Ujlaki, Rick Bayless, Barbara Haber, Phyllis Bober, Mildred Berman, Dahlia Carmel, Clara-Maria de Amezua, Hoppin' John (John Martin Taylor), Dr. Lawrence Kushi, Aziz Osmani of Kalustyan's grocery, Marisel Presilla, Donna Bayliss, Tim Lang, and Sara Baer-Sinnott, Dun Gifford, and Annie Copps of Oldways Preservation and Exchange Trust.

Many thanks to the editors and staff at *Food & Wine, Food Arts, Gourmet,* and *Eating Well* magazines for your interest and support over the years, and for publishing our thoughts on rice, our recipes, and often our photographs, too.

To various companions in our travels through the rice-eating world, many thanks for your curiosity and good humor, especially to Tashi and Dominic, and to Rocky Dang, Saratwadee Asasupakit, Nancy Harmon Jenkins, Lee Day, Rajan Gill, Ethan Poskanzer and Judy Nisenholt, Dina Fayerman, Mel Green and Allyson Tache and family, and Clare Ann Harff. Thanks, too, to many other travelers met on the road, for your good company.

In Wyoming and California, thank you to Jack and Ann Alford and Robin and Earnie Nelson, for so many times making us feel so warmly welcome.

Back home, we have been helped with information, advice, translation, and more, by many people over the years. They include Dina Fayerman, Cassandra Kobayashi, Hilary Buttrick, Miho Sawada, Molly Tharyan, Ramsay Derry, Sujitra Pornprasitt, the Leuang Thong family of the Vientiane grocery, Ferri Marzban of Alvand grocery, Grace Buie, Bahargul, Morgan Miya, Sam Miya, Luigi Orgera and Adriano at La Fenice, Françoise Ducret, Astrid Vargas, and Deb Olson. Thank you, all.

Recipes developed and tested in our kitchen are always helped by a reading and testing elsewhere. Big thanks to Cassandra Kobayashi for your imaginative testing and useful suggestions and to Hilary Buttrick for all your help with matters Chinese. Thank you to Judy Stevenson and Morgan Miya for testing and feedback and to Dina for tasting everything we put in front of you.

We are grateful to our very gifted agent, Liv Blumer, for navigating us with deftness through sometimes complicated waters. And in Canada, thank you to Doug Pepper and Sarah Davies at Random House for believing in rice.

Books begin with an idea that in time becomes a manuscript, but they really take shape in the hands of editors and designers. A big thank you to the team at Artisan: Deborah Weiss Geline, Susi Oberhelman, Trish Boczkowski, and copyeditor Judith Sutton. Huge thanks, too, to designers Alison Lew and Renata De Oliveira of Vertigo Design. In Toronto, many thanks to photographer Colin Faulkner and food stylist Jennifer McLaggen, and to Sandy Price, Trisha Jackson, and Susan Dicks for generously lending props.

We consider ourselves the world's most fortunate cookbook writers: Ann Bramson, our editor and publisher, and Kim Yorio, director of marketing at Artisan, are very simply the best. Kim and Ann, for your never-ending hard work, insight, friendship, and support, thank you.